CW01466994

CHECKMATE

THE WALLACE MURDER MYSTERY

MARK RUSSELL

MANGO BOOKS

First Edition published 2021.

Copyright © Mark Russell, 2021

The right of Mark Russell to be identified as the author of this work has been asserted in accordance with the Copyright, Designs & Patents Act 1988.

All rights reserved. No part of this book may be reprinted or reproduced or utilised in any form or by any electronic, mechanical or other means, now known or hereafter invented, including photocopying and recording, or in any information storage or retrieval system, without the prior permission in writing of the publishers.

Unless otherwise stated, images are from the author's collection. Whilst every effort has been made to credit all images to the appropriate source/copyright holder, the author apologises for any oversight, which we would be happy to correct in future editions.

ISBN: 978-1-914277-00-9 (hardcover)
ISBN: 978-1-914277-01-6 (softcover)

Published by Mango Books

www.MangoBooks.co.uk
18 Soho Square
London W1D 3QL

CHECKMATE

THE WALLACE MURDER MYSTERY

This book is dedicated to my parents,
and also in memory of Harry Williams and Marie Brennen.

CONTENTS

ACKNOWLEDGEMENTS

First and foremost I would like to thank Adam Wood and David Green at Mango Books. I would also like to thank Kate A. McNichol and Merseyside Police for their invaluable assistance. Thanks also to James Murphy for help, advice and the use of sections of his excellent book *The Murder of Julia Wallace*.

Thanks also to Caroline Champion, Phil Bunford, Ged Fagan, Linda Williamson, Gaynor Boyle, Alexandra Beechey, Anita Smith (photography), Chris Kelly and Brian Starkey; the late Jonathan Goodman; Roger Wilkes; Alan Hayhurst; The National Archives, Kew; Sandra Donaldson, Marion Ely, HM Courts & Tribunals Service; Staff at St George's Hall; Hill Dickinson LLP.

I would also like to thank Pete Wildman and James Allison Wildman for allowing me the use of sections from Al's memoirs online; Harry Williams (one of the funniest men I have had the privilege of knowing) for assistance and insight; Roger Hull and staff at Liverpool Record Office and Libraries; Morgannis Graham and John Porter (Group Archivists, Prudential PLC); James Sedgwick and George Cogswell. Sincere thanks also to Dave Shawyer, BT Heritage Curator for information regarding telecommunications in 1931. I would also like to thank Ken Kenny, Gary Billington, Nick Bunning and Lindsay Smith for their continued interest and support.

The number of people who have assisted me has been immense, and I apologise to anyone that I might have overlooked.

ABOUT THE AUTHOR

Mark Russell is a local historian and researcher. Since viewing the Yorkshire TV docu-drama *Who Killed Julia Wallace?* in 1975 he has had a great interest in the case. His interests include music, films, history and true crime. He lives in Liverpool.

INTRODUCTION

On 20th January, 1931 the city of Liverpool was to witness one of the most brutal and infamous of murders. 69-year-old Julia Wallace was bludgeoned to death in the front parlour of her home in the Anfield district of the city. From early on the case was referred to by the Press as the Anfield Murder Mystery.

The pattern of events was triggered by a telephone call made the previous evening by a mysterious caller by the name of R.M. Qualtrough. He left a message for the victim's husband, William Herbert Wallace, at the Central Chess Club in the city centre. Wallace was a club member and was scheduled to play a tournament match that evening, but had yet to arrive at the club when the call was made. He eventually arrived at the club where the message was conveyed to him.

Other areas of Liverpool would also be significant to the Wallace case; Clubmoor; the leafy suburb of Allerton in the south of the city and also the Dale Street/North John Street area of the city centre. Two triangular-shaped grassed areas would be crucial to the case – one in Anfield, the other in Allerton.

My first real recollection of the Wallace case occurred in late October 1975. A trailer for an upcoming documentary drama was aired on Granada TV. I was mesmerised as I was confronted with the image of a woman lying on the floor and what looked like a poker being brandished back and forth. The programme was the Yorkshire TV-produced *Who Killed Julia Wallace?* This was long before the advent of home VCR, so you could only watch it once.

I became even more intrigued when my mother stated that the murder had taken place not that far away. We watched the programme when it was aired and my parents thought that it would be a good idea to go up to Wolverton Street the following night. I can remember my father driving my mother, my two brothers and myself up Richmond Park and turning into Wolverton Street. I personally thought the street looked dark and quite sinister. My father drove up the street and parked on the left-hand side near the top. My mother pointed out the house and said "That's number 29..." It seemed to be in total blackness, which added to my uneasiness. After a few minutes we drove away, to my relief. That moment was to have an indelible impact on me – an impact that has stayed with me ever since.

I found out that my mother was born in Clarendon Road (less than 200 metres from the telephone box which was pivotal to the case) and was christened in the Holy Trinity Church three years after the murder. I also discovered that my grandparents (and other relatives) would see both Wallace and Julia regularly on Breck Road, and also pay Wallace on his collection round. My great-aunt (who was obsessed with the case) attended the trial of Wallace.

The weeks following the murder my grandfather and great-aunt would avidly discuss it. My great-aunt was utterly convinced of Wallace's guilt. Although my grandfather always found Wallace rather aloof, he was convinced of his innocence.

A lot has been written about the Wallace case – full-length books, magazine articles, essays and anthologised accounts, and whilst a few are admirable works, practically all of them suffer from the same thing: what the author considered happened – a natural bias.

There also seems a preoccupation with sensation-seeking, particularly with regards to criminology and crimes in general. You only have to look at the copious amounts of books published in the field, and the Wallace case is no different. This preoccupation with sensationalising undermines the dignity of the victim. It is a sad fact that there are more known photos of Julia in death than there are of her in life and, in many cases, the victim is frequently overlooked.

The conspiracy theory hasn't been ignored either, but I am utterly convinced there is no conspiracy regarding the Wallace case. It is sheer wishful thinking on the part of the author wanting to see such conspiracies, some of them of *The Da Vinci Code* proportions. These accounts are completely unfounded, and in actuality have no basis in fact. This phenomenon is not solely limited to the Wallace case though – it prevails in practically anything and everything – be it the Titanic, JFK and NASA, to name a few. The public in general love a good mystery and, dare I say it, almost want the murder to remain unsolved.

Joseph Caleb Marsden had only ever been known by his surname, and remained virtually an unknown until I named him on several forums some years ago and, like Jonathan Goodman did with Richard Gordon Parry in 1981, brought him to wider public knowledge via radio in January 2011, but I cannot claim any ground-breaking credit there – after all, Wallace named both Marsden and Parry.

The writing of this book has taken over ten years and in the process I have consulted all contemporary newspaper accounts available and accessed the files and records of Merseyside Police, the National Archives at Kew, the records held at Hill Dickinson LLP and previously never-before-seen documents, including records of Parry's court appearances, the coroner's inquest report and the service record of Police Constable Fred Williams.

1

OPENING MOVES

Mention the name Anfield and most people, certainly those from outside the city, will immediately think of the home of Liverpool FC (and former home of Everton FC). Bordered by the districts of Walton, Clubmoor, Tuebrook and Everton, Anfield can be described as a Victorian area as it was largely developed during that time. The area leading from Walton and Everton was principally farmland, and it was the sloping or 'hanging' fields from which Anfield is believed to have derived its name. Bennison's Survey of 1835 shows the whole area, with the exception of a few farms and mansions, to be devoid of buildings. Once described by a local writer as 'a rural haven, picturesque in the extreme with Breck Road over-arched by trees' it would by the 1880s be overtaken by construction. A considerable contributor to the building boom was the 'Welsh builders' – men of Cambrian birth or extraction who erected many of the houses in the area. There are several 'group' street names in the area; ecclesiastical groups (which led to that area of Anfield being nicknamed the 'Holy Land'), Welsh associations, Girls' names, Lake District place-names, and months of the year. There are also streets prefixed by the word 'Red' and connections to the author Thackeray.[1] The district is also home to, as Picton once put it, the 'Pere Le Chaise of Liverpool' – Anfield Cemetery. The major priority of the newly-appointed Liverpool Burial Board in 1856 was to find a suitable location for the poorer

1 Sedley, Pendennis, Becky, Esmond, Newcombe and Castlewood are all named after characters in the works of William Makepeace Thackeray. Castlewood Road was previously known as Osborne Road, also named after another Thackeray character.

classes, and Anfield seemed ideal. The design and layout of the cemetery was by Edward Kemp. The Church of England division was consecrated by the Bishop of the Diocese on 27th April 1863. On the following day the Roman Catholic Bishop consecrated the division appropriated for the burial of Roman Catholics, and on 4th May the non-consecrated division was opened for general burials in which nonconformist ministers of various denominations took part in the proceedings.

Opposite the cemetery on Priory Road stands Stanley Park. In the mid-1860s there was great outcry by ratepayers in Liverpool for the construction of parks and places of recreation. When the demand was first made the Corporation of Liverpool was a very wealthy body, and therefore voted large sums of money to the cause without much persuasion. The park's hundred acres were set out in 1867-70 by Edward Kemp; the original estimate of £42,792 was not exceeded. The octagonal open shelter houses, bridges, boat houses and other architectural objects were designed by the borough surveyor E.R. Robson. The park opened to the public on 14th May 1870.

On earlier maps of the area the football ground is listed as 'Everton Football Ground.' This is not a misprint. It was originally the home ground of Everton FC. In 1891 Everton became League Champions and were flourishing. The club could afford to pay its top players up to £3 a week. In 1892 a dispute erupted when the club fell out with its president and main benefactor, John Houlding. His plans for the club were rejected, and the club purchased a new site on the other side of Stanley Park. Houlding was left with a ground but no team, so Liverpool FC were formed. Anfield is unique in the fact that it has been the home ground of two top-flight football league champions. As well as football, the district has an equally famous (or more accurately infamous) location. It was at this location in 1931 that one of the most brutal murders took place. Wolverton Street,[2] a cul-de-sac of thirty four red brick houses, was listed in

2 The street had seen its fair share of tragedies over the years; 52-year-old Frederick William Warwood lived at 21 Wolverton Street. He committed suicide by inhaling gas at his home on 17th September 1921; 40-year-old Ellen Williams committed suicide on 4th March 1926 by

Gore's Directory in 1910, but it was in 1912 that the street saw its first residents move in.

William Herbert Wallace was born in Millom, Cumbria on 29th August 1878 to Benjamin and Margery Wallace (*née* Hall). His father was a printer and stationer and also a part-time agent for the Prudential Assurance Company. The birth of Wallace was followed by that of his brother Joseph (17th December 1879) and sister Jessie (19th October 1882). All three children were born at 44 Newton Street.[3] When Wallace was ten years old the family began a series of moves, first to Blackpool (where Wallace was struck down with typhoid fever) and then to Dalton-in-Furness. The 1891 census has the Wallace family living at 151 Chapel Street. By 1901 the family had moved to 19 Victoria Street, where the children attended the local Board School in Broughton Road.[4] After leaving school aged fourteen, the family moved across the peninsular to Walney Island to live at 89 Dominion Street. It was here that Wallace first gained employment, as an apprentice draper's assistant on 3 shillings a week at Messrs Tenants of 72-74 Cavendish Street, Barrow.[5] After completing his apprenticeship in 1898, he moved to Manchester where he was engaged as a draper's assistant with Messrs Whiteaway, Laidlaw and Company, outfitters to Her Majesty's Armed Forces and the Colonial, Indian and Foreign Services.[6]

hanging at her home 26 Wolverton Street; 39-year-old commercial traveller James Green lived at 37 Wolverton Street. He died outside Anfield Football Ground before the Liverpool v Burnley match on 26th December 1928. Green, who was accompanied by two companions, was near to the turnstiles when he leaned against the wall and then collapsed. Liverpool FC doctor Louis Curwen was quickly summoned but Green was already dead due to auricular fibrillation. The tragedies connected with the street continued; on 29th April 1942 56-year-old Wolverton Street resident Minnie Kirkman committed suicide by throwing herself from the 112 feet high roof of the Bon Marché store on Church Street, and just over a year later another Wolverton Street resident, John William Garth, hanged himself at Broadgreen Hospital.

3 Newton Street has been given the sobriquet 'Murder Alley' in recent times, as there have been three murders committed there. Bizarrely they occurred in neighbouring houses, on the same side of the road as number 44 and were down to domestic violence.

4 The 1901 census has Wallace and sister Jessie both listed as draper's assistants and Joseph as a printer compositor.

5 James Murphy, *The Murder of Julia Wallace* pp.75.

6 According to Jonathan Goodman, Joseph embarked on Shanghai, where he took up the position of printer for the Chinese Government service. Goodman also claimed that Joseph had married Amy prior to his journey to the Orient but this is untrue. Joseph actually married Amy in 1909 in Ulverston. Goodman *The Killing of Julia Wallace* pp.106.

After working in Manchester for several years Wallace decided to leave for Calcutta after a vacancy arose in that city's Whiteaway, Laidlaw and Company branch on Chowringhee Street. In 1902, aged twenty-three, he set sail for India.[7] He worked and lived in the stifling heat of Calcutta for two years. The heat of India would not be the only thing that would bother him – a recurring kidney complaint would compound his misery, necessitating several visits to the British Hospital. During his time in India Wallace had continued his correspondence with Joseph, who was in Shanghai working as a printer for the Chinese government, and sought a transfer there. He arrived in 1905, but was plagued by kidney trouble. The following year his left kidney was operated on, and three weeks later he had an abscess on his right kidney. Three weeks after that, his left kidney was again operated on due to a urinary fistula. While in Shanghai he was operated on four times at the German hospital.

Wallace left China in March 1907 on board the Norddeutscher Lloyd SS *Gneisenau* (which travelled from Yokohama to Bremen via Southampton). Wallace claimed he had to disembark at Hong Kong for surgery before re-joining to make the trip home, an experience he had a mind to 'complain to the British Government about.' On 3rd April 1907 he was admitted to Guy's Hospital, London. There, he underwent an operation for the removal of his left kidney on the 12th April and was discharged on 18th May.

In 1910 Wallace was working as an election agent for the Liberal Party, at their offices at 5 Raglan Street, Harrogate. According to the census of 1911, the family (minus Joseph) was living at 9 Belmont Road. At the time, Wallace's sister Jessie was working as a nurse in the vicinity. Running parallel to Belmont Road was St Mary's Avenue, and it was to number 11 that Julia Dennis had moved from her flat in 5 Dragon Parade.

In 1911 Wallace met Julia and after three years of courtship they were married on 24th March 1914.[8] After a brief honeymoon,

7 Goodman *The Killing of Julia Wallace* pp.106.

8 St Mary's Church in Low Harrogate was originally built in 1824. It proved to be too small for the congregation so a new church was built nearby in 1915-16, using stone from the old

Wallace and his father moved in with Julia (Wallace's mother Margery had died in December 1913, aged 62). With the outbreak of the First World War all political party activity ceased. Through his father's long-standing connections with the Prudential, Wallace gained employment with the assurance company exactly a year after his marriage to Julia – 24th March 1915 – as collection agent in Liverpool. Benjamin Wallace died the same month, aged 79. An affirmed agnostic and stoic, Wallace's favourite book was Marcus Aurelius' tome *Meditations*. His bookshelves included Lewis Carroll's *The Hunting of the Snark*, Köhler's *The Mentality of Apes* and Homer's *Iliad* and *Odyssey*. Wallace also read the *Financial Times* daily, and also the *Armchair Scientist*.

Julia Wallace was born on 28th April 1861 at Bruntcliffe House in East Harlsey, Northallerton, Yorkshire. She was the second of seven children born to William George Dennis and his wife Annie Teresa (*née* Smith). Annie Teresa actually died aged 32 giving birth to the seventh child, Herbert William, on 18th April 1871. Julia's birth certificate lists her father's occupation as farmer (her marriage certificate has him as a veterinary surgeon). He died on 19th February 1875 aged 40, the death certificate recording the causes of death as jaundice and dropsy.

Julia has always had a somewhat mystical status. She has been described invariably as reserved and old-fashioned. Wallace claimed she was fluent in French; a watercolour artist who specialised in landscapes, seascapes and flowers; an accomplished pianist and former singer. She was religious and a regular churchgoer, with an abiding belief in the hereafter. Aged 10, she is listed in the census as living at Number 5 Farm House (in the township of West Harlsey). Ten years later she was an Assistant Governess/Teacher at Keswick House Ladies School, Keswick Road, Wandsworth, living with Banker's Clerk Robert G. Smith and his wife Charlotte (who was also a Governess) and their four daughters. In 1891 Julia was living at Elm House, Daltons Yard, Oulton with Woodlesford, Leeds. She

demolished church. A 'Tin Tabernacle' was erected as a stop gap. It was here that the Wallaces were married in 1914.

was employed as a governess to, curiously, another Robert Smith and his family. The 1901 census has Julia 'living on own means' at 182 Stroud Green Road, Hornsey. The Burgess Roll of 1910 has her living at 5 Dragon Parade, Harrogate, and it was there in 1911 that she met William Herbert Wallace. Strangely, the 1911 census (which was taken on the night of Sunday 2nd April) lists Julia under the name Jane Dennis, living at 11 St Mary's Avenue, Harrogate as 'Apartment House Keeper'. The document also contains other inaccuracies; 32 years of age (when in actual fact she was nearly 50), and her birthplace as Hexham, Sussex.

On their relocation to Liverpool in March 1915, the Wallaces moved into 26 Pennsylvania Road in the Clubmoor district. They stayed there for four months before settling into 29 Wolverton Street. The houses had three bedrooms, and with the Wallaces having no children there was adequate room, so much so that the scientific-minded Wallace converted the back bedroom into a chemistry laboratory where he would conduct his experiments. The usual practice would be to eat in the kitchen (which also doubled as the living room), prepare the meals in the back kitchen/scullery and entertain visitors in the front parlour, which, in the instance of the Wallaces, was also used as a music room. Music featured largely in their lives. Against the wall opposite the fireplace stood an upright piano[9] which Julia played. Wallace would play the violin, but with far less musical dexterity than his wife. They would play sonatas by Beethoven and Mozart, and would also attend many classical music concerts together. They slept in the upstairs middle bedroom, with the front spare bedroom being used more for storage. The house also had an upstairs bathroom. The Wallaces rented the house from landlord Samuel Evans for 14s 3d a week, and were comfortable enough financially to have a weekly cleaning lady, Sarah Jane Draper, who called every Wednesday morning and was paid 2s 6d.

In 1931 Britain was still in the middle of the Great Depression,[10]

9 Emblazoned with medallions and candelabras, the piano was built by manufacturer H. Matz & Co. Berlin, Germany.

10 Also known as the Great Slump.

with unemployment at two million. It was the largest and deepest economic depression for Britain in the whole of the 20th century, and no doubt had its sources in the Great Depression of 1929. King George V was on the throne and the Prime Minister was Ramsay MacDonald, with a Labour (and then) National Coalition Government. In September the National Government took Britain off the gold standard, following panic on the world financial markets. Under Labour, the Greenwood Housing Act of 1930 addressed slum clearance by providing subsidy and obliging local authorities to re-house tenants.

There was widespread sickness on Merseyside around the month of January 1931, the cause being the spell of fog followed by cold weather (the weather the previous winter had been milder). This also contributed to the high increase in the death-rate. There was an epidemic of measles, and hospitals were full of pneumonia cases following influenza. Thousands of children were ill with influenza and measles, and death was rife among adults due to respiratory ailments, bronchitis and pneumonia. On average, ninety adults per day were admitted to municipal hospitals suffering from pneumonia, and some schools were closed due to the outbreaks of influenza and measles. Although diphtheria showed a decline and inoculation was advised as a preventive, between five and ten percent of those affected died, of which two-thirds were children. Newspapers were advising the general public on how to combat illness with their advertisements for Hall's Wine Tonic, Bovril, Angier's Emulsion and Peps Tablets.

Dense fog and frost caused chaos around Merseyside in early January, with many pedestrians suffering broken limbs due to falls on slippery surfaces and ice-coated pavements. Eight degrees of frost were registered, with transport services almost crippled. The severe weather was also responsible for numerous collisions between various types of motor vehicles. On the Mersey, shipping was almost at a standstill with visibility so bad that it was impossible to see from one side of the river to the other for several days. The city also saw disruption to rail and tram services, causing delays.

57-year-old Charles Earl's body was recovered from the Leeds and Liverpool Canal. He had been a lockgate keeper for twenty four years and was believed to have drowned after falling into it due to fog.

In the world of sport, Arsenal were crowned champions of the First Division. Liverpool finished 9th and Everton (after a brief sojourn to the Second Division) were promoted to the top league as champions. In cricket, Yorkshire won the County Championship and the Boat Race saw Cambridge win for an eighth time in succession.

1931 would turn out to be a somewhat vintage year regarding crime and murder. Precisely a fortnight before the death of Julia Wallace, Evelyn Foster was almost burned beyond recognition in Northumberland. She claimed to have given a lift in her car to a 'smartly-dressed man who wore a bowler hat.' He was never found and no-one was ever arrested. In March Alfred Arthur Rouse was executed for his involvement in the 'Blazing Car Murder' that occurred near the village of Hardingstone in Northamptonshire some four months prior; in Germany Peter Kürten, 'The Vampire of Düsseldorf', was found guilty of some of the most atrocious crimes on record. Like Wallace, he went on trial in April 1931 and was found guilty, but unlike Wallace Kürten was not reprieved – he was executed by guillotine in Cologne. On 8th June, 25-year-old Starr Faithfull's washed up body was discovered at Long Beach, New York, and in Europe Symphorophiliac Szilveszter Matuska used dynamite in the derailment of the Vienna Express near Budapest on 13th September. Twenty two people died and over one hundred others were injured. Matuska was arrested a month later and sentenced to death, which was commuted to life imprisonment. In October Al Capone was sentenced to 11 years in prison for tax evasion in Chicago, and in December the body of 10-year-old Vera Page was found in undergrowth in Addison Road, London. She had been raped and strangled. Suspicion fell upon Percy Orlando Rush but there was insufficient evidence to charge him with the murder. That same month Jack 'Legs' Diamond was shot dead in

Albany, New York.

1931 saw the publications of Dorothy L. Sayers' *Five Red Herrings*, Dashiell Hammett's *The Glass Key* and Agatha Christie's *The Sittaford Mystery*. It was also the year that Salvador Dalí painted one of his most recognisable works – The Persistence of Memory – which incorporated his surrealistic concept of time complete with melting pocket watches.

During the year of 1931 two new cinemas were opened in Liverpool; the Forum on Lime Street and the Princess in Selwyn Street. In addition to these, the King's Hall Cinema on Oakfield Road was demolished and a new one, the Gaumont Palace, was built in its place. The Granby cinema on Granby Street was closed for extensive alterations and was reopened as the Princes. The film-loving public flocked to the picture houses in their droves to be gripped by the Universal horror films *Dracula* and *Frankenstein*; Fritz Lang's ground-breaking *M*, Rouben Mamoulian's *Dr Jekyll and Mr Hyde*, Hitchcock's *The Skin Game* and James Cagney's *The Public Enemy*. The film world also saw the release of the Marx Brothers' *Monkey Business*, Chaplin's *City Lights* and the first starring feature film of Laurel and Hardy, *Pardon Us*. Picture houses were advertising two stars who finally gave in to the talkies – Garbo in *Anna Christie*, with the tagline 'Greta talks!' and Lon Chaney in 'the only Talking Picture of a great artiste', *The Unholy Three*. The world of music saw the releases of *Goodnight Sweetheart*, *Dream a Little Dream of Me*, *As Time Goes By*, *Minnie the Moocher* and *Mad Dogs and Englishmen*.

1931 saw the deaths of Russian ballerina Anna Pavlova, Australian soprano Dame Nellie Melba, German film director F.W. Murnau, novelist Arnold Bennett, jazz musician Bix Beiderbecke, Danish composer Carl Nielsen and inventor Thomas Edison.

Throughout the year, aviation, water and land speed records were broken at a regular occurrence. In February Malcolm Campbell broke the land speed record at Daytona Beach, Florida with a speed of 246mph. On his return to England he was knighted. In April C.W.A. Scott flew to Australia in 9 days 4 hours, establishing a record. In June he flew back in just under eleven days. This return record was broken in August by Jim Mollison, who managed the feat in 8 days 19 hours. In the autumn the water speed record was achieved by Kaye Don travelling at 110mph in his *Miss England II* on Lake Garda. In winning the Schneider Trophy George Hedley Stainforth set a new air record, which he himself broke a month later with a speed of just under 408mph. In November 19-year-old Peggy Salaman and her co-pilot Gordon Store broke a record by flying from England to Cape Town in just over five days.

In the world of architecture the Empire State Building and George Washington Bridge were opened in New York City, as was the statue Christ the Redeemer overlooking Rio de Janeiro.

The year also had its fair share of disasters. February saw an earthquake hit New Zealand, with a loss of over 250 lives in the towns of Napier and Hastings. Damage was estimated at well in excess of two million pounds. In June the excursion steamer *Saint-Philibert* overturned in heavy seas five miles off the coast of St Nazaire, with hundreds losing their lives. Only eight survived. China suffered some of the deadliest natural disasters in history when catastrophic floods hit between July and November. Estimates of the total death toll ranged from over 100,000 to several million. November saw the Bentley Colliery explosion, in Doncaster in which 45 men and boys were killed.

Britain's population stood at 46 million. That of Liverpool peaked in the 1930s with 855,539[11] recorded in the census of 1931. The birth rate in Liverpool for that year was the second lowest on record (behind that of 1918). The Housing Act of 1919 resulted in large-scale council housing building during the 1920s and 1930s. Thousands of families were rehoused from the inner-city to new suburban housing estates. Speke Airport began service flights on 17th June 1930,[12] while the Overhead Railway rattled along the dock road and the Mersey Tunnel was in construction – a massive undertaking which used the labour of 1,700 at its peak. During

11 *Liverpool Red Book 1932*. Incidentally, the Anfield population in 1931 was 24,261, with an electorate of 10,867. *Liverpool Labour*, Sam Davies, Keele University Press 1996.

12 The airport opened proper on 1st July 1933.

work on the tunnel, a subsidence of the road occurred on 29th October 1930 in Dale Street, leading to fires and explosions which resulted in damages to the cost of £50,000.

Although UK driving licences were introduced by the Motor Car Act 1903, no test was required. Legislation for compulsory testing was introduced for all new drivers with the Road Traffic Act 1934. Until well into the 1930s motorists enjoyed the freedom of the road. From 1931 to 1934 there wasn't even a speed limit on British roads. As the number of cars grew – over 1 million cars on UK roads in 1930 – accidents increased. There were over 7,300 fatalities in that year. The inevitable would happen, as safety regulations were multiplied. The speed limit was set at 30mph in built-up areas (which was unpopular with some drivers but favoured by the police). By mid-March 1935 the first 30mph signs were put up around Liverpool. Incredibly, there were more fatalities on Britain's roads in the 1930s than today. The Morris Minor was introduced in 1931, it being the first £100 car. 1931 saw the first schematic London Underground tube map designed by Harry Beck, and also the first publication of the Highway Code. The three local newspapers, the *Liverpool Post & Mercury*, *Echo* and *Evening Express* each cost 1d. The cost to post a letter in the United Kingdom was 1½d. Smokers could obtain 10 Player's for 6d (20 for 11½d); a Lotus all-electric transportable radio set (usually costing £24) could be purchased at half the price at George Henry Lee; a complete oak dining room suite cost 10 guineas. Meanwhile, the average house cost £600.

Children of the 1930s didn't have the luxury of internet, DVDs and computer games – they had to make do with the theatre of the streets and their own imagination. Games like Rounders, Hopscotch, Follow My Leader, Kick the Can and Stroke the Bunny were favourites. The girls would play skipping games, the streets echoing to 'Raspberry Gooseberry my jam tart – tell me the name of your sweetheart,' 'Grandmother, Grandmother Gray, may I go out to play? I won't go near the waterfall to drive the ducks away' or 'Sam, Sam, the dirty old man, washed his face in a frying pan, combed his hair with a leg of a chair...' Indeed, to have a bicycle in the 1920s or '30s was like being a millionaire.[13]

Companies were offering the populace the option of having electricity installed into their homes for an initial payment of £2. By 1931 the number of homes with electricity had risen to 33% (approximately 1 in 3). By 1931 all of the principal streets in the most important areas of Liverpool had been electrically-lit (a process which amounted to over 10,000 metal filament lamps being used). C&A, Owen Owen, Lewis's and other big stores[14] were advertising their wares in the pages of the local newspapers. Meanwhile, thrift was advised as the keystone for the coming year. The Liverpool Savings Bank,[15] Halifax,[16] Martins and others were encouraging the public to save their hard-earned money in their saving schemes. 1931 saw the first unit trust launched in Britain, the M&G[17] the First British Fixed Trust. The idea was brought to Britain by a stockbroker impressed by the way that American mutual funds (the US equivalent of unit trusts) had withstood the shock of the 1929 Wall Street Crash.[18]

Established in 1848 the Prudential[19] was founded to provide professional people with loans secured by life assurance. This market broadened during the second half of the Nineteenth century, when insurance policies – penny premiums collected by agents – were sold to the working classes. In 1931 the Prudential was the largest insurance institution in the British Empire, and had a Staff Union membership of over 7,000. The country was split into regional divisions; Scotland being 'A', Wales 'E', the West Country 'N' etc. Liverpool and the North West was 'G' division. The number of Ordinary Branch policies issued during the year of 1931 was 76,719, assuring the sum of 18,006,386 which produced a new annual premium income of £1,126,040. The Industrial Branch

13 Liverpool's Vanishing Street Games, Leonard Franklin, *Evening Express* 12th July 1935.
14 Blackler's, Bon Marché, George Henry Lee and the three mentioned stores are no longer extant in Liverpool.
15 The oldest of the principal thrift agencies in Liverpool, founded in 1815.
16 The largest building society in the world in 1931.
17 Municipal & General Securities Company Limited.
18 Prudential plc. Directory.
19 Originally known as the Prudential Mutual Assurance Investment and Loan Association.

premiums received for the year were £18,804,288, which was an increase of £682,433 over those of the previous year. The number of Life policies in force at the end of the year was 1,028,613, assuring with bonus £197,370,838 which produced a premium income of £11,089,049 per annum.[20] There were 10,000 Prudential agents in 1931.

John Paterson was employed by Condliff & Co, Jewellers and Opticians, of 93 Dale Street. It was part of his duty to wind and correct the clock of the Holy Trinity Church[21] on the corner of Breck Road and Richmond Park on the Friday of each week. On Friday 16th January Paterson wound the clock and set it at the correct time of 12.50pm, as it was two minutes fast. On Friday 23rd January Paterson again wound and set the clock at 12.25pm. The clock showed the correct time and did not need adjustment.

The Liverpool Central Chess Club[22] would meet at Cottle's City Café, which was situated at 24B North John Street.[23] The evening of Monday 19th January saw the continuation of the chess championship. The Chess Club would meet on Thursdays as well.

20 Prudential Assurance Company Limited 83rd Annual Report.

21 This fine landmark building was built in Decorated Gothic style and designed by William and James Hay. The first founding stone was laid on 13th August 1845. It finally opened for divine service on Easter Sunday, 4th April, 1847. In the 1920s and up to her death Julia Wallace was a regular member of the congregation. The Vicar from May 1928 to July 1934 was the Reverend Robert Barrow. Before entering the ministry he was in the insurance business. He went to India in 1903 at the age of 23, and served as a pioneer missionary in the Central Provinces for ten years. On his return to England he became curate at Holy Trinity Church, St Anne's Street for three years, and was then appointed curate at St Cleopas, Toxteth becoming vicar in 1916, a post he held for fourteen years.

22 The Central Chess Club was formed in March 1893 and held its meetings at the Central Café. This was situated on the fourth floor of the Central Building, 43c North John Street. Here, the club would meet on Tuesday and Thursday evenings. The annual subscription was 2s 6d, and the membership numbered 44. The club's first secretary was F.L. Ball. They played regular fixtures against the Liverpool Chess Club, the Sandon Club and the Manchester Club on a home and away basis. In 1901 world chess champion Emanuel Lasker gave a lecture to a large and interested audience at the club. By 1909 the club had moved to 24B North John Street. Among those who visited the Central Chess Club were Polish Grandmaster Akiba Rubinstein, Bohemian chess master Oldřich Duras, leading British players Joseph Henry Blackburne and Amos Burn, and Russian chess master Eugene Znosko-Borovsky. The Liverpool Chess Club was originally founded in 1837 at the Lyceum Building, Bold Street and was claimed by its members to have been the oldest in the country. In 1931 that club's venue was No. 45, The Temple, Dale Street.

23 Situated in the Harrington Chambers buildings. Incidentally, the Club was not listed in the telephone directory at the time.

The café was accessible down a dozen steps to the basement, and had four rooms with the tables being set out for games to be played. On the wall was a noticeboard which displayed, among other things, the chess fixtures that had been prepared in October to be played. To the right of the noticeboard, a telephone box with the number 3581 Bank emblazoned on the glass of the door. About a hundred people used the restaurant daily. William Herbert Wallace was a member of the club, and although very passionate about the game was only a second- to third-class player. The café was also used by the Mersey Amateur Dramatic Society, which held its rehearsals there on Tuesdays and Thursdays.

Rain and sleet covered the city as Club Captain Samuel Beattie[24] left work at Orleans House[25] and made his way to the Club. He would set up the chess boards and tables in time for the arrival of the club members. Wallace's attendance record was sporadic to say the least, his last visit to the club being two months before on a night which saw him defeated by E. Lampitt,[26] but he decided to make a visit to the Chess Club. He was scheduled to play a match that night against F.C. Chandler.

At approximately 7.15pm, at the telephone exchange in Anfield[27] operator Louisa Alfreds received a call asking for Bank 3581 – the number of the Chess Club. It was a man's voice. She made the connection then continued with her other work. Two minutes later a second operator, Lilian Martha Kelly, received a call from the same caller. He notified her that he had pressed button 'A' but had not had his correspondent. She asked him to press button 'B' to receive his two pennies back[28] which he did, the light in

24 Samuel Beattie won the Second Division in 1909, gaining 20 shillings in the process. He also won that year's 'C' knockout tourney, the prize being 31s 6d. He actually drew a game with the aforementioned Blackburne during a simultaneous chess challenge at the Central Chess Club in October 1912. Beattie died on 11th February 1946 at his home, 24 Warwick Drive, Wallasey. He was 73 years of age and had spent nearly 60 years on the Liverpool Cotton Market. He left a wife, Isabella, and four daughters.

25 Beattie worked for cotton brokers George Langley & Co. Their offices were situated on the first floor of Orleans House, Edmund Street (about 700 yards from North John Street).

26 In the knockout tournament the first round matches had to have been played by 30th November 1930. Wallace, at the time a third rate player, was eliminated in the first round by first class player Daniel Baruch.

27 The Anfield telephone exchange was at 5 Richmond Terrace.

28 The cost of a call from a kiosk in 1931 was 2 pence (2d) for a local call. If the exchange was

the exchange indicating so. She asked the caller if there ought to be a reply, to which the caller said yes – that it was a restaurant and there should be plenty of people there. She tried again to attain the number, but without success. Exchange supervisor Annie Robertson was then informed and she finally put the call through. By reason of the complaint of the caller not having had his conversation for the first call, a record was made for his second call at the exchange. Robertson made a note of it, pencilling the time (which was showing 7.20pm on the exchange clock) with the letters N.R. (no reply) in the margin.

Wallace had had a slight attack of flu on the Saturday previous and did not do his usual collection. He had stayed at home and steeped his feet in mustard and hot water, then followed this up with a cupful of whisky with hot water. The remedy seemed to do the trick as Wallace was then well enough to make a visit to the Chess Club. He claimed he left his house by the back door at 7.15pm and made his way along Richmond Park to the tram stop at the corner of Breck Road and Belmont Road, where he took a No.14 tram. He alighted at the corner of Lord Street and North John Street. Sometime that same evening Julia called at her doctor, Louis Curwen.[29] Over the weekend she'd had a bad cough and had been unable to sleep properly.

At 7.20pm waitress Gladys Harley answered the telephone. She heard a voice saying "Anfield is calling you." The next voice she heard was deep and spoke very quickly. The caller asked if Wallace was there, and said that it was with regard to the Chess Club. The waitress told the caller that she would fetch the Captain, Beattie. Beattie had known Wallace for eight years but did not know what he did for a living. Beattie made his way over to the telephone. In a gruffish, strong voice the caller asked if Wallace was there and if

from an automatic exchange and the call could be self-dialled, then for this fee it could last as long as the caller desired. With operator-connected calls, 2d bought three minutes during the day and six minutes in the evening/night. Dave Shawyer email to the author, 4th August 2014.

29 A graduate of Dublin University and Trinity College, Curwen came to Liverpool in 1925. During the First World War he served in the R.A.M.C. in France and also at Salonika, attaining the rank of captain. He was the Medical Officer to Liverpool Football Club (a position he held for almost 20 years). Curwen died of a heart attack at his home, 111 Priory Road on 13th January 1952. He also had a practice at 59 Anfield Road.

he could speak with him. Beattie notified the caller that Wallace had yet to arrive:

"Will he be there?"

"I cannot say," replied Beattie.

"Can you give me his address?"

"I am afraid I cannot."

"Will you be sure to see him?"

"I don't know. I cannot say."

"Could you get in touch with Wallace? It is a matter of importance for him."

"I'm not sure," replied Beattie again.

"I will be busy and do not know if I can contact him. It is my daughter's 21st birthday and I want to do something for her which would be in the nature of business for Mr Wallace."

Beattie then told the caller that if he couldn't get the message to Wallace himself, he could do it through a friend.[30] The caller then left Beattie instructions for Wallace to call on him the following evening – 20th January. Being an agent for the Prudential Assurance Company Wallace had the authority to go to any part of the city to get new business in connection with ordinary branch Insurance and general branch Insurance, but with regard to Industrial Branch business it was not general practice, but not against the rules, for an agent to conduct business in another district. The caller gave his name – R.M. Qualtrough – and an address – 25 Menlove Gardens East – with the instruction for Wallace to call on him at 7.30pm. Beattie asked the caller to spell the name and then wrote the details down, repeated the information back to the caller and said that he would pass the message on to Wallace. Beattie then went back to his game of chess.

At approximately 7.35pm James Caird arrived at the Chess Club. He was a friend of Wallace and lived in Letchworth Street, not far from Wolverton Street. They had known each other for well over a decade[31] and had joined the Club together. Caird wandered

30 James Caird was a grocer by trade, his shop being at 113 Stanley Road, Kirkdale. He won the Class 1 Chess Championship in 1933.

31 In his statement to the police conducted at the City Café on 26th January Caird said he

around the club, looking at some of the matches in progress. At about 7.45pm he went over to Wallace, who had by then arrived,[32] and asked if he would play a game. Wallace politely refused, knowing that he was well behind in his rota of games, so wanted to get a championship game scratched off. As Chandler was absent, Wallace saw Thomas McCartney (who was in his section of the championship) and asked him to play. McCartney, who hadn't seen Wallace for exactly a year, agreed and they commenced.

Caird walked around the tables, watching other games in progress. When he reached the table occupied by Beattie, the Captain asked him if he had Wallace's address. Caird notified Beattie that Wallace had arrived and was sitting at a table behind. Beattie made his way over and had to attract the attention of an absorbed Wallace, who was contemplating a move:[33]

"Oh, Mr Wallace, I have a message for you."

"Oh, who from?"

"From a man named Qualtrough."

"Qualtrough, Qualtrough, who is Qualtrough?" replied Wallace.

"Well if you do not know who he is I do not. He said that he wished to see you tomorrow evening at 7.30. The address is 25 Menlove Gardens East. He said it is in the nature of your business."

"I don't know the chap. Where is Menlove Gardens East? Is it Menlove Avenue?" asked Wallace.

"No. Menlove Gardens East," replied Beattie.

had known Wallace for 12 to 14 years. In his testimony at the trial he stated 14 or 15 years. Trial Transcript p.27.

32 In his police statement Caird said that he actually saw Wallace arrive. In *The Murder of Julia Wallace*, James Murphy states that the usual club rule that games had to start before 7.45pm was waived in the event of arranged games due to non-attendees, thereby making it possible that Wallace could have arrived later than 7.45pm. While this is a valid point, it presupposes Wallace's knowledge – he did not know that F.C. Chandler would not arrive. If Chandler had arrived and Wallace would have been late it surely would have been noted and deemed highly suspicious. Incidentally, tournament games had to start by 7.30pm.

33 There are contradictory reports of the game between Wallace and McCartney. Wallace was scheduled to play black for their game on 24th November 1930, yet at the trial Beattie said that Wallace was thinking out the opening move. In 1931 it was recognised that white made the first move [Trial Transcript p.24]. Wallace's opponent Thomas McCartney said that they had commenced playing for five or ten minutes before being approached by Beattie. [Thomas McCartney Witness Statement, 26th January 1931]. Wallace said they had been playing about ten minutes when Beattie delivered the message to him. [William Herbert Wallace Witness Statement, 22nd January 1931].

"Where is Menlove Gardens East?"

"Wait a moment. I will see whether Deyes[34] will know where Menlove Gardens East is. I know that one comes into Menlove Avenue and the other one, I think, goes into Queens Drive. It is an awkward place to be knocking about in the dark for. I will just see whether Deyes knows where Menlove Gardens East is."

"I belong to Liverpool," replied Wallace.

Wallace wrote the details down in his memorandum book across the spaces for the dates 26th and 27th January. He uttered 'Menlove Gardens West' and was immediately corrected by Beattie that it was 'East.'[35] After the words 'Mossley Hill' Wallace wrote 'East' in block letters. Beattie then went to ask Deyes, but although he knew Menlove Gardens, Deyes did not know whether there was an East.

Beattie's advice was for Wallace to take a car to Penny Lane but to get the location first and then enquire.

McCartney asked Wallace where he lived and then suggested that he should take a car which ran from Spellow Lane to Smithdown Road.

"I have a tongue in my head. I can ask when I get there," was Wallace's reply.

At about 10.15pm Wallace, accompanied by others, left the club. Wallace, Caird and another member named H.M. Betton[36] boarded a West Derby Road tram and made their way home, Caird and Betton sitting together. Betton stayed on the tram as Wallace and Caird alighted at Belmont Road. As they walked Wallace discussed his game with McCartney, which he was pleased to have won. The talk then went to the subject of the telephone call and the name Qualtrough:

"Qualtrough," said Wallace, "have you heard of that name before?"

34 Edgar Bertram Deyes lived in Beech Lane, Menlove Avenue at the time, but did not know if Menlove Gardens East existed or not.

35 There was no reason for Wallace to have thought it was Menlove Gardens West. When spoken, west sounds nothing like east. In any case, Beattie gave Wallace the envelope on which he had written down the details so it was visible to him.

36 Harold Melbourne Betton. He was a first class player and lived at 51 Guernsey Road. He won the Chess Championship two consecutive years; 1932 and 1933.

"I have only heard of one person of the name of Qualtrough," replied Caird.

They then discussed the address. Caird suggested that Wallace should go on the bus along Queens Drive. Wallace, uncertain whether he would even make the journey, said that if he did decide to go he would take the most direct course by going into town and from there to Menlove Avenue. They walked down Letchworth Street where Caird bid Wallace farewell before entering his home at number three. Wallace continued home, placed his key in the door and opened it without any difficulty.

2

TUESDAY 20 JANUARY 1931

At 10.30am Wallace left the house to go collecting on his rounds in the Clubmoor[37] district adjacent to Anfield. He was dressed in a tweed suit and, as it was drizzling and a grey sky covered the city, he decided to wear his mackintosh and bowler. Julia stayed at home doing her household duties. He didn't work on Fridays, but collected on Saturday mornings.[38] He would make over 560 calls a week. Three weeks out of four he could collect between £30 and £40. Each fourth week it might be anything between £80 and £100 – possibly even more on occasions.[39] This was referred to as a 'monthly week' and had fallen on the 12th January, the previous week. Wallace remitted the money to the Prudential Offices in Dale Street each week, and although it had to be paid in by Wednesdays the practice was not enforced. Sometimes he paid in on Thursdays.

At about 10.30am a man selling laces called at number 27

37 As the name suggests, Club Moor was a rough uncultivated area of moorland. A haunt of robbers and outlaws, it became a more cultivated and enclosed area in the 18th century. At the turn of the 20th Century it remained a hamlet with a rural backdrop.

38 His weekly salary was £3 16s 0d per week, and his average commission and bonus was about £2 per week.

39 The first Prudential agents were appointed in 1848 (the year the company was founded) before the company's registration was complete. At first the company had a very small team of agents, but after the Industrial Department opened in 1854 to sell insurance to the working classes, the team grew into a sizeable number. By the turn of the century there were 10,000 Prudential agents and they had sold insurance to one third of the population. In the 1960s, six million homes in Britain were visited by the Prudential agent. The agents were issued with regularly updated instructions which contained precise details about conducting business, filling in forms and keeping accounts. Any agents who broke the rules were dealt with severely. The directors were anxious to achieve a reputation for fair dealing that would differentiate the Prudential from its rivals. 'The Man from the Pru' became part of the national vocabulary. He was referred to in nineteenth century music hall tradition, most memorably in Stanley Holloway's recitation about *Young Albert*, recorded in the 1930s, which gave the Prudential a great deal of gratuitous publicity [Prudential Group Archives History Sheet].

Wolverton Street, the home of Walter and Bertha Holme. Mrs Holme didn't buy any from him.

At approximately 11.00am window cleaner Arthur Hoer[40] called at 29 Wolverton Street. Julia opened the front door and handed him a bucket of water. He had known Mrs Wallace for a number of years and was there for a few minutes, cleaning the outside front windows. His wife Emily occasionally assisted him when he was behind in his work. They spent several hours on the houses in Wolverton Street. Arthur Hoer cleaned the back windows of number 27 before leaving at 2.00pm to attend a meeting of the Marketing Committee at the Municipal Offices.

About midday another man called at number 27 Wolverton Street. He was selling bootlaces and buttons. Mrs Holme informed the man that she didn't want anything, and that another man had already called earlier.

Shortly before 2.00pm Wallace made his last call at 177 Lisburn Lane. He then took a tram to Holy Trinity Church on Breck Road. He arrived home at approximately 2.10pm and had dinner. Ten days earlier Julia had to see her doctor regarding a touch of bronchitis, but apart from a slight cold she was otherwise well.[41] At 2.30pm Arthur Hoer's brother-in-law Charles Bliss arrived in Wolverton Street to take the ladders away. As the front windows had all been done and several top windows were in need of doing, Emily Hoer asked her brother if he would do them.

At 3.15pm Wallace returned to Clubmoor to continue his rounds. He was then wearing a light fawn overcoat and trilby, as the weather had turned out finer.

At approximately 3.30pm Police Constable 206G James Edward Rothwell left his house at 30 Craigs Road to sign on duty at Anfield Road Police Station. He cycled along Antrim Street, Finvoy Road into Knoclaid Road, then onto Maiden Lane to Townsend Lane.

40 Arthur Brian Hoer was born in Truro, Cornwall in 1899. He represented Labour in the Vauxhall Ward in the Liverpool City Council. He was first elected in November 1928, when his return was uncontested. During his time he was a member of the Markets, Water, Cemeteries and Allotments Committees.

41 The Wallaces were constantly afflicted by some sort of ailment or other on what seemed a weekly basis.

About 30 yards from the end of Maiden Lane he saw Wallace walking towards him, hands in his overcoat, looking down towards the ground. Rothwell had been a client of Wallace's and had known him for about two years. The constable had also been on uniform duty at Anfield Road Police Station for about eight months, working the No. 2 beat which included Richmond Park and Wolverton Street. It appeared to Rothwell that Wallace looked distressed and was crying.

At about 3.30pm Wallace's sister-in-law Amy[42] called at 29 Wolverton Street (she had also visited Julia on the Sunday 18th). She was married to Wallace's brother Joseph, and had returned to England from the Orient in June 1929. In the summer of that year she went to Anglesey on holiday with the Wallaces and had also stayed with them at their home for a fortnight before eventually moving to Ullet Road in September 1929. Julia offered her tea, but Amy declined. During their conversation Julia told Amy of the telephone message left for Wallace the previous evening, and notified her of Wallace's planned visit to Menlove Gardens that evening. Julia told Amy that neither she nor her husband knew anyone in that area. Amy Wallace noticed that, apart from a slight cold, Julia was her usual self.

Just after 3.30pm Wallace called at 11 Pennsylvania Road, the home of Letitia Harrison. She had known Wallace for about three years. She noticed nothing unusual about him – in fact he had a joke with her. He also called on Alice Addey of 32 Pennsylvania Road. She had known Wallace for 16 years and claimed he appeared the same as usual.[43]

42 Amy Margaret Blackwell was born in Ulverston in 1877. It was there that she married Joseph Wallace in 1909. In 1911 they were living at 137 Cambridge Street, Pimlico in London. That same year their son Edwin Herbert was born. She died on 14th August 1960 at Stanley Hospital, Ulverston.

43 As well as the mentioned clients, Wallace also called at the following on Tuesday 20th January; Maud Muir, 42 Pennsylvania Road (at about 4.00pm). Emily McParlin (who had known Wallace for 14 years), 5 Worcester Drive (3.30-3.40). George Boyd, 6 Worcester Drive (4.00-4.30). Blanche Elizabeth Richards, 17 Worcester Drive. Gertrude Phythian, 10 Worcester Drive (4.30-4.45). Lottie Lowry (who had known Wallace for 12 years), 40 Worcester Drive (about 3.45). Caroline Keill, 6 Worcester Drive North. She had known Wallace for 3 years and claimed it wasn't unusual for him to wipe his eyes with a handkerchief. Matilda Smith, 8 Worcester Drive had known Wallace for 10 months and claimed he 'definitely called after 4pm.' Jane Elizabeth Harbord, 15 Worcester Drive (3.30). John Burton (he had known Wallace for a few

At approximately 3.45pm a motor car pulled up outside number 27 Wolverton Street. Two men got out and knocked at the door. Mrs Holme answered it. She noticed a woman sitting in the back seat. One of the men informed Mrs Holme that they were from Electrolux, and that she had made a complaint about her appliance. The men were invited into the parlour to look at her machine. After examining it one said that the machine was alright but she could always exchange it for a new one and pay the difference. The man said he would call in a few days' time.

Between 4.00-4.15pm Wallace called at 8 Londonderry Road. Edith Earnshaw had known Wallace for 15 years. He also called at 16 in the same road, home of Amy Lawrence. He was asked in and Mrs Lawrence's husband offered him a cup of tea, which he accepted. Mrs Lawrence had known Wallace for twelve months.

At approximately 4.15pm baker's errand boy Neil Norbury[44] knocked at 29 Wolverton Street to deliver a loaf. Julia answered. She was wearing a scarf wrapped around her neck to protect her from the cold. She was always nice to the boy. Norbury noticed that Mrs Wallace didn't look too well. She told him that she thought she had bronchitis. At approximately 4.30pm Amy Wallace left.

Between 4.15-4.30pm Emily Hoer was cleaning the bottom back windows of 73 and 63 Richmond Park, with Bliss cleaning the back tops of Wolverton Street.

At 4.30pm Bliss was at the back of No. 29, after having cleaned the top windows. When he finished he was pulling the ladders over the dividing wall into No. 31 when Mrs Wallace came to the back kitchen door. He was then standing on the ladder in No. 31 when she asked him where Mr Hoer was. Bliss told her that Hoer

months), 64 Glengariff Street (5.00-5.15). Ann Miller, 4 Brookbridge Road (she said Wallace asked her the time, she looked at the clock and noticed that it was 6 o'clock). Other clients in the Clubmoor area (but who did not see Wallace on the Tuesday) were Margaret Prince, 8 Pennsylvania Road and Minnie Palmer, 27 Missouri Road (she had known Wallace for 14 years).

44 The *Evening Express* erroneously reported that apart from Wallace, Norbury was the last person to see Mrs Wallace alive (*Evening Express,* 21st January 1931). Neil Norbury was born in 1915. He married Mary Rimmer in 1936, joined the Territorials before the war then became Gunner 1082653 in 3 Regiment, Royal Horse Artillery. He died on active service in the Middle East on 28th January 1943.

had to leave. Mrs Wallace said that she would pay him then (this conversation was heard by Florence Johnston from No. 31). Mrs Wallace gave him a shilling and Bliss gave her 3d change. Mrs Wallace, who appeared to Bliss to be in her usual spirits, went back into the kitchen. He then cleaned numbers 31 and 33 Wolverton Street and 63, 73 and 77 Richmond Park.

At 5.00pm Emily Hoer was cleaning the ground floor windows at No. 31, and at about 5.15pm was at No. 29. Here she cleaned the bottom back windows, the kitchen and back kitchen. The back yard door and back kitchen door were both shut. She noticed the light on in the kitchen, but the blind drawn. She heard no sound from the house, but noticed a light in the back bedroom. Mrs Hoer had known Mrs Wallace for about ten years. She assumed Mrs Wallace must have been ill, as she always spoke to her when she was cleaning the windows. There was no light from the back kitchen/scullery. At 5.20pm Mrs Hoer finished. She took the ladders out of the yard and met Bliss in the entry.

Sometime after 5.30pm Wallace called at 19 Eastman Road, it being his last call of the day. Mrs Margaret Martin answered the door. Wallace had called at her house for over two years, once a fortnight, and usually called at about 6.00pm on Mondays. His call was with regard to Mrs Martin's daughter Marguerite surrendering her insurance policy to the Prudential. Wallace left papers and said he would call back at about 5.00pm the following evening to pay Miss Martin £5 17s 0d. Mrs Martin noticed that Wallace appeared calm, collected and the same in appearance. It was 5.55pm when he left.

Wallace boarded a bus at Queens Drive and Townsend Avenue and alighted at Cabbage Hall. He arrived home by the back door at 6.05pm. After having tea of bread, scones and a cup of tea with Julia, he gathered some of the papers and forms that he required before going upstairs to the bathroom to wash his hands and face. He then went into the bedroom, changed his collar, brushed his hair then came back downstairs.

At 6.30pm Benjamin Wade left his house by the front door of 16

Wolverton Street. He was on his way to the Picturedrome. Crossing the road and entering the passage between numbers 19 and 21 Wolverton Street, he passed a man who had come from the entry at the back of the houses numbered 21 to 37. The man appeared to be about 29 years of age, 5 ft 10 to 11in, wearing a black overcoat, trilby hat and black boots. He had a dark slight moustache and was sharp-featured.

Sometime between 6.30-6.35pm David Jones delivered a copy of the *Liverpool Echo* to 29 Wolverton Street. He had delivered the paper there for four or five years, and usually at 6.30pm. He entered Wolverton Street through the middle entryway leading from Richmond Park. He did not notice anyone in the entry. When he put the *Echo* through the letterbox of number 29 he did not notice any lights on, nor heard or saw anyone in the house. Jones then delivered another paper at number 12 before exiting through the entry into Redbourne Street. He did not see anyone else in the street while he was there.

16-year-old James Allison Wildman[45] delivered newspapers mornings and evenings for his uncle, William Wildman.[46] He usually started his evening round at 6.20pm and first delivered at numbers 11, 19, 21 and 28 Suburban Road, then at 42 Winchester Road, 34 Clarendon Road and 52 and 48 Claude Road. Wildman

45 James Allison Wildman was born at 5 Twickenham Street on 7th December 1914. Better known as 'Al,' he started school in January 1919 at Anfield Road Council School. When he was seven he joined the Rawdon Library, where he spent a lot of his time. He was quite good at sport and played at Anfield in the final of the Under Twelve football competition. His team won and he was presented with a silver medal. He also excelled at cricket, opening the batting for the school. Two of Wildman's classmates made names for themselves; Alex Scott played in goal for Wolverhampton Wanderers in their glory days, and Raymond Crane grew up to be Lord Mayor of Liverpool. Al left school in December 1928. It being the height of the great recession, he found a temporary position with a firm of importers, Scoff Bros, but this only lasted six weeks. After being out of work for six months he was taken on at Cowan and Co. Haulage Contractors on the East side of No. 1 Canada Dock in Bootle, at the foot of Canada Dock Overhead Station. Road Transport was a reserved occupation, which was why he was not called up at the outbreak of World War Two. However, in April 1942 he received his call-up papers, and duly reported to Catterick Camp to the Royal Armoured Corps at Menin Lines. He saw service in South Africa, Egypt, Palestine, Iraq, Lebanon, Jordan, Italy and Germany. After the war he returned to his job with Cowan & Co. He married his sweetheart Myra on 3rd April 1948 at St Cyprian's Durning Road. Al and Myra had three children: Peter, Christopher and Alison. Al died on 27th October 2005 in Liverpool while visiting relatives.

46 Bill Wildman was a professional footballer who numbered among the clubs he played for Everton and West Ham United. He had to retire due to a very bad knee injury. The compensation he was awarded enabled him to buy the shop at 156 Lower Breck Road.

then went back to the shop, unpacked more newspapers and began the second part of his round, which incorporated four newspapers in Hanwell Street, one in Taplow Street, and two in Richmond Park. As he walked through the entry between Twyford Street and Richmond Park Wildman would always cast a glance at the Holy Trinity Church clock,[47] and on this night noticed that the time was 6.35.[48] It usually took him 2-3 minutes to reach Wolverton Street from here. He continued along Richmond Park to Campbell's Dance Hall and cut through the entry into Wolverton Street. Here, he delivered papers at numbers 28, 27, 22, 20 and 18. As he delivered the paper into number 27 Wildman noticed the door of 29 open and a milk-boy standing on the top step with two or three cans in his hand. The milk-boy was wearing a Collegiate cap. Wildman did not know the boy, but had seen him on his bicycle in Richmond Park. As Wildman left the milk-boy was still standing there. Wildman walked down the entry from Wolverton Street into Redford Street, down Richmond Park and onto Lower Breck Road.

Another paperboy, Douglas Metcalf,[49] delivered newspapers for confectioner John James Yates of 51 Breck Road. He delivered Mrs Davies's newspaper at the Parochial Hall. As he was hoping to go to attend a football match he asked a man there the time. The man told Metcalf it was twenty to seven. Metcalf then made his way over to Campbell's Dance Hall, and stood talking with some other boys. During the time he was there he noticed James Allison Wildman going down an entry off Wolverton Street.

13-year-old Alan Croxton Close[50] lived with his parents at 51

47 The tower has three clock faces. Contrary to belief they were not illuminated in 1931.

48 Wildman told his mother the following morning that he had been in Wolverton Street at about 6.35 the previous evening.

49 Douglas Metcalf was born on 22nd January 1917. He died on 13th April 1993, aged 76.

50 Alan Croxton Close was born on 10th February 1917 at 51 Sedley Street, Anfield to master carter and dairyman Henry and Agnes Ann (née Kettlewell). Alan was a pupil of the Liverpool Collegiate. The burden of the actual murder and subsequent trial must have had a profound effect on someone of such a young age. He met his future wife Daphne Edith Warren in Llandudno. They were married at St. Paul's Church, Sale on 15th March 1940, residing at 3 Baxter Road. Close was Sergeant Pilot 566591 in 23 Squadron, Fighter Command in the RAF with six years' service. At the beginning of the Second World War 23 Squadron undertook shipping protection and intruder missions in a night-fighter role, and from 31st May 1940 he was stationed at RAF Collyweston, Northamptonshire. Close's death certificate states that he died on 19th June (the cause of death being 'Air Combat with Enemy'). It was issued from the

Sedley Street, which doubled as a dairy. He delivered milk for his father and his round was usually from 5.30-6.30pm, but he was half an hour late due to his bicycle being damaged. He would also walk his round if it was raining. Close said he walked past Holy Trinity Church and noticed the clock, which read 6.25pm. He walked to the dairy, put the cans onto the counter and picked up fresh cans of milk. He then walked along Sedley Street to Letchworth Street, knocked on the door and handed a can of milk over, waited to get the can back, then walked down Letchworth Street to Richmond Park. There he saw 13-year-old Elsie May Wright.[51] The two exchanged greetings before carrying on. Close set down two bottles of milk in the garden of a house in Richmond Park, then walked across the road to the narrow entryway leading to Wolverton Street. He had delivered milk to number 29 for about two years. There, he knocked on the knocker, left a can of milk on the doorstep then went to No. 31. Mrs Johnston's regular practice was to leave a jug in the hallway, with the front door ajar. Close filled the jug from a can of milk, pulled the front door to and then returned to No. 29. He noticed the front door was open and that the can had been taken in. As far as the milkboy could see, there was no light in the parlour but one on in the kitchen. A moment or so later Julia returned to the front door, gave Close the can back and told him hurry home out of the cold. Close bid Mrs Wallace 'goodnight' before continuing on his way.

At 6.35pm Walter Holme was having his tea. He heard the front door of number 29 closing. It sounded to him like someone entering or leaving the house. Bertha Holme also heard the noise. She asked her husband if it was someone knocking at their front door. He replied in the negative, saying that it was someone at the Wallaces.

RAF Station Sutton Bridge, Marsland, Norfolk. He died just west of King's Lynn at Terrington, St. Clements, Lincolnshire. Flying with 23 Squadron he took off as the pilot of a Bleinham Mark If (call sign 'S' for a night patrol). They were shot down early am (which means he was killed on the 19th, not the 18th as stated on his gravestone). His companion LAC Lawrence Robert Karasek bailed out and survived the crash, but was killed in action three months later on 25th September 1940. C.W. Clough & Son were the funeral directors, and they arranged to collect Close's remains from Sale railway station on 21st June. He was buried the following day at Brooklands Cemetery, the coffin being draped by a Union Jack.

51 Elsie May Wright was born on 25th May 1917 and ended up working as an assistant shop worker in a drapery. Her father John was a widower and former chef on the RMS *Transylvania*.

The couple heard no other noise for the rest of the evening.

The night was damp, dark and moonless. Wallace left the house by the back door at approximately 6.45pm. Wearing a dark overcoat and trilby, he turned left into the alleyway, continued along, then right, through the narrow entryway between numbers 79 and 81 Richmond Park.[52] From there he crossed the road and walked up the narrow alley alongside the Parochial Hall, up past the steps at the top before emerging into Sedley Street. From there he walked straight ahead, turned left into Pendennis Street, continued along, and then turned right into Castlewood Road.[53] Continuing to the top, he turned left into Belmont Road[54] and walked down the left-hand side to the corner of St Margaret's Church.[55]

Here Wallace then boarded the number 26 tram. It took him along Sheil Road, right into Kensington, left into Holt Road and across the junction of Edge Lane into Durning Road,[56] then across the junction of Wavertree Road and onto Tunnel Road. The tram travelled up to the top of Tunnel Road, where Wallace alighted.[57]

He crossed over the road to the tram stop on Smithdown Lane. At 7.06pm the number 5 tram stopped. A sizeable crowd was waiting to board. Wallace was about the last to board, and in an excited manner asked conductor Thomas Charles Phillips if the car went to Menlove Gardens East. Phillips informed him that it did not and that a 7 or 5w would. Phillips then told Wallace that he could give him a transfer ticket or penny fare and he could change. Wallace boarded, telling Phillips that he was a stranger in the district and

52 Retaining their character are the streets leading to and around Wolverton Street; Sedley, Letchworth, Taplow, Twyford and Twickenham amongst others. The erecting of security alley gates in recent years though has rendered the maze of entries inaccessible.

53 Castlewood Road was formerly called Osborne Road, the name change occurring in 1914/15.

54 Convicted poisoner Frederick Henry Seddon lived at 88 Belmont Road in 1901. He eventually lived at 63 Tollington Park in North London, and was hanged in 1912 for the murder of Eliza Mary Barrow.

55 The distance from the back door of 29 Wolverton Street to St Margaret's Church was 605 yards.

56 In 1900 Herbert Rowse Armstrong was living at 52 Durning Road. He was the only solicitor in Britain to have been hanged for murder. He lived in Hay-on-Wye and was arrested in December 1921 for the attempted murder of rival solicitor Oswald Martin by arsenical poisoning. He was later also charged with the murder of his wife Katherine.

57 The distance was 1.7 miles.

that he had an urgent call at Menlove Gardens East. He then took the first seat on the right-hand side of the car. Phillips punched him a penny ticket. Wallace then again reminded the conductor that he wanted to get to Menlove Gardens East. Phillips continued collecting fares inside and outside. When he reached the platform Wallace repeated his appeal to the conductor. Phillips told him that he would have to change at Penny Lane. At Earle Road ticket inspector Edward Angus boarded, the tram continuing along Smithdown Road. Angus alighted at the stop at Portman Road[58] at 7.10pm. When the tram reached Penny Lane, Phillips shouted "Menlove Gardens. Change here," Wallace alighted.[59] He then boarded a number 5a and sat on the left-hand side of the car which left Penny Lane at 7.15pm. He asked conductor Arthur Thompson to put him off at Menlove Gardens East. When the car reached Menlove Gardens West, at the junction of Menlove Avenue, Thompson beckoned Wallace over to the platform and told him this was his stop. Wallace thanked him, said "I am a complete stranger in the area," then alighted.[60]

At 7.20pm – precisely twenty four hours since the telephone call to the Chess Club – Wallace walked along the right-hand side of Menlove Gardens West and turned right into Menlove Gardens North, still on the gardens side. At about the sixth to eighth house along he saw a woman exiting the gate. He stepped into the middle

58 Not far from Portman Road stood the Cameo Cinema, which was situated on the corner of Bird Street and Webster Road. On 19th March 1949 manager Leonard Thomas and his assistant Bernard Catterall were counting the evening's takings in an office upstairs when a masked gunman entered the office to rob them. Both men were fatally shot. The money was left behind and the gunman was chased where he escaped onto Smithdown Road. During the investigations information was received alleging George Kelly and an accomplice, Charles Connolly, were responsible. After two trials, both men were convicted. Kelly was hanged and Connolly received ten years' imprisonment. In 2003 the convictions for both men were deemed to be unsafe and were quashed. On 16th April 1951, 55-year-old Lillian Harris Parr and her 25-year-old daughter Lillian Beryl Beech were both shot dead in the back kitchen of their home at 32 Underley Street (also along Smithdown Road). The killer was younger Lillian's 29-year-old estranged husband (Ray) Walter Richard Beech. The following day Beech killed himself with a single bullet from a Colt .45 to the brain in the Princes Park Hotel, 118 Upper Stanhope Street. On 19th August 1951 Beatrice Alice Rimmer was bludgeoned to death in the hallway of her home at 7 Cranborne Road (adjacent to Webster Road). Two Mancunians, Alfred Burns and Edward Devlin, were arrested. Both men were denied reprieves and were hanged at Walton prison.

59 The distance from Smithdown Lane to Penny Lane was 1.6 miles.

60 The distance from Penny Lane to Menlove Gardens West was 0.4 miles.

of the road and enquired of her the whereabouts of Menlove Gardens East, but she did not know where it was. Wallace tracked back and turned right into Menlove Gardens West to the corner of Dudlow Lane. It was here that he met 23-year-old clerk Sydney Hubert Green.[61] Wallace asked him directions, but Green notified him that there was no East as far as he was aware. Wallace thanked him and said he would try 25 Menlove Gardens West, where he rang at the address. Katie Ellen Mather was listening to *The Geisha* on the radio when Wallace called. She answered the door. Wallace asked her if there was a Mr Qualtrough there, and that he was looking for Menlove Gardens East. Mrs Mather told him that there was nobody there of that name, and that there was no such place as Menlove Gardens East. Wallace exclaimed that it was funny there being no East. He thanked Mrs Mather then walked back along Menlove Gardens West and turned into Menlove Gardens South. As he walked along here Wallace realised that the house numbers were all even. He carried on along and onto the junction with Menlove Gardens North, but again the houses here were also even-numbered. Puzzled, he walked onto Menlove Avenue and asked someone standing under a shelter, but he was also a stranger in the area and could not help. Wallace walked across Menlove Avenue and into Green Lane. He later claimed that he then recognised where he was – it was the street on which Joseph Crewe,[62] his Superintendent at the Prudential, resided. Wallace called at Crewe's house at number 34 but received no answer – unbeknownst to him, Crewe was spending the evening at the cinema. Wallace walked down Green Lane and arrived at the junction of Allerton Road. It was here that he encountered Constable 220F James Edward Serjeant, who had just left Allerton Road police station. Wallace asked Serjeant to direct him to Menlove Gardens East. Serjeant

61 Green died on 16th January 1981.

62 Joseph Crewe was born on 4th April 1875 and was a weaver before starting with the Prudential. In March 1898 he was an agent, Fulwood; January 1903 Assistant Superintendent, Blackley; January 1910 Assistant Superintendent, Windsor; August 1914 Assistant Superintendent, Dingle; January 1919 Superintendent, Anfield; January 1927 Superintendent, Everton. He resigned December 1934 due to the limit on age. He was married to Agnes (*née* Dearden), who was born on 4th November 1874. They had two daughters, Jean and Marie. Joseph Crewe died on 18th December 1942 at a Blackpool nursing home and was buried at Preston Cemetery.

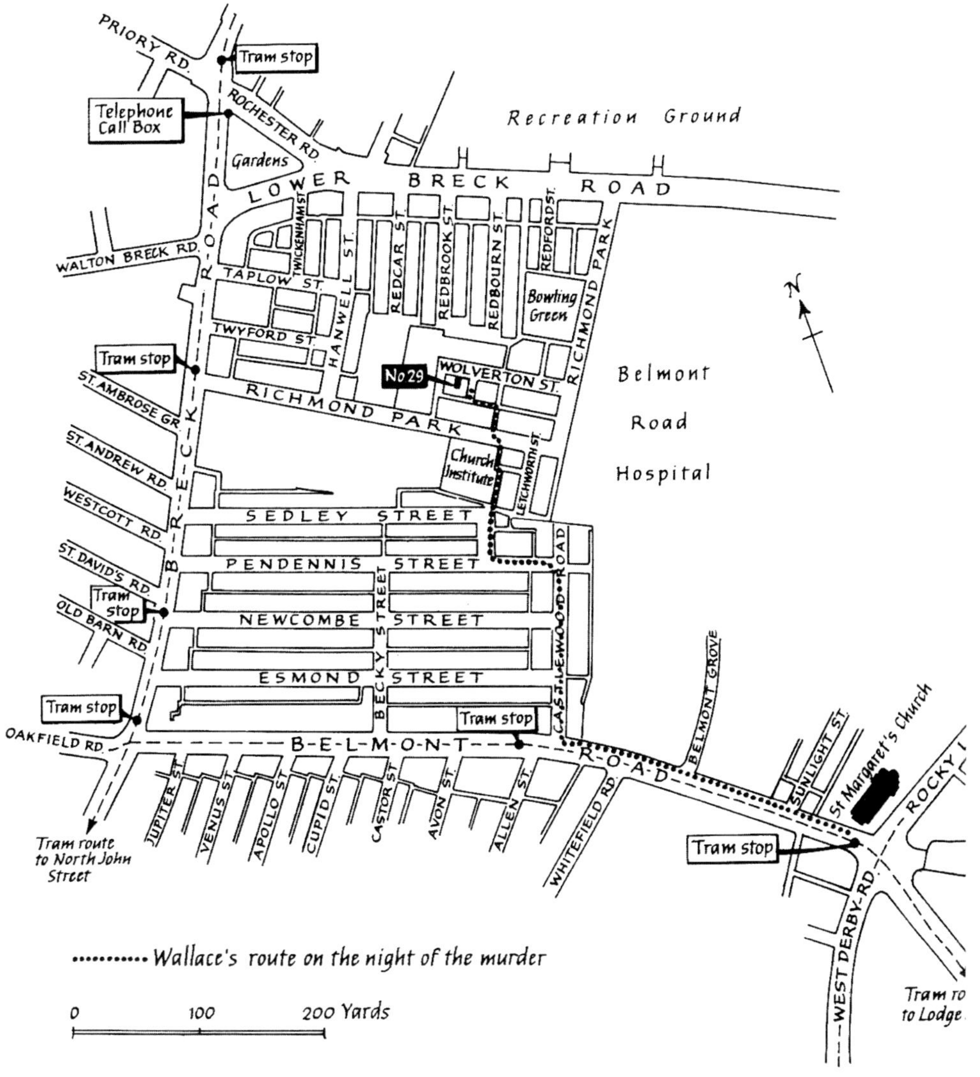

Map of Anfield (Courtesy Roger Wilkes)

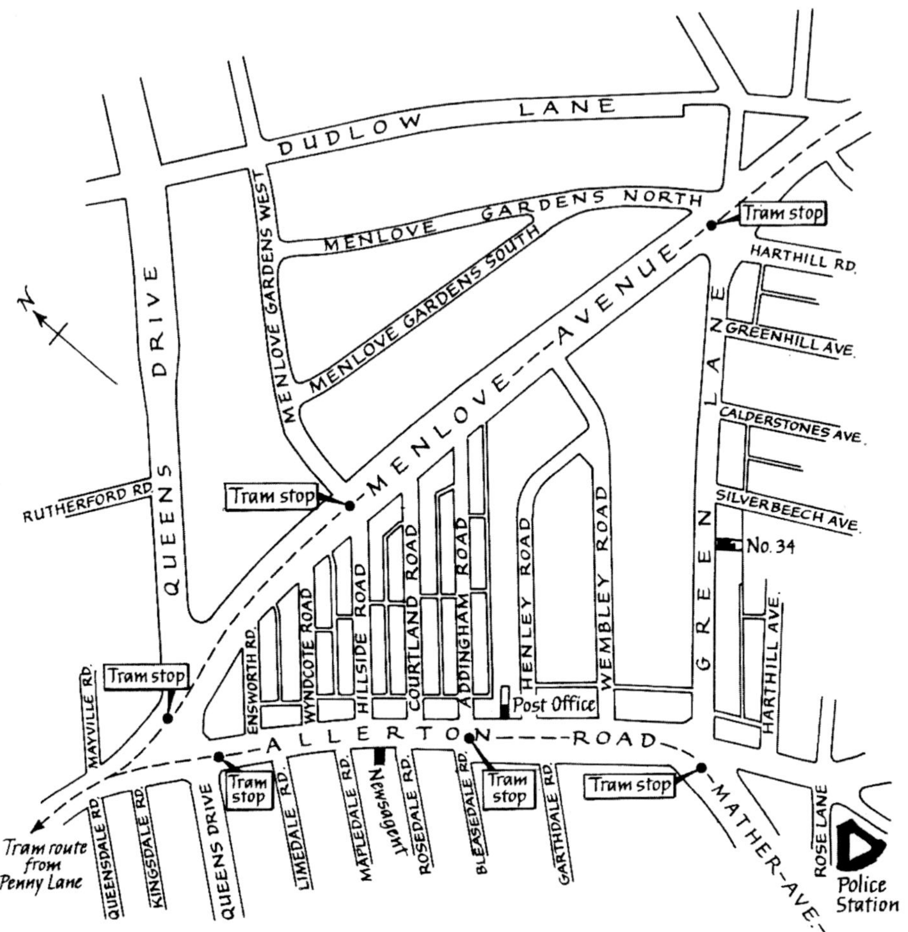

Map of Allerton (Courtesy Roger Wilkes)

informed Wallace that there was no such place as Menlove Gardens East, but there was a North, South and West. Wallace told the constable that he had been to 25 Menlove Gardens West but the person he was looking for didn't live there. Wallace mentioned his business and the potential client 'Quallthorp.'[63] Serjeant suggested that Wallace should try 25 Menlove Avenue. "Is it far away?" asked Wallace. At first Serjeant replied that it was in the first or second block, but then remembered correctly that it was the third house in the second block. Wallace thanked him, half turned away, then turned back and asked if there was anywhere where he could consult a directory. Serjeant advised him that the Post Office might have one. Barring that, the police station[64] might let him use one. Wallace compared the time with Serjeant. It was then 7.45pm.[65]

Wallace walked along Allerton Road to the Post Office, but was told by the man serving that they didn't have a directory. He advised Wallace to try the newsagents on the opposite side of the road. Wallace crossed the road and made his way to Allday's Newsagents at 130 Allerton Road. It was sometime about 7.55pm. He spoke to shop assistant, Nancy Collins, who fetched a directory. Manageress Lily Pinches made her way over to the cigarette counter where Wallace was standing, browsing the directory. He informed the manageress of his intention of finding the client and the address. Pinches notified him that there was no East – only a South and West. She also looked in her account book but said that the residents of 25 Menlove Gardens West were not listed – they were not customers of hers. Wallace told her that he had been to that address but it wasn't the person he was looking for. He left the shop and made his way to the tram stop near to the Plaza cinema. At about 8.10pm he boarded the number 8 tram, which took him back along Penny Lane and Smithdown Road. He then took the number 27 tram along Tunnel Road and the same route in which

63 James Edward Serjeant Witness Statement, 21st January 1931. Serjeant was born on 30th March 1898 and died in 1968.

64 Allerton Police and Fire Station was opened on 23rd October 1930.

65 It has been argued that Wallace was comparing the time with Serjeant in order to establish his whereabouts at the time. The defence claimed that Wallace was asking the time merely in innocence, as he was not sure whether the shops would still be open.

he made his outward journey.

At about 8.15pm Ann Jane Parsons of 281 Lower Breck Road was walking along Hanwell Street, where she saw a man 'racing like mad' down towards Lower Breck Road. Shortly afterwards she saw another man running in the same direction. James S. Wood of 303 Walton Breck Road also witnessed a man running.

Between 8.25-8.30pm Florence Johnston was in her kitchen. She heard two thumps. She attributed the noise to her father (who lived in the front room) taking off his boots. She didn't hear any other unusual noises all the other time.

At approximately 8.35pm 38-year-old Henry Harrison Greenlees of 95 Richmond Park said that the Holy Trinity Church was lightly illuminated and that he was accosted by a stockily-built man wearing a felt hat. The man asked for 54 Richmond Park, but Greenlees notified him that no such number existed. Greenlees saw no-one else in Richmond Park as he entered his house at about 8.40pm.

Wallace arrived at his front door at about 8.45pm. He tried his key but found he could not open it. He knocked gently but got no answer. There was no light from the house. He then walked around the alley[66] to the back entry, opened the back yard door, which was unbolted, walked up the yard and tried to open the back door, but was unable to gain access. He noticed a small light in the back kitchen, but no light in the kitchen. He knocked on the back door. Florence Johnston heard this but thought nothing of it as she recognised his knock, having heard it on numerous occasions. Wallace received no answer so went back to the front of the house and tried the key again. The lock did not work properly – the key turned then unturned without unlocking the door. Wallace again went to the back of the house. As he walked past the back door of No. 31 John and Florence Johnston were coming out of their house:

"Good evening, Mr Wallace," said Mrs Johnston.

66 From the front door of 29 Wolverton Street to the back door there were two ways; 1) by an entry on the south side (which was paved and dry at the time), and 2) by an entry to the north side. This was twelve yards further and unpaved and muddy.

"Have you heard anything unusual?" replied Wallace.

"Why, what has happened?" asked Mrs Johnston.

Wallace related to the Johnstons that he had tried both front and back doors but was unable to get in either. Mr Johnston suggested that Wallace try again, and if it didn't work he would get his key and try it. Wallace opened the back yard door and walked up the yard to the back kitchen door. He looked over his shoulder and told them that his wife wouldn't have gone out as she had a bad cold. He turned the handle and found that the door unlocked: "It opens now," he exclaimed. Before entering the kitchen Wallace asked the Johnstons to wait while he had a look inside the house.

The Johnstons waited in the entry as Wallace went in. In the back kitchen a small light, almost out, was by the gas over the sink. Wallace lit the light in the middle kitchen then went upstairs. There was a light on in the middle bedroom which, after a few moments, went up. From outside the Johnstons saw the light of a match in the room that had been converted into a chemistry room. John Johnston heard Wallace call out twice.

Minutes later he exited the back door in an upset and distressed state: "Come and see. She has been killed," he said in a raised voice.

He then led the Johnstons through the kitchen and into the front parlour.[67] Mrs Johnston had been in the front room on three occasions in ten years, and on all three occasions Mr Wallace was out. Julia's body was lying diagonally across the black rug in front of the unlit Sunbeam gas fire, face down, looking towards the piano. Her head was about eighteen inches from the open door, to one side, with portions of brain matter and large quantities of blood at a radius of nine inches on the floor. Her feet were close to the right-hand fender. From the dimly-lit right-hand gas mantle on the wall could be made out a huge wound above her left ear which had shattered her skull, revealing bits of brain. The blood was up the walls at an average of four feet and up to seven feet in areas. Taking the room with the fireplace to the north, a large patch of blood clot was on the north-western edge of the hearthrug, a large patch

67 The front parlour measured 11ft x 11ft, with a height of 9ft 4½in.

of blood clot and brain substance and bone by the south-western corner, on which the head was lying, and a little east of this a large patch of blood clot.

To the left of the fireplace, a two-seater chair, on the arm of which rested Wallace's violin case. Against the left-hand side of the room stood a sideboard and in front of this, near the doorway, a chair. The room was cluttered with photographs, paintings, furniture and ornaments. A table in the bay window held a potted aspidistra; a chaise longue in front and to the left of that; another table in front of that, on which stood another potted aspidistra plant. Against the wall adjacent to the door the piano stood with the lid open, holding sheets of music in its rack. Standing on top of the piano was an ornament in the shape of a shoe and four photographs, one of which was of Julia. On the wall above the piano hung a print of William Hatherell's *Lord Kitchener's 1902 homecoming from South Africa*. To the side of the piano, behind the door, were two chairs, one of which held a stack of sheet music on the seat. In front of the piano, an empty music stand. Two spent matches were in the doorway, a Bryant & May matchbox was on the table by the bay window.

Mrs Johnston asked Wallace if the matches were Mrs Wallace's, to which he replied, "Yes." Wallace bent down to grasp his wife's lifeless left hand. Florence Johnston followed suit muttering, "Oh you poor darling." John Johnston told Wallace not to touch anything, and that he would fetch the police and a doctor. The three of them then left the room and went into the kitchen.

Florence Johnston noticed a spent match in the doorway. On the floor was a small door which had been wrenched off a cabinet that contained photographic items belonging to Wallace. He reached up to the shelf and took a cash-box down, the hinge on the lid broken. Wallace had had it 16 years. Mr Johnston asked Wallace if there was anything missing. Wallace said about £4 was missing, but could not say for definite until he had checked his books. Mr Johnston then asked Wallace to check upstairs to see if everything was alright. Wallace went upstairs and came back down within minutes. He said that there was £4 in a jar that had not been taken.

John Johnston[68] hurried down Lower Breck Road to the home of his then GP, Dr Dunlop,[69] who advised him to report the matter to the police. Johnston ran to Anfield Road Police Station, arriving there at 9.05pm. He informed Constable 99G Saunders of the murder. Saunders, who was in charge of the station, immediately informed Constable 191G Frederick Roberts Williams,[70] who proceeded by bicycle to Wolverton Street. At the same time Saunders also telephoned for an ambulance as a precautionary measure.

Meanwhile, after spending a few minutes in the kitchen Wallace and Mrs Johnston went back into the front parlour. Wallace walked around to the window side, stooped over the body and said, "They've finished her. Look at the brains." He then held his wife's hand again, as did Mrs Johnston. She noticed that Mrs Wallace's hand had gotten colder. Mrs Johnston then glanced round the room and uttered "Whatever have they used?"

68 It must be assumed Johnston went out the back way on his journey to notify Dr Dunlop and the police.

69 The practice on Rochester Road had two doctors – John Dunlop and William Laing Dunlop.

70 PC Frederick Roberts Williams was born in Liverpool on 27th February 1900. He served in the Royal Navy on board HMS *Neptune* from April 1916 until 19th February 1919. His trade was clerk, and rank that of stoker. Auburn-haired with grey eyes, Williams stood 5ft 10½ and was an all-round sportsman – he boxed for the navy, played cricket for the police and was proficient at billiards and snooker. Appointed as a Police Constable on 7th April 1919, he was the first policeman to arrive at 29 Wolverton Street on the evening of 20th January and was subsequently commended for exercising thoroughness at the crime scene. He was also awarded a Vote of Thanks by the Liverpool Shipwreck and Humane Society in 1926 for using his initiative in stopping a runaway horse on Townsend Lane the previous year. At the time of the Wallace murder Williams was number 191G and lived with his family in Lowerson Crescent. In September 1937 he was given the number 193G. He resigned from the force on 22nd August 1946, and ended his days on the investigation department at Littlewoods, Walton Hall Avenue. Fred married Annie Pascoe on 19th May 1923 and they had two sons, George and Harry. George served on the HMS *Charybdis* during the Second World War. The *Charybdis* was a Royal Navy Dido-class cruiser built by Cammell Laird Shipyard in Birkenhead. The ship's motto was 'Just Another Day's Work.' On 21st October 1943, *Charybdis* was torpedoed in the English Channel by the German torpedo boats *T-23* and *T-27* during Operation Tunnel, with the loss of 30 officers and 432 others. George's action station was in the ammunition locker below X turret, aft. Sadly, George was among the casualties. In *The Killing of Julia Wallace* Jonathan Goodman claimed that sometime during the mid-1950s Dr Robert Coope was making a ward round in Broadgreen Hospital. There he was approached by a patient who gave his name as Fred Williams. Williams said that he believed Wallace to have been innocent, and that he wanted to discuss the case with Coope as there was a lot he could tell him. Due to a bout of influenza Coope himself was laid up in bed for three weeks. When fit again he went back to Broadgreen Hospital and to the ward but Williams was not there – he had apparently passed away a fortnight before. This account has no veracity whatsoever. Fred Williams died on 26th December 1947, and never shirked from his belief that Wallace was guilty of the murder.

Wallace fingered the crumpled mackintosh underneath the body and said, “Why, whatever was she doing with her mackintosh and my mackintosh?” Mrs Johnston held Mrs Wallace’s hand for the second time. “Is it your mackintosh?” replied Mrs Johnston. “Yes,” said Wallace, “it is mine.”

Wallace rose and left the room, followed by Mrs Johnston. They went back into the kitchen, the fire embers nearly out. Wallace twice showed emotion, sobbing and putting his hands to his head. Mrs Johnston suggested making the fire. She placed the wood on to the live embers as Wallace stirred it up and added the coal.

At 9.10pm there was a knock at the front door. Mrs Johnston went to answer it but had difficulty with the lock. Her house had previously had the same type of lock, but had been replaced by a Yale one which consisted of a knob that had to be turned, whereas the lock in number 29 had to be slid along. She was also slightly agitated, which was understandable under the circumstances. She moved aside to let Wallace open it. He beckoned PC Williams inside, notifying the constable that something terrible had happened.

Williams went into the front parlour. There he saw the body lying on its stomach in a twisted position on the mat in front of the fireplace, the head turned slightly towards the door, the feet towards the fireplace. The head was covered with blood, quantities of which were spattered across the floor and on the walls to the left of the fireplace. A small pad of hair or ‘chignon’ lay inches away from the head. A mackintosh, partly under the body and shoulder, blue-grey in colour, was rumpled and covered with blood. There were fragments of burnt mackintosh on the floor near the fireplace. The window blinds were drawn and the right-hand gas-jet above the mantelpiece was lit. Williams leaned over the body and felt the right wrist. The flesh was slightly warm but he detected no pulse. Wallace gave PC Williams his account of what happened; his journey to Menlove Gardens, his return to the house and the subsequent discovery of his wife’s body in the front parlour.[71]

71 PC Williams did not take any written notes during his investigation of the house, but made rough ones at about 10.30pm.

Armed with his torch, Williams closed the parlour door and was accompanied by Wallace in his investigation of the house. They went upstairs and into the middle bedroom, where a gas-jet was lit. Williams asked Wallace if the light was burning when he entered the house. Wallace said that he changed himself in the room before leaving for Menlove Gardens, and probably left the light on himself. On the mantelpiece was a jar with four £1 notes protruding from it. The money was savings Wallace and Julia had made from time to time and put there for convenience. Wallace took hold of the ornament, partly extracted the notes and said, "Here is some money which has not been touched." Williams requested Wallace to replace the notes and put the jar back in its place.[72] A curtained recess on the right of the fireplace contained Mrs Wallace's clothes, which had not been touched. Williams and Wallace then went into the back bedroom that had been converted into a laboratory. There was nothing unusual in its appearance. They then went into the bathroom, where a small light was burning very low. Wallace said that they usually kept a light on in there. They then went into the front bedroom. There was no light on. The room was in a state of disorder: bedclothes half off the bed and half on the floor; a couple of pillows lying by the fireplace. The drawers of a dressing table in the room were shut, as was the door of a wardrobe.

They then went back downstairs to the kitchen. A copy of that evening's *Liverpool Echo* was on the table, opened at the centre. Some of Julia's needlework was there as well as a sugar basin, but the tea things had been cleared away to the basin in the back kitchen. In the corner, to the left of the range was a cupboard, approximately seventeen inches deep (from back to front of the wall) and approximately three feet wide; on top of that a small cabinet, of which a door had been forced open and broken in two pieces, and over that four rows of shelves, which contained Wallace's diaries. Wallace indicated to Constable Williams the small black cash-box on top of the bookcase shelves and commented

72 Also contained in the vase was a postal order for 2/-, No. C/29.451809 issued on 3rd January 1931 [Moore Report, 28th January 1931].

that about £4 was missing. Also on the left, behind a black curtain, was a box roughly the same size as the cabinet with the broken door containing Wallace's microscope; in front of that was a box measuring 2½ inches by 2 or 3 inches wide and the same depth containing chess pieces. A chair was halfway under the table, with a lady's handbag on it.[73]

Wallace then followed Williams back into the front parlour. The Constable noticed the window blinds drawn and the right gas-jet over the mantelpiece burning. Wallace passed Williams, stepped to the left past the body and lit the left-hand gas-jet. They then left the parlour, the constable closing the door behind them, and went back to the kitchen. Noticing the window of the kitchen covered with heavy curtains, Williams parted them slightly and said to Wallace, "Did you notice any lights in the house when you entered?"

"With the exception of the lights upstairs, the house was in darkness," replied Wallace.

In the meantime Constable Saunders endeavoured to get in touch with the Divisional CID, and failing to do so telephoned CID Central at 9.40pm. Detective Superintendent Hubert Moore[74]

73 Afterward DS Harry Bailey found that the handbag contained the sum of £1 5s 10½d in one compartment and a George half-crown in another. The handbag also contained some letters, which were subsequently examined.

74 Born on 16th July 1879 in County Leitrim, Hubert Moore joined the Liverpool Police in 1900. He served as a constable in A Division for three years, when he was transferred to the warrant department. He was a court official for seven years at Dale Street, and began his career as a detective in 1912. The efficient manner in which he carried out his work and natural gift for criminal investigation brought him early promotion. Within six years he was drafted onto the permanent staff of the CID at Dale Street Detective Office, and it was here that well-earned promotion came to him – first as Sergeant, then Inspector, and later as Chief Inspector. He played a conspicuous part in the investigation of numerous serious crimes. As an Inspector, he was part of the investigative team that traced murderer Edouard Charles Braem to Belgium. Braem murdered Mary Sarah Clarke in an apartment in Brownlow Street in July 1921 before fleeing to the Continent. The crime was traced to Braem by a laundry mark on a shirt and he was arrested in Belgium. The Belgian authorities refused extradition, and Braem was tried in Belgium a year later, where he was found Guilty. As Belgium did not carry the death sentence, Braem was sentenced to penal servitude for life. In another case Moore was one of the officers responsible for the apprehension of William Kennedy in January 1928, who, along with Frederick Guy Browne, was hanged for the murder of Constable George William Gutteridge. Always popular with both uniformed and plain-clothes officers, Moore was appointed Chief Superintendent in February 1930. During the First World War he undertook onerous duties at the Landing stage in the supervision of aliens, and also provided valuable service during the Sinn Fein troubles which followed in Liverpool. Moore specialised in police inquiries arising out of industrial disputes. These were duties which called for the exercise of tact and intelligence. Moore enjoyed the confidence of both employers and workers so much so that on one occasion he acted as peacemaker in an unofficial capacity. A trade deadlock had been

was informed at his home by telephone immediately afterwards.[75] Following this, Moore telephoned CID Central with instructions for Constable Harrison to send a multiple call to all CID Inspectors in the city, informing them of the contents of the call from Constable Saunders and asking them and their staffs to stand by for instructions.

9.50pm saw the arrival of Sergeant Joseph Breslin at 29 Wolverton Street. PC Williams answered the door to his superior in G Division. They entered the front parlour. Williams said "That looks like a mackintosh." Wallace, standing in the doorway, looked in the hallway and replied, "It is an old one of mine. It usually hangs here."

Professor John Edward Whitley MacFall,[76] who had been notified

averted, with both parties being brought together. One of his most exciting police experiences occurred in July 1903. As uniformed constables Moore and Hugh Lamont Burgess (who would go on to become Chief Inspector) were set upon by a gang of ruffians in Soho Street. They were slashed at with razors, narrowly escaping with their lives. Despite the heavy odds, the two officers put up a remarkable fight. The perpetrators were subsequently arrested and convicted at the following Spring Assizes; nine men received sentences ranging from five to seven years. On 31st March 1939 Moore took what he described as 'the biggest risk of his life' when he seized an unexploded bomb placed by the IRA in Bold Street. Moore noticed smoke rising from behind a chromium-plated barrier in front of the shop window of gas stove manufacturers John Wright & Co. He found a small brown paper parcel, which sizzled as he picked it up. He threw it into the road, where it exploded seconds later. Responsible for the successful investigation of many cases and for his work in preparing important cases for trial, he was complimented by judges on many occasions. His work was also officially recognised and he was commended on more than forty occasions, where he received bronze and silver medals for meritorious service for the knowledge displayed of travelling racecourse thieves and also on the occasion of provincial Royal visits. When the Mersey Tunnel was opened on 18th July 1934, Moore carried out the security operations of the Royal visit with meticulous detail. These operations included specially-trained officers searching cellars, attics, empty houses, shops and warehouses throughout the Royal route. For days before the visit, a vigil was kept at every dock, railway station, on every incoming ship and in every street for possible political fanatics. Every overhead tramline wire over the Royal route was thoroughly checked, and in many cases new wires replaced old ones. While the King and Queen were on their tour the current in each place through which they passed was automatically switched off. Hubert Moore retired from the force in July 1939. He died aged 72 in hospital on 24th August 1951, leaving a wife Ann, three daughters Imelda, Elsie and Veronica, and a son Hubert.

75 There are conflicting views on the actual whereabouts of Moore on the night in question. There was talk that he was in the Liverpool Press Club Bar (which was situated at St George Building, 24-32 Lime Street) but in his report Moore claimed he was notified of the murder at 9.50 while at home. He lived at 25 Belmont Drive.

76 MacFall was born in Liverpool in 1873. His father John MacFall was a Freeman of the City of Liverpool. MacFall was educated at Liverpool College, St Bartholomew's and University College, Liverpool. At the age of 26 he gained his M.B. and Ch.B. at Victoria University, Manchester and M.B. and B.S. of Liverpool University in 1904. He studied law as well as medicine, becoming a barrister in the Inner Temple. In World War One he served with the Royal Army Medical Corps 3/1st West Lancashire Field Ambulance in France and was wounded in Arras. He retired with the rank of Major. An athletic man, he held the university

by telephone, arrived shortly afterwards. He observed that the head had been badly battered in by the left side. Above, and in front of the ear, was a large open wound measuring ½ an inch by 3 inches with blood and bone tissue protruding. At the back of the left side was a great depression of the skull with several wounds. MacFall inspected the hands of the victim, but there was nothing clutched in them and nothing under the fingernails to indicate that there had been a struggle. The hands were cold, but the body was warm. Rigor mortis at this time was only present in the upper parts of the left arm, but by about 1 o'clock had extended to the right arm and right leg but in no part was there any very marked rigidity. From these observations MacFall formed the opinion that death had occurred approximately two hours before his arrival.[77] A large number of typical blood splash marks formed in a circle from the edge of the sideboard round the north-west corner and above the marble shelf, also a few small blood splashes between the door and the piano. MacFall was of the opinion that it was possible the victim was sitting in the chair in the north-west corner of the room with the head lowered and turned to the right, as if talking to somebody. He also believed that the blood splashes were not produced by the whirling round of the weapon due to the 'soda water bottle' effect of the direction of blood splashes; they just seemed to concentrate

record for putting the weight and also counted tennis, riding and swimming among his recreations. He became Professor of Forensic Medicine and Toxicology, University of Liverpool in March 1925 and was Examiner in Forensic Medicine at the Universities of Glasgow, Manchester, Birmingham, Edinburgh and Aberdeen. He became Divisional Surgeon to Liverpool City Police and Senior Medical Adviser to the CID of Liverpool, Birkenhead and Lancashire County Police. He was also the Medical Officer at the Liverpool City Police Children's Remand Home, 31 Derwent Road. He resided at 'Rose Brae', Green Lane, Stoneycroft and built up a large private practice. He once recounted an amusing story in which he was called to the police station one night to examine a motorist alleged to be drunk. He entered the room, walked up to a man sitting on a table swinging his legs, and asked him to kindly stand up and put out his tongue. The man replied that he was in actual fact the Inspector and the man sitting on the bench opposite was the prisoner. MacFall was also involved in the aforementioned Braem case. He performed the post-mortem on Mary Sarah Clarke, and gave evidence as an expert witness at the trial in Antwerp the following year. MacFall said that in the investigation of crime comedy and tragedy went hand-in-hand, and the comedy was often emphasised by the awful tragedy before them. Among his publications was *The Textbook on Forensic Medicine* and he also contributed papers to various medical journals. MacFall died at his home in Holywell, North Wales on 30th September 1938. He left a widow and one son and two daughters from a previous marriage.

77 In other words at approximately 7.50pm [John Edward Whitley MacFall Report].

on the area in front of the chair. During the time MacFall was examining the body and the blood marks he noticed Wallace come into the room smoking a cigarette. Seemingly unmoved, Wallace leaned across to flick ash into a bowl on the sideboard.

At 10.05pm Detective Superintendent Hubert Moore and Sergeant Fothergill[78] arrived at 29 Wolverton Street. They entered the front parlour, where Professor MacFall was sitting on the arm of the easy chair making notes. Moore made a brief inspection of the upstairs of the house then went into the kitchen, where he found Wallace and John and Florence Johnston. "Julia would go mad if she could see all this," remarked Wallace. Moore asked him if he had seen anybody hanging about the house or in it when he returned. Wallace said that he thought someone might have been in the house when he arrived but could not be sure. Moore then asked the Johnstons if they had seen anybody in or around the house. Mrs Johnston said she hadn't.

Detective Sergeant 114H Harry Bailey[79] had now arrived on the scene. Moore then went to Anfield Police Station, where he

78 Adolphus Worthington Fothergill was born in 1894 and served four years with the Liverpool Scottish and Machine Gun Corps in France and Mesopotamia during the First World War, attaining the rank of Sergeant. He joined the Liverpool Police in August 1919. After a short spell as a uniformed constable, he was transferred to the CID at the end of 1920. He showed such versatility and skill that within four years he had risen to Sergeant in November 1924. He became Inspector in May 1933, and two years later was given the rank of Chief Inspector. He became Superintendent in 1939, Chief Superintendent of the CID in December 1945 and was appointed Deputy Chief Constable in succession to the late Edward Nichols in 1952. Fothergill was commended on many occasions and held many police awards, which included the Merit Badge for courage and coolness in arresting an armed bank robber in 1933. The target was the Midland Bank in Great George Street, where Fothergill took charge. As the robber stepped into the bank intent on blowing the safe, Fothergill secured his revolver and trussed him up in a corner. After donning the robber's cap Fothergill coolly signalled to the robber's accomplice to enter the bank. He was then captured by other detectives, and after escaping again was caught by a police cordon round the bank. Fothergill led the inquiries in the Hanging Boy case on Edge Lane in 1946. Within 48 hours he traced and arrested men who had been to the premises. He was also one of the first on the scene after the discovery of Beatrice Alice Rimmer's murdered body in Cranborne Road in 1951. In that same year's Royal Birthday Honours Fothergill was awarded the King's Police Medal for distinguished service. He retired in 1956 and died at his home in Meols on 10th January 1967 aged 72 years of age, leaving a widow and a daughter.

79 Harry Bailey was born on 5th December 1885. He retired from the Police Force in 1935 after which, he joined the investigation department of the Littlewoods pools firm. He was a member of the Cycling and Athletic Lodge No. 2335. He died at the age of 64 on 12th March 1950 at Ormskirk Hospital. Along with Inspector Herbert Gold, Bailey was complimented by Hubert Moore for the intense work he carried out during the investigation, both mental and physical. In fact Moore sent Bailey home on a few occasions due to his worn and haggard appearance. After Wallace's arrest Bailey was put on the sick list by the Medical Officer.

telephoned Inspector Wallace of CID Special Branch and gave him the particulars of the murder. Immediately, all Divisions were instructed to enquire at lodging houses, railway stations, night cafés and other likely places, at the same time intimating that the assailant would have considerable bloodstaining on his person/clothing.

Moore telephoned Assistant Chief Constable Glover, who arrived shortly afterwards and after a consultation with MacFall, telephoned Police Surgeon Hugh Pierce. Liverpool City Police official photographer Harry Hewitt Cooke was ordered to Wolverton Street and the fire brigade were instructed to supply a set of floodlights. Detective Sergeant Bailey discovered two spent matches in the folds of the mackintosh and took possession of them.

Superintendent Broughton, Assistant Chief Constable Glover and Detective Superintendent Moore were all at the scene of the crime when Inspectors Herbert Gold[80] and Thomas Langford[81] arrived. Detective Inspector Gold noticed how cool and calm Wallace appeared under the circumstances. Sitting in the kitchen with the cat on his knee, stroking it, Wallace seemed oblivious.

A thorough search and examination of the premises commenced with the view to discovering any instrument with which the crime had been committed. Fingerprints or anything else of that nature that might assist in the identity of the murderer were also looked for.

While the search of the premises was in progress Amy Wallace and

80 Gold was born on 14th June 1883 and was no stranger to Wallace – he was his Prudential agent (and had been for about nine or ten years). At the time of the murder, Gold was living at 95 Queens Drive. He found Wallace very reserved – the sort of person who went about his business and who did not encourage conversation. Gold retired from Liverpool City Police in 1936. Following his retirement, he also worked on the investigation department of the Littlewoods pools firm. In 1940 he moved to the tiny Wiltshire village of Christian Malford, where he commanded the Home Guard during the war. He died on 11th May 1963.

81 Langford was a member of the Metropolitan Police Force before joining the Liverpool force. He served at Dale Street Detective Office, then became inspector in charge of CID at Prescot Street in 1928. He took a prominent part in the IRA arrests in 1921 when the Republicans were setting fire to warehouses and other premises. In 1933 Langford took charge of the Flying Squad, and continued there until the outbreak of WWII. He retired in 1943 after 31 years in the Liverpool force.

her 19-year-old son Edwin arrived at the house. They remained in discussion with Wallace, but along with the Johnstons were asked to leave sometime afterwards. Moore also noticed that Wallace didn't appear to be in the least disturbed, and asked him how he found the house on his return. He gave an account of his actions to Moore. As he did so he pointed to the wooden cabinet, the door broken off and lying on the floor. Moore, noticing a half crown piece and two one shilling pieces about eight or nine inches apart and away from the base of the cabinet, asked Wallace where he found the cash-box when he returned. Wallace replied "Where it is now." Moore took the box down, opened the three compartments and found a one dollar bill in the middle one. Replacing the lid, Moore was baffled as to why a thief would put it back in its original place.

Moore was then accompanied by Wallace upstairs. In the back room which was used as a laboratory there were several tools, among them two hammers. There were also photographic materials and a case containing a number of bottles. After looking around and examining several boxes, Wallace said that nothing was missing. They then went into the bathroom but Moore didn't notice anything amiss there. In the middle bedroom the light was burning; on the dressing table stood a few photographs and trinkets but nothing seemingly out of place there either. Moore noticed the notes protruding from the jar but did not touch it. They then proceeded into the front bedroom. The bedding disturbed, it appeared to Moore as though someone had just come in and taken the two pillows and thrown them across the bed to the window side of the fireplace – one practically on top of the other, the bed clothing pushed over the fireplace exposing some of the mattress. On the mattress were two lady's handbags and two lady's old hats, and on the bed clothing close to those hats was another hat. Moore noticed articles undisturbed on the dressing table and that the drawers were shut. He then looked in the wardrobe, saw that everything seemed intact then closed it. Moore immediately formed the opinion that the room did not resemble one of a thief looking for valuables. The blinds had not been drawn. There were two suitcases on top of a box in the corner, a fairly thick layer of dust on them. Wallace told Moore that he had not been in the room for about a fortnight so could not comment on it.

Moore and Wallace then headed back downstairs and examined the front door. Inspector Gold was present as Moore paid particular attention to the front door lock and the wood surrounding it, but there were no traceable marks of any description. Moore asked Wallace for his latch key then placed it into the lock. The Detective Superintendent stood on the doorstep and pulled the door closed, locking it. He worked the key in the lock for a few seconds and, with a little care, opened the door and re-entered the house. Moore said that he could open the door all right but the lock was defective. Wallace said that it had not been like that that morning. Moore retained the key then went into the front parlour.

MacFall made a careful search of the house for bloodstains. Behind the back door he found two suspicious-looking marks but they were not blood – to MacFall they appeared more like tea or coffee. He then headed upstairs. Between 10.35 and 10.45, with the aid of a pocket torch he discovered a small clot of blood measuring three-sixteenths of an inch in diameter and one-eighth of an inch in height on the rim of the lavatory pan. From it there was a light streak of blood towards the centre of the pan. Although the lavatory seat was raised, the clot was not easily seen in the ordinary bathroom light due to the shadow cast by the wash basin. The clot was subsequently photographed by Police Photographer Harry Hewitt Cooke before MacFall gathered it up in a piece of glazed paper and placed it in his velvet-lined silver spectacle case. Also in the bathroom hung a dry, unclean towel, and on the edge of the bath, a damp nailbrush.

With the aid of a torch Moore made a further examination of the mackintosh which was placed on the right side of the deceased, the body not resting on it. Moore was of the opinion that no-one had disturbed the mackintosh. To him, it looked as though someone had tucked the garment in by the body and round the

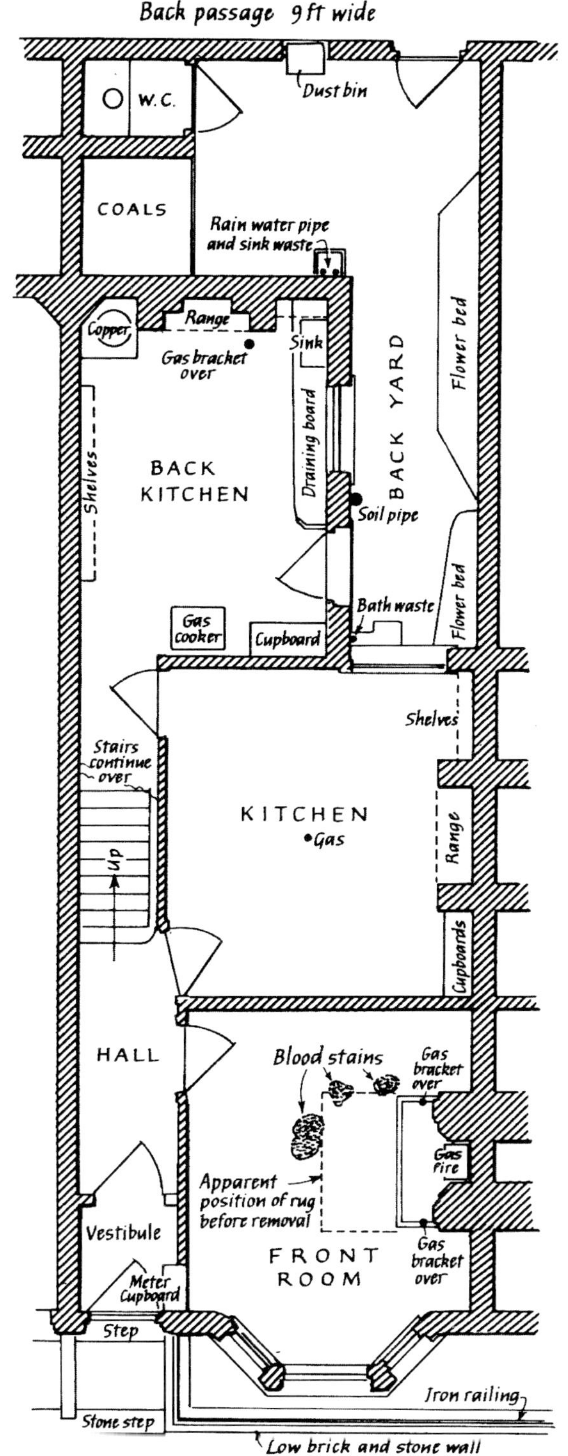

Ground Floor Plan of 29 Wolverton Street (Courtesy Roger Wilkes)

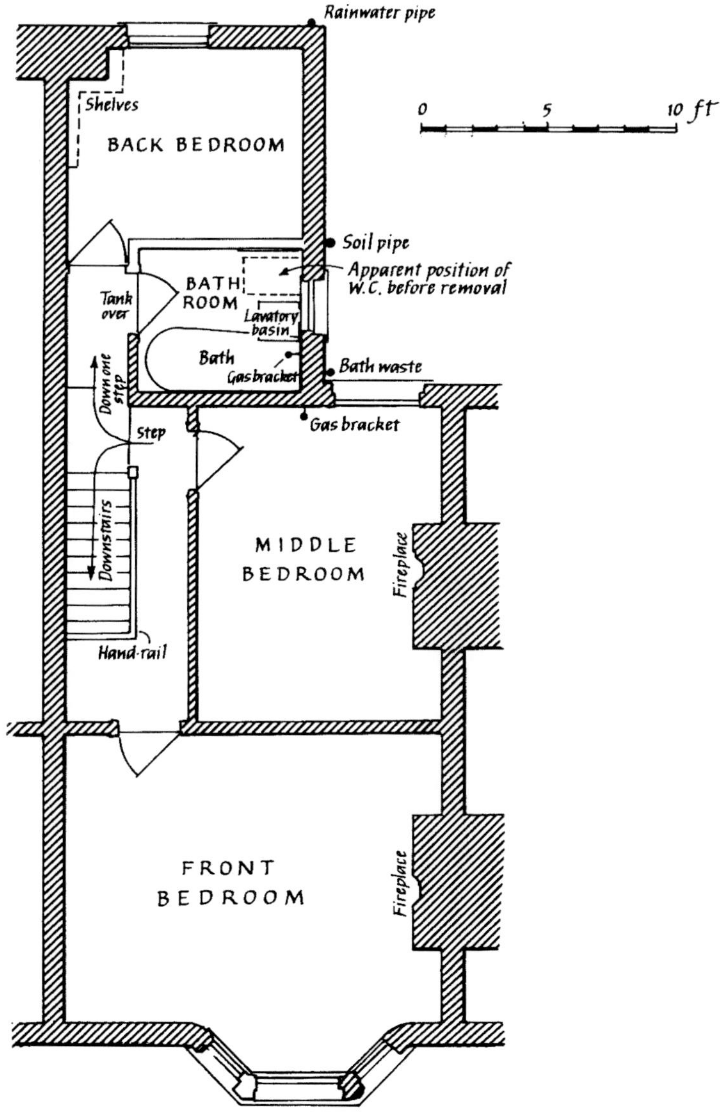

First Floor Plan (Courtesy Roger Wilkes)

shoulder. It had numerous splashes of blood on the front and on and inside the sleeve cuffs. A portion of the bottom-left side had been burned. Moore asked Wallace if the mackintosh was his. Wallace was hesitant in his reply. Moore then asked if Mrs Wallace had a mackintosh like it but again, Wallace did not reply. Detective Sergeant Harry Bailey was then asked by Moore to take the mackintosh up so they could examine it. Wallace then identified it by two patches that were on the garment.[82] Wallace claimed that he had left the mackintosh on the hall rack opposite the parlour door at half past one.[83]

The investigation was then aided by the arrival of the two powerful electric lights. The search commenced at the parlour door, on the floor, the kitchen floor, the carpet on the stairs, the banister, the landing area, the bathroom door, washbasin and bath, but no bloodstains were found. Moore examined Wallace very closely but found no traces of blood on him. Inspector Gold checked the windows and doors for possible signs and examined the back yard walls, but found no indication of anyone having climbed them.[84]

82 A lot was made by the police of Wallace's hesitancy in identifying the mackintosh in their presence, but it is unfair to suggest that Wallace was reluctant to admit ownership. He had after all already admitted earlier the mackintosh was his to Mrs Johnston, Constable Williams, Sergeant Breslin and another officer.

83 Wallace could hardly have left it there at 1.30pm. He didn't arrive home from Clubmoor until 2.15pm.

84 There had been a spate of burglaries in the area (which dated from 1st January 1929 to 17th January 1931). These were attributed to the 'Anfield Housebreaker', but there is a strong possibility that the crimes were perpetrated by more than one person and were possibly even unconnected. Several of the houses in streets adjacent to Priory Road were targeted by burglars. 17 Wolverton Street was targeted during the evening of 20th December 1930. The methods used in the approximate 100 cases were usually by duplicate front door key (as in the case of 17 Wolverton Street) and back door key, back window or back door. The majority of the burglaries were committed in the evening and at night. In fact the term 'Anfield' is also a general reference and quite inaccurate. While many burglaries were conducted in the area (some where even the same house was burgled twice), they were also carried out in West Derby, Clubmoor, Walton, Tuebrook and even as far as Old Swan. A robbery occurred at 32 Snaefell Avenue, Tuebrook where burglars stole money, jewellery and clothing (which included an overcoat). The house was left in a state of disorder. When the owners returned at about midnight they had difficulty in gaining admission through the front door (which the burglars had partly bolted). The owner forced it open and found the house in a state of chaos. The thieves had worked in complete silence, the neighbours either side hearing nothing. Anfield and its surroundings were not the only areas that were targeted – the leafy suburb of Allerton was to fall prey to a 'Reign of Terror' as an outbreak of burglaries gripped the area in 1930. Between 5th and 23rd December there had been 26 cases of housebreaking, and three of handbag-snatching in the district. Police believed these burglaries were committed by a gang of Wavertree youths (whose nine members were subsequently remanded in custody). 38 Menlove Gardens South was targeted on 21st December, where jewellery worth £243 belonging

Throughout the night all members of the CID made diligent enquiries. Known thieves of violent tendencies were looked up and questioned, but no useful information was obtained.

At approximately 11.45pm Inspector Gold and Sergeant Bailey accompanied Wallace to Anfield Police Station. Word had spread around the area and a sizeable crowd had congregated in Wolverton Street. The belief among them was that Wallace had been arrested.

On the way Wallace related his story of receiving the telephone message. On reaching the station Sergeant Bailey commenced to take the statement.[85] Wallace then related to Gold what had been stolen from the cash-box.[86] During his interview Wallace said that he knew of no one who would have been likely to send him the telephone message and that no-one knew that he would be at the club.

Gold then examined Wallace's clothing, boots and hands but could find no traces of blood upon him.

At 11.50pm Police Surgeon Hugh Pierce[87] arrived at 29 Wolverton Street. From his observations he said that rigor mortis had progressed to the extent of the neck and upper part of the left arm. During the time he was there Pierce did not make any notes.[88]

At approximately 1.00am Harry Hewitt Cooke set up his camera to photograph the parlour. The door was removed to allow the shot to be taken.[89] Cooke then moved over to the other side of the room to take another shot.[90] Both photographs were taken in the dark by

to resident Amy Morrison was stolen. The jewellery was recovered from bushes at the corner of Menlove Avenue and Menlove Gardens the following day. Meanwhile, a group of six youths from Norris Green who operated in separate gangs were charged in January 1932 for a spate of burglaries on houses in Norris Green, Knotty Ash and Fazakerley.

85 Wallace's first statement at Anfield Detective Office, Tuesday 20th January 1931.

86 The actual contents – a £1 Treasury note; three 10 shilling notes; 30 or 40 shillings in silver; a postal order No. 65/5.491246 for 4s 6d from W.L. Springer, 51 New Road; four penny stamps and a cheque No.19318 dated 16.1.31 for £5 17/- made payable to W.H. Wallace from his employers, The Prudential Assurance Co, drawn on the Midland Bank, 62 Castle Street. The four penny stamps had not been taken [Hubert Moore Crime Report, 28th January 1931; Herbert Gold Deposition 4th March 1931].

87 Pierce was Police Surgeon from 1919 to 1948 and then Medical Superintendent for the Elder Dempster Lines from 1948 to 1956. He died on 8th May 1956.

88 During the time they were present, neither MacFall nor Pierce took the temperature of the body or the room.

89 Police Photograph 6.

90 Police Photograph 7.

Top left: 5 Dragon Parade, Harrogate. Julia lived here (Author's Collection) Right: Julia Wallace
Bottom: Bruntcliffe House, birthplace of Julia Wallace (Courtesy Jim Sedgwick)

Top left: William Herbert Wallace Right: 9 Belmont Road, Harrogate. Wallace lived here with his parents and sister Jessie (Author's Collection)
Bottom: Newton Street, Millom. Wallace's house is indicated by the 'X' (Author's Collection)

Top. Pennsylvania Road. The Wallaces' first address when they moved to Liverpool in 1915. They lived at number 26 for four months before moving to Wolverton Street (Liverpool Record Office)

Bottom left: 11 St Mary's Avenue, Harrogate. This is where William and Julia Wallace began their married life. Right: 29 Wolverton Street (both Author's Collection)

Top: Cottle City Café. Home to the Central Chess Club (Merseyside Police)
Bottom: Central Chess Club Report (Author's Collection)

President—T. H. STOREY.

Vice-Presidents—

MR. J. E. SQUIRES. MR. C. T. MOBBS. DR. AMYOT.
MR. WALTER HARRIS. MR. A. SLATER. MR. C. BOYCE. MR. R. W. SAWNEY.
REV. H. PEACH. MR. E. B. DEYES. MR. J. E. PARRY.

Captain—MR. S. BEATTIE. *Sub-Captain*—MR. P. M. V. HURLEY.

Hon. Secretary—MR. P. M. V. HURLEY.

Hon. Treasurer—MR. H. F. THORNE.

Committee—MESSRS. A. E. HAINSWORTH, W. E. ROBERTS, W. R. VASS, W. T. ROBERTSON, H. MUNRO, T. P. WILLET, F. FISH, H. BETTON.

Delegates to Lancashire Chess Association:

MR. S. BEATTIE. MR. M. KRESNER.
MR. H. F. THORNE. MR. E. B DEYES. MR W. T. ROBERTSON.
MR. W. R. VASS. MR. W. E. ROBERTS.

TELEPHONE: BANK 3581.

THE CITY CAFE,
24 NORTH JOHN STREET,
LIVERPOOL,
September 21st, 1933.

General Meeting
Thursday. 28. 7.30.

Dear Sir,

The past season has been quite satisfactory from most points of view, although there is no outstanding feature to bring to your notice. The Club maintains a high position in the League, the players, as usual, responding loyally to the call and giving of their best. That fickle jade, "Fortune," however, refused to smile on our efforts on at least two occasions, or the highest honours might have been attained.

Top left: Fixture list for the 1930/31 season (Merseyside Police)
Right: Chess club member E.B. Deyes. He was asked where Menlove Gardens East was but did not know (Evening Express)

Bottom: Central Chess Club noticeboard inside café (Merseyside Police)

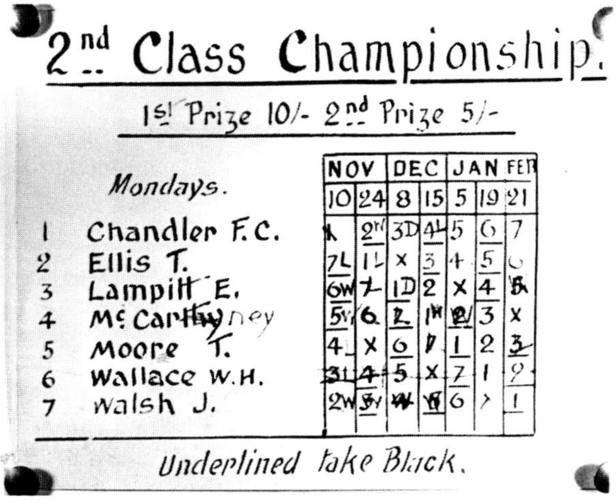

2nd Class Championship.

1st Prize 10/- 2nd Prize 5/-

Mondays.		NOV 10	NOV 24	DEC 8	DEC 15	JAN 5	JAN 19	FEB 21
1	Chandler F.C.	1	2W	3D	4L	5	6	7
2	Ellis T.	7L	1L	x	3	4	5	6
3	Lampitt E.	6W	7	1D	2	x	4	5
4	McCartney	5W	6	2	1W	2	3	x
5	Moore T.	4L	x	6	7	1	2	3
6	Wallace W.H.	3L	4	5	x	7	1	2
7	Walsh J.	2W	3W	4	6	6	7	1

Underlined take Black.

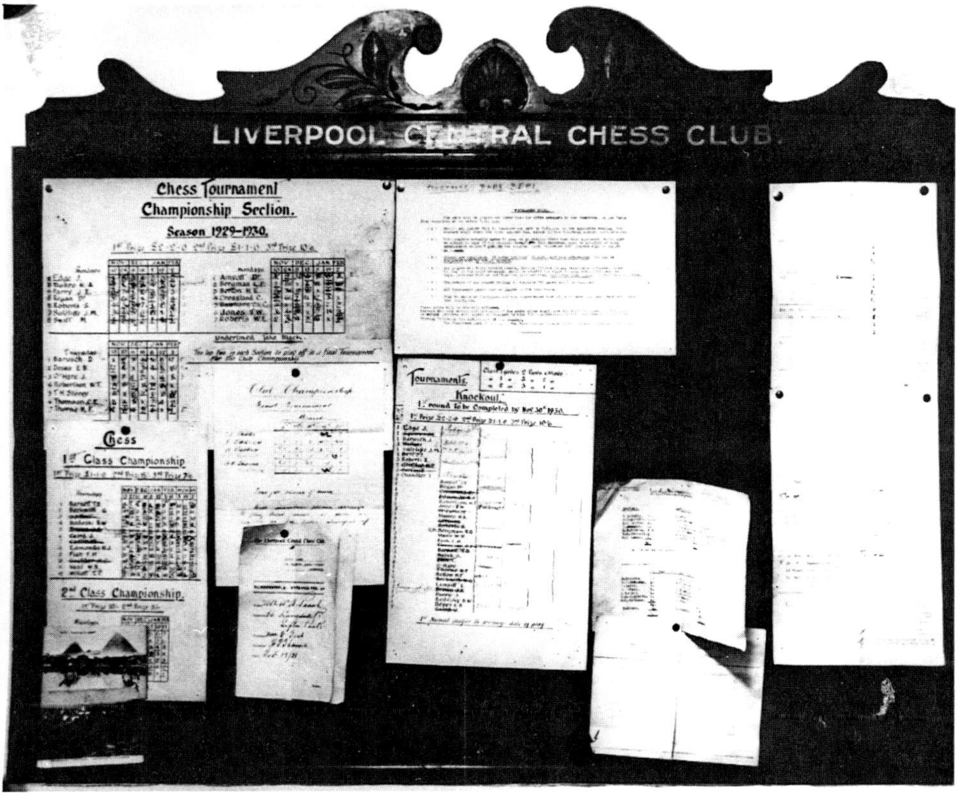

LIVERPOOL CENTRAL CHESS CLUB.

Top left: David Jones delivered the newspaper to 29 Wolverton Street on 20 January (Evening Express). Right: Bread delivery boy Neil Norbury. Newspapers erroneously reported that he was the last person to see Mrs Wallace alive (Evening Express)

Bottom: Sedley Street Steps. Wallace made his way up these on the evening of 20 January (Author's Collection)

Top: Menlove Gardens West (Author's Collection)
Bottom left: Alan Close. He delivered the milk on 20 January (Author's Collection)
Right: James Allison Wildman, taken on his 90th birthday in December 2004 (Courtesy Pete Wildman)

Top left: Sydney Hubert Green. He spoke with Wallace near to Menlove Gardens on the evening of 20 January (Liverpool Daily Post)
Right: 25 Menlove Gardens West. Home of Mr and Mrs Mather (Author's Collection)
Bottom: Menlove Gardens South on the left and North to the right (Author's Collection)

Top: Allerton Road Post Office. Wallace enquired about a street directory here (Author's Collection)

Bottom : The former Allday's Newsagents. Wallace consulted a directory here before making his way back home (Author's Collection)

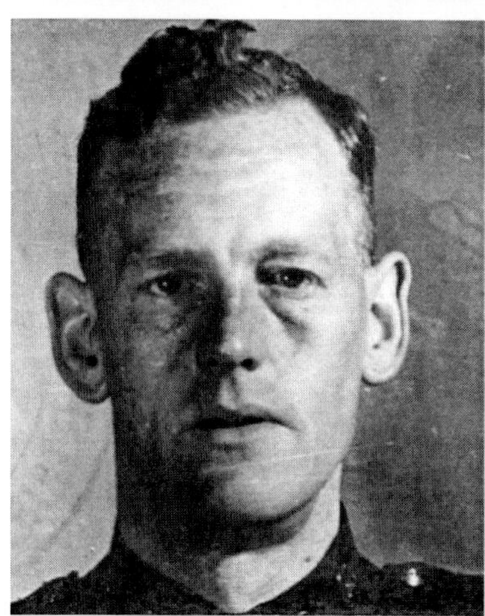

Top: Allerton Road Police Station (Liverpool Record Office)

Bottom left: PC Fred Williams. The first policeman on the scene after the discovery of the murder (Merseyside Police)
Right: The back doors to 29 and 31 Wolverton Street (Author's Collection)

Back yard of 29 Wolverton Street (Merseyside Police)

Reverse shot of back yard (Merseyside Police)

The crime scene photographed by Harry Hewitt Cooke (Merseyside Police)

Top: Reverse shot of the same scene (Merseyside Police)
Bottom: The living kitchen. The cash-box can be seen on the very top shelf on the left (Merseyside Police)

Blood clot can be seen to the right on toilet pan (Merseyside Police)

Bathroom of 29 Wolverton Street (Merseyside Police)

flashlight.

At about 1.15am, Bailey returned to Wolverton Street to tend to the removal of the body. The victim was wearing earrings, a brooch on her neck and a wedding ring. In a pocket inside her corsets (which was secured by a safety-pin) Bailey found £1 and 10/- treasury notes. He also noticed that the skirt was burnt at the front, directly opposite the groin area. Coroner's Beadle Inspector William Gleeson had the body removed to Princes Dock Mortuary.

The circumstances of the murder led the CID to strongly suspect Wallace, but they took precautionary measures. The investigation was ongoing throughout the night. The carpet on the stairs, the bannister and the bathroom floor were all examined, but no blood was found whatsoever. Detective Superintendent Moore was at 29 Wolverton Street until about 4 o'clock in the morning. Leaving police officers at the scene, he returned to Anfield Police Station. Wallace asked if he could return to his house to sleep, but Moore notified him that it was completely out of the question. Wallace was driven to Amy Wallace's flat at 83 Ullet Road to catch a few hours' sleep.

3

INVESTIGATION AND ARREST

WEDNESDAY 21 JANUARY

The police investigations continued throughout the night. Hour after hour the Liverpool Police scoured the area – the new police motor patrol car was also brought into service. In addition to that police motorcyclists patrolled the districts of Anfield and Old Swan.[91] The newspapers were onto the story as well: the copy of that morning's *Liverpool Post and Mercury*[92] bore the headline:

TRAGIC DISCOVERY IN LIVERPOOL –
HUSBAND FINDS WIFE FATALLY WOUNDED

The paper reported:

> "A Liverpool insurance agent, Mr William H. Wallace, of 29 Wolverton Street, Richmond Park Anfield, Liverpool, on returning home from business about quarter to eight last night, found his wife, Julia, lying dead on the floor of a front room with severe wounds to the back of the head.
>
> How Mrs Wallace, who was about fifty years old, came by her fatal injuries is being investigated by the police. No signs of any struggle were found and no weapon lay near the body. The street is in a quiet neighbourhood, and unusual sounds would have been noticed by the neighbours."[93]

91 *Evening Express*, 21st January 1931.

92 In *The Killing of Julia Wallace* Jonathan Goodman claims that the murder received no mention in that morning's *Daily Post*. Liverpool's morning paper in 1931 was the *Liverpool Post and Mercury*, and it did actually mention the murder [Goodman *The Killing of Julia Wallace* pp.70].

93 *Liverpool Post and Mercury*, 21st January 1931.

Dale Street Police Headquarters was a hive of activity. The twelve lines on the switchboard increased with calls as the day wore on. Detective Superintendent Hubert Moore opened a new file: No.13641G.C. Murder/Julia Wallace. At 10.00am Wallace reported to Dale Street Police Headquarters and remained there until 10.00pm that night. Throughout the day CID Officers made house-to-house enquiries in Wolverton Street, and the area was searched for any possible weapon or bloodstained clothing. The house was again thoroughly examined, the Chief Constable Lionel Everett, Assistant Chief Constable Herbert Winstanley, Professor MacFall and City Analyst William Henry Roberts all visiting it. Fingerprint expert Harry Hewitt Cooke conducted an examination. Water tanks, the lavatory and outside area were searched, but nothing was found. The wash basins and kitchen sink of the house were removed for microscopic examination to ascertain any traces of blood. No fingerprints were found. The grounds of the nearby Belmont Road Institute[94] were subjected to intensive searching, in the hope of discovering any clue or possible weapon. Bushes and hedges were uprooted and scrutinised carefully, but without success.

Both recipients of the telephone message were traced. Waitress Gladys Harley was interviewed and made a statement at Cottle's City Café. Samuel Beattie was interviewed at the offices of George Langley & Co in Orleans House, where a statement was also taken.

At 11.00am Herbert Gold arrived at 29 Wolverton Street. He took possession of thirteen of Wallace's books from the kitchen. Among them were diaries for the years 1928, 1929, 1930 and 1931, and other books which appertained to business matters. He also took possession of several items, which included the mackintosh, cash-box and jar which included the four £1 notes. Gold also took the front door lock and key and back kitchen door lock and key. Sometime later, Gold was handed the victim's skirt from Sergeant

94 Originally the Belmont Road Workhouse, it was built by the West Derby Board of Guardians in 1890 and was extended in 1894 and 1910. It also became known as the Belmont Road Institution and Belmont Road Hospital. It was designated a general hospital in 1948 and was renamed Newsham General Hospital in 1950. It finally saw closure in 1988.

Bailey.

At about midday at Princes Dock Mortuary Amy Wallace made the formal identification of the body. Harry Hewitt Cooke then took three photographs[95] of the deceased. The body was then prepared for the post mortem. MacFall's report read as follows:

> On 21.1.31 at Princes Dock Mortuary, I made a P.M. examination of the body of Julia Wallace. Woman about 55 years, 5 "3 to 4 inches, lightly built, prominent abdomen. No linea ablicantes.[96] The external genital orifice was quite clean with no evidence of blood. There was a small recent bruise mark on the inside of the left upper arm. There were no other external marks of violence on the trunk or limbs. The hair was matted with blood and brain tissue. The hair was removed. Two inches above the zygoma[97] was a large lacerated wound 2" x 3" from which brain and bone were protruding. On the back of the head on the left side were ten diagonal apparently incised wounds. On removal of the scalp the left frontal bone was driven into the front of the brain corresponding to the external wound. The whole of the left side of the back of the skull was driven in and broken into pieces. The injury extended into the middle and rear fossae,[98] fracturing the base of the skull breaking up the rear part of the cerebellum[99] bursting the tentorium cerebelli[100] and breaking up the left side of the cerebellum. The left lateral sinus was broken across also the meningeal arteries. The appearance was as if a terrific force with a large surface had driven in the scalp bursting in parallel lines, with the appearance of several incised wounds, but the edges of these wounds were not sharp.
>
> The lungs, heart, kidney and spleen were normal. The stomach[101] contained about four ounces of semifluid food consisting of currants, raisins and unmasticated lumps of carbohydrate. The

95 Police photographs 10, 11, 12.

96 Lines, white to pink or grey that occur on the abdomen, buttocks, breasts, and thighs and are caused by the stretching of the skin and weakening or rupturing of the underlying elastic tissue. The condition is usually associated with pregnancy, excessive obesity, rapid growth during adolescence, Cushing's syndrome, or prolonged adrenocortical hormone therapy.

97 The part of the temporal bone of the skull that forms the prominence of the cheek.

98 Small cavities or depressions in the bone.

99 The trilobed structure of the brain.

100 The tentorium cerebelli is an arched layer, elevated in the middle and inclining downward toward the circumference. It covers the superior surface of the cerebellum.

101 Goodman erroneously states that MacFall did not think of examining the stomach, but in actual fact he did [Goodman *The Killing of Julia Wallace* pp.73-74].

> small bowel was normal, the caecum[102] ascending and transverse colon were enormously and chronically distended (typical constipation bowel). Uterus virginal clean and no evidence of bleeding. The right ovary normal, left ovary 3½ by 2½ fibroid.
>
> I am of the opinion that death was due to fracture of the skull by someone striking the deceased three or four times with terrific force with a hard large headed instrument.

MacFall was then driven to the University to conduct his experiments on the clot of blood found on the rim of the lavatory.[103] He used the Kastle-Meyer's, Teichmann's and Guaiacum test, the microscopic test to determine the size and shape of the corpuscles and the Precipitin Test to determine whether the blood was human or animal. The blood contained typical red cells and white corpuscles. No epithelial cells were found. MacFall said that the blood was not menstrual,[104] and when seen and examined with the lens appeared to be the same time as the blood clots found near the body.

Meanwhile Moore received a telephone call claiming that the Wallaces employed a maid. Wallace notified Moore that the house cleaner was called Sarah Jane Draper. She had been recommended to the Wallaces by Mrs Jenkinson, a friend of theirs. She was located, interviewed at her home in Tollerton Road and then driven to Wolverton Street and shown around the house by Inspector Gold. There she said that a poker about nine inches long with a small knob on it was missing from the kitchen fireplace, and also absent was a straight piece of iron about a foot long and the thickness of a candle which stood by the parlour fireplace. She used to clean the front bedroom and said the bed was always kept made with blankets, sheets and pillows, and that Mrs Wallace would have her hats spread out upon it. She said that she had never seen it in the state it was currently in. Mrs Draper said that she had recently

102 The first portion of the large intestine.

103 Goodman *The Killing of Julia Wallace* pp.74.

104 The blood not being of menstrual origin was to dismiss the possibility of it being deposited there by accident and in that manner. Julia's advanced age would render her past menstruation. The menopause can occur between the ages of 45 and 55, usually around age 50. In his post mortem report MacFall was of the belief that the victim was 'of about 55 years' [John Edward Whitley MacFall PM Report].

lost her husband and that she had sent a postcard to the Wallaces on 20th January notifying them that she would not be calling the following day. She always found the Wallaces to be on friendly terms when she was there.

Over the following days the house would be subjected to close inspection. The fittings and fixtures of the front parlour were removed and the room examined for any possible traces of a weapon.

Detective Sergeant Harry Bailey was assigned the job of looking up and investigating anyone with the name Qualtrough.[105] There were fourteen families of that name in the Liverpool area,[106] but none of them could shed any light with regards to the telephone call.

Wallace's movements on the evening of the murder were traced and verified to be consistent with his statement.

The story was the talk of the city and all over the evening's newspapers, with some of them reporting that Wallace had left the house at 6.15pm. The *Evening Express* reported that "There never has been a more baffling murder in Liverpool."

On Breck Road near Richmond Park, fourteen-year-olds Douglas Metcalf, Harold Jones,[107] Kenneth Caird[108] and Elsie May Wright were talking. As they were discussing the murder they saw Alan Close walking up to them. Metcalf asked Close if he delivered the milk at 29 Wolverton Street the previous night. "Yes. At a quarter to seven," came the reply. Close had already visited No. 29 that afternoon with Elsie Wright to deliver milk but it was not wanted. Metcalf then asked him if he had notified the police of it. "No,"

105 Qualtrough is of Manx origin, and originally had the prefix 'Mac.' MacWalter dropped the 'Ma' and the 'c' and 'w' spoken together would form the sound of a 'q' hence Qualtrough.

106 It would seem strange that Wallace had not heard the name Qualtrough. He was, to all intents and purposes, a seemingly well-educated man and also well-travelled. One of the names on the list was Richard James Qualtrough. He was insured with the Prudential, although he didn't know Wallace. Another listed name was William Qualtrough – he was a contractor who lived in Molyneux Road but had his business at 74 Windermere Street, Anfield. There was also a butcher's shop at 108 County Road, Walton by the name of Thomas John L. Douglas Qualtrough.

107 Harold Jones lived at 7 Redcar Street, was the best friend of Douglas Metcalf and also delivered papers for Mr Yates of 51 Breck Road.

108 Kenneth Campbell Caird was born on 24th September 1916. He was the son of James Caird. He died in Rhuddlan, North Wales in 1988.

Close answered. Metcalf told him the importance of telling the police, and stated that they would accompany him to Wolverton Street. They headed there together, Close remarking on the way that he was the 'missing link'. When they knocked the door was opened by a constable. Close related to him that he had seen Mrs Wallace the previous evening. The milkboy was then ushered into the house.

At Allerton Police Station PC James Edward Serjeant made a statement. In it he recounted his encounter with Wallace at the junction of Allerton Road and Green Lane. Serjeant said that Wallace stammered a little and appeared to be a nervous type of man.

After approximately twelve hours Wallace left Dale Street Detective Office. He was allowed to stay the night at Wolverton Street due to the arrival of his sister-in-law, Amy.[109] She stayed in Amy Wallace's flat overnight before leaving to return to the South Coast. She gave a brief statement to the police, and an even briefer one to Wallace requesting him to send on her sister's fur coat.[110]

THURSDAY 22 JANUARY

At the Coroner's Court,[111] situated in the Police Court[112] on Dale Street, the inquest into Julia Wallace was opened by Coroner George Cecil Mort.[113] The only witness was Amy Wallace. Dressed in a fur coat and hat, she was called to establish identity. She told of her visit to Wolverton Street on the evening of the murder, and her subsequent identification at the Princes Dock Mortuary on 21st January. On leaving the dock Mrs Wallace made a complaint to the

109 Amy Dennis. She lived at 4 Denmark Terrace, Brighton.

110 Goodman *The Killing of Julia Wallace* pp.83. Among the documents held at Hill Dickinson is a letter of acknowledgement regarding the fur coat dated 25th February 1931.

111 In May 1961 the Coroner's Court became Court No. 6.

112 Subsequently the Magistrates' Court.

113 Born at Stroud, Gloucestershire, Mort became Liverpool City Coroner in 1928. For eight years previously he had been in private medical practice at Menlove Avenue. He saw service as a Surgeon-Lieutenant in World War One and was in action at the Battle of Jutland aboard HMS *Cochrane*. Known for his compassion, the Coroner's Court during his time was a model of human kindness. His reassuring demeanour immediately put the witness at ease. After 25 years he retired from the post in 1953.

Coroner. She said that she objected to a report that appeared in a newspaper gleaned from her, when she was under the impression the reporters were the police. Mort told her that if the press thought they were doing their duty a complaint could not be made. Mrs Wallace then signed the depositions of evidence and left the court. The inquest was adjourned until 5th February.

At 10.45am Wallace reported again to Dale Street Detective Office. There, he told Inspector Herbert Gold that he had some important information. Wallace gave the name of Richard Gordon Parry,[114] a 22-year-old former Prudential co-worker who Wallace had known since September 1927. Wallace told Gold that Parry was employed by the Gresham Insurance Company, and that he had previously collected on Wallace's round when he (Wallace) was ill with bronchitis in December 1928. Parry did part of the collecting for two or three days a week for about three weeks. When Wallace checked the accounts there were several slight discrepancies. Parry was short of small amounts, and had not entered all of the amounts collected in the book. When Wallace spoke with Parry about the matter he was told that it was an oversight; Parry was sorry and said he would put it right. Wallace also related to Gold that Parry called frequently at Wolverton Street concerning business and, was well-acquainted with the Wallace's domestic arrangements.

Wallace then mentioned another former Prudential worker, 30-year-old Joseph Marsden.[115] He had been an agent for the company for just over three years. Like Parry he also collected when Wallace was ill, but had already left the Prudential at the

114 Wallace gave Parry's address as Derwent Road. Although a William Parry lived at 28 Derwent Road at the time, this was not Parry's father. In actual fact, Parry lived at 'Bryn Eden', 7 Woburn Hill [William Herbert Wallace Witness Statement, 22nd January 1931]. Incidentally, the statement was read out on the first day of the trial and included the wrong address. Parry was born on 12th January 1909. He was employed by the Prudential from 19th September 1927, and resigned 28th of December 1929 (services were terminated on 4th January 1930). He died on 14th April 1980. Gwilym A. Davies of Llangernyw handled the funeral arrangements. Parry was cremated at Colwyn Bay on 21st April.

115 Joseph Caleb Marsden was born on 21st September 1900. He worked for the Prudential from 16th March 1925 to 21st May 1928, when he resigned. He worked out of the districts of Anfield and Everton. In January 1931 Marsden was living with his parents Harold and Margaret at 24 Adelaide Road in the Kensington area of the city. On the evening of 20th January he was suffering from flu and was confined to bed. He married Sylvia Alberta Taylor at the Church of St Mary, Edge Hill on 7th June 1932. Marsden died on 23rd June 1967.

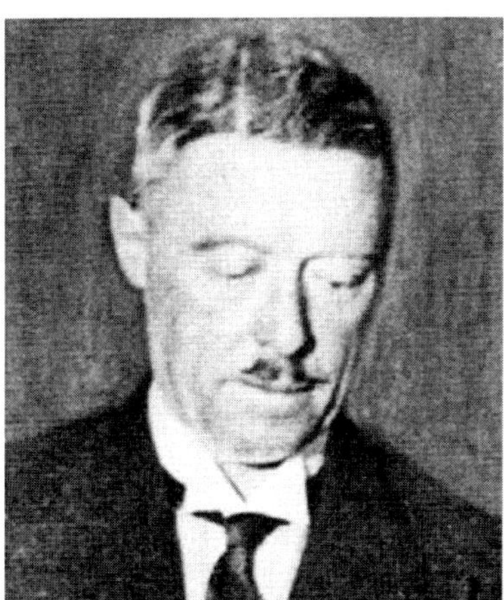

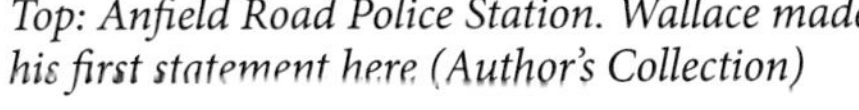

Top: Anfield Road Police Station. Wallace made his first statement here (Author's Collection)

Bottom Clockwise from left: Detective Sergeant Harry Bailey (Merseyside Police); Detective Superintendent Hubert Moore (Courtesy Roger Wilkes); Detective Inspector Herbert Gold (Liverpool Echo)

Top: Dale Street Detective Office (Liverpool Record Office)

Bottom left: John Edward Whitley MacFall (Liverpool University Library)
Right: 29 Wolverton Street (National Archives)

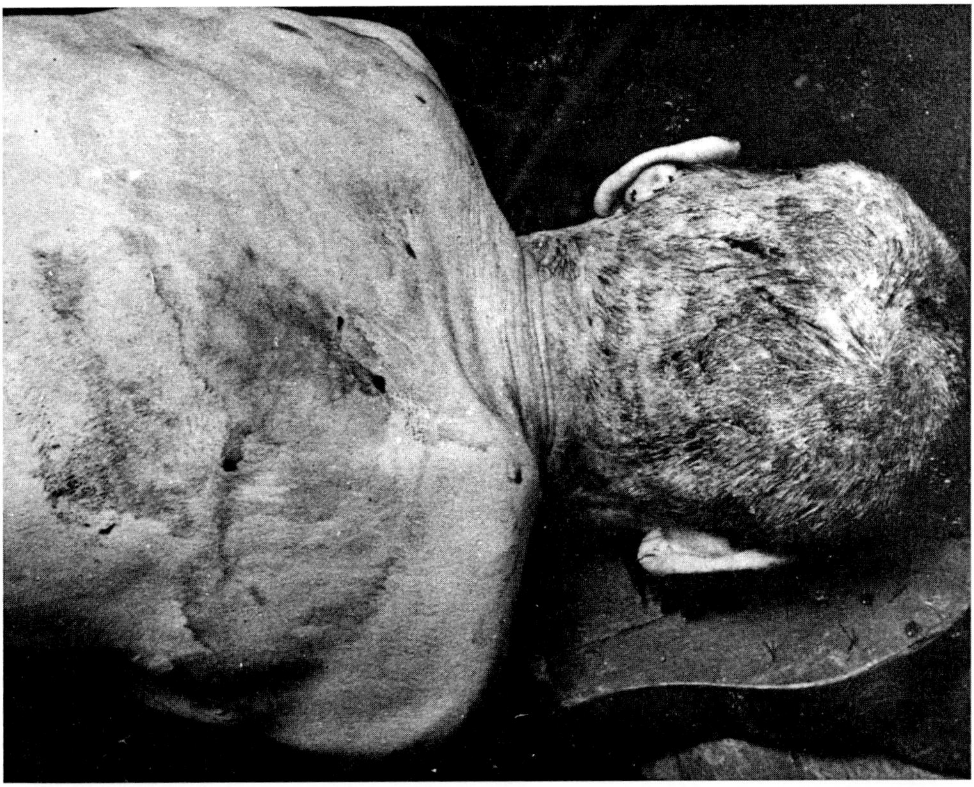

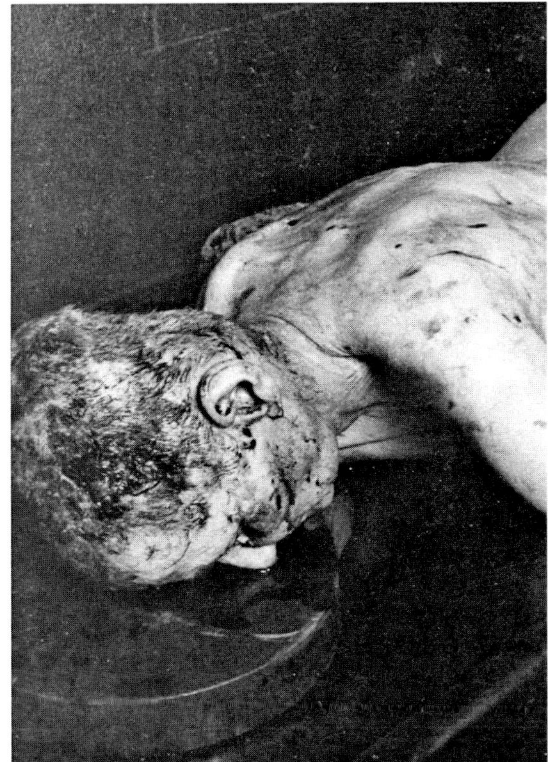

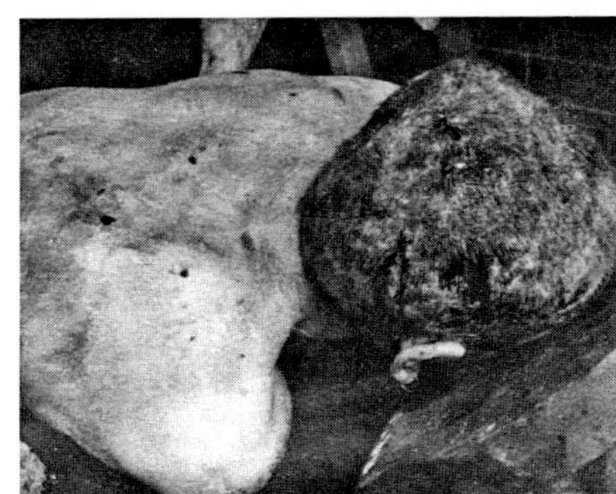

The three photographs taken at Princes Dock Mortuary (Merseyside Police)

Top left: Liverpool Coroner George Cecil Mort (Liverpool Record Office)
Right: Dr Hugh Pierce (Liverpool Record Office)
Bottom: Coroner's Court (Author's Collection)

time of the murder. Marsden was also well-acquainted with the Wallaces' house. Wallace said that Marsden was recommended to him by Parry, and that he had finally left the Prudential due to financial irregularities. Wallace also said that his wife would have had no hesitation in admitting Parry or Marsden into the house.

Wallace then gave a list of other persons who would have been welcomed into the house by Mrs Wallace; the list included Albert Wood,[116] Joseph Bamber,[117] Gilbert F. Davis,[118] James Heyes,[119] and Stanley Young.[120]

The Postmaster of the General Post Office was contacted by letter from Chief Constable Lionel Everett. He said that the call had been sent from the Anfield district at about 7.15pm on the Monday, and that it was of great importance that the number of the telephone from which the call was made was ascertained.[121]

Assistant Chief Constable Herbert Winstanley wrote a letter to the Director of Public Prosecutions at Whitehall, London. He said that they were enquiring into the murder but no arrest had been made, and that statements were continuously being taken and a full report would be forwarded at the earliest possible moment.

Sydney Hubert Green was interviewed at Dale Street Detective Office. He gave a statement about his encounter with Wallace on Menlove Gardens West on the evening of 20th January.[122]

During the investigations Police conducted a minute search on two areas of wasteland near Wolverton Street. The earth was sifted

116 He was Assistant Superintendent under Joseph Crewe. Wood, who lived at 26 Ellerslie Road, had seven agents under him, one of whom was Wallace. He had visited 29 Wolverton Street when Wallace was not present. Julia showed him into the front parlour, got matches to light the fire with and pulled the blinds down. He said that Wallace always spoke highly of Mrs Wallace. Wood left the Prudential in September 1929.

117 Bamber was also an Assistant Superintendent for the Prudential. He lived at 45 Kingfield Road. On the evening of 20th January he was at home from 5.45 until 7.30. He then visited his parents at 26 Cedar Road in Walton. In a diary extract dated 18th December 1928 Wallace mentioned that Bamber was suspicious of Parry and that he 'wanted watching with insurance work.'

118 Teacher of music, 448 Queens Drive.

119 Wallace's tailor, 99 Breck Road.

120 Young was born in Manchester on 7th September 1874 and joined the Prudential in February 1910 as an agent in the Liverpool area. After retiring briefly in March 1920 due to ill health, he came back in November of the same year. He retired again in August 1930, but came back as a temporary collector (though not authorised to sell new policies) in January 1938. He died on 26th October 1944.

121 Lionel Everett Letter, 22nd January 1931.

122 Sydney Hubert Green Witness Statement, 22nd January 1931.

and shrubbery carefully examined for traces of the weapon, and also any bloodstained clothing that the murderer may have discarded in his disappearance. The police even searched the dustbins and alleyways in the surrounding streets, but these proved fruitless.

As a result of enquiries through the Intelligence Department of the Post Office, it was ascertained that the call had been made from a public telephone box situated on the corner of Rochester Road[123] and Breck Road, some 400 yards from Wolverton Street. A record of the call was made at the exchange due to the fact that the caller complained of not being connected properly on the first call, thereby necessitating having his two pennies returned. This required the Supervisor to write out a note showing the numbers, the time and nature of the complaint.[124]

Accompanied by Detective Sergeant Harry Bailey, Wallace visited 29 Wolverton Street to make an examination of the property. There, he stated that his wife's jewellery appeared intact, and

123 Rochester Road was incorporated into Lower Breck Road c.1928. The kiosk that was used on the corner of Rochester Road and Breck Road was the K1 mark 2 style. It was made of concrete with a wooden door. The door could have been grey or ultimately red. It was constructed in concrete and had a three-panel back, metal-framed windows, metal signage and pyramidal roof. It was topped by ornate metal scrollwork and a finial. Two insulators were affixed on the top of the decorative iron work. These brought the telephone line to the kiosk from a nearby pole. By 1931 there were 10,255 of these on Britain's streets [Dave Shawyer email to the author, 5th August 2014].

124 In 1931 both Anfield and Bank exchanges were manual exchanges. This meant the caller didn't dial anything, and all the connecting was done via operators (if there were no direct lines between two exchanges then a third operator would have been involved in a central exchange). When the caller wanted to make a call he lifted the receiver and inserted two one-penny coins. These combined actions caused an electrical connection to be made, and the calling condition to be made (in this case) to the Anfield operator. Before the operator answered, the transmitter (microphone) on the telephone was disconnected. When the operator answered her actions connected the transmitter and the caller and operator could then speak to each other. To get this far she knew that he had deposited the minimum fee, and in this case that would be all that was required. If more money was required she would have asked him to deposit more coins. She would know this had taken place because the coins would hit a bell or a gong on their way into the coinbox, and a transmitter inside it allowed the operator to hear the tones. When satisfied the correct fee had been deposited, and with the help of the bank operator, she would have connected the call and rung the Chess Club. When answered, the operator would have asked the caller to press button A on the coinbox. This did two things; firstly, it deposited the coins from the holding mechanism into the money box, making a refund impossible, and secondly, it allowed the connection of the transmitter in the phone to be activated without the operator having to be on the line. If the customer didn't press anything when the operator dropped out of the connection, the caller would only be able to hear the Chess Club but not be able to speak to them. If instead he had pressed button B, then the coins so far deposited would have been returned, but in doing so would have disconnected the telephone line (for seven seconds) which would have lit a lamp on the operator's switchboard [Dave Shawyer email to the author, 8th March 2013].

nothing appeared to be missing from the cash-box beyond £4, the postal order for 4s 6d and a cheque for £5 17s 0d payable to May and Frost. Particulars of the postal order were left with the Post Office Intelligence Department for notification as soon as it was cashed, and payment of the cheque would be stopped. The cheque was not endorsed, and should it be presented the police would be immediately informed.[125]

Late in the afternoon Detective Superintendent Moore, Superintendent Thomas and Assistant Prosecuting Solicitor J.R. Bishop left Dale Street Police Headquarters and paid a visit to the scene of the murder. While in the house they reconstructed the crime according to a hypothesis already formed by them. Moore told the *Evening Express* that as far as the police were aware, the only thing missing from the house was £4. No items of furniture were missing from the house.[126]

That evening at Dale Street Detective Office, Superintendent Thomas informed Wallace that the telephone call had been made at about 7.00pm and traced to a call box near to his home in the Anfield area. At 9.40pm Wallace looked at his watch said to Gold that he didn't want to be late getting to Ullet Road as his sister-in-law would be going to bed. Gold told Wallace that he could leave.[127] Wallace made his way down to the tram stop at the corner of North John Street and Lord Street.

At approximately 10.20pm Samuel Beattie, James Caird and Daniel Baruch left the City Café after that night's Chess Club meeting. At the corner of Lord Street Caird recognised Wallace. Caird turned to Beattie and notified him of Wallace's presence. Wallace looked at Beattie, said hello and asked him if he could

125 Hubert Moore Crime Report, 28th January 1931.
126 *Evening Express*, 22nd January 1931.
127 Herbert Gold, Trial Transcript pp.223-224. There is no doubt that Wallace intended to speak to Beattie after hearing the news of the traced call. It has been claimed that Wallace was shadowed when he made his way to the tram stop and his meeting with Beattie. Gold said that Wallace had not been followed, but said at the trial that he knew how they came to know. In all likelihood Wallace *was* followed, and Beattie approached sometime after and questioned with regards to the conversation. Jonathan Goodman claimed that three plain clothes detectives, Frederick Austin, Thomas Cleater and Thomas Hudson, were assigned the task of shadowing Wallace. Detective Frank Elsworth was another who followed Wallace from the time just after the murder up to his arrest [Goodman *The Killing of Julia Wallace* pp.98].

remember the actual time he had received the telephone message. Beattie said the time was about 7 o'clock. Wallace pressed him as it was of importance, but Beattie replied that he couldn't say for definite. Wallace said that he had just left Dale Street Detective Office and that they had cleared him. Beattie said that he was very pleased to hear it, but advised Wallace to not say anything else as the discussion could be misconstrued. Wallace said that he was going to Ullet Road as the police wouldn't let him stay at his own address that night. Caird then asked when the funeral would be. Wallace said that he did not know, but would be trying for Saturday. He then boarded a number 8 tram.[128]

FRIDAY 23 JANUARY

Wallace was again accompanied by Inspector Gold and Sergeant Bailey around 29 Wolverton Street. He was asked to check if anything was missing. He took possession of some jewellery from a drawer in the chest of drawers in the middle bedroom, and a Post Office Savings Bank Book in Julia's name (which had a credit of £90[129]) from a drawer in the front bedroom. A thorough examination of the house was made, and Wallace claimed that the only thing missing was a small axe for chopping wood from the back kitchen which he had not seen for about twelve months. A further search was made, and the axe was found in a basket under some old clothing under the stairs. In reply to Inspector Gold, Wallace said that Mrs Draper must have thrown the poker away with the ashes and that he knew nothing about the iron bar. Gold saw an insurance policy in Julia Wallace's name with the Prudential Assurance Company for £20[130] and asked if there were any others. Wallace told him that was the only one. In the middle bedroom Gold took possession of the suit of clothes Wallace was wearing on the 20th January, and also took the towel from the side of the bath in the bathroom.[131]

128 Samuel Beattie Witness Statement, 24th January 1931.
129 Today this would amount to £4,120 (National Archives).
130 Approximately £915 in today's money (National Archives).
131 Police photographer Harry Hewitt Cooke took another photograph of the bathroom on 18th

Meanwhile, Richard Gordon Parry was interviewed at Tuebrook Police Station. In his statement he said that on the evening of the 19th January he took Lily Lloyd to her home in Missouri Road at about 5.30pm and remained there until about 11.30pm, when he went home. The following night, Tuesday, he finished work for the Standard Life Assurance Company at about 5.30pm and called upon Olivia Alberta Brine of 43 Knoclaid Road. He remained there in the company of Mrs Brine, her thirteen-year-old daughter Savona and nephew Harold Dennison until about 8.30pm. Parry then made his way to Hodgson's post office at 50 Maiden Lane, where he bought a packet of Players No. 3 cigarettes and a copy of the *Evening Express*. On his way to Lily Lloyd's he realised he had to pick up his accumulator at Hignett's, 513 West Derby Road, which he duly did. From there he went along West Derby Road to 49 Lisburn Lane, where he spoke for about ten minutes to Annie Williamson with regards to a 21st birthday party. From there Parry went to Lloyd's at 7 Missouri Road and remained there until about 11.00-11.30pm. He then headed home.[132]

Wallace went back to his collecting round, where the police shadowed him.[133] They claimed that it was purely in his own interests in view of the hostility he was bound to encounter on his rounds, and not because of their suspicions of him.[134] Telephone supervisor Annie Robertson and operators Louisa Alfreds and Lilian Martha Kelly were interviewed and gave statements at the General Post Office in the City Centre. They said that the call they received was from call-box 1627 in Anfield, and that the caller's voice was 'quite ordinary and used to using telephones.' Alfreds and Kelly commented on the way in which the caller pronounced the word 'café.'[135]

The Assistant Chief Constable wrote a letter to the Land Steward

February. Trial Exhibit number 13.

132 Witness Statement of Richard Gordon Parry, 23rd/24th January 1931.

133 See note 127.

134 This is highly unlikely. If they were acting in the interests of Wallace, why did they not notify him of their surveillance of him?

135 The caller pronounced the word "ca-fay".

& Surveyor[136] Municipal Offices requesting a representative of the Offices to prepare plans of 29 Wolverton Street and the immediate vicinity.

The search in and around the Anfield area continued. Drains and sewers in the immediate vicinity of Wolverton Street were opened and inspected by sanitary officials of the Liverpool Corporation and the police.

At 6.30pm Wallace reported to Dale Street Detective Office. There, in the presence of Inspector Herbert Gold, he was questioned by Detective Superintendent Moore about his conversation with Beattie on the corner of Lord Street the previous evening;

"You saw Mr Beattie at the Chess Club last night?"

"Yes, while I was waiting for a tram in Lord Street," replied Wallace.

"You asked him what time did he receive the telephone message?"

"Yes. Mr Beattie said seven o'clock or shortly afterwards."

"You told him the time was important," asked Moore.

"Yes."

"In what way was it important?"

"I had some ideas of my own," replied Wallace. "We all have ideas. It was indiscreet of me. I can't say why I asked him. I admit it was an indiscretion on my part. I cannot say anything further."

Wallace made his third statement to Inspector Gold. In it he gave details concerning the tram journeys from Smithdown Road and Penny Lane, and the approximate time he alighted at Menlove Gardens West.

The *Evening Express* reported that faint fingerprints far from perfect in outline were discovered on certain articles in the house, and that the articles had been removed the previous night and submitted for microscopic examination.[137] The paper also said that the telephone message was sent by some person who spoke with a gruff and what seemed disguised voice,[138] and that the black

136 Albert D. Jenkins.

137 *Evening Express*, 23rd January 1931.

138 It would seem this was sheer speculation on behalf of the police. In none of Beattie's statements does he say that the voice appeared to be disguised (although Beattie used the term 'gruff',

tabby cat of which Mrs Wallace was so fond could not be found on the night of the crime, but had finally returned to the house the previous day (22nd January).[139]

SATURDAY 24 JANUARY, 10.30AM

In a ceremony conducted under the utmost secrecy, Julia Wallace was buried in Anfield Cemetery. There were few people about and the identity was known only to the three mourners, the detective in attendance, clergyman and the undertakers.[140] The official list of the persons to be buried that day did not include the name of Mrs Wallace. The coffin, bearing a simple inscription, was covered in wreaths. The service in the chapel and at the graveside was conducted by the Reverend James Edward Stevenson.[141] During the sermon Wallace wept uncontrollably.[142]

At Dale Street Detective Office Detective Superintendent Moore received a statement from Professor MacFall and Police Surgeon Hugh Pierce. In it, they said that they had considered the possibility that the murderer might not have been covered in blood, and due to the appearance of the splashes in the corner of the room thought it quite likely that it might have spurted away from the assailant and therefore might have been little blood about his body.[143]

At Wolverton Street Harry Hewitt Cooke took photographs of the outside of the house. These included shots from the back yard door towards the house, and a reverse shot from the house towards the back yard door.[144]

which could have intimated to the police that it was disguised). A police report written by Hubert Moore claims that Beattie said the voice was disguised [Hubert Moore Report, 28th January 1931].

139 The cat (which was called Puss) had actually belonged to a neighbour who gave it to Julia to mind while the original owner went away on holiday. Julia became so fond of the cat that it was agreed she should keep it. Incidentally, the cat was at the house on the night of the murder. Sergeant Harry Bailey gave it the milk (in three bowls) that Alan Close had delivered earlier that evening.

140 The cost of the grave and burial was £6 16s 0d. The undertaker was John Leary, 188 and 190 Breck Road and 7a Lodge Lane.

141 Reverend, Congregational Church, Queens Drive.

142 Goodman ,*The Killing of Julia Wallace,* footnote pp.113.

143 MacFall and Pierce statement, 24th January 1931.

144 Police photographs 3 and 4.

At Smithdown Road depot Arthur Thompson gave a statement with regard to his encounter with Wallace. Thompson stated that he relieved a guard on the 5a tram at Penny Lane at 7.13pm, and that he was asked by a gentleman sitting inside the car for Menlove Gardens East.[145]

At the City Analyst's Department on Mount Pleasant, William Henry Roberts[146] examined fifteen articles that were handed to him by Inspector Herbert Gold. Roberts said that the mackintosh had been extensively and heavily stained with human blood on the right side, both inside and outside, and on the upper inner side of the right sleeve. The outside of the left cuff and a large area near the left pocket were similarly stained. Roberts also said that a considerable portion of the bottom right side had been recently burned away. The piece of hair was matted together with several human blood clots, and the two pictures were spattered from all angles with human blood. The two photographs were also examined, and one had four blood splashes on it and the other had a bloody smear on the bottom right-hand side of the glass. The outside of the violin case had numerous blood splashes and spots upon it, mainly on the upper wide end of the case. The front of the outside brown paper cover of the sheet of music was spotted with blood. The cushion had numerous blood stains on one side, together with particles of the burnt mackintosh. One corner of the hearthrug was soaked with human blood, there also being many small bloodstains on other parts. The blood had not soaked right through the hearthrug. Roberts also examined the cash-box and

145 Liverpool Corporation Tramways Witness Statement Arthur Thompson, 24th January 1931. Thomas Charles Phillips made two statements regarding his encounter with Wallace on the No. 5 tram. Due to the police investigations and their cooperation, both Thompson and Phillips lost five hours wages at 6s each. Hubert Moore suggested they be given 10s each to cover the costs.

146 Professor William Henry Roberts was born in Liverpool on 11th January 1877 and educated at the Liverpool Collegiate and Liverpool College University. In 1904 he became a master of science at Liverpool University, and the next year a Fellow of the Institute of Chemists. Known to friends as Bobs he became Chief Assistant three years after joining the staff in the service of the Liverpool Corporation. He became City Analyst in 1912 at the age of 34. Like MacFall, he too appeared at the trial of Edouard Charles Braem in Antwerp in 1922. In March 1938 Roberts was elected President of the Society of Public Analysts and other Analytical Chemists in succession to Dr Gerald Roche Lynch. Under Roberts' guidance, the Liverpool Civic Laboratories became the best-equipped and largest in the country outside of London.

dollar bill but found no blood, and the suit of clothes Wallace wore on the evening of 20th January was scrutinised and subjected to the benzidine test but, with the exception of two minute old stains in the right-hand trouser pocket, they were free from blood. The carpet, towel, lock and key were also free of blood. The skirt that Mrs Wallace was wearing was examined. There were three recent horizontal burns which could have been caused through contact with the hot fireclays of the gas fire in the front parlour. The front of the skirt was heavily bloodstained.

Detective Superintendent Moore was of the opinion that Wallace himself made the telephone call from the Anfield call-box and then took the tramcar to the City Centre. He appeared to be over-anxious to establish an alibi, on account of the number of people he asked regarding the address and the name Qualtrough. Moore was also of the opinion (due to the bloodstain found on one of the notes) that after committing the murder, Wallace took the notes from the cash-box to support his allegation of a robbery, and later placed them in the jar. Moore was convinced a thief would not do this.[147]

Moore received another piece of news. Joseph Hall[148] called at Dale Street Detective Offices to deliver a letter, which he had intended posting. It was a statement from his daughter Lily, in which she claimed to have seen Wallace talking to another man in Richmond Park at about 8.35pm on the evening of 20th January.

Samuel Beattie arrived at Dale Street Detective Office to make a second statement. He told of his meeting with Wallace on the corner of Lord Street on the Thursday evening, and their subsequent conversation with regard to the telephone message. Beattie also stated that since making enquiries at the Chess Club and thinking the matter over, he could say that Wallace was not in the club earlier than 7.45pm.[149]

147 Hubert Moore Report, 28th January 1931. One has to question though why Wallace would do this. He would surely have known a police investigation would cover the whole of the house.

148 55-year-old Joseph Hall committed suicide at his home at 9 Letchworth Street by coal gas inhalation on 15th June 1931.

149 Samuel Beattie Witness Statement, 24th January 1931. It would be interesting to know what the exact evidence was for Beattie to say that Wallace did not arrive before 7.45pm.

Meanwhile, a story had circulated in the press regarding a mystery man acting in a suspicious manner in the Anfield area, but this had nothing to do with the murder.[150]

SUNDAY 25 JANUARY

The Liverpool CID continued to ponder over the murder. They were convinced that Wallace committed the crime. The fact that there was no indication of forcible entry and no sign of a struggle led them to believe that the motive was not one of robbery. The fact that the four £1 notes were left untouched upstairs indicated the same. They were also highly suspicious of the cash-box being placed back in its original position. The top of the bookcase measured 7ft 2½in. A lower shelf (on which the cabinet rested) was seventeen inches deep from the back to the front, and three feet wide. The shelves above were eleven inches deep. That meant there were six inches that could be used as a foothold, something that Detective Superintendent Moore believed would be highly unlikely to be attempted by a burglar.[151] Although the motive was obscure regarding Wallace, Moore was of the opinion that a solution could be found in Wallace's affliction – his one kidney, which Moore believed was often associated with insanity. The search for the weapon failed, and the police knew that, up to then, nothing definite had been found to bring the crime home to him.

Detective Inspector Gold visited Lily Hall at her home in Letchworth Street. She was confined to bed due to illness. She said that on the Tuesday night she had alighted from the tram she took home from work. As she walked past Holy Trinity Church she noticed that its clock showed the time was 8.35pm. She continued along Richmond Park, and as she passed the entry leading into Wolverton Street noticed Wallace standing on the pavement

150 This story was sheer sensationalism on behalf of the press probably with the authorisation of the police. The description given in the newspaper was uncannily like that of Wallace.

151 Wallace said that the chair could have been used to stand upon. There are a couple of points to ponder here: a) There would surely have been foot marks left on the seat of the chair; b) The police photo (8) in the kitchen was taken on Friday 23rd January. It could have been moved during that time from the Tuesday evening. If a burglar had used it to stand on, it would be unlikely he would be bothered putting the chair back by the table.

opposite, talking to another man. As she walked past Wallace was facing her and the other man had his back to her. Wallace was wearing a trilby and dark overcoat. The other man was about 5ft 8in tall, wearing a cap and dark overcoat, and was of a stocky build. She continued home to Letchworth Street.[152]

Inspector Herbert Gold and Sergeant Harry Bailey accompanied Alan Close on a reconstruction of his milk round. The distance that he had to cover was 500 yards.[153] The reconstruction was timed, and it took Close 5 minutes.[154]

Police conferences were held throughout the day and right up to a late hour at Dale Street Detective Office. Present were Assistant Prosecuting Solicitor J.R. Bishop and CID Officers.

MONDAY 26 JANUARY

It was reported in that morning's *Liverpool Post and Mercury* that the mysterious man taking the taxi to Smithdown Road had come forward in response to the police appeal. The situation had been satisfactorily explained to the police. The man had in fact reported to them on the Saturday night, and police were happy he had no connection with the crime.[155]

The Assistant Chief Constable notified the GPO, Holloway, London of the stolen postal order and the number, and asked that he be informed immediately should it have been cashed in.

Assistant Prosecuting Solicitor J.R. Bishop sent a letter to the Director of Public Prosecutions, requesting to see him at the earliest possible time. He also sent proofs of witness statements and a précis of the facts.

A police conference was held early that day. Detectives in charge of the case investigated and inquired into nearly 200 items of information, and sifting through them involved an enormous

152 Witness Statement Lily Hall, 25th January 1931.

153 The distance was measured by the Surveyor.

154 Harry Bailey, Trial Transcript pp.209. Close says that in company of the police it took him six-and-a-half minutes to complete the route, and that on another occasion he timed himself and it took him 5 minutes [Witness Statement Alan Close].

155 *Liverpool Post & Mercury*, 26th January 1931.

amount of inquiry. Police were of the opinion that Wallace was responsible for the crime, but they continued with other lines of enquiry. A search continued for the possible murder weapon and articles of bloodstained clothing. Patrol police and detectives again searched side-streets, backyards and waste-grounds of Anfield and other surrounding districts, but found nothing of material value.

Locksmith James Sarginson received the rim latch. He found it dirty and rusty. Two wards appeared to be missing, and the springs were also missing from the remaining two wards. Sarginson said that the cause of stiffness was due to dirt and the absence of springs.[156]

Inspector Gold visited the City Laboratories and handed City Analyst William Henry Roberts more articles from 29 Wolverton Street. Included were two small stained pieces of plaster from the landing just outside the front bedroom door, the four £1 Bank of England notes, a postal order for 2s 4d and a half-crown from the middle bedroom, and a short-handled sledgehammer with a head 2" square from the room which Wallace used as a laboratory. Roberts found no blood on the pieces of plaster or hammer, but said that the front of the top note of the four £1 notes[157] contained several smears of blood, on the extreme left-hand edge extending from the 'O' in 'One' diagonally upwards. Such smears would be caused by drawing a bloodstained thumb across the note. Roberts was of the opinion that the smears were recent, and consistent with having been made on January 20th.

At 7 Missouri Road both Josephine and Lilian Lloyd gave statements. Josephine claimed that Parry called at her house at approximately 7.15pm on the evening of 19th January. She said he stayed about 15 minutes then left to make a call at Lark Lane. He returned sometime between 9.00-9.15pm, and stayed until about 11.00pm. She said that Parry called about 9.00pm on the Tuesday

156 Witness Statement James Sarginson, 26th January 1931. Sarginson Brothers was situated at 86 & 88 Dale Street.

157 The numbers of the four £1 notes were G56 593125, G31 172893, H92 267210 and F98 294738. The four notes had been folded, and when opened No. G56 593125 was the top note with the blood smear.

evening, and remained there until about 11.00pm.[158] Lilian said that she was giving a music lesson to Rita Price of Clifton Road and at about 7.35pm heard Parry's car, then his knock and then conversation at the door. She did not see him. He left and then returned between 8.30-9.00pm, and left again at about 11.00pm. She said that Parry called between 8.30-9.00pm on the Tuesday evening and remained until approximately 11.00pm.[159] Mrs Lloyd said that he was wearing a dark overcoat, black jacket and waistcoat, striped trousers and spats when he called on the Monday and Tuesday. She said Parry was wearing a navy blue suit at the end of the week.

At 43 Knoclaid Road Olivia Alberta Brine and her nephew Harold Dennison were interviewed. Mrs Brine said that Parry called at her home between 5.00-5.30pm on the evening of 20th January and remained there until about 8.30pm.[160] Harold Dennison claimed he called at his aunt's at 6.00pm on the same evening and Parry was there, staying until about 8.30pm.[161]

That evening saw the Anfield tram tests. They were conducted to determine the time Wallace could have left home in order to get the tram at the fixed point of time; namely Smithdown Lane at 7.06pm.[162] According to the working timetable of the Liverpool Corporation Tramways, the time allowed for a tramcar from St Margaret's Church to Smithdown Road was 12 minutes. The number 26 tram ran every 4 to 5 minutes during traffic hours, and every 6 minutes at other times of the day. The three sets of Police Officers left at different times. They took the exact route Wallace said he took on the evening of 20th January. The first pair assigned was Assistant Prosecuting Solicitor J.R. Bishop and Inspector Herbert Gold. They left from the back of 29 Wolverton Street at 6.45 and reached the destination of Smithdown Lane at 7.04. The time taken was 19 minutes. The next to go were Sergeants Harry

158 Witness Statement Josephine Ward Lloyd, 26th January 1931.
159 Witness Statement Lilian Josephine Moss Lloyd, 26th January 1931.
160 Witness Statement Olivia Alberta Brine, 26th January 1931.
161 Witness Statement Harold English Dennison, 26th January 1931.
162 Amateur sleuths also ended up carrying out their own investigations by re-enacting and timing the various tram routes made by Wallace on the evenings of 19th and 20th January.

Bailey and A.W. Fothergill. They left at 6.49pm. They took the same route, but boarded a tram at the request stop 50 yards to the right of Castlewood Road at 6.52pm. This was the same tram Bishop and Gold boarded at the corner. The tram reached its destination (as above) at 7.04pm. Time taken: 15 minutes. Detective Constables William Brown Gilroy[163] and Christie set off at 6.53pm. They walked to the tram stop at the corner by St Margaret's Church and boarded the number 26 tram at 6.57pm. They alighted at the corner of Tunnel Road and arrived at Smithdown Lane tram stop at 7.10pm. It had taken them 17 minutes.

TUESDAY 27 JANUARY

The investigations were continued throughout the night and day, and that evening's edition of the *Evening Express* reported that the police were confident that the present line of inquiry would yield a result. It was evident that the police enquiries were strictly limited to Wallace, with particular emphasis on the alleged sighting of him by Lily Hall in Richmond Park on the evening of 20th January. A conference between CID Officers was held at Police Headquarters in Hatton Garden. J.R. Bishop telephoned the Director of Public Prosecutions in Whitehall to make an appointment for the following day. Meanwhile, the police had received offers of help from spiritualists and clairvoyants, but these were declined.

That afternoon Bishop was accompanied by Inspector Gold and they departed for London. There, they submitted the police file to the Director of Public Prosecutions.

At approximately 6.00pm Wallace called at Dale Street Detective Office. There he enquired about a change of clothing, as the police had the only key to 29 Wolverton Street. Detective Superintendent Moore asked Wallace if he spoke to anyone on the way home after the tram car on the evening of the murder. Wallace said that he didn't.

The tram tests continued that evening. At 6.45 Sergeant Fothergill

163 Gilroy died on 27th February 1955 leaving a wife, Nancie, a son and a daughter.

and Detective Constable 95E William Prendergast[164] set off from the back of Wolverton Street. They made their way to the corner of St Margaret's Church, Belmont Road, and after a two minute wait boarded the number 26 tram at 6.52, before finally reaching the destination of Smithdown Lane at 7.03. The journey took them 18 minutes. Detective Sergeant 120H James Reginald Hill and Detective Constable 431H William Brown Gilroy were the next to go. They left at 6.49 and jumped on a tram at the corner of Castlewood Road at 6.52. They alighted at the junction of Tunnel Road and Earle Road and walked over to Smithdown Lane tram stop, reaching the destination at 7.06. Time taken: 17 minutes. Detective Sergeant Harry Bailey and Constable 409H Walter Stanley Oliver[165] were the final pair. They left at 6.53pm, walked

164 William Prendergast was born in Liverpool on 21st December 1904. Criminals feared him and nicknamed him 'The Ace.' Because of his skill at interrogation, his services were often sought by Superintendents of other divisions. During the Second World War he worked in close cooperation with MI5 and was involved in a case which ended in a spy being hanged for selling information to the Germans about British troop movements. Prendergast became the first member of the famous wartime anti-IRA Squad. The city's streets erupted into IRA violence, whose members carried out bomb attacks on postal communications and shops practically every night. One night at the outset of the Second World War there was a midnight bomb attack on a shop in Bold Street. The call received by the police was for a gas explosion. The Squad raced to the location and found the street in chaos. There was no trace of a gas explosion but the whole front of a shop had been demolished, with glass and debris littering the street. Amongst the debris Prendergast spotted the tarred remains of a balloon. He knew it was a desired method of the IRA to use such balloons – they contained acid which would eat through the balloon to a small detonator which would then set off the explosive. The quick-thinking Prendergast knew in all likelihood other devices would be in the area, so immediately raced from shop to shop. He noticed one in a shop doorway further up the street and wrenched it from its hiding place. As he shouted to the other Squad members Prendergast threw it into the roadway. All the members threw themselves to the floor as the bomb exploded with a terrific roar. Prendergast was congratulated on his actions directly from the Home Office. He was in the Liverpool Police for 32 years, 28 of them in the CID, and was commended on numerous occasions. A formidable detective with a phenomenal memory, he never had to make a note of anything. Judge Neville Laski claimed he was one of the finest detectives he had ever met. A compassionate and humorous man, Prendergast once stated that he felt sorry for the thief, because 'once you have found out his background, you come to understand why he is a thief.' He retired from the force on 18th May 1959 and went on to contribute storylines to the television series *Z Cars*, on which he also acted as a technical advisor. He died in Aintree Hospital on 9th October 1969.

165 Educated at the Liverpool Collegiate School, Oliver began as junior clerk in the office of the Clerk to Justices. He joined the Liverpool City Police in 1924 and after a short period in uniform was transferred to CID. He served in practically every department during his 27 years with the police. He was also prosecutor in the Stipendiary Courts and Committal Courts for some years. In July 1939 he was promoted to Detective Inspector and helped in the organisation of the Special Branch and Intelligence Department prior to the outbreak of the Second World War. He was delegated by the Director of Intelligence to oversee important enquiries nationwide during the war. In 1951 he was appointed by the Admiralty as Officer Commanding Police at the Royal Naval Base, Simon's Town, South Africa.

to St Margaret's Church and after a two minute wait boarded the number 26 tram at 7.00pm. They reached the destination at 7.13pm. The time taken was 20 minutes.

From these and the Monday's timings, Detective Superintendent Hubert Moore and the CID calculated that the average time was between 17-20 minutes, meaning that Wallace could have left the house as late as 6.49pm (and even as late as 6.51). Coupled with the estimated time that the milk boy Alan Close spoke to Mrs Wallace – 6.30-6.35pm – they believed Wallace had time enough to commit the murder.

WEDNESDAY 28 JANUARY

Numerous letters and other pieces of information relating to the case were received again at police headquarters and were thoroughly checked. Police conferences continued throughout the day.

That evening J.R. Bishop and Inspector Gold arrived at Lime Street on the 9.35 train from London. Bishop had been in conference with officials at the Home Office and had put the facts regarding the death of Mrs Wallace before the Assistant Director of Public Prosecutions, Seward Pearce.[166] Pearce said that he would not advise proceedings on the present evidence, and suggested that if further enquiries yielded no additional evidence that the question of charging Wallace would be left for the Coroner to decide at the adjourned inquest. After some consideration it was decided that the matter should be left in the hands of the police authorities in Liverpool.

During the course of the investigations, examinations of the fingerprints found at the scene were made but proved to be of no value.

THURSDAY 29 JANUARY

An early conference between J.R. Bishop and the Liverpool

166 The Director of Public Prosecutions was Edward Hale Tindal Atkinson (1878-1957).

CID was held. Bishop notified them of his consultation with the Assistant Director of Public Prosecutions in London and the decision to leave the matter in the hands of the Liverpool Police.

The police had now come to the conclusion that the murderer could have avoided blood spatter during and after the attack. Professor MacFall and Police Surgeon Hugh Pierce were both of the opinion that the avoidance of blood by the murderer could not be ruled out. The enquiries were ongoing with regards to the alleged man who was seen talking to Wallace, but no-one came forward.

Wallace made a fourth statement to Inspector Gold at his temporary abode at 83 Ullet Road. Gold was anxious to discern Wallace's movements after alighting at Belmont Road on his return journey from Menlove Gardens. Wallace stated that he knew nobody by the name Hall in the neighbourhood of Wolverton Street, but had a hazy recollection that he may have heard Julia mention the name Hall in connection with the Holy Trinity Church. Wallace also mentioned that on one occasion during the summer of 1929 both he and Julia went out for a walk and realised that he had forgotten to take his key. He knocked at the home of Percy Henry Gosling[167] and had to borrow his key to gain admittance. Wallace also mentioned that Richard Cadwallader[168] had a key that opened the door to number 29. Cadwallader used to drink and on several occasions on returning home had inadvertently entered number 29 instead of his own house.

MONDAY 2 FEBRUARY

It was a day that saw Winston Churchill in Liverpool. That evening, he would address a meeting at the Philharmonic Hall where he would speak in support of Patrick Buchan-Hepburn and the By-election that would take place on 5th February. The talk that would spread throughout the city would not be about Churchill's visit, however; something of far more greater public interest was

167 28 Wolverton Street.
168 33 Wolverton Street.

about to surface.

Police were still eager to contact the man that Lily Hall claimed she had seen speaking to Wallace in Richmond Park on 20th January, and the newspapers reported that the CID were appealing to a 'stockily-built man' to come forward.

After several days of police conferences and sifting through witness statements, Inspector Herbert Gold finally received instructions to charge and arrest Wallace.

At 7.00pm a police car pulled up outside 83 Ullet Road. Detective Superintendents Hubert Moore and Charles Thomas and Detective Inspector Herbert Gold stepped out and made their way to the first-floor flat of Amy Wallace, who was out shopping. Wallace was sitting in the drawing-room writing letters, and Edwin was in his bedroom studying. There was a knock at the door. Edwin answered it. Wallace heard footsteps and voices and then the drawing-room door opened.

"Someone from the police station wants to see you, Uncle," said Edwin.

The three detectives entered behind him, not waiting for any invitation. Wallace rose to his feet.

"Take a seat, gentlemen," he said. They remained standing. Then the three of them neared Wallace, almost surrounding him. Gold waited for Edwin to leave the room before continuing.

"You know who I am?"

"Yes," replied Wallace.

Gold then carried out the formality of the arrest.

"William Herbert Wallace, it is my duty to arrest you on the charge of wilful murder of your wife, Julia Wallace, at 29 Wolverton Street on the 20th January."

Looking at the three detectives, a perplexed Wallace replied:

"What can I say in answer to this charge of which I am absolutely innocent?"

Gold calmly noted the reply in his book, while Thomas and Moore examined and collected all the papers on the table, including the unfinished letter Wallace had been writing to a personal friend.

Top: Telephone box Anfield 1627 (Merseyside Police)
Bottom: Anfield Telephone Exchange, Richmond Terrace (Courtesy of BT Heritage & Archives)

Top left: Wolverton Street alleyway (Liverpool Record Office)
Right: Richmond Park alleyway leading into Wolverton Street (Liverpool Record Office)
Bottom: Wolverton Street waste ground (Liverpool Record Office)

Left: City Analyst William Henry Roberts. He analysed items taken from the murder scene (Liverpool Record Office)
Right: Richard Gordon Parry (Courtesy Jonathan Goodman)

Left: A.W. Fothergill. He was one of the detectives who conducted the tram tests (Liverpool Record Office)
Right: William Prendergast. Another of the detectives who conducted the tram tests. He went on to become an advisor for television's Z Cars (Liverpool Record Office)

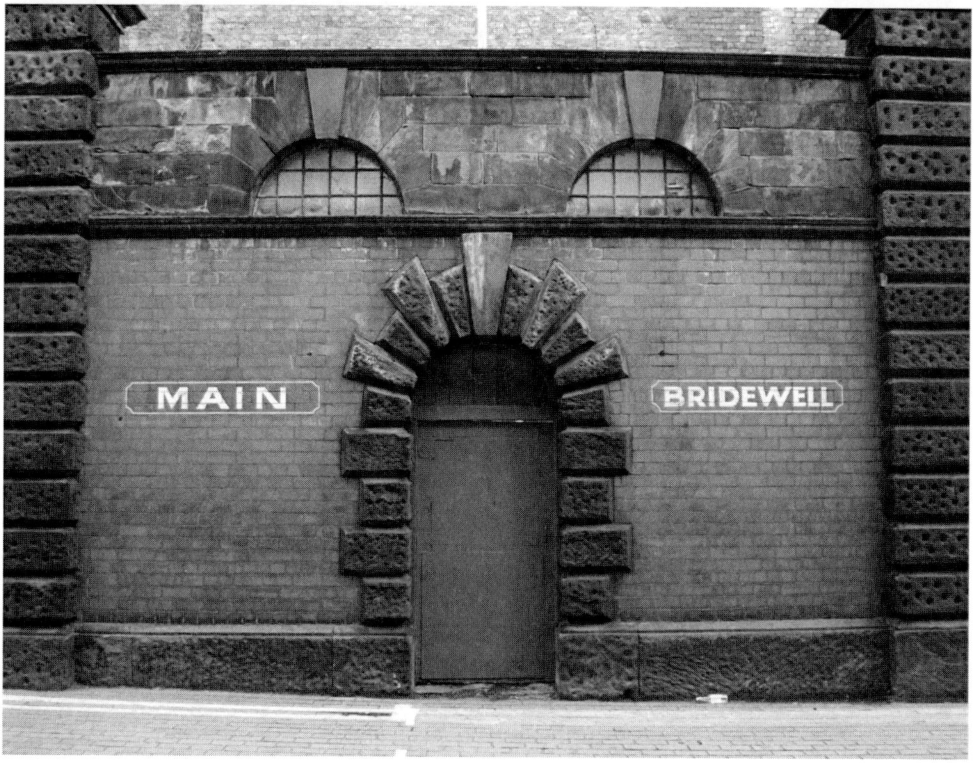

Top: 83 Ullet Road. Wallace was arrested here on the evening of 2 February (Author's Collection)
Bottom: Cheapside Bridewell. After his arrest, Wallace was taken here (Author's Collection)

Wallace was allowed to get his hat and overcoat and speak with his nephew.

"They have come to take me away," said Wallace.

"I'm awfully sorry, Uncle. Is there anything I can do?" whispered Edwin.

"No. Tell your mother not to worry. It will be all right."

Wallace was then ushered out of the flat, into the car and driven to the Main Bridewell, Cheapside.[169] There, Gold cautioned and charged him. Wallace made no reply. Wallace was searched and every article in his possession was taken from him with the bare exception of his clothing. Even his spectacles were taken. He also had in his possession the diary which included the details of his Menlove Gardens appointment.

He was then led downstairs and placed in a cell which at that moment was absolutely empty, containing no furniture of any kind. According to regulations a prisoner was entitled to have clean drinking water in his cell, and the warder in charge brought Wallace a large tin pannikin containing about half a gallon of drinking water.

Later on in the evening, bedding which consisted of a fibrous mattress and a couple of blankets was brought in. Wallace lay down in his clothes, but did not sleep a wink.

169 On 2nd February 1904 the famous escapologist Harry Houdini visited the Main Bridewell, Cheapside to demonstrate his prowess. The 'Handcuff King' was performing at the Liverpool Empire that week and was permitted to exhibit his skills by Head Constable Leonard Dunning. Houdini astounded all present, including Dunning himself and twenty-five other police officials. The demonstration actually began at the main door of the Bridewell, where he managed to place his hand underneath a coat and open the door. Doubts were expressed concerning the veracity, some claiming the gates had been left open, but these were immediately dispelled when Houdini repeated the feat. Three pairs of handcuffs were put round his wrists and he was placed nude in an empty cell which had been searched. Within six minutes he was free from the handcuffs, had escaped from the cell and had managed to open all the other cells in the corridor. He had also moved one inmate to a different cell and locked him in so securely he had to be asked to unlock the door. The demonstration was certified and signed by Leonard Dunning.

4

COMMITTAL PROCEEDINGS

TUESDAY 3 FEBRUARY

At 10.00am, half an hour before the court was fixed to open, the gallery in the Stipendiary's Court[170] was crowded with spectators – mostly men of the labouring class, with one or two youths. Only half a dozen women were among them.

The police had to disperse a crowd of about 200 that had filled the ante-room in the hope of getting into the court. At 10.30am there was a stir in court when Wallace's name was called. Wearing a dark suit and heavy black overcoat he stepped calmly into the dock of Court No. 1, holding his bowler hat in his hand and leaning on the dock rails as the charge was read. Wallace's was the eighth case of the day and he glanced interestedly around the court through his gold-rimmed spectacles, listening attentively. He appeared calm as he rested his face on his left hand.

Prosecuting Solicitor J.R. Bishop[171] outlined the case against the

170 Designed by John Weightman and built 1857-59, the Police Court on Dale Street was claimed to be the second largest in the world only behind the famous Bowery Court in New York. The building was subjected to severe bomb damage during the Second World War. In 1952 the Police Court became known as the Magistrates' Court.

171 Born in London on 3rd June 1886, Joseph Richard Bishop was educated at Merchant Taylors' School and was admitted solicitor in 1908. He served articles with his uncle in Abergavenny and before the First World War was assistant solicitor to the L.B. and S.C. Railway Co, London. He saw war service overseas as a Royal Engineers Officer, first in the Signals, and later on the Staff. After the war he was appointed Prosecuting and Chief Solicitor to the Brighton Corporation and Solicitor to Shoreham Harbour Board. He became Assistant Prosecuting Solicitor to Liverpool Corporation in April 1929, and in 1936 took up the position as Solicitor to the Police. The Wallace case was his first big trial. During the Second World War he did a great deal of work on behalf of the Director of Public Prosecutions with regard to the IRA

accused, and Wallace must have looked on in perplexity as Bishop proceeded to make one distortion after another. In his opening statement Bishop said that he proposed to offer only evidence of arrest and to ask for a remand.

Stipendiary Magistrate Stuart Deacon[172] asked if Wallace was represented.

Bishop: "Not as far as I know."

Deacon: "What is Wallace?"

Bishop: "He is an insurance agent."

During Bishop's speech Wallace fingered his moustache and scratched his head, scarcely altering his expression. On one or two occasions he shook his head and even objected (but was immediately silenced), but generally he seemed to be composed.

"The accused was arrested about seven o'clock last night. His business takes him about Liverpool at various times in the day."[173]

Bishop said that the telephone message was sent by Wallace himself with the preconceived intention that, in committing the crime, he would be able to establish an alibi about his position at the time. The prosecution also believed that after Alan Close had delivered the milk on the Tuesday evening Wallace committed the murder then made his way to the tram stop.

"After the accused the last person to see the unfortunate woman alive was a milkboy at 6.31 and it is the suggestion of the Prosecution, that after the boy called the accused murdered his wife and left the house at about 6.55.[174] He had an appointment which required him to leave the house about seven o'clock and it is

movement. He retired in April 1952 after serving 23 years, during which time he built up a dossier of over 20,000 cases, approximately 50 of them being for murder. His last duty before retiring was attending the Burns-Devlin appeal in London. Bishop believed that the most interesting case he was personally involved in was that of the Cameo Murders. He died in North Wales on 28th January 1977.

172 Born in Widnes on 29th May 1868, Deacon held the office of Stipendiary Magistrate for 36 years – longer than any of his six predecessors, and at Dale Street had dealt with over 250,000 offenders. A Liberal, he administered justice in a fair-minded and humane manner. His great passion in life was golf. He died on 29th November 1947. As the name suggests, the position of a stipendiary was that of a professional nature. They had to have a substantial knowledge of law and legal proceedings. Stipendiary magistrates are now referred to as district judges.

173 Wallace's business was confined to the areas of Clubmoor, Anfield and Stoneycroft.

174 The tram tests proved that the latest Wallace could have left the house would have been 6.51.

a fact that he was seen a short distance away[175] at 7.10.[176] To get to that spot he may have left the house at any time from five to four minutes to seven.[177]

On the previous evening at about 7.45 the accused was in a café and while he was there a friend of his gave the accused a message requesting him to go the next night to a house in the Sefton Park district[178] and call upon a prospective client."

Bishop said that the telephone message was sent by Wallace himself, and that it could be proved that the message emanated from a call-box two or three hundred yards from his house.[179]

"It would have taken him just as long to get from that call-box in time to reach the café where he received the message, as did time elapse between the time the message was received and the accused arrived at the café."[180]

Bishop then moved on to the subject of the call:

"One curious fact is this – but for the fact that that message was sent from a call-box, and that the number to which it was sent was engaged,[181] one could never have traced the call box from which the message was sent. You will hear that the message to the telephone operator was given in one voice, but it was a totally different voice which was given to Beattie.[182]

The prosecution says that sometime before seven o'clock he went to keep this appointment which he said had been made in Menlove Gardens."[183]

Bishop stated that the elaborate and persistent inquiries made by

175 Not a short distance away – Smithdown Lane is almost two miles away.

176 The time the tram left the junction was about 7.06.

177 See note 174.

178 Not Sefton Park but Mossley Hill.

179 In actual fact 400 hundred yards.

180 This was never determined. The police never bothered to ascertain the duration of the journey from the call-box to the café. The road subsidence that occurred in Dale Street in October 1930 caused disruption to traffic. Traffic was diverted via Tithebarn Street and Moorfields and via Whitechapel and Lord Street. Dale Street reopened for light traffic on 8th December, and opened for all traffic on 5th February 1931.

181 The number was not engaged. Neither Gladys Harley nor any members of the chess club had used or answered the telephone for at least half an hour prior to the Qualtrough call.

182 Telephone operators Alfreds and Kelly both said that the caller's voice was an ordinary one – certainly not gruff. Café waitress Gladys Harley said that the voice was deep, and that the caller spoke very quickly. Captain Beattie said the voice was 'gruffish.'

183 Not Menlove Gardens but Menlove Gardens East.

Wallace on his way to and in the Mossley Hill area pointed to guilt. The suggestion of the Prosecution was that Wallace's inability to gain access on his return to his house was a charade, and in actual fact he was waiting to meet one or two neighbours to go into the house with him:

"On his return he says he went to the front door. That is a curious fact, as he said later that he was always in the habit of going in by the back door.[184]

It is a curious thing that the accused, having gone into the house, asked the neighbours to wait in case there was anything wrong.[185] He goes into every room in the house before going into the sitting-room where his wife lay battered to death. Lying beside the victim on the carpet was a mackintosh which belongs to the accused and which he had been wearing earlier in the day. For some reason or other when he went out after tea he did not wear the mackintosh, but put on his coat. Perhaps it was colder.[186]

Now this mackintosh, had been hanging up on the rack. Accused immediately remarks to the neighbour, 'What is my mackintosh doing here?'[187] When the police arrived and saw this mackintosh they held it up and examined it. There was blood all over it and blood up the sleeves."[188]

Bishop moved to the subject of the cash-box, claiming that Wallace found that four £1 notes had been stolen.[189] This was disputed by Wallace and he was immediately silenced by an officer.

184 Wallace said no such thing. What he said was that it was his usual practice to use the front door late at night and the back door in daylight.

185 Bishop was correct with this point. In statements dated 21st January both of the Johnstons claimed Wallace asked them to wait while he went into the house on his return from Menlove Gardens. They altered their evidence after speaking to Wallace's solicitors.

186 Wallace did not wear his mackintosh in the afternoon or evening for the simple reason that it had stopped raining.

187 In actual fact it wasn't until Wallace and Mrs Johnston went to the parlour the second time that Wallace mentioned the mackintosh. At the trial, Wallace admitted that he noticed the mackintosh after he had lit the gas during his first visit to the sitting-room and the discovery of the body [Trial Transcript pp. 278-279].

188 The mackintosh was extensively and heavily stained with human blood on the right side, both inside and outside, and on the upper inner side of the right sleeve. The outside of the left cuff and a large area near the left pocket were similarly stained [William Henry Roberts Analyst Report, 20th February 1931].

189 After checking his insurance books Wallace informed the police of the contents. See footnote 85.

"Later it was found that four £1 notes were in a vase in a bedroom upstairs and on one of these notes there was some human blood. I need say no more about that. In the bathroom of the house on the first floor, there is a water closet, and on the top rim of that there was found a bloodstain which, there is no doubt at all, was of the same period of time as the murdered woman's death.[190] It is the suggestion of the Prosecution that whoever murdered the woman went up into the bathroom and washed away all stains of blood from his person."

Bishop said that no weapon could be found, and that was a most significant fact:

"The suggestion is put forward that if a stranger broke in and robbed and murdered the woman he would not take his weapon away."

This concluded Bishop's statement.

Inspector Herbert Gold addressed the court, and said that at 10.30pm on 20th January he went to 29 Wolverton Street where he saw the dead body lying on the parlour floor. Inquiries had been made, and at 7.00pm on 2nd February, in company with Superintendents Moore and Thomas, he went to Ullet Road where he issued the arrest.

Deacon then spoke: "I am asked to remand you for eight days, Wallace. Have you anything to say against that?"

Wallace, gripping the rails of the dock tightly with long hands, pulled himself up to his full height and replied dramatically; "Nothing Sir, except that I am absolutely innocent of the charge."[191]

Deacon then remanded Wallace for eight days.

At Dale Street Detective Office Assistant Chief Constable W.E. Glover wrote a letter to the Director of Public Prosecutions, notifying him of the arrest of Wallace the previous evening. Enclosed were copies of statements taken during the investigation.

At 2.30pm, at the Main Bridewell, Wallace was placed with

190 The only undoubted facts about the bloodstain were; (a) That it was of human origin, and (b) That it was not of menstrual origin.

191 *Liverpool Echo*, 3rd February 1931.

nine other men of similar age and appearance. In the presence of Detective Superintendent Moore, Inspector Gold, Sergeant Heatley and Governor of the Main Bridewell Superintendent Gill, both Lily Hall and tram conductor Thomas Charles Phillips identified Wallace as being the man they saw on the evening of the murder. Although not legally represented, Wallace was satisfied in the presence of Governor Gill.

Wallace was driven to Walton Gaol where he was taken to the reception room. It was a procedure that Wallace had to repeat over the next three weeks. All the prisoners carried in the police van were taken there and had to stand in line, answering to their names, occupation, religion, etc., and the charge against each read out at the same time. The prisoners were then placed temporarily in open cells and there sat awaiting the doctor who was to examine them. On his arrival they were stripped absolutely naked and compelled to take a hot bath, before being medically examined. Being a prisoner on remand, Wallace was dressed in a dark blue uniform and given number 282. As the charge against him was a capital one, he was placed under the supervision of the senior medical officer, William Davies Higson and his staff.

That evening Wallace was handed a very greasy pan containing a pint of very greasy cocoa, eight ounces of bread in one rude chunk with half an ounce of margarine on top of it, and gruffly informed that this was supper and that he would get nothing more until six o'clock the following morning.

After passing through several iron-barred gateways, Wallace was put in the charge of the chief hospital warder and conducted to the room in which he was destined to spend the next few weeks.

The room contained a dozen beds. Wallace was to occupy the last remaining vacant one of the twelve. The other occupants of that room were mainly mental defectives, some of whom had been in prison at least once before. Like Wallace, these prisoners were on remand awaiting trial. The bed Wallace was to occupy was indicated to him and, as it was then eight o'clock, was told it was bedtime.

The man in the next bed to Wallace was charged with housebreaking. Another was there on a charge of bigamy. A third, an old soldier, obviously insane, was also charged with housebreaking and was subsequently transferred to an asylum. Another man was charged with manslaughter, having stabbed a woman in the throat. He was later sentenced to seven years' penal servitude. There were also two cases of vagrancy against individuals of the very lowest type of mentality. Another prisoner, an epileptic, startled everyone in the room by rolling out of his bed in the middle of the night in a fit.

During the whole fourteen or fifteen weeks Wallace was in the hospital, cases were continually coming in and going out; all varieties of male human beings, charged with every sort of crime. Three men in addition to Wallace were charged with murder and passed through that hospital ward during his time there.

The inmates all dined at one long table in the centre of the dormitory, and although they were supposed to be shaved by the officers, they were allowed to use the safety razors for themselves. Wallace also had plenty of books to read, the prison library being a fairly extensive one. The only games were draughts and dominoes, for which Wallace had little regard.

During this time Wallace was allowed visitors for up to twenty minutes a day, and he was cheered by their support. His legal team could come at practically any time, and the duration of their visits was not curtailed. For exercise Wallace was allowed an hour's walk around circular concreted pathways in the grounds during the morning, and for half an hour in the afternoon. Two or three warders were always in attendance. Talking was against the regulations, but that rule was often overlooked. As long as the prisoners did not walk too closely together, talking was accepted.

A report written by Physician and Neurologist William Johnson of the Royal Southern Hospital gave a brief history and summary of Wallace's kidney illness, and stated that an abnormal mental condition would be associated with a defective renal function. One would expect certain symptoms would be present, mainly headache, vomiting and restlessness. Johnson's report said that it was possible that seven months after admission to hospital Wallace 'may be in a physically debilitating state which would be contributory to mental disturbance.'[192]

THURSDAY 5 FEBRUARY

Liverpool City Coroner George Cecil Mort formally adjourned the inquest of Julia Wallace until 25th February. The firm of Herbert J. Davis, Berthen and Munro[193] was instructed to defend Wallace, and Hector Munro[194] appeared on his behalf. Mort said that in view of the criminal proceedings in connection with the case, he proposed to adjourn it until such a time as the proceedings would be likely to be concluded.

Munro suggested an adjournment for two months, but the Coroner, in fixing February 25th, said he would then probably know the result of the police court proceedings.

Wallace wrote a letter to Julia's sister Amy. He said that although his arrest was such a blow that he could hardly think coherently, he was absolutely innocent of the charge.

At Dale Street Detective Office Joseph Crewe was interviewed. He said that Wallace had worked for the company for 16 years and

192 Medical Report William Johnson, 3rd February 1931.

193 In all probability Wallace knew Munro, as both were members of the Central Chess Club and, coincidentally, the offices of Davis, Berthen and Munro were situated on the first floor of the Prudential Assurance Buildings, Dale Street.

194 Hector Alfred Munro was born in Liverpool on 28th September 1899 to William Hector Bryden Munro and Evelyn Fairfax. He was educated at Liverpool Collegiate, and in 1917 enlisted in the famous Artists Rifles infantry regiment. He was shot in the head and seriously wounded in France, but recovered after a year in hospital. Hector followed his father (who died in 1916) into the legal profession. He practised in London for a time in partnership with Edith Annie Berthen (who was the first woman solicitor in Liverpool, second in the country and also the first female to set up practice of her own account). In 1927 she was asked by Herbert John Davis to join him in partnership. She would accept, but only on the condition that Hector Munro be included so the firm Herbert J. Davis, Berthen and Munro was formed. The firm acted as solicitors to the French, Portuguese, Swiss and Liberian consulates and had offices at 4 Rue Say, Paris. Politically Munro was a socialist and a member of the Fabian Society. He was married three times and had a son, Donald. Munro had an avid interest in chess and, like Wallace, was a member of the Central Chess Club. He was one of the club's better players (ranked in the 1st Class), and also one of the members of the club's committee. He also represented Lancashire in the game. His other great interest was literature. Hector Munro died peacefully at his home in Hampstead, London on 14th February 1981. He maintained his belief in Wallace's innocence throughout his life.

under his supervision for 12 years, and that Wallace's accounts with the company were in perfect order. Crewe went to live at his present address – 34 Green Lane – about three-and-a-half years previously, and since then Wallace had visited him on business on many occasions and for about a period of about two months, about a year and a half before, visited him once a week.

SATURDAY 7 FEBRUARY

Prosecuting Solicitor J.R. Bishop and Inspector Herbert Gold visited London to see Assistant Director of Public Prosecutions Seward Pearce. There they discussed the medical examination of Wallace, the taking of a blood test and blood pressure as well as a urine sample in order to assist in forming an opinion to his mental condition. Pearce advised that the question should be delayed until after the committal, and said that the Home Office could then be approached on the subject. Pearce told Bishop and Gold that they had a fairly good case against the accused.

Whilst in London, Gold visited Guy's Hospital with a view to consult Wallace's medical history from that institution, but was unable to obtain any information as officials in charge of the records were unavailable on Saturdays.

MONDAY 9 FEBRUARY

At Dale Street Detective Office Arthur Thompson, conductor of the third tram Wallace boarded on the evening of 20th January, gave a statement. He told of his encounter with Wallace on the 5a car, and that the tram journey from Penny Lane to Menlove Gardens West where Wallace alighted took two to three minutes.

The following day Hector Munro visited 29 Wolverton Street, accompanied by a photographer and surveyor. A plan of the house was drafted, and photographs of the parlour and front and back of the house were taken.

WEDNESDAY 11 FEBRUARY

A long queue of would-be spectators formed outside No. 1 Court for over an hour before the court opened, and many were eventually turned away by the police. But even the early-comers were to be disappointed, for the Stipendiary sat in No. 2 Court on Wednesdays. Only a few spectators were present there.

Wallace was remanded again for eight days by Stipendiary Magistrate Stuart Deacon. Prosecuting Solicitor Bishop applied formally for the remand, and stated that Wallace would be represented by Hector Munro.

Munro said that the remand would suit him and it was granted without comment.

Wearing gold-rimmed spectacles and dressed in a black overcoat and tie, Wallace appeared calm and collected and occasionally glanced around the court. He bowed slightly to the Magistrate when he was remanded.

A week later Hector Munro visited James Allison Wildman at his home to interview him and take a statement. Wildman told Munro that he noticed the time on the clock of Holy Trinity Church and that it was 6.35 when he looked at it. Wildman then said that it usually took him two to three minutes to reach Wolverton Street. This was news Munro was looking for. If Wildman was correct, the time Alan Close was delivering the milk to number 29 would have been more like 6.37-6.38, and not 6.31 as Close claimed.[195]

While Wallace was in custody the gas in 29 Wolverton Street was cut off. The police had to put on a special supply to conduct tests. The Wallace defence team, however, was unable to make tests of

195 Having personally timed the route several times it is highly unlikely that Close completed the round in six minutes. It took on average 5–5½ minutes, and without the stops Close made. It is possible Close could have completed it in the time he says, but in all likelihood he was escorted around at an unlikely speed to that which he originally took on 20th January. In *The Murder of Julia Wallace* James Murphy correctly states that Close wore a wristwatch, thereby Close was more likely to be correct in the timings. There are a couple of points to this; a) His wristwatch may have been wrong (either way, it has to be said). Close did say that it was usually a minute or two fast. b) Close said that he walked along Richmond Park to Redford Street and it was then 6.45. This is contradictory with Close's testimony; it would certainly not take ten minutes to get to Redford Street from Wolverton Street, and even more unlikely in the prosecution's claim that it was 6.31 when he was at number 29. Wildman was a very observant and intelligent boy. He managed to notice that Close was wearing a Collegiate cap.

its own.

On Monday 16th February James Sarginson received the back door lock from Inspector Gold. He examined it and found it rusty. The locking bolt was in good working order, but stiff and in need of oil. The spring bolt was extremely stiff to make work, owing to the crank which operated the spring bolt binding on the case of the lock. There was a loose spring inside the lock. When the knob was turned (with difficulty) the spring bolt remained inside the lock and the knob returned to its normal position. A knock was necessary to return the spring bolt to its normal position.

THURSDAY 19 FEBRUARY

By ten o'clock, half an hour before the Court opened, hundreds of people had gathered in the courtyard. A dozen constables formed them into a queue upstairs to the lobby leading to the court. Similar scenes had been witnessed the week before when Wallace made his previous appearance, and there was a repetition of the public misconception as to which court the accused was to be brought up. As the doors to the Stipendiary's Court opened about half of the crowd managed to obtain standing room in that court, the remainder being shepherded back into the street. But Wallace was to appear in No. 2 Court, where few, besides witnesses, had gone.

Again, it was J.R. Bishop to prosecute on behalf of the police. Representing Wallace, instructed by Herbert J. Davis, Berthen and Munro, was Sydney Scholefield Allen.[196]

Brought up into the dock between two officers, Wallace was wearing a black overcoat and black tie and appeared brisk and cheerful. He answered "Yes" when his name was called.

Scholefield Allen said that it would be a convenience for Wallace to take a seat immediately behind him, and understood the

196 Born in Birkenhead on 3rd January 1898, Sydney Scholefield Allen was educated at Birkenhead Institute and the University of Liverpool. He served in the First World War, first in the ranks and later as an officer in the Royal Field Artillery 55th West Lancashire Division. He was called to the Bar in 1923 and practised on the Northern Circuit and North Wales. He held the post of Recorder of Blackburn from 1947-69 and was Labour MP for Crewe from 1945-74. He died on 26th March 1974.

police would not object. Magistrate Ward[197] agreed and Wallace, accompanied by the two constables, left the dock to sit behind his defending solicitor. As he took his seat Scholefield Allen asked him how he felt. "I am quite all right," replied Wallace.

Before outlining the evidence in the case Bishop handed the Magistrate a plan of the house and surrounding area, numerous photographs and further plans of the Wolverton Street and Menlove Avenue areas and also a plan of the tram routes from Wolverton Street to North John Street and Menlove Avenue.

Bishop said that the victim had been murdered sometime between 6.30pm and 8.40pm on 20th January and that she was last seen alive by any person other than the accused no later than 6.35. He also said that the murder had been premeditated 24 hours before it was committed, and the Prosecution suggested that that message was sent by Wallace himself as the first step in establishing an alibi.

With regards the telephone call, Bishop had this to say:

> "It is a curious fact that there would have been no record of that call if it had not been that when it was first put through the number was engaged.[198] For that reason a record was made by the operator. I suggest that he walked from the house to that telephone box and rang up the café leaving a message to be delivered to himself when he arrived. He, in fact, arrived in such time as it would take him to get from the telephone box comfortably by tramcar.[199] When he arrived at the café the message was delivered to him."

As on 3rd February Bishop's factual errors were again present, with a few more thrown in for good measure:

197 A native of Liverpool, Richard Joseph Ward was born on the site of the Municipal Buildings on 5th January 1854. His shop R.J. Ward and Sons was situated on St Anne's Street. Established in 1803, they were manufacturers of musical instruments. Greatly interested in the conditions of prison life, he was chairman of the Convict Board and chairman of the Visiting Justices at Walton Prison. It would seem somewhat bewildering that Ward would preside over the Wallace committal proceedings with the more qualified and legal-minded Stuart Deacon disregarded. Ward was another associated with the Braem case and was present at the trial in Antwerp in 1922. He died on 1st July 1940 in his 87th year.

198 See note 181

199 See note 180.

"It is very strange that not only did he not know the name of Qualtrough, but he appeared not to know the district of Menlove Gardens at all.[200] It is curious because his chief, in fact, lives in a house in Green Lane, which runs out of Menlove Avenue and Menlove Gardens North, South and West all run out of Menlove Avenue on the opposite side.[201]

Wallace has been in the habit of visiting his chief at his house, and must have known the district well. Apart from the fact that he has lived in Liverpool for many years,[202] when his chief was ill about two years ago[203] he used to go to the house regularly. When he began to make inquiries where Menlove Gardens were he was only beginning to establish in the minds of other people that he would be in Menlove Avenue the next night."

Bishop then moved on to the evidence of Rothwell:

"The policeman saw him walking along with his face turned to the ground and actually crying. I suggest that at that time he had made up his mind what he was going to do.[204] It was weighing on his mind, and he was feeling remorse."[205]

Bishop then came to later in the evening:

"The accused says he left the house again about a quarter or ten minutes to seven,[206] but when he was first asked when he last saw his wife he said at once: "She came down the yard with me and a little way along the entry[207] and then she went back and bolted

200 Wallace never said that he didn't know the district. He said in the Chess Club; "Is it Menlove Avenue?" He might well not have known it that well. Both Deyes and Joseph Crewe lived in the district, and neither of them knew whether Menlove Gardens East existed or not. The Menlove Gardens area and other streets in the district were fairly modern. Katie Mather herself said that there were streets she didn't know. From a neutral point of view though, it is surely stretching the boundaries of belief that anyone other than Wallace would use a fake address, especially to go to the lengths of plotting murder.

201 Menlove Gardens South does not.

202 Many Liverpool residents at the time in all likelihood didn't know the veracity of a Menlove Gardens East. This more than likely still applies.

203 This had no basis in fact whatsoever. Crewe said at the committal proceedings that he had never been ill a day in his life. Joseph Crewe Witness Testimony 23rd February 1931.

204 Noted barrister and crime writer Edgar Lustgarten called the inference of Rothwell and the notion that Wallace was on trial for a crime about to happen farcical [Lustgarten, *Verdict in Dispute* pp.193].

205 This would appear to be doublethink – the prosecution never moved away from the opinion that Wallace was cool, calm and collected – too collected, yet believed Wallace would show remorse pre-murder.

206 6.45pm.

207 Wallace never said that she went down the entry with him – it was PC Williams who claimed Wallace said that.

> the yard door. I went off.[208]
>
> At 6.31 a boy delivered milk at the accused man's house. Wallace is next seen about ten minutes past seven."[209]

Bishop said it was curious that Wallace did not speak of a possible mistake in the reception of the message, but at once called it a 'bogus one'[210] and that 'finding the message was a bogus one, he became suspicious that something was wrong at home,' and so he hurried home. When he gets home he does not go to the back door[211] but round to the front door. He finds his key will not open the door, but he is not sure whether the door is bolted or not. Then he goes to the back and says he found that door bolted and he cannot get in. He went to the front door again, but could not open it, then he says, 'I rushed round to the back door, and on the way I met Mr and Mrs Johnston, the next door neighbours, and asked them to wait because I was afraid something was wrong indoors.'

> "The neighbours wait, and Wallace goes into the house. He goes all over it before he goes to what you will see would be almost the first room he would reach,[212] and that is the sitting-room quite close to the kitchen. He goes upstairs into every room apparently before he thinks of going into the sitting-room, where his wife was lying dead.[213] He calls his neighbours in, and Mr Johnston goes away to bring a police constable and a doctor, while Mrs Johnston remains with Wallace.
>
> One of the first things Wallace says to Mrs Johnston, and I find this very important, is, 'What is my mackintosh doing beside

208 Wallace never said he heard Julia draw the bolt. He just told Julia to bolt the back yard door after him.

209 See note 176.

210 It is unfair to suggest Wallace should have thought there might have been a mistake in the reception of the message conveyed to him and not thought it was a bogus message. There was no Menlove Gardens East, no-one at 25 Menlove Gardens West by the name of Qualtrough, and the houses of Menlove Gardens North and South were even-numbered, thereby it is reasonable for an innocent Wallace to believe it a false message.

211 This is a contradiction – Bishop says that "Mrs Wallace bolted the back door," so why would Wallace try to enter through a bolted door?

212 Certainly not the first room, unless you were entering the house from the front door. It is unreasonable to suggest that Wallace should have looked in the parlour as it was probably the last place he would have expected to find Julia if she was alive.

213 This is typical double-thinking by Bishop. If Wallace would have entered the parlour first the prosecution would have regarded it highly suspicious that a man should first enter a room singled out mostly for musical interludes and the visit of guests.

> her?' Wallace recognised it as his mackintosh. That is important for this reason, that when the police draw his attention to this mackintosh, he hesitates for a considerable time before he admits it is his."[214]

Bishop said that an attempt had been made to destroy the mackintosh by fire, but whoever did it had failed in obliterating certain identifying patches on it.[215] In the court a police officer held up the blue-grey garment, ragged in appearance, for the Magistrate to inspect.

Bishop said that Wallace was not wearing the mackintosh at Menlove Avenue because it had played some part in the crime.[216]

This was too much for Scholefield Allen, who protested vehemently:

> "Time after time Mr Bishop is suggesting things. It is his duty to present this case fairly, without bias, and on the facts. This case is for Committal Proceedings, and my friend is not entitled to put suggestions against Wallace in this manner. Wallace is on trial for his life and my friend seems to forget that."

Scholefield Allen said it was Bishop's duty to present the case for the Crown as the minister of justice. Facts were needed, and not things that were prejudicial to Wallace. What was said in court would be taken down by the press and there would be full reports of Bishop's speech in the evening's newspapers – reports that would be read by people wise and people ignorant – people that would be among the twelve men and women of a jury that would try Wallace at a later stage for his life.

Bishop said that it would be very difficult for him to produce a statement without giving the reasons.

Mr Ward intervened: "It must be realised that there is a Prosecution and a Defence."

214 See note 83.

215 The patches (which were on the inside of the arm) were almost certainly due to an accident Wallace had in Knoclaid Road on 3rd September 1928. The mackintosh was damaged from a protruding nut on a barrier that had been erected in connection with a sewer construction. Wallace was unsuccessful in his claim for compensation. Incidentally, the length of the mackintosh was 50 inches.

216 If Wallace was bothered about the mackintosh, why on earth would he leave it behind? Surely he would have disposed of it with the murder weapon.

Scholefield Allen said that the serious responsibility lay upon both himself and Bishop as cold, remorseless instruments of justice, to present the facts and not to attempt to flare up the imagination of the public.

Continuing, Bishop said that Professor MacFall put the time of death as somewhere between six and seven o'clock, and that the only bloodstains found in the house with the exception of those in the parlour was the one on the rim of the lavatory. It was the suggestion of the prosecution that whoever committed the crime must have gone upstairs to the bathroom to wash.

Bishop came to the subject of the replaced cash-box:

> "Whoever had stolen this money from the cash-box had not only got up[217] taken the cash-box down and taken the money out, but they had put the tray back into the box, closed it and put it back on the shelf. A person breaking into the house would not go to all that trouble.
>
> When the upstairs portion of the house was examined again it was found that four £1 notes were in a vase in the middle bedroom. On further examination one of the notes had a bloodstain upon it. You can draw your own inference from that."

Bishop said the front door lock was defective at times. When Superintendent Moore tried the key he found some difficulty with it, and when he did Wallace said, 'That is strange; it was not like that this morning.'

Bishop concluded by stating that these were the details with which he thought it necessary to open, and he hoped Scholefield Allen was not serious in suggesting that he had been unfair, as it would be useless to open the case without explaining as much as he possibly could.

Harry Hewitt Cooke gave evidence regarding the photographs he had taken. He said that the door was removed in order for him to get a better view for photograph 6 and that nothing had been moved.

William Henry Harrison, Liverpool Corporation surveyor,

217 The shelf was 7 ft 2½ inches high.

produced plans and gave measurements relating to the Wallaces' home. He said the distance from 29 Wolverton Street to the telephone box was 400 yards.

Scholefield Allen: "Not two or three hundred?"

Harrison: "No."

Scholefield Allen said that a great point was being made of the distance between the house and the telephone box, but the point lost much of its significance if it was stated and proved that there were two other telephones within a radius of 400 yards.[218]

Post Office engineer Leslie Heaton said he could not say if the nearest public telephone to Wolverton Street was in the public library. He did not know if there were any other public telephones in Breck Road, but there might be.

Telephone operator Louisa Alfreds said that the voice she heard was a male and it was 'quite an ordinary voice.' She plugged straight through to Bank 3581 and heard a voice at the end of the line. About two minutes later telephone operator Lilian Martha Kelly made a communication to her that she was apparently trying to get Bank 3581. Kelly told her the call had been cut off. Alfreds said she did not hear the voice on the telephone the second time.

Lilian Martha Kelly said that it was a man's voice she heard. He did not ask for a number, but she replied and had a conversation with Miss Alfreds. She later spoke to the subscriber and a light on the board indicated that he had pressed button B and got his two pennies back. After a further conversation with the subscriber she tried again to get Bank 3581, but failed. She then referred to the supervisor Annie Robertson and two or three minutes later she connected Anfield 1627 to Bank 3581.

Annie Robertson said that about 7.20pm Kelly referred a call – Bank 3581 – to her. Robertson got the call and the connection was made.

Gladys Harley said that she answered the telephone and heard a gentleman's voice. In consequence of what was said she spoke to

218 Qualtrough could hardly have used any of the other telephones as they were indoors in public areas – one in the library, one in the Anfield Post Office and others in shops.

Mr Beattie, who then went to the telephone. Harley said that the telephone was free for half an hour. It was untrue to say, as had been claimed, that the line had been engaged. She knew Wallace but did not recognise the voice on the telephone.

At this point Scholefield Allen referred to a statement made by Miss Alfreds that the voice was an 'ordinary' voice. This was questioned by the Clerk of the Magistrates, Henry Harris. On being recalled Alfreds said that the voice she heard was a "quite ordinary voice."

Samuel Beattie said he took the telephone message from the person who called and relayed it to Wallace. He said he handed Wallace the envelope which contained the details. Wallace said he did not know where the place was, but supposed he would find it. Beattie said he would make enquiries from fellow member Deyes, but he was unable to assist him. Beattie said Wallace's reply was, 'Oh, I belong to Liverpool. I suppose I will find it.' Beattie indicated the tram car to Penny Lane as a means of reaching the district and advised him to enquire on arrival there. Beattie then resumed his own game and did not speak to Wallace again that evening.

Continuing, Beattie recounted his meeting with Wallace on the Thursday evening of 22nd January, and Wallace's 'discreet conversation.'

Scholefield Allen: "It is said that the voice on the telephone was disguised."

At this point Henry Harris interjected: "I do not think you ought to refer to that because that expression has not been used in this court."

Scholefield Allen: "It has been used in an application for remand, and it has been stated against the accused man. I am pleased to hear there is no suggestion that it was a disguised voice."

In reply to Scholefield Allen, Beattie said that the voice he heard on the telephone was strong, gruff and confident, and that the speaker spoke readily.

Scholefield Allen: "Was he ever surprised or expressed any lack of knowledge about Menlove Avenue?"

Beattie: "I cannot say that. He said 'Menlove Avenue?' and was corrected."

Scholefield Allen: "It is quite incorrect to say, as Mr Bishop said in opening, that Wallace did not know the name or even the district of Menlove Avenue?"

Beattie: "I have never said that."

Scholefield Allen: "It has been said that Wallace was so callous he went to the Chess Club on the Thursday night, January 22nd. Is that true?"

Beattie: "It is not."

Beattie said that when he saw him on Lord Street on the Thursday night Wallace did not seem changed, upset or shaken.

The next witness to give evidence was James Caird, friend and neighbour of Wallace. He told of his visit to the Chess Club on the Monday evening, and corroborated the evidence given by Beattie. Caird also said that Wallace rarely visited the Chess Club on Thursday evenings, the reason being that he did not like leaving Mrs Wallace alone. Caird also alluded to the encounter with Wallace on the Thursday evening, and that he looked like a man under great strain, upset and shaken, and that he was in mourning. In answer to Scholefield Allen, Caird said that there was not the slightest truth in a rumour that there was another woman involved.

FRIDAY 20 FEBRUARY

About 200 people were in the public gallery of No. 2 Court when Mr Ward took his seat for the resumption of the hearing. Wallace, accompanied by a police officer, again sat behind his counsel and smiled frequently as he spoke with Sydney Scholefield Allen and Hector Munro. He took off his overcoat before the proceedings began, revealing that he was dressed in mourning.

The day's hearing opened with the calling of a new witness – PC James Edward Rothwell. He was asked by Prosecuting Solicitor J.R. Bishop if he remembered Tuesday 20th January.

At this juncture Scholefield Allen protested, claiming the

question was a leading one.[219]

Assistant Clerk to the Magistrate Henry Harris agreed, and said the witness should not be led.

Rothwell recounted his sighting of Wallace on the afternoon of the murder, claiming that the accused was wearing a tweed suit and a light fawn coat or mackintosh. He said Wallace appeared to be distressed, his face 'pale, haggard and drawn.'

There was laughter in the court and Ward rebuked the spectators: "Do not let us have so much humour. Take this thing seriously."

Continuing, Rothwell added that he looked round at Wallace a second time, as it was not Wallace's manner. He then went on duty at Anfield Bridewell and never thought any more of the incident.

Cross-examined by Scholefield Allen, Rothwell said that Wallace passed him on his left side as he was cycling along Maiden Lane. Wallace was walking in the opposite direction.

Alan Croxton Close was the next to give evidence. He said it was his usual practice to take the milk round between 5.30 and 6.30 each night. Close said it was 25 minutes past six as he passed Holy Trinity Church on the evening of the 20th.

John Paterson said it was his duty to wind and regulate the clock of the Holy Trinity Church once a week. He examined the clock on 23rd January and found that it was accurate.

Conductor Thomas Charles Phillips said that shortly after seven o'clock on 20th January a man came forward and asked him if the tram went to Menlove Gardens East. Phillips told him that he would have to get on a 5w or 5a, but changed his mind and said that Wallace could board his tram and change at Penny Lane. Phillips said Wallace enquired about Menlove Gardens East. He punched a penny ticket for Wallace then went upstairs to collect fares. When he came back down, Wallace again asked him not to forget, reminding the conductor that he needed to change at Penny Lane. When the car reached Penny Lane, Phillips said he shouted for Wallace to change for Menlove Gardens, at which Wallace alighted.

219 A question worded in a manner that suggests the proper or desired answer.

Arthur Thompson said he was on a 5a car which left Penny Lane for Calderstones at 7.15pm on 20th January. He said Wallace asked him if he could put him off at Menlove Gardens East. When the tram approached Menlove Gardens West, Thompson beckoned Wallace to the platform and told him this was the stop. On alighting, Wallace said he was a complete stranger to the area.

Katie Mather said that someone called at her house on 20th January. She did not recognise the man as she did not turn the light on, but said he was "a tall, slight man, dressed in a hat and coat. He made an enquiry for a Mr Qualtrough."

Police Constable James Edward Serjeant was the next witness. He said that on 20th January he left Allerton Police Station at 7.40pm and crossed over to the junction of Allerton Road and Green Lane, where Wallace asked him to direct him to Menlove Gardens East. Serjeant said he told him there was no such place, but there was a North, South and West.[220] Serjeant told Wallace to try Menlove Avenue. Wallace thanked him, half turned away, then turned back and asked where he could see a directory. Serjeant told him to try the Post Office or Allerton Police Station. Wallace compared the time with Serjeant, pulled out his watch (as did Serjeant), the time being a quarter to eight.

Lily Pinches, manageress of Allday's newsagents, told the court that she was in the shop on the night of 20th January when a man called 'a good while after eight' and asked for a directory.

Bishop: "Do you know who he is?"

Pinches indicated: "He is sitting next to the constable there. He was looking for Menlove Gardens East but I told him there was no East. I told him there was no 25 Menlove Gardens West in the book. He said he had been there and they weren't the people he wanted. The man then said 'Good night' and left the shop."

Sydney Hubert Green, clerk, said that he spoke to a man in Menlove Gardens West sometime after 7.10pm on 20th January:

Bishop: "Who was the man?"

Green also indicated Wallace: "I think it was that man there with

220 Wallace said he was looking for a 'Mr Qualthorp' (as it was spelled to Serjeant).

the white hair. He asked me if I could tell him where Menlove Gardens East was. I told him there was no such place. He then said he would call at either number 16 or 26 – I don't remember which – Menlove Gardens West. The man then said 'Good night' and then left me."

Typist Lily Hall said that she had known Wallace by sight for three or four years, and that she last saw him on 20th January:

Bishop: "Where was he when you first saw him?"

Hall: "At the bottom of the entry by the Parish Hall. He was thirty or forty yards away. I had walked along Richmond Park from Breck Road towards him. He was standing talking to a man by the entry. I was on the pavement on the opposite side. I passed him before I crossed over to the side on which he was. When I passed I saw them part. One went down the entry opposite the institute and the other along Richmond Park."

Hall said she knew it was 8.35pm because she looked at the clock on the Holy Trinity Church as she passed.

Police Constable Frederick Roberts Williams said he went to 29 Wolverton Street and knocked at the front door. After a few seconds' fumbling by someone inside the house the door was opened by Wallace. Williams then told of his sighting of the body of Mrs Wallace:

> "She was lying in a twisted position with her head towards the sitting-room door and her feet towards the fireplace. I felt her right wrist, but could feel no movement of the pulse. The flesh was slightly warm.
>
> I questioned Mr Wallace. I said, 'How did it happen?' and he replied, 'I don't know. I left the house at a quarter to seven to go to Menlove Gardens. My wife accompanied me to the back door and walked a little way down the entry with me. She returned and bolted the backyard door. She would then be alone in the house. I went to Menlove Gardens, but found that the message which I received was wrong. Becoming suspicious, I returned home. I inserted my key, but could not open the door. I went round to the back of the house and found the back-yard door on the latch, but not bolted. I went up the yard and tried the back-kitchen door, which would not open. I returned to the front, again tried the

> door, and found it was bolted. I hurried round to the back again and this time found the back kitchen door would open. I entered the house, and this is what I found.'
>
> Accompanied by Wallace, I searched and examined the house. In the middle bedroom, over the kitchen, the gas-jet was burning. I asked Mr Wallace if the light was burning when he entered the house, and he replied, 'I changed myself in this room before leaving the house and probably left the light on myself.'
>
> On the mantelpiece in that room I noticed a small ornament from which protruded five or six £1 notes. Wallace took hold of the ornament, partly extracted the notes, and said, 'Here is some money which has not been touched.' At my request Wallace replaced the notes and ornament in their original positions."

Williams identified the jar produced as being that he had seen in the middle bedroom.

> "In the corner of the room to the right of the fireplace was a curtained recess. I approached this, and Wallace remarked: 'My wife's clothes are kept there. They have not been touched.'
>
> I looked into the recess and saw that, apparently, the clothes had not been touched. Wallace said, 'There appears to have been no one here.' I went with Mr Wallace to the back bedroom, which had been converted into a laboratory. Wallace said, 'Everything is all right here.'
>
> We then went to the bathroom, in which there was a low light burning. I asked Wallace if the light was usually left burning and he replied 'We usually have a low light here.' We then went to the front bedroom, which was in a state of disorder and in darkness.
>
> The bedclothes were half on the bed and half on the floor, and there were two pillows lying near the fireplace."

Bishop asked what other furniture there was in the room beside the bed.

"A dressing table with a mirror and drawers and a wardrobe," answered Williams.

> "The front of the wardrobe and the drawers in the dressing table were shut. I went downstairs with Mr Wallace, and in the kitchen I noticed the door of a small cabinet had been broken in two pieces.

> Mr Wallace pointed out to me a small black cash-box which lay on top of a bookcase to the left of the fireplace. Wallace said there was about £4 in the box which had gone. Mr Wallace next picked up a woman's handbag lying on a chair near the table. He opened the handbag and took out a £1 note and some silver. He said something which I do not remember, referring to his wife's money. We then went into the sitting-room and both stood near the door. The window-blinds were drawn and a gas-jet above the fireplace and to the right was lit and showing a good light.
>
> I looked round the room, and Wallace stepped round the body near the sideboard and lit the gas-jet to the left of the fireplace. We left the room, and I closed the sitting-room door.
>
> We then went to the kitchen. I asked Wallace if there were any lights burning when he entered. He said that apart from the two lights upstairs the house was in darkness. The kitchen window was covered with heavy curtains. I parted these slightly.
>
> I asked Mr Wallace: 'When you first came up the yard did you notice any light shining through the curtains?' Wallace replied: 'The curtains would prevent a light from escaping.' I said; 'I'll try them,' and Wallace replied, 'It's no use now. You have disturbed them.'
>
> About five minutes later we again entered the sitting-room. This time Police-Sergeant Breslin was with us. I pointed to what appeared to be a mackintosh, and said, 'This looks like a mackintosh.' Wallace, who was standing near the door, looked into the hall and said: 'It is an old one of mine. It usually hangs here.'
>
> The mackintosh was a blue-grey colour. I did not examine it. The one produced resembles it. The mackintosh was lying near Mrs Wallace's head. It was all rumpled and spattered with blood. Shortly after this Professor MacFall, Superintendent Moore and other officers arrived, and they carried on the examination."

Scholefield Allen: "Did you ask Wallace if the mackintosh was his?"

PC Williams: "No."

Scholefield Allen: "Is it true to say, as opened in this case, that there was no doubt that he recognised it at once, although later, in the presence of the police, he hesitated a considerable time before he admitted it was his?"

"He did not hesitate in my presence," replied Williams.

The hearing was adjourned until Monday.

MONDAY 23 FEBRUARY

Long before Magistrate Ward took his seat for the resumption of the hearing, a long queue had formed outside the main entrance on Dale Street. Only a small proportion of the public could be accommodated in the gallery of the court, with hundreds turned away.

Wallace again sat behind his counsel accompanied by a constable, and watched the proceedings composedly and with close attention.

Joseph Crewe, Wallace's Superintendent, said that he had known Wallace for twelve years. He said he had moved to his current address three-and-a-half years before, and that Wallace had visited him perhaps four or five times.[221] Crewe said that the friendship came about two years previously when Wallace asked him if he knew anything about the violin. Crewe said that he did, and suggested he should go with Wallace to buy one. Crewe said he could give Wallace a few lessons until he found someone to teach him. When Crewe was asked how many times Wallace had visited him, he replied: "Four, five or perhaps six times."

Bishop repeated this and Scholefield Allen objected. "Mr Crewe said four or five times." Turning to Bishop, Scholefield Allen continued: "Do not put words into his mouth he did not use."

Bishop retorted: "Will you please sit down, Mr Scholefield Allen."

Crewe said that Wallace was a man of the highest character in every respect, and that the Wallaces were all in all to each other.

"On the few occasions Mr Wallace visited you, did you give him directions as to how to get there?" asked Scholefield Allen.

"Yes," answered Crewe.

"When did he visit you?"

221 This is contradictory to Crewe's statement at Dale Street Detective Office: 'Mr Wallace has visited me on business at my home on many occasions.' [Witness Statement Joseph Crewe, 5th February 1931].

"I cannot say exactly, but it was in the winter."[222]

"Did these visits take place at night?"

"Yes. About 8.00pm I should say."

"Was Mr Wallace familiar with this district?"

"No."

Assistant Clerk to the Magistrates Henry Harris intervened: "How can the witness say what Mr Wallace knew?"

Scholefield Allen re-phrased the question: "Was the Menlove Avenue district in Mr Wallace's insurance round?"

"No, his round was Clubmoor."

"Did you know before this case whether there was a Menlove Gardens East?"

"No."

"You would not think," continued Scholefield Allen, "with Mr Bishop, that it was very strange Wallace did not know Menlove Gardens East?"

Henry Harris again intervened: "Does it matter what Mr Bishop thought?"

Scholefield Allen continued: "It was put in as prejudice. Here is a witness who lives within 1,500 feet of this place, and he has said in evidence that he did not know the place."

"We have no evidence as to the witness's intelligence," interjected Bishop.[223]

Scholefield Allen said that he doubted the insurance company were lacking in intelligence when they appointed Mr Crewe as Superintendent. He then asked Crewe if he was ill two years previously.

"I have never been ill a day in my life," came the reply.

Crewe said that the nearest tram stop to his house on Green Lane was situated on Allerton Road at the corner of Mather Avenue, while the next nearest was the tram stop at the corner of Menlove Avenue and Green Lane corner.

222 Wallace's first violin lesson with Crewe was on 28th November 1928. On 5th December Wallace visited Crewe again for another lesson, and afterwards they went to the Plaza on Allerton Road together. His third lesson was dated 12th December 1928.

223 This remark by Bishop must have rankled with Crewe.

When Crewe was asked the question by Bishop, the witness replied; "I suppose I have the intelligence to answer it?"[224]

Detective Chief Inspector Alfred William Roberts said that he had received a lock from Detective Inspector Gold on 26th January and handed it to locksmith James Sarginson the same morning.

Sarginson said that the front door lock he examined was a two-lever nightlatch-type which he found dirty and rusty. After taking off the cover he found that there was a considerable amount of dirt inside. The pin hole in which the key fitted was worn. The part which the key operated and turned back the latch was also worn, with the result that when the key was turned past half-way it allowed the latch to slip back to its normal position. It appeared to have been out of condition for a considerable time and there was no evidence of recent damage. With regards to the lock from the back kitchen door, Sarginson said that the locking bolt was in good working order but stiff for want of oil. The spring bolt was very stiff to work due to the crank which operated the spring bolt binding on the case of the lock. A loose spring was inside the lock (and was still there). When the knob was turned, with difficulty, the spring bolt remained inside the lock and the knob returned to its normal position. A tap or knock was necessary to return the spring bolt to its normal position.

John Sharpe Johnston said that at 8.45pm on 20th January he was leaving the house with his wife by the backyard door leading to the entry. "As I opened the door to let my wife into the entry, I saw Mr Wallace pass the threshold of my door towards his own entry door. My wife said 'Good evening Mr Wallace.' He replied 'Have you heard anything unusual tonight?' My wife said, 'No, why? What has happened?' Mr Wallace said: 'I have tried the back and the front, and they are locked against me.'"

Johnston added that he suggested to Wallace that he should try again, and if he failed (Johnston) he would get his key and try it.[225]

224 This was a classic moment. It would have been nice to witness Bishop's reaction to this remark from Crewe.

225 It wasn't inconceivable for door keys to fit locks on other doors at that time. Wallace even mentioned this in his statement dated 29th January, that both the door keys belonging to Percy

Johnston continued:

> "Mr Wallace opened his door and went into the yard, then went to the kitchen door and said, 'It opens now.' He went in and I said, 'I'll wait here.' I saw a light in the middle bedroom and in the bathroom. I did not see any other lights. In about five minutes I saw Mr Wallace again. He called a name twice, but I could not catch the name.
>
> Before he called I saw the light go up in the middle bedroom. A light flickered, as if from a match, in the small back bedroom. Then Mr Wallace came out saying: 'Come and see – she has been killed.' That was about a minute and a half later. Mrs Johnston and I went into the house and right to the front sitting-room. There was a gas light burning on the right hand side of the fireplace.
>
> I saw a body lying across the floor. I stooped down and knew it was Mrs Wallace. Her body was lying diagonally across the floor."

Looking at a photograph, Johnston was of the opinion that the feet were further apart than shown, and Mrs Wallace was lying with her right arm underneath and her left arm was across her chest.

He continued:

> "The gas fire was not lit, and the room was not brightly lit. I told Mr Wallace to touch nothing and I would go and inform the police and bring a doctor. My wife felt Mrs Wallace's left hand. The three of us left the front room and went into the kitchen. There Mr Wallace drew our attention to the broken door of a cabinet which was on the floor. Mr Wallace pointed to the cabinet door, saying that it had been wrenched off. He then reached up to a top shelf of a bookcase, and lifted down a cash-box. He opened it and I asked him if there was anything missing. He said about £4, but couldn't say for definite until he had checked his books. I said to him 'Is everything all right upstairs before I go for the police?' Mr Wallace went upstairs, came down again and said, 'Everything is all right; the £5 in a dish, they haven't taken.' I then left the house and went for the police."

Johnston said that he did not see the mackintosh when he went

Gosling (No. 28) and Richard Cadwallader (No. 33) opened the door to No. 29 [William Herbert Wallace Witness Statement, 29th January 1931]. The scenario is not like modern locks that are individual – it was a feature of the times that keys did actually fit other locks.

into the parlour.

Scholefield Allen: "How long have you been neighbours?"

Johnston: "About ten years."

Johnston said it was incorrect that Mr Wallace asked them to wait.[226] Scholefield Allen said this contradicted Bishop's remark in his opening statement.

Ward: "Does it make much difference? We are getting it now from the witness."

Scholefield Allen: "The suggestion is that Mr Wallace waited there for someone, and when he got someone to go into the house with him he asked them to wait while he made the discovery."

Ward: "I have not got that idea."

Scholefield Allen said that idea had gone out to the public, and that idea was now proved to be entirely inaccurate.

Ward: "But the public are not dealing with this matter."[227]

Scholefield Allen: "Some members of the public will have to deal with it."

Bishop elicited from Johnston that he made a statement to the police in the early hours of the morning after the discovery and signed it.

Johnston then identified the signature on the statement, and Henry Harris noted this on the depositions.

Florence Sarah Johnston said she and her husband formerly lived next door[228] to the Wallaces in Wolverton Street. She corroborated her husband's evidence regarding their encounter with Wallace in the entry and their entry into the house:

> "We saw Mrs Wallace on the black rug. Mr Wallace stooped down on the side of the body nearest the window and felt her hand. I also felt her hand and said: 'Oh, you poor darling.' Mr Wallace said, 'They have finished her.' The gas bracket near the window was lit. Mrs Wallace was lying almost on her right arm."

226 Whether it was Wallace who asked them to wait is irrelevant. It wouldn't have been unreasonable for an innocent Wallace to actually ask them to wait if he was genuinely anxious.

227 A jury made up of twelve people would eventually have to deal with the matter– obviously what Scholefield Allen was alluding to in his reply.

228 The Johnstons moved out on the night of the murder to 358 Townsend Avenue.

Describing the position of the body on the floor Mrs Johnston said, “I shall always see it. There was no disturbance of the furniture in the room.” She was then handed photographs of the crime scene, which she scanned.

> “To me the picture does not look like Mrs Wallace’s room. It looks like a faked-up room. I am just saying what I think. I suppose it is the conditions in which the photograph was taken.”

“I want this put on the depositions,” said Scholefield Allen, “I shall have something to say about these pictures.”

“We will take the photographs bit by bit,” said Bishop.

Looking again at the pictures, Mrs Johnston said that she did not remember a chair being where it was situated, while the violin stand was immediately behind her head.

Bishop: “Did you see who moved that out of the way?”

Mrs Johnston: “No, we did not move it. Mr Wallace and I were the only people there before the police came. We touched nothing.”

Mrs Johnston also said that the position of the body was different to that in the photograph. She supposed rooms did not look the same in photographs, but the position of the body did not seem the same.

“You see, I was there twice. That is why I noticed so much.”

Bishop: “Did you see a mackintosh?”

Mrs Johnston said the mackintosh was almost hidden under Mrs Wallace’s body on the side nearest the sideboard, and sometime later Wallace identified it as his.

It was intimated that there were five more witnesses to call – the next being Professor MacFall – but as it was indicated that his evidence would take more than half an hour the Magistrate deferred the Professor’s evidence until another day.

Sarah Jane Draper said she went to 29 Wolverton Street with Inspector Gold on 21st January and noticed that a small poker was missing from the fireplace in the kitchen, and that a piece of iron that was kept in the fireplace in the front room was also missing. Mrs Draper said that it was a large piece of iron, about a foot long and thick as a candle, and that it always stood in the fireplace.

TUESDAY 24 FEBRUARY

The fourth day of the hearing saw the same public interest as evidenced by the long queue assembled in the main archway of the Police Court building. The public gallery was crowded with spectators – mainly men – while many were unable to obtain admittance.

Wallace took off his overcoat as soon as he came into court, and occupied his usual seat behind counsel.

It was the evidence of Professor MacFall that was most eagerly-awaited and the spectators didn't have long to wait.

MacFall said that he was called to Wolverton Street on the night of 20th January. He said he saw the body of a woman lying on the hearthrug of the floor in the front parlour:

> "She was laying face downwards with the face turned to the left. The left arm was extended and the right arm was by the side of the body. The body was fully clothed and lay diagonally across the hearthrug. The head, by the corner of the rug nearest the door, was badly battered in on the left side. Above and in front of the ear, there was a large open wound, half an inch by three inches from which, bone and brain substance protruded.
>
> At the back of the head on the left side, was a great depression of the skull, with several wounds. There was a large patch of blood – a blood-clot – on the edge of the hearthrug on the floor, and extended round the edge of the hearthrug. The hands were cold but the body was warm.[229] The head was turned to the left and fixed by post-mortem rigidity of the neck. Post-mortem rigidity was present also in the upper part of the left arm.
>
> By about 1.00am post-mortem rigidity extended to the right arm and leg. From the evidence of this rigidity and the condition of the blood I formed the opinion that death had taken place about four hours before my arrival about 10.00pm.[230]

229 The extremities are often colder than other parts of the body.

230 This totally contradicts MacFall's first statement: 'From my observations I formed the opinion that death had taken place approximately two hours before my arrival.' [Witness Statement John Edward Whitley MacFall]. In fact MacFall contradicted himself on several occasions. From his post mortem findings he claimed that there had been two main blows struck with terrific force with several smaller ones, only to state later that it was one main blow followed by ten smaller ones. In his post mortem report he claimed the victim's hands were free from blood, only to claim otherwise at the trial [John Edward Whitley MacFall PM Report; Trial Transcript pp.121].

> There was blood-staining of the hands but nothing clenched in them, and there was nothing beneath the fingernails.
>
> A large number of typical blood-splash marks were in a circle from the edge of the sideboard round the corner of the room to above the mantelshelf. A few of these marks – one or two only – reached as high as seven feet but the majority were about four feet high. There were also a few small blood splashes between the door and the piano near the door. The splashes were on the wall, while typical splashes on the sideboard gave the direction of blood spurts."

As blood and brain matter was arced around the head and not underneath it, MacFall came to the conclusion that the last blows had been administered while the body was on the floor, the front of the head being bludgeoned first.

"There was an old mackintosh," said MacFall, "bundled up a little beneath the right shoulder of the woman. This mackintosh was partly burned on the lower and front part."

Bishop: "Were there any blood splashes on the sideboard?"

MacFall:

> "Yes. A careful observation of the direction of the splashes on the sideboard and wall by the left side of the fireplace showed three varieties of blood marks: 'Soda-water bottle' spots – the usual description – round spots, and the partly diagonal spots. Consideration of these showed the direction to concentrate to a point, or focus, in front of the chair in the corner of the room by the fireplace.
>
> I left the room and made a careful search of the house for bloodstains, especially. Several suspicious stains which were not blood were found. I thought that other people might think they were stains. In the bathroom, on the edge of the lavatory pan – in a position shown on a photograph[231] – a circular clot of blood, three sixteenths of an inch in diameter and an eighth of an inch in height, was found. Its appearance coincided in coagulation, serum exudation, therefore, time of the blood seen in the clots by the body."

MacFall said that he performed the post-mortem examination

231 Police Photograph 9.

of Mrs Wallace's body at Princes Dock Mortuary. The back of the head toward the left side bore ten diagonal incised wounds. The whole of the left side of the back of the skull was driven inwards and broken into pieces. The appearance was as if a terrific force, with a hard instrument, had driven in the skull. The body itself was in general good health and death was due to fracture of the skull by someone striking the woman eleven times on the head with terrific force. In reply to Bishop, MacFall said the opening blow would have most certainly caused death alone and in less than one minute.

> "When I first examined the bathroom I found a nail brush on the side of the bath – by the wall – the bristles of which were moist and the wood partly dry. Its appearance was as if it had been used within a few hours.[232] There was no sign of any colouring – blood or otherwise – on the brush."

Scholefield Allen asked MacFall if he could remember what time it was that he first observed the spot of blood.

"Perhaps about a quarter of an hour after I examined the body," said MacFall.

Henry Harris: "Does it come to this, that you finished your examination of the body in half an hour?"

MacFall: "Yes."

Scholefield Allen: "Then you found this spot about 10.45pm?"

MacFall: "Perhaps about then, or a little before it. Between 10.35 and 10.45."

MacFall said the spot of blood was removed immediately after the photograph was taken at 12.45am.

Scholefield Allen: "You will see the advantage the police have. The accused had no medical representative there. When did you carry out the tests?"

MacFall: "On the Wednesday afternoon."

"I am told that, chemically, the time at which the examination is made is of some importance," said Scholefield Allen.

"I tested about 4.00pm on Wednesday."

232 It is possible Julia could have used it.

MacFall said that he kept the spot of blood in his possession until he tested it. It had in actual fact remained in his silver spectacle case in his pocket (which he produced in the court). He also described the different blood tests he had applied: "I examined it microscopically for blood cells. I applied the Guaiacum and Kastle-Meyer. There was also the Precipitin Test. In addition, I also applied the Frothing Test."

Scholefield Allen: "Have you given all the facts for your opinion that this blood clot was of the same time as the blood about the body?"

"Yes."

"Is it possible to be able to tell the difference between male and female blood?"

"No, it is not."

"What was the temperature of the bathroom?"

"Just an ordinary temperature," answered MacFall, ambiguously.

"I want to know whether scientifically you took the temperature of the bathroom and the room downstairs," asked Scholefield Allen.

"No I did not. The temperature of the bathroom and the room downstairs were about the same. It was not very cold."

"Did you weigh the body?"

"No."

MacFall said that he came to the conclusion of the time of death through rigor mortis and clotting of the blood, adding that the body was that of a frail woman, her physique was poor, but otherwise healthy.

Scholefield Allen: "What degree of accuracy can you get in estimating post-mortem rigidity?"

MacFall: "It is within one hour and a quarter and three-quarters of an hour."

Scholefield Allen then asked MacFall what the temperature of the body was when he examined it.

"I did not take the temperature, but it was warm."

MacFall said that he relied upon the corroborative evidence of both post-mortem rigidity and the blood clots. He also said that he examined the body frequently at intervals for three hours, and the changes in post-mortem rigidity assisted him in estimating how long Mrs Wallace had been dead.

Hugh Pierce, Police Surgeon, said that he arrived at Wolverton Street at approximately 11.50pm on 20th January. There he found the body of the victim which he examined with Professor MacFall. Pierce said he made a rough guess as to the height of the body, but did not measure it. He did not take the temperature of the body or the sitting room, as he had not taken a thermometer with him. Pierce said that rigidity had set in in the neck and upper part of the left arm. The body was examined from time to time to see the advancement of rigor mortis, and by 1.00am rigidity had extended to the right arm and right leg. From these facts he formed the opinion that death had occurred about six hours previous to his arrival.[233]

In reply to Scholefield Allen Pierce said that between half a pint minimum and two pints maximum blood had been shed. He also said that rigor mortis was complete at 12 noon, and it did not alter his opinion on the time of death. He based it on rigor and rigor alone.

Scholefield Allen: "You used the nebulous phrase, 'I examined the body from time to time.' What were the times?"

Pierce: "Every quarter of an hour."

Scholefield Allen: "What happened at 12.10am?"

Pierce: "Rigor Mortis was about the same."

Scholefield Allen: "What was the body like at 12.25am?"

Pierce: "The right arm was almost completely rigid, the right leg, slightly. Professor MacFall and I did not make careful notes on these periodic observations."

Scholefield Allen: "That is very important. You go there as scientific witnesses, forming expert opinions, and you do not take careful notes."

"You do not take notes about little observations in these periods,"

233 Approximately 5.50pm.

replied Pierce.

Scholefield Allen had discredited the evidence of MacFall and was now doing the same with Pierce.

Bishop cut in: "If you would ask questions and not make so many speeches to the witness we would get on better."

Scholefield Allen (to Pierce): "Do you realise this man's life may depend on what you say? Then you will appreciate why I am so anxious to get at the facts."

Pierce said that he wished to amend his previous statement and that what he should have said was not 'careful notes', but 'detailed notes.'

Pierce said that when he next examined the body at 12.40am the right leg was more rigid. He said that he last observed the body at 1.00am and the right leg was then almost completely rigid.

When asked by Scholefield Allen if that was the only fact at that time which helped him to confirm his opinion, Pierce proceeded to say, "It was the chief fact –"

"I'm not having that," interrupted Scholefield Allen. "If it was the chief fact, I want all the others."

"You will take his words instead of him taking yours," said the Magistrate.

"I would be delighted to take his words," said Scholefield Allen. "In truth and fact, this witness ought to have detailed notes here with the various facts."

"He is an experienced man, and knows," said the Magistrate.

Pierce said that he observed the blood clot on the lavatory rim at about 12.10am and two other occasions. When asked if he could give an opinion on the time of the clot in the bathroom being the same as the clots around the body, he said that he could not give an opinion. He also said that it was very hard to give an accurate estimate on the time of death. If there was a violent struggle rigor mortis may come on quickly, starting to set in an hour from death perhaps, but normally the time was fixed between four and eight hours in a normal individual.

"Are these the outside limits for a healthy, normal person?" asked

Scholefield Allen.

"I should say so," replied Pierce.

"Would you say that a person who might have lost two pints of blood was a normal healthy person? Would rigor mortis set in earlier or later after that loss of blood?"

"I do not think it would make any difference."

"Assuming that she had lost the blood," continued Scholefield Allen, "would it affect the time of rigor mortis setting in?"

"I would not like to express an opinion," said Pierce.

Scholefield Allen drove the point home: "How then could you form an opinion as to the time of Mrs Wallace's death?"

"By the progress of the rigor mortis," offered Pierce. "I based my opinion about the time of death on the fact that she was a normally-built person."

Wednesday saw the adjournment of the inquest into the death of Julia Wallace for another seven days. Hector Munro said he thought the Committal Proceedings would be concluded in a week's time. Coroner Mort said that, in any case, the inquest proceedings would be a pure formality. He would not reopen the inquest except to close it, whatever the result of the Committal Proceedings.

On the same day, Amy Dennis wrote a letter to Davis, Berthen & Munro acknowledging receipt for Julia's fur coat.

THURSDAY 26 FEBRUARY

Hundreds of people waited in a downpour of rain outside Liverpool Police Court two hours before the resumed hearing. They were doomed to disappointment, however, for after waiting for some time, they were dispersed by an officer who informed them that the proceedings would in all likelihood be formal and that the hearing had been adjourned until the following Monday.

There were only a few people in court when the Magistrate took his seat.

Wallace took off his overcoat as soon as he left the dock and took his usual seat behind that reserved for counsel and solicitors. He had a few moments' conversation with Hector Munro before an application was made to the Magistrate.

Munro said: "It has been arranged between my friend [Bishop] and me, subject to your worship's approval, that this case shall be remanded until Monday next at 10.30am, for the convenience of counsel."

Ward: "I know of no arrangements. You cannot make them without consulting me."

Bishop: "I have made no arrangement, but the matter has been mentioned to me."

Ward: "I am always ready and willing to help you gentlemen, but I like to know something about it before you make arrangements. I agree to the remand until Monday."

The proceedings lasted a minute, and Wallace then left the court. Before he went down the dock stairs he waved his hand to someone in the public gallery.

Sydney Scholefield Allen was engaged in a case in the Crown Court at Manchester Assizes.

MONDAY 2 MARCH

The fifth day of the Committal Proceedings saw the same public interest. Hundreds of people were unable to be accommodated in the public gallery. A long queue assembled in the main entrance to the courts, and many of those who could not get into the court tried to obtain admission to the other courts.[234]

Wallace smiled to his counsel and took his usual seat behind the solicitor's bench, keeping his overcoat buttoned up as he listened to the evidence.

Recalled, William Henry Harrison, surveyor, said the shortest route between the back door of 29 Wolverton Street and the corner of Belmont Road was 605 yards. The distance between the tram

234 The *Liverpool Echo* dated 2nd March 1931 reported the Court being besieged by crowds of spectators.

stop on Belmont Road and the tram stop on Smithdown Lane was 1.7 miles.

In reply to Bishop, Harrison said that there was a nearer tram stop at the junction of Castlewood Road and Belmont Road than the one Wallace claimed he used – the nearer one being 375 yards from the back door of 29 Wolverton Street.

Liverpool City Analyst William Henry Roberts gave evidence. He said the mackintosh was heavily bloodstained on the right side, both inside and outside, and on the upper inner side of the right sleeve. The outside of the left cuff and a large area near the left pocket were similarly stained. A considerable portion of the bottom right side had been recently burned away and was so pliable that when shook, fragments fell from it. He also said the piece of hair found inches from the head was matted with several blood clots, and both pictures were spattered at all angles with human blood. One photograph had four human blood splashes on it and the other had a smear of human blood on the bottom right-hand side of the glass.

Roberts said the outside of the violin case and the front of the brown paper cover of the piece of music had blood splashes and spots upon them. On one side a cushion had numerous small human bloodstains, together with burned particles of the mackintosh. One corner of the hearthrug was soaked with human blood, there being also numerous small human blood spots on other parts of the rug. The blood had not soaked right through the rug. The cash-box and dollar-bill were free from blood.

The Analyst said the suit Wallace wore was free of bloodstains with the exception of two minute old stains in the right-hand trouser pocket, and these had nothing to do with the case as they were too old.

Roberts also said that the skirt was heavily bloodstained, and at the bottom of the placket[235] were three horizontal burns which could have been caused by contact with the hot clays of the gas-fire. Roberts was of the opinion that the blood smears on the £1 note

235 An opening at the top of a garment for ease in putting on and removal.

could have been caused by the drawing of a slightly bloodstained thumb across the note. After examining the notes he said that the bloodstain was consistent with those at the crime scene on 20th January, and that they might have been consistent with the 'day before, perhaps two days, but not three days.'[236]

Roberts added that about a pint and no more than one and a quarter pints of blood had been spilled in the murder.[237]

It was the turn of Detective Superintendent Hubert Moore to give evidence.

> "At about 10.05 I arrived at 29 Wolverton Street. The door was opened by Constable Williams. I made a thorough examination of the house. I found the front door locked, but it had no marks on it. The furniture in the sitting-room appeared to be in perfect order and undisturbed. The chairs, table, pictures and ornaments appeared to be as they ordinarily would be. The hearthrug was also undisturbed.
>
> Going into the kitchen I saw Wallace and asked him how he had found the house on his return. He said, 'I was called by telephone to a business appointment in Menlove Gardens East at 7pm tonight. I went there but could not find the address. I hurried home; I tried the key in the front door, but the key would not act. I went round to the back door but I could not open it. I returned to the front door and again tried the key, which would not act, went round to the back door, which opened easily. I met Mr and Mrs Johnston and asked them to wait while I came in. I found my wife murdered in the parlour and this just as you see it.'
>
> Pointing to a small cash-box Wallace said, 'About £4 has been stolen from the box.'
>
> On the floor I saw a half-crown piece and two separate shilling pieces. I asked Wallace where he had found the cash-box. He said; 'Where it is now.' It was then at the top of the bookcase. I reached the box down and took out the money container. In one of the compartments I found an American dollar bill. The other

236 It is difficult to comprehend how Roberts could say that the notes could not have been bloodied three days before the evening of January 20th. It was almost a week after the killing that he received the notes and conducted his tests (which included staining and examining other notes). At the committal proceedings, Roberts said that it was impossible to state with certainty the exact age.

237 This included the blood found on the articles [William Henry Roberts Witness Evidence, 2nd March 1931].

> two compartments were empty. I said to Wallace that I could not understand why a thief would go to all the trouble of fixing the lid on and putting the box back where he had found it."

Moore said that he then accompanied Wallace upstairs. In the room used as a laboratory nothing appeared to be missing. In the middle bedroom nothing appeared to be disturbed either. Moore said that he noticed the small jar on the mantelpiece, the notes visible.

> "I next went into the front bedroom with Wallace. There I found the bed in disorder. Two pillows were on the floor between the fireplace and the window. The clothing had been pushed towards the fireplace from the door, exposing a portion of the mattress. On the mattress there were two women's handbags. There was also a woman's hat on the mattress, and two other women's hats on the disturbed bedclothes. I asked Wallace if this room had been used recently, or if he could say the bedding was like that that day. Wallace replied, 'I cannot say – I don't think I have been in this room for a fortnight.'"

The clothing in the wardrobe and in the drawers of the dressing-table had not been disturbed," said Moore. "We then returned downstairs and made a further examination of the parlour. In consequence of a communication made to me, I later went into the bathroom where I saw a small clot of blood on the lavatory pan. Later I saw MacFall remove the clot and in so doing leave a distinct moist stain about half an inch long."

Moore said he next examined the front door lock. Using Wallace's key he found it would turn to a certain point, but if it was turned too far round the lock would slip and the door would again be locked. Moore managed to open the door, where he then said to Wallace: "I can open the door all right, but the lock is defective." Wallace replied: "It was not like that this morning."

Moore said he then examined the parlour. There, he noticed the crumpled mackintosh tucked up and slightly underneath the right shoulder and head of the victim. No part of the body was resting actually on the mackintosh.

"Between the body and the sideboard was a considerable quantity of blood, which would necessitate any person wishing to reach the fireplace stepping over it.[238] On the right hand side of the room between the piano and the body there was a considerable quantity of brain matter.

I asked Wallace if the window blinds were drawn when he entered the room. He replied, 'Yes, I lit a match and put the gas on.' I then asked him if he screamed or shouted; 'No,' Wallace replied, 'I thought she might have been in a fit. I lit the gas to go to her assistance. Of course, I found she was dead.'"

Moore said that when he asked Wallace about the mackintosh the accused seemed reluctant to admit ownership:

"He put his left hand to his face, stooped slightly and looked towards the body but made no reply. About thirty seconds later I said: 'Had Mrs Wallace a mackintosh like that?' Wallace made no reply. I said to Sergeant Bailey: 'Take it up and let us have a look at it.' Sergeant Bailey lifted up the mackintosh."

At this point an officer in the court held up the mackintosh, and Moore continued.

"I said: 'This is a gent's.' Wallace got hold of the mackintosh and said: 'If there are two patches inside it is mine.' "He then said: 'It is mine. I wore it this morning. The day turning out so fine, I wore my fawn coat this evening. Of course, it was not burned like that when I wore it.'

A little later I asked Wallace to accompany a police officer to Anfield Road Police Station, telling him that there were better facilities there for taking a detailed statement from him. He left in the company of Inspector Gold. By this time Wallace's sister-in-law had arrived, but as the house got overcrowded I asked them to leave. I gave instructions to the police."

Moore said that a thorough search of the house was made throughout the night but other than those in the parlour (and the one on the lavatory pan) no bloodstains were found. There were also no signs of forcible entry.

238 Every one of the other visitors to the room managed to negotiate their way around it without contaminating themselves with the blood or brain matter. Wallace, though, would have had to do this in a dimly-lit room which would have also necessitated avoiding the chair in front of the sideboard.

"We left the police officer in charge of the house," continued Moore. "On January 21st I visited the house again and made a further search of the house interior and exterior. We again failed to find any weapon or bloodstains outside the parlour. I was present when the drains were searched."

In reply to Bishop, Moore said that he saw Wallace that morning (the 21st) and that the accused was in and out of Dale Street Detective Office all day on both 21st and 22nd January. Moore also said that he saw Wallace on the 23rd at 6.30pm:

> "I said to him 'You saw Mr Beattie of the Chess Club last night?' He said, 'Yes.' I said, 'You asked him about the telephone message and what time he received it?' The accused said 'Yes.' I said, 'You told him that the time was important? In what way was it important?' He replied, 'I had an idea. We all have ideas. It was indiscreet of me.' I said, 'I wish you would tell me what your idea was. It might help me in the inquiry.' He replied, 'I cannot explain any further. I recognise now it was an indiscretion on my part.'"

The Detective Superintendent said that Wallace called at Dale Street Detective Office at 6.00pm on 27th January. There he asked Wallace about Lily Hall's alleged sighting:

> "I asked him if he had spoken to anyone on the way home on the night of the murder after leaving the tramcar. Wallace said 'No.' I said, 'Are you quite sure? A lady who has known you for years stated that she saw you at 8.35pm speaking to a man on the footway in Richmond Park by the entry near Letchworth Street.' He replied: 'I was not so alarmed that I would not raise my hat or speak to anybody, but I did not.' After a short pause he said 'I am positively certain.'"

Moore then told of his accompaniment of Superintendent Thomas and Inspector Gold on 2nd February and the ultimate arrest:

> "Inspector Gold cautioned the accused, who then said: 'What can I say in answer to such a charge, of which I am absolutely innocent?'
>
> Later that same evening, I was present at the Main Bridewell when Inspector Gold cautioned and charged him with the wilful

> murder of Julia Wallace at 29 Wolverton Street on 20th January. The accused did not reply."

Moore said that he saw the clot of blood at about 11.30pm.

"I am told that in these cases it is important to have photographs taken of the clot. Did you take photographs in this case?" asked Scholefield Allen.

"No," replied Moore. "Professor MacFall took possession of it and I do not know what he did with it. It is not usual for the CID to make enlargements of bloodstains."

Moore said that the he was unable to say if the mackintosh had been touched before Bailey had handled it, and that he was unaware at the time that Wallace had admitted ownership.

"Do you know that at that time he had identified and acknowledged the mackintosh as his to Police Constable Williams and Sergeant Breslin?" said Scholefield Allen.

"No," replied Moore.

In reply to Scholefield Allen, Moore said the police had issued an appeal in the Press for the man that was seen by Lily Hall near Wolverton Street to come forward, but this had been unsuccessful.

The Court was adjourned until the following day.

TUESDAY 3 MARCH

Public interest was maintained. Long before the court was opened a long queue of people waited for admission. Again, many were to be greatly disappointed as they were turned away.

The first witness on the penultimate day of the hearing was Detective Sergeant Harry Bailey. He said that he went to 29 Wolverton Street on the night of the murder at about 10.25pm. When he arrived there Professor MacFall and Detective Superintendent Hubert Moore were present:

> "I examined the house for evidence of forcible entrance, but found none. In the parlour I found the body of Mrs Wallace. Tucked up against it, at the back, I saw a mackintosh which was much bloodstained. Looking closely at the mackintosh, I saw two burned matches inside a fold. I observed that the mackintosh

> was burned down the right side."

Bailey corroborated Moore's evidence regarding Wallace's reluctance in admitting ownership of the mackintosh. He also said that when he held up the mackintosh and showed the burned side, Wallace said that it was not burned like that the morning when he wore it.

"What condition was the room in?" asked Bishop.

> "There was no sign of disorder or a struggle. In the kitchen I saw the broken cabinet while the cash-box was on the shelf. On the floor I saw a half-crown and two separate shillings. On a chair inside the kitchen and partly below the table I saw a leather handbag. It contained altogether £1 8s 4½d. The evening newspaper lay on the kitchen table. I could see the handbag as I entered the kitchen.
>
> Upstairs I went into the middle bedroom and could see no sign of disorder, but I saw a jar containing Treasury notes on the mantelpiece. In the front bedroom I saw the tick was pushed towards the middle of the bed. The drawers were shut."

Bailey said that he later went to Anfield Road Police Station with Wallace and Inspector Gold, and then produced the statement Wallace had made there and proceeded to read it out in court.[239]

Bailey said that he later returned to 29 Wolverton Street and had the body removed to Princes Dock Mortuary. It was at the mortuary that he noticed the burning on the skirt, but no burning on the corresponding part of the underskirt. The Detective Sergeant also told of his visit to Wolverton Street on 21st January and his taking possession of the articles for analysis.

"On January 23rd I was with Inspector Gold at the house when he said to the accused; 'Mrs Draper has stated that there is a poker and a piece of iron missing from the parlour.' Wallace replied: 'She must have thrown the poker away with the ashes and I do not know anything about the piece of iron in the parlour.'"

Bailey told of the tram test he conducted with Sergeant Fothergill on 26th January, the time taking fifteen minutes. He also said

239 Witness Statement William Herbert Wallace, 20th January 1931. See Appendix I.

that he had conducted a second test the following night and that he made the journey from the back of 29 Wolverton Street to St Margaret's Church in three minutes and the overall journey took twenty minutes.

Scholefield Allen: "You are quite certain you took three minutes from the back door to St Margaret's?"

Bailey: "Yes. I walked all the way."[240]

Scholefield Allen: "What pace of walking did you do that night?"

Bailey: "About 4½ miles an hour."

Scholefield Allen: "The distance from that back door to the church is 605 yards, and you walked that in three minutes. That is at the rate of seven miles an hour?"

Bailey: "I believe it is getting near that."

In reply to Scholefield Allen, Bailey agreed that it would have been a fairer comparison had he waited at Smithdown Road corner, boarded a Menlove Avenue car, and *then* taken the time.

Scholefield Allen moved on to the question of the poker in the house.

"You have been to that house and there is a poker in the kitchen?"

"Yes, so far as I know," said Bailey.

"It was there on the night of January 20th?"

"Yes."

"There is a gas fire in the sitting-room, so there was no necessity for a poker?"

"That is so," replied Bailey.

Scholefield Allen then asked the Detective Sergeant about the name Qualtrough: "It is not an unusual name in Liverpool, is it?"

"No. There are fourteen families of that name in Liverpool."

Scholefield Allen: "Wallace says he has been on the best of terms with his wife during the whole of their married life. Have you investigated this statement? Is it true?"

Bailey: "As far as I can find out, it is true."

240 It is astonishing that the test from Wolverton Street to St Margaret's was made in three minutes. It most certainly would not have been walked in the time. You would think a guilty Wallace would surely have brought attention to himself travelling at such a speed.

After the luncheon interval Bailey said (in reply to Scholefield Allen) that he had made a mistake concerning the time with regard to the second test journey to St Margaret's Church – the time was 6.58 – two minutes later than he had previously said. He made no note of the time and did not consult his watch.[241]

Detective Sergeant Fothergill said he accompanied Detective Sergeant Bailey on the tramcar journey to Smithdown Lane and Lodge Lane on 26th January. They jumped a tramcar at the request stop near Castlewood Road in Belmont Road at 6.53pm and arrived at Smithdown Lane at 7.04pm. Fothergill said that the following night he again made the test, in the company of Police Constable Prendergast. They left the house at 6.45pm and arrived at the corner of Smithdown Road and Tunnel Road at 7.03pm.

In reply to Scholefield Allen, Fothergill said he left the house for the tram journey at 6.45pm (the time that coincided with Wallace's journey), and that when he arrived at Lodge Lane corner at 7.03pm did not wait to board a tramcar heading towards Menlove Avenue, but the next Smithdown Road car was a number 7 at 7.04pm.

Scholefield Allen asked Fothergill if his test did not confirm Wallace's statement as to the time he left his house and the time he boarded a car at Smithdown Road:

Bishop: "Do not answer that question until I have argued it, if it is allowed."

Ward: "I don't see how the witness can prove that."

Scholefield Allen: "The time given by the witness was within two minutes of the time at which Wallace was seen on the tramcar."

Ward: "But the witness cannot confirm another man's action."

Scholefield Allen put the question to Fothergill a second time.

"All I can say is, I saw a Number 7 tramcar approaching this stop," said Fothergill.

Scholefield Allen: "There is a great reluctance on the part of the police to help me."

Ward: "I don't think you ought to say that. This man can only

241 The tram report says that Bailey and Constable Oliver boarded the tram at St Margaret's at 7.00pm.

answer as to what he knows."

Scholefield Allen then asked the witness that if a man left the house at 6.45pm what time would he expect him to be on that tramcar on the corner.

"About 7.04pm," replied Fothergill.

Scholefield Allen: "It takes a long time to get what I want."

Bishop: "The remark is more comment than question."

Scholefield Allen: "It is comment, but justifiable comment."

Ward: "I do not agree. You must put your question, and please let the witness answer."

Scholefield Allen: "I have put the question twice, and he will not answer it."

Henry Harris: "He has said he saw a tramcar come along at 7.04, and left a second or two later. He took a note of the time, but did not board the car."

Scholefield Allen: "That confirms what the accused said."

Constable William Prendergast confirmed the times of the tests he made with Detective Sergeant Fothergill.

Detective Sergeant James Reginald Hill and Detective Constable William Brown Gilroy gave evidence of the test times of their journey by foot and then tramcar from the house to Smithdown Lane. Hill said that a cross-country tram was approaching, going towards Lodge Lane, which they boarded at 6.52. Gilroy corroborated Hill's evidence and then spoke of another test he made in which he walked from the house to St Margaret's Church, in four minutes.

Scholefield Allen: "I am going to have this mathematical operation this time. Have you worked out how many miles an hour that is?"

Gilroy: "I have not."

Scholefield Allen: "Will you take my figures?"

Gilroy: "Yes."

Scholefield Allen: "What pace did you walk?"

Gilroy: "A fast pace."

Scholefield Allen: "Come on, I want more than that. Was it a very fast pace, such as the Liverpool athletes do in their competitions?"[242]

Gilroy was silent. Scholefield Allen then said that Gilroy must have walked at five miles an hour. Bishop objected to Gilroy being made to answer. Mr Ward said the question should not be put as both men would do it as quickly as possible.

As Scholefield Allen claimed, there was a reluctance to help the Defence; not only by the Police and Prosecution, but also the Magistrate.

Detective Constable Walter Stanley Oliver gave evidence of the tram test he made on 27th January. Oliver said that, accompanied by Detective Sergeant Bailey, he left the rear of 29 Wolverton Street at 6.53pm. They walked to St Margaret's Church, and after a two minute wait boarded a tram at 7.00pm. It was 7.13pm when they finally reached Smithdown Lane.

Detective Inspector Herbert Gold next gave evidence as to what happened at the house after he arrived there at 10.30pm on 20th January.

The hearing was adjourned until the following day.

The seventh and final day of the Committal Proceedings saw public interest as great as ever, with hundreds forming a queue but not being able to gain access to the court.

Continuing his evidence, Detective Inspector Herbert Gold said that he examined the back yard and wall to see if there were any traces of forcible entrance but found none. Gold also said that he asked Wallace if he had seen anybody loitering about his house on the evening of the murder and Wallace said he hadn't, and that the first people he spoke to were the Johnstons.

> "I asked Wallace if he thought anyone was in the house when he got back, and he replied: 'I think someone was in the house when I went to the front door, because I could not open it, and I could not open the back door.' I asked if he had heard anybody moving about in the house and he said, 'No, I heard no noise in

242 The police that conducted the tram tests were nicknamed the Anfield Harriers.

the house.'"

Continuing, Gold said that he asked Wallace if it was likely anyone would call when he was out, and Wallace's reply was: 'Only the paper boy from Cabbage Hall. I am not sure whether he had delivered the paper or not before I left.'

> "I asked him to tell me exactly what was stolen from the cash-box, and he said: 'There was a £1 note, three 10s notes, 30s to 40s in silver, a postal order for 4s 6d from W.L. Springer, 51 New Road,[243] and four penny stamps, a cheque on the Midland Bank, Dale Street, for £5 17s 0d, payable to me and crossed, in the cash-box, and that is missing, except the four penny stamps – I have them.'"

Gold said Wallace could not think of anyone who would be likely to send him a message at the Chess Club, and that Julia would not admit anyone to the house in his absence, unless she knew them personally – if she did, she would show them into the parlour. Wallace also said that he could not think of anyone (besides the paperboy) who would be likely to call either to see him or his wife.

"I asked him who gave him the message at the Chess Club," said Gold, "and he replied, 'Captain Beattie.' I asked if anyone knew he was going to the club or had he told anyone he was going there, and he replied: 'No. I had not told anyone I was going, and I cannot think of anyone who knew I was going.'"

Gold then told the court that he examined Wallace's clothing and hands but found no bloodstains on them.

Continuing, Gold said that on Wednesday 21st January he went to Wolverton Street with Superintendent Moore at about 11.00am and made a further examination of the premises. There, he took possession of various articles.

> "I saw Wallace again on January 22nd at Dale Street Detective Office at about 10.45am. He said to me that he had some

243 In her statement Florence Leonard Springer said she posted the cheque from her husband John Leonard from Tuebrook Post Office to Wallace on 19th January. On the accompanying note, Mrs Springer spelt the name 'Wallis' [Witness Statement Florence Leonard Springer, 22nd January 1931].

> important information for me. Wallace related it to me verbally and I wrote it down in the form of a statement."

Bishop said that the statement by Wallace mentioned the names of various people, and these perhaps might not be given as it tended to incriminate others.[244] Scholefield Allen agreed – from the point of view of the accused.

Assistant Clerk Henry Harris conferred with the Magistrate and then said, "The witness had better leave out the names."

Gold then read out the statement that had been signed by Wallace. The statement explained Wallace's visit to the Chess Club on 19th January and his visit to the Menlove Gardens area the following evening.

Gold said that he visited Wallace's house on 23rd January with the accused and Sergeant Bailey, and that Wallace took possession of some of Julia's jewellery and a Post Office Savings Bank book which were in a drawer in the middle bedroom. After a thorough search of the place Wallace said that nothing appeared to be missing, with the exception of a small wooden axe.

> "We made a further search and found the chopper in a basket under some old clothes under the stairs. I told Wallace that the charwoman had said the poker and iron bar were missing from the house and he said: 'Perhaps she has thrown the poker away with the ashes. I do not know anything about a bar of iron in the parlour.'"

I saw an insurance policy in the name of Mrs Wallace," said Gold, "and I asked Wallace if there were any others. He replied: 'That is the only one.'

Later I took possession of the suit Wallace was wearing when I first saw him on the night of January 20th, and also a towel from the bathroom.

On February 2nd I went to Ullet Road where I saw Wallace and cautioned him. I told him I was going to arrest him for the wilful murder of his wife, and he said: 'What can I say in answer

244 Parry and Marsden among others. See Appendix II, Wallace Statement (II).

to this charge of which I am absolutely innocent?' When formally charged, he made no reply. I found in his possession a diary, which has this entry written across the spaces for January 26th and 27th: 'R.M. Qualtrough, 25 Menlove Gardens East, Mossley Hill, 7.30, Tuesday.' The word East is in block letters. The handwriting of the entry is that of Wallace, with the exception of the word in block letters."

Bishop: "In the accused's statement of January 22nd, the names of three or four men are mentioned. Have you made inquiries as to these men?"

Gold: "Yes."

Bishop: "Are you satisfied with your inquiries?"

Gold: "Yes."

Bishop: "Has any action been taken by the police following these statements?"

Gold: "No."

Bishop: "Are you prepared and ready to give the results of your inquiries?"

Gold: "Yes."

In reply to Scholefield Allen, Gold said that he was very much surprised to learn that the mackintosh had been previously identified by Wallace; Gold thought from the position it was in when he first saw it seemed that it would be almost impossible for anyone to have identified it at all.[245]

Scholefield Allen cross-examined Gold about the pad of hair found by the head. Gold said that it was hair that might have been worn by a lady. When Scholefield Allen suggested that it was false hair, there was laughter in the public gallery of the court and the Magistrate was quick to admonish those responsible: "I do wish everyone would treat this inquiry quite seriously. It is serious, and I want the people at the back of the court to realise that."

245 Gold said that the mackintosh would have been almost impossible to identify due to its crumpled condition, and that in his opinion it could have been a piece of mackintosh material, a cycling cape or an old army groundsheet. In Wallace's defence though it was not unreasonable for him to have recognised it. It was after all his mackintosh, and thereby not suspicious that he identified it under the body.

Scholefield Allen then asked Gold if he had the business diaries kept by Wallace from 1928, 1929, 1930 and 1931.

"Yes."

"Are these diaries of events, thoughts and opinions?"

"Yes," replied Gold, "and of daily occurrences. There is an entry relating to a falling out with his wife on January 7th 1928. There are records of visits to the Calderstones district and there are many entries relating to the illnesses of himself and his wife."

There was more laughter in the court and Mr Ward said that people in the court were trying to take advantage of the position: "If there is any more of it, I will clear the court."

Gold continued.

> "There is an entry relating to an anxious time Wallace spent during that evening, because it appears that his wife had gone to Southport and she was very late getting back because there had been an accident on the railway.[246] He says in his diary he went to the police station at 1.00am to see if there was any news of her."

Scholefield Allen:

> "This entry also says: 'I went back home and found her ladyship had just turned up. It seems a laundry van had been smashed up on the railway line, the train derailed, and the line blocked. Julia waited at Southport station until after 10 o'clock, and as she had apparently no hope of getting a train, she decided to take a bus. She arrived at Liverpool at 12.30 and reached home at 1am. It was a relief to know she was safe and sound, for I was getting apprehensive, feeling she might have been run over by a motor car or something.'
>
> There is an entry on January 7th 1931, exactly three years after the one entry about the falling out with his wife, in which the accused writes: 'A night of keen frost. The heavy fog gives a wonderful appearance to all plants and trees. Every twig and

246 The actual date of the accident was 15th December 1930. 18-year-old Percy Bennett was killed when the van he was driving was hit by an empty express train travelling at fifty miles an hour. It occurred at Roy's Crossing, about 600 yards from Ainsdale Station in thick fog. The scene was witnessed by Geoffrey Bond, a boy travelling with Bennett. He had got out of the van to close the gate of the level crossing. Bennett died at Southport Infirmary. Bizarrely, the driver of the train, Edward Holt, was to have retired on superannuation the previous Saturday but due to the date being the 13th, asked for permission to stay on longer.

> leaf was most beautifully bordered and outlined with a white rim of frost. Holly leaves, owing to their wavy edges, presented a most charming appearance and I cannot recollect an occasion on which the hoar had produced such a wonderfully beautiful effect. After dinner I persuaded Julia to go into Stanley Park. She was equally charmed. A gradual thaw seems to be setting in now.'
>
> That is a most beautiful and tender incident."

While his Counsel was reading the extract, Wallace wept uncontrollably, and held his handkerchief to his face. He was so affected by emotion that he sat for a few moments in court after Mr Ward had adjourned for lunch. Wallace finally walked away, his solicitor saying to him: "All right now, Wallace?"

On the resumption, Scholefield Allen said that the diary entry for 7th January was only thirteen days before the 'unfortunate happening.'

Scholefield Allen (to Gold): "There are many references in the diaries to their happy family life together?"

"Yes."

"Do you find this entry on March 25th, 1929: 'Julia reminds me today it was 15 years ago yesterday since we were married.[247] Well, I don't think either of us regrets the step. We seem to have pulled well together and I think we both get as much pleasure and contentment out of life as most people. Our only trouble is that of millions more, shortage of £ s d'?"

"Yes."

Gold said that the falling out between Wallace and his wife in January 1928 arose because Mrs Wallace had been buying too many newspapers. Other entries in the diaries included essays on scientific subjects written by Wallace.

"That is the case for the Prosecution," said Bishop, as Gold left the witness-box.

Wallace stood as Clerk Henry Harris[248] read the formal terms of

247 It could be said that for such a blissful life together, Wallace needed reminding of their anniversary.

248 During the committal Harris took down the depositions directly in longhand as the witnesses gave their evidence, an incredible feat that amounted to over 50,000 words.

the accusation. In a firm voice, Wallace replied:

> "I am not guilty to the charge made against me, and I am advised to reserve my defence. I would like to say that my wife and I lived together on the very happiest of terms during the period of some 18 years[249] of our married life. Our relations were those of complete confidence in and affection for each other. The suggestion that I murdered my wife is monstrous. That I should attack and kill her is, to all who knew us, unthinkable and unbelievable; all the more so when it must be realised that I could not gain one possible advantage by committing such a deed. Nor did the police suggest I gained any advantage.
>
> On the contrary, in actual fact, I have lost a devoted and loving comrade. My home life is completely broken up, and everything that I held dear has been ruthlessly uprooted and torn from me. I am now left to face the torture of this nerve-wracking ordeal. I protest once more that I am entirely innocent of this terrible crime."

As he made reference to his married life, Wallace's voice shook. There was complete silence in the court when he sat down.

The Magistrate, Mr Ward, said that he had followed the case clearly and taken notes, mental and otherwise, from the outset to the conclusion: "You must go for trial at the next Liverpool Assizes."

Before he left court by way of the dock Wallace had a brief discussion with Scholefield Allen and Hector Munro.

Meanwhile, at the Coroner's Court, the inquest on Julia Wallace was again formally adjourned for another week: "I have received a declaration from the Clerk to the Justices that the case is now being heard, and I adjourn the inquest in order to hear the result of that case," said Mort.

The following Tuesday, Wallace's solicitors sent a letter to J.R. Bishop, saying that they wished to see the diaries that had been taken by Inspector Gold. They also wanted to examine the mackintosh, clothes and all other exhibits. Copies of all the statements were also requested to be seen.

On Wednesday 11th March the inquest into the death of Julia

249 Almost 17 years.

Wallace was again adjourned. Mort said that he had received a communication that Wallace had been committed to the next Assizes, therefore, adjourned the inquest until 21st May.

A week later, the *Liverpool Echo* reported that the Recorder of Liverpool, Edward George Hemmerde K.C.[250] had been chosen to lead for the prosecution.[251]

THURSDAY 26 MARCH

At the Prudential Staff Headquarters in Holborn Hall, Gray's Inn Road, London, a unique and extremely secretive development was about to unfold. A secret 'trial' was to take place in an upper room there.

Wallace was once Chairman of the organisation's Liverpool branch, and Hector Munro had contacted the Prudential Staff Union to determine whether Wallace could expect help from them.

It was Norman Allsop who had started Wallace in the Prudential services sixteen years before, and it was both he and August Evans who took up Wallace's defence and brought the case before the members of the union (Evans had been visiting Wallace regularly at Walton Gaol and had been keeping him in good spirits). Executive members travelled from all over the country to London to attend the hearing.

Allsop and Evans reported that Wallace was an educated and cultured man, who had lived in complete happiness with his wife. Statements were produced from Wallace's acquaintances in Liverpool claiming that none of them believed he had committed murder. Hector Munro presented all the available evidence, and made a passionate appeal for help for Wallace. He said he was convinced that his client was innocent and equally convinced he would be acquitted and declared that 'no court in the land could

250 *Liverpool Echo*, 18th March 1931. It was also reported in the following evening's edition of the *Evening Express*. In *The Killing of Julia Wallace*, Jonathan Goodman claims that the announcement of Hemmerde appeared on April Fools' Day. This is inaccurate. [Goodman, *The Killing of Julia Wallace* pp. 159].

251 The *Evening Express* dated 19th March claimed that R.S.T. Chorley had been briefed to act as Junior Counsel to Hemmerde. Leslie Walsh was the Junior Counsel.

convict Wallace.' He also said that Wallace would need the best possible legal assistance.

"When he is acquitted," said Munro, in a tense atmosphere, "he will be a ruined man all the same. All his savings will be gone. He has put all he has – roughly £400 – into his defence and it will be at least twice this amount on a modest estimate."

Members of the Executive fired a series of questions at Munro and the Liverpool members of the union. The interrogation lasted for hours. At the conclusion there was not a single person present who was not convinced of Wallace's innocence.

The Wallace Defence Fund was set up immediately, and one of the most remarkable trade union manifestoes of modern times was drafted and written out. It stated:

> 'We are, as we write, sitting in session of Executive Council in Holborn Hall, and have under our consideration a matter of life and death. One of our members, an agent, Mr William Herbert Wallace, of Liverpool, is in Walton Gaol, charged with the murder of his wife. Those who know him think it inconceivable that he could be capable of such an atrocious murder. No motive has been assigned or suggested, except robbery, which would clear Mr Wallace. The Executive Council recognises that our duty to Mr Wallace does not arise out of the fact that we are a Trade Union, and he is our member, although that makes us stand related as brothers, but on the broader, stronger ground of human brotherhood and Christian charity. The Executive Council has agreed to guarantee the whole cost of the defence and to raise what money will be required. We have placed a duty on the conscience of each member, and trust whole-heartedly that there will be a response, immediate and ample, to the needs of this supremely serious occasion. Every person is held innocent until guilt is proved in British law and equity.'

The manifesto was signed by the President, J.C. Kinniburgh, and Joint Secretaries E.T. Palmer (who was the MP for Greenwich) and W.T. Brown, and circulated to members. It quickly produced £500.

Wallace put £100 of his own money to the defence fund and his brother Joseph (who had, in the meantime, arrived from the Malay States) contributed £300. Wallace's position was kept open and a temporary agent had been put on his round.

On the Tuesday, 31st March, Wallace's solicitors sent a letter to town clerk Walter Moon, drawing his attention to the letter they received from him on 16th March with regard to the viewing of Wallace's diaries. J.R. Bishop notified Hector Munro that all documents could be inspected, but he could not part with the diaries as they were exhibits in the case.

SATURDAY 4 APRIL

Senior Medical Officer William Davies Higson wrote a letter to the Director of Public Prosecutions with his findings with regard to Wallace's health. He noted that the prisoner was rational, generally cheerful and philosophical, and a lot better generally over the last six months than for some time previous. Although there were slight attacks of vertigo due to quick movements of the head, at no time had Wallace shown any undue mental depression since his admission on 3rd February. Higson was of the opinion that Wallace was mentally fit to plead to the indictment, and that any sign of insanity due to renal deficiency on the day of the murder would have hardly escaped notice.[252]

It was reported that Roland Oliver KC and Sydney Scholefield Allen were to undertake the defence for Wallace.[253]

On 11th April Blackpool Police served a Witness Notice to Joseph Crewe. He was on holiday at the time, staying at the Norbreck Hydro Hotel and scheduled to return on Monday the 13th.

The Liverpool Spring Assizes opened on Monday 13th April at St George's Hall. Wallace was brought down from Walton Gaol along with other prisoners to the Court in the Black Maria van and placed in a cell below. At half past ten all the prisoners were taken up and stood by stairs near the prisoner's entrance to the court, to await the decision of the Grand Jury. It was an anxious

252 W. Davies Higson Medical Report, 4th April 1931.
253 *Evening Express*, Friday 10th April 1931.

time for Wallace. Mr Justice Wright told the Grand Jury that the calendar contained thirty seven names and charges customarily to Liverpool.[254] Two of the cases were for charges of murder.[255]

Justice Wright said that the evidence in each of the cases was, as far as he could see, circumstantial, and that such evidence could vary from something as strong as that of an actual eyewitness to that of doubt and uncertainty:

> "I imagine in both these cases you will return a true bill, and then the matter will be investigated by the Petty Jury. I shall leave the matter to you."

It was not until after five o'clock in the afternoon that Hector Munro came and informed Wallace that the Grand Jury had returned a true bill and that the hearing of the case had been fixed. The date of the trial would be Wednesday 22nd April.

254 Some of the offences of those charged were bigamy, incest, perjury, arson, forgery, armed robbery, assault and burglary.

255 Apart from the trial of Wallace, 25-year-old James Litherland (a builder from Earlestown) was charged with the murder of 26-year-old Annie Taylor. She was found by her husband at their home on the evening of 23rd February. At his trial the jury, after retiring for twenty five minutes, found Litherland guilty of manslaughter and he was sentenced to five years' penal servitude. Professor MacFall performed the post-mortem on Mrs Taylor and said that death had been due to asphyxiation by strangulation.

Top: Magistrates' Court, Dale Street. At the time of the Wallace case it was called the Police Courts (Author's Collection)

Bottom left: Stipendiary Magistrate Stuart Deacon (Liverpool Record Office)

Right: Court number 1 (Liverpool Record Office)

Left to Right: Magistrate R.J. Ward (Liverpool Record Office); J.R. Bishop (Evening Express); Clerk of the Court Henry Harris (Evening Express)

Court number 2 (Author's Collection)

5

THE TRIAL

The trial of William Herbert Wallace took place on Wednesday 22nd April. Drizzling rain did not deter the masses from congregating outside the imposing grandeur of St George's Hall.[256] Long before the trial began many people tried to gain admission into the court. The queue, which contained a large proportion of women, extended from near the main entrance of the hall to right round the steps of the side entrance facing St John's Lane, about 500-600 eagerly awaiting admission to the No. 1 Court. There was room for about 300, and in consequence many hundreds were turned away. The public gallery was occupied to the limit of its standing room. Those who didn't gain entrance stood about on St George's Plateau, watching the arrival of the legal representatives and officials.

Superintendent Hubert Moore was an early arrival at the court. He was followed by J.R. Bishop.

The trial was presided over by Judge Robert Alderson Wright,[257]

256 Designed by Harvey Lonsdale Elmes, St George's Hall was built in 1854. The Crown Court, former jury room, cells and the grand jury room are located in the southern part of the building. The Prosecuting Solicitor's Office was also located at St George's Hall.

257 He was appointed a judge of the King's Bench Division of the High Court in 1925 at the age of fifty-six and created a Life Peer (of Durley) in 1932. In 1945 he became chair of the UN War Crimes Commission which involved the collection of material that was subsequently used in the trials at Nuremberg. Much-travelled, he continued regular trips overseas well into old age (he flew to India aged 88). He died aged 94 on 27th June 1964.

with Edward George Hemmerde K.C.[258] and Leslie Walsh[259] (instructed by the town clerk Walter Moon on behalf of the Director of Public Prosecutions) for the Prosecution and Roland Giffard Oliver K.C.[260] and Sydney Scholefield Allen (instructed by Messrs Herbert J. Davis, Berthen and Munro) for the Defence.

Oliver and Scholefield Allen were the first of the legal luminaries to take their seats. They were followed by Hemmerde and Walsh. Wallace's brother Joseph sat in the well of the court, side-by-side with Wallace's solicitors. A number of people watched the proceedings from the seats usually occupied by the Grand Jury, and they were mainly women.

Justice Wright took his seat promptly at 10 o'clock. He was accompanied on the Bench by Sir Frederick C. Bowring, the High Sheriff, Canon Dwelly, the High Sheriff's Chaplain, and the Under-Sheriff, G.L. Wright.

There was a hush in court when the Clerk of Assize W.J.H. Graham[261] directed the Chief Warder to 'Put up Wallace.'

Dressed in a smart dark suit, black tie and stiff linen collar, Wallace stepped slowly from the stairs of the cell to the dock. He entered slowly and calmly. As he reached the rails of the dock he

258 Called to the Bar in 1897, Hemmerde quickly made his mark on the Northern Circuit. One of his most important briefs as a junior counsel was in the successful defence of Sir Edward Russell (later Lord Russell of Liverpool), then editor of the *Daily Post*, in the 1905 action brought against him by eight Liverpool licensing justices for alleged criminal libel. He became Recorder of Liverpool in 1909, but his relations with the civic authorities were constantly strained. He was unable to bear grievances with dignity and was not afraid to utter complaints in the loudest of manners. On one occasion he objected being invited to the Town Hall as 'E.G. Hemmerde Esq K.C.' unless the title 'Recorder of Liverpool' was added. He won the Diamond Challenge Sculls, Henley in 1900 and was also a successful playwright. For the Wallace trial Hemmerde's fees came to £353 6s 0d. He died on 24th May 1948.

259 Leslie Walsh was born in Wigan on 6th May 1903. Called to the Bar in 1927, he practised on the Northern Circuit. He was Stipendiary Magistrate first for Salford (1951-1974) and then Greater Manchester (1974-75). He died on 4th January 1986.

260 Quiet in manner and softly spoken, Oliver was thought by many to be one of Britain's greatest criminal lawyers. In 1921 he was appointed Third Junior Prosecuting Counsel for the Crown at the Central Criminal Court. He was associated with many notable trials of the time – he was part of the prosecution team in the Thompson-Bywaters murder trial in 1922; junior to Sir Henry Curtis Bennett for the defence at the trial of Ronald True in 1922, and part of the defence team (which included Sir Edward Marshall Hall and Sir Henry Curtis Bennett) for Madame Fahmy in 1923. He was the judge at the first Cameo Murders trial of George Kelly and Charles Connolly in January 1950. An excellent carpenter, he was also extremely fond of music and, like Wallace, played the violin. He died on 14th March 1967.

261 William James Holmes Graham. He was Clerk of the Assize 1927-47.

clasped his hands behind his back, and gave a nod of recognition to Scholefield Allen.

The Clerk of Assize spoke:

> "William Herbert Wallace, you are indicted and the charge against you is murder, in that on the 20th day of January, 1931 at Liverpool you murdered Julia Wallace. How say you, William Herbert Wallace, are you guilty or not guilty?"

Wallace replied in a quiet but firm voice: "Not Guilty."

When the jury was sworn in Wallace watched with keen interest. He was asked by the Clerk of the Court if he had any objection to make of the jury. After consulting his solicitor Wallace made no objection. Occasionally he raised his bespectacled eyes to the glass roof of the court. The jury, which included two women, were informed by Justice Wright that the case would probably last until Friday, and he adjourned the court for fifteen minutes to enable the jury members to send home for anything they might require for one or two nights.

The Clerk of Assize addressed the Court again:

> "Members of the Jury, the prisoner at the bar, William Herbert Wallace, is indicted and the charge against him is murder, in that on the 20th day of January, 1931, at Liverpool he murdered Julia Wallace. Upon this indictment he has been arraigned, upon his arraignment he has pleaded that he is not guilty and has put himself upon his country which country you are, and it is for you to enquire whether he be guilty or not and to hearken to the evidence."

There was a tense atmosphere as Hemmerde rose to give his opening speech for the Crown. Wallace looked on through horn-rimmed spectacles as Hemmerde, speaking in deliberate grave tones, outlined the case for the Crown. He said that although Wallace and his wife appeared happy together, the Prosecution would lay before the jury evidence that would lead them irresistibly to the conclusion that the murder was committed by Wallace.

Hemmerde produced plans which he handed to the judge and the jury, explaining them in detail, mentioning the house back and front entrances, the yard which included an ashbin,[262] the back kitchen, the front kitchen, the front sitting-room (looking onto Wolverton Street), the upstairs rooms, including the bathroom, front and back bedrooms, and the room Wallace used as a laboratory. Also produced were photographs showing views of the house, the back of the house, the yard and outside the back door, the sitting-room from two angles, and the kitchen.

Hemmerde recounted the message left for Wallace at the Central Chess Club and that, due to the difficulty the caller had in getting through, the call was traced:

> "That message came through about 7.20. When Wallace arrived he was told by Mr Beattie that someone wanted him to call at 7.30 at 25 Menlove Gardens East and that it was something in the nature of Wallace's business. Wallace writes it down and says he does not know where it is, and as a result of not knowing, a certain amount of conversation is brought about."

Hemmerde said that it was the Crown's suggestion that Wallace sent the call himself and that the message was a carefully-laid plan to create an alibi for the following evening:

> "A person unknown to the prisoner rings up the City Café and leaves a message that he is expected the next night to call on someone he does not know at an address which you will find does not exist."

Hemmerde said that one would have expected Wallace to have known the Menlove Gardens area, and that in actual fact he was not a stranger to the area – as his visits to his Superintendent Joseph Crewe proved.

> "The position then is that here is a message from a call-box 400 yards from his house, asking him to meet a man whom he had never seen, and with whose name he is not familiar, at a place, Menlove Gardens East, which, as a matter of fact did not exist. You might think that someone wanted to get him out of the way the next night. You might think he wanted people to believe that someone wanted to get him out of the way the next night. Now,

262 These were fitted into the back wall of a property and could be emptied from the alleyway.

> follow what happens the next day. On January 20th, Tuesday, the next day, at 3.30, a police officer named Rothwell, cycling along Maiden Lane, saw Wallace, apparently distressed and apparently wiping his eyes. I won't go further into that; you will hear it from the policeman.
>
> At 6.30 a boy called to deliver the milk at the house in Wolverton Street. According to him it must have been within a minute or two one way or the other, of 6.30 when he delivered the milk. That was the last time that Mrs Wallace was seen alive. We know that at that time, from Wallace's own statement, he was there and apparently left the house somewhere about 6.45. You may take it that if he is guilty of this atrocious crime – because whoever is guilty it was a most atrocious crime – it must have been committed within the time from 6.30 to about 6.50. At a time between 7.06 and 7.10 Wallace boarded a tramcar at the junction of Smithdown Lane and Lodge Lane. He boarded the tramcar and says: 'Does this car go to Menlove Gardens East?' The conductor says: 'No, but you can board my car and I can give you a penny ticket or transfer.' Wallace boards the car and says: 'I am a stranger in the district, and I have important business.' You will remember that he did not know Qualtrough by name, or what his business was. When the conductor went for fares, just afterwards, Wallace again said: 'You won't forget, guard, that I want to go to Menlove Gardens East.' At 7.15 Wallace is on another car which runs from Penny Lane. He asks the conductor to put him off at Menlove Gardens East."

Plans of the route were shown to the jury at this point.

Hemmerde said that he would have expected Wallace to have walked the short[263] distance from the stop on Penny Lane to Menlove Gardens West.

> "We then come to the next stop. The conductor beckons him at Menlove Gardens West and gives him some directions, and Wallace says: 'Thank you, I am a complete stranger round here.' You might think all these conversations with conductors are natural or unnatural. Wallace calls at 25 Menlove Gardens West. At about 7.20 he meets a man in the street and that man says that there is no Menlove Gardens East. Twenty minutes later he sees a police constable and asks him for directions to Menlove Gardens

263 Not a short distance – over 400 yards.

> East. The officer tells him there is no such place and Wallace then says to the officer that he has been to Menlove Gardens West, that he is an insurance agent looking for a Mr Qualtrough, that Mr Qualtrough had rung up his club leaving him a message; and then Wallace says, taking out his watch: 'It is not eight o'clock yet.' The officer looks at his watch, and says, 'It is just a quarter to eight.' Remember that Wallace was told at 7.20 there was no such place as Menlove Gardens East, and that is confirmed to him by the police officer at 7.40. You may think that is perfectly natural. On the other hand, you may think it is over-elaborated – the taking out of his watch by Wallace so that the officer would know exactly what time it was. You may think that of some importance.
>
> Next we find Wallace in a newsagent's shop in Allerton Road. He asks for a directory and says to the manageress: 'Do you know what I am looking for?' The manageress says: 'No,' and Wallace replies: 'I am looking for 25 Menlove Gardens East.' The manageress tells him that there is no East, but only North, South and West.
>
> You follow Wallace, therefore, in conversation with tramcar conductors, and finally reaching Menlove Gardens West. You follow his enquiries from a clerk, a police officer, and the manageress of the newsagent shop, who all tell him there is no Menlove Gardens East, and that is the last we know of him there."

Hemmerde said that the tram tests proved that Wallace could have made the journey to Smithdown Lane tram-stop in the time suggested.

> "The next thing is that he is seen just outside his house talking to someone, and the only importance of that is that he says subsequently he talked to no one on the way back. He returns to Wolverton Street somewhere about 8.30 or 8.35.
>
> Now remember he is living at his home with his wife, who, so far as we know, did not have an enemy in the world. He had left her in the house in one of those little streets where you would hardly expect robbers or burglars would find a very rich harvest.[264]
>
> Immediately Wallace found out there was no Menlove Gardens East, he hurried home, he says, because he felt suspicious. Why on earth he should have felt suspicious because someone had

264 This is nonsense. There was a spate of burglaries in the area and the districts surrounding Anfield. Burglars are also opportunists. They will burgle for the most unlikely of amounts.

given him a wrong address is difficult to gather.

At 8.45 Mr Johnston, was leaving his house with his wife by the back door, and Wallace was coming towards his own entry door. The prisoner says to Mr Johnston: 'I have only just come, have you heard anything unusual tonight?' Mrs Johnston replied: 'No, what has happened?' Wallace says: 'I have tried the back and the front, and they are locked against me.' Mr Johnston suggested that he should try again, and Wallace opened the yard door, went into the yard up to the kitchen door, and said: 'It opens now.' Mr Johnston said: 'Look round and we will wait.'"

Hemmerde said that Wallace's inability in gaining admission to the house was a complete charade. He could perfectly well get in, but was pretending that he could not. Hemmerde also said that when Wallace did gain entry the natural place to look first would be downstairs.

"Mrs Wallace was lying across the room with her head battered in, with apparently one terrific blow, then ten others; eleven terrible blows. You will hear from the medical evidence that when Professor MacFall arrived at 9.50 this unfortunate woman had been dead at least three hours. There are certain matters connected with what is known as rigor mortis that makes it a scientific certainty[265] that there must have been a certain time elapsing between Mrs Wallace being alive and the time that Professor MacFall saw her dead."

Hemmerde made the point that on entering the room Wallace managed to avoid stepping on the body and also the pools of blood.

"They go into the front room, and they find this unfortunate woman lying like that. Mr Johnston says: 'We must telephone the police,' and they go into the kitchen. There, Wallace says that the door of a cabinet has been wrenched off. He then reaches up to the top shelf, which is 7ft 2½in from the ground and takes down a metal cash-box."

At this point Hemmerde held up the cash-box before the jury.

"He takes down a cash-box. Mr Johnston asks: 'Is anything

265 Not a scientific certainty at all. Rigor mortis was then, as it is now, a fallible method taken on its own on which to base the time of death.

missing?' Wallace replies: 'About £4. I cannot say exactly until I see my book.' Mr Johnston says: 'Is everything all right upstairs, before I go for the police?' Wallace goes upstairs and comes down and says: 'Everything is all right. There was £5 in a dish. They have not taken it.' Mr Johnston then went for the police. Mrs Johnston started to light a fire in the kitchen and Wallace helped her. Then Mrs Johnston and Wallace returned to the sitting-room, and stood by the body. Then Wallace remarked: 'Whatever was she doing with her mackintosh and my mackintosh?' Mrs Johnston said: 'Is that your mackintosh?' and he stooped down and looked at it, and said: 'Yes, it is mine.' That mackintosh was covered with blood. It was also badly burned. Had it taken fire by accident? If so, what through? Had it been fired by someone on purpose? If so, who had fired it? This mackintosh was hanging up in the passage. Wallace had worn it that day. It was found there against the body. There was blood upon it, and apparently it had been rolled up, and pressed against the body. Just consider at this moment who had an interest in destroying that mackintosh. Assuming that someone had broken into that house – there is no trace at all that anyone did – but assuming that they did, and then killed this woman, it is possible that such a person might have taken down the raincoat to prevent blood getting upon their clothes. Having done that, why should a stranger to the house want to destroy a mackintosh?[266] It is apparent that an attempt had been made, unless there had been an accident, to set fire to that mackintosh and destroy it.[267]

If the theory of the Prosecution is right, the creation of the necessary alibi would leave very little time for attention to detail. Let me say now that so far as this coat is concerned, there is plenty of blood upon it, but there is no blood whatever to be found upon Wallace's clothes. There is blood in the sitting-room in great quantities, and although it was believed that Wallace, after committing this deed went upstairs immediately afterwards, there was not a trace of blood anywhere on the stairs. The man, who struck that woman and left her in a pool of blood, went upstairs without leaving the slightest trace, but in the lavatory, in the pan of the water closet, there was a clot of blood. The

266 As stated previously, why would a guilty Wallace want to destroy the mackintosh? Surely he would have gotten rid of the mackintosh when he disposed of the weapon.

267 See note above. It was a ludicrous suggestion by the prosecution that the burning on the mackintosh was the intention of the destruction of it.

> same blood as you will hear that the woman bled downstairs.[268] That was the only trace of blood in the bathroom or anywhere upstairs."

Hemmerde then held up a thin iron poker for the inspection of the jury. Proceeding, he said: "There was in the room and there had been for some time close to the gas stove an iron poker, amply sufficient to have done this deed."

Roland Oliver intervened. "May I ask my friend if he is suggesting that this is a similar implement? I was under the impression that no poker was found."

Hemmerde: "One of the witnesses will give evidence as to a poker being usually kept in this room. I am only producing this one to give some idea of what it is like. I am not suggesting it was the poker in question."

Justice Wright: "I was wondering why Mr Hemmerde had produced that poker. It was not the poker in question, it was simply an illustration."

Hemmerde said that while a woman who cleaned the house had been coming there a poker of that kind had been kept by the fireplace for some time, and that the day after the tragedy it was gone.[269]

> "Whoever did this crime may perfectly well have done it with that weapon, and you will realise that anyone who had done it with a weapon like that would have had no difficulty in getting rid of it. They could have pushed it into the ground. At any rate, it is missing."

Hemmerde drew the attention of the jury to the photographs of the bathroom and said that the murderer went to elaborate precautions in avoiding the blood:

268 There were three characteristics that led MacFall to the opinion that the clot on the WC was of the same time as those in the sitting-room; serum exudation, contraction of the blood, and moisture. Serum is a yellowish substance which gets squeezed out of blood.

269 The last time Sarah Jane Draper was at the Wallace house was 7th January, almost two weeks before the murder. If there was a poker or iron bar missing, it could have been thrown out in that fortnight, possibly even by Julia.

> "In one of the most famous criminal trials[270] it was shown that the man committed the crime when he was naked. A man might perfectly well have committed that crime wearing a raincoat. He might have worn it like a dressing gown, and come downstairs as though he was going to have a bath with nothing on upon which blood could fasten. If he were naked and simply wearing the raincoat he could have left the raincoat there, and then performed the necessary washing, without leaving any stains, if he was very careful."

Hemmerde said that the disruption in the front bedroom was created merely to give that impression.

> "In the room where they slept a very curious thing was found. You remember that there was £4 said to be missing from downstairs. Upstairs in a vase on a mantelpiece in the bedroom were five Treasury notes, and on one of them was a spot of blood. How did this get there?[271]
>
> When Police Constable Williams arrived Wallace opened the door and said: 'Come inside officer, something terrible has happened.' The police constable comes in and goes straight to the body. He says to Wallace: 'How did this happen?' Wallace says: 'I don't know. I left the house at a quarter to seven. My wife accompanied me to the back door and walked a little way down the entry with me. She returned and bolted the back-yard door.'
>
> Remember that if a person is telling a story of what actually happened the last time he saw some loved companion, he would not be likely to forget it.[272]
>
> 'My wife accompanied me to the back door and walked a little way down the entry with me. She returned and bolted the back door.' – Note the details; 'She would then be alone in the house. I went to Menlove Gardens and found that the message I had received was wrong. Becoming suspicious, I returned home.' Why on earth should he become suspicious? Had his wife enemies? How

270 Generally regarded to mean the murder of Lord William Russell by his Swiss valet François Benjamin Courvoisier. Hemmerde was also alluding to similar crimes having been committed by naked people in India. At the Police Courts there was no mention of the naked man theory.

271 The mystery of the Treasury notes was not the spot of blood on one of them, but the actual amount of how many there were there – a mystery that even followed itself into the courtroom. There were, in actual fact, four.

272 At the appeal Justice Branson commented that it was not unreasonable for an innocent person in shock to forget certain actions. While that may be true, it would appear that it didn't affect Wallace's remembrance of his actions on the way to, in, and around the Menlove Gardens area. He managed to recount his actions with minute detail and precise times.

often must he have left her in the house alone, and while I am on the subject why should anyone in the first place have troubled to ring up an insurance agent at his chess club if the object of doing so was to get the agent's wife alone, when there must be times without number during the day[273] when an observance of the agent's movements would have left the field absolutely clear.

A police constable then went upstairs with Wallace. He said he changed himself in the little bedroom before leaving and probably left the light on. Notice that he changed his clothes there before leaving the house. On a mantelpiece the policeman noticed a small ornament there from which were protruding five or six one pound notes.[274] Wallace took hold of the ornament and said, "Here is some money which has not been touched.' The policeman requested him to replace the ornament.

They then went into the little laboratory, and Wallace said: 'Everything is all right here.' Then into the bedroom where there was a low light burning and the officer asked if it was usually left burning, and Wallace said: 'We usually have a low light here.'

Then into the bedroom.[275] I can only summarise its condition by saying that it was not one which suggested to experienced police officers that anyone had been searching, but that someone had been tumbling the room about.

They then went downstairs into the kitchen, and Wallace pointed out the cash-box, and said: 'There was about £4 in the box and it has gone.'

They then went into the sitting-room and Wallace proceeds to light the other light. Then they go to the kitchen where the window which looks out into the yard was covered with heavy curtains. The police constable pulls them apart slightly and says: 'When you first came into the yard did you notice a light shining through the curtain?' and Wallace says: 'The curtains would prevent the light from escaping.'

About five minutes later another officer[276] arrived. PC Williams says: 'This looks like a mackintosh.' Wallace, standing by the door, says: 'It is an old one of mine. It usually hangs there,' pointing where it hangs.

At 9.50 Professor MacFall arrives. He says that one terrific blow

273 Not to mention the Monday night.
274 Those enigmatic notes again.
275 Front bedroom.
276 Sergeant Joseph Breslin.

had produced an open wound in the front, and must have caused death in less than a minute. He will tell you that the condition of the body showed that death had taken place at least three hours previously. You will note that because you will find it suggested at one time by the prisoner that the reason why he could not get into the house at one time, and could get in at another, was that there must have been someone in the house who at some moment had released the back door.

If this murder takes place before 7 o'clock, do you think it even possible that the murderer would have been still there some two hours later? Nothing whatever was taken from the house except some small sum and a small cheque. Is it likely that anyone would have remained there that time?

The fact that will be spoken to by Professor MacFall and another doctor[277] that this woman had obviously been dead at least three hours becomes of the greatest significance.[278]

Remember, not only had the thief, if it was a thief, the murderer who had come there for some reason, killed this woman, but he had taken down the cash-box with the broken lid. He had left in it a dollar bill, and had taken some other things, and apparently having gone upstairs, had put the same amount of money in a vase on the mantelpiece, which does not look very much as though his object was robbery.

At 10.05 Detective Superintendent Moore arrived. On his arrival he made a thorough examination of the house. Everything was in the position one would expect.

On going into the kitchen he saw Wallace and asked him how he had found the house on his return. He (Wallace) said: 'I was called by telephone to a business appointment at 25 Menlove Gardens East at 7.30 tonight. I went there but could not find the address. I hurried home and tried to get in by the front door, but the key would not go. I went round to the back door, but could not open it. I returned to the front door and again it would not go, and I went round to the back door, which opened easily. I met Mr and Mrs Johnston and asked them to wait while I came in. I found my wife murdered in the parlour and this just as you see it.'

He pointed to the cabinet and the cash-box, and said, 'About £4 has been stolen from that box, which included one Treasury £1

277 Dr Hugh Pierce.

278 Pierce said that in his opinion, the time of death could have been two hours either way – as early as 4.00pm or as late as 8.00pm.

> note, three 10s Treasury notes, about 30s or 40s in silver, and a postal order. That is my company's money.'
>
> On the floor the Superintendent found a 2s 6d piece and two separate shilling pieces. He asked the accused where he found the cash-box, and he said: 'Where it is now.'
>
> Superintendent Moore thereupon took down the cash-box and said to the accused: 'I cannot understand why a thief should go to all this trouble fixing the lid on, and putting the box back on the shelf where he had found it.'"

Hemmerde said that Moore was accompanied by Wallace upstairs and that nothing appeared to be missing.

> "After the discovery of the clot of blood, Superintendent Moore went downstairs and examined the lock very carefully. He asked Wallace for his key and tried the lock, and found that it would turn to a certain point, but if the key was turned too far the lock would slip and the door remained locked. A person has to know the lock to be able to do it each time," said Hemmerde, holding up the lock and demonstrating the action.
>
> Superintendent Moore pointed this out and found that he could do it quite easily. He said to the accused: 'I can open the door all right but the lock is defective.' Accused said: 'It was not like that this morning.' You will hear that it must have been like that for a very long time.
>
> Then they went into the sitting-room and made a further examination and the Superintendent said: 'Didn't you scream or shout?' Wallace said: 'No, I thought she might have been in a fit. I lit the gas to go to her assistance, but, of course, I found that she was dead.'
>
> A little later he called Wallace into the sitting-room and asked: 'Is this your mackintosh? Has Mrs Wallace a mackintosh like this?' and accused made no reply. Then Superintendent Moore said to another officer: 'Take it up and let's have a look at it.'
>
> Wallace said he left it hanging on the wall. A little later, Detective Sergeant Bailey arrived, and after making an examination went with the accused and Inspector Gold to Anfield Bridewell, and there Wallace makes a statement."

At this point Hemmerde read out the statement, commenting that the jury would see that what Wallace said about the way the lock worked was exactly what Moore had pointed out to Wallace, and was not what Wallace had pointed out to the Detective Superintendent.

"On January 22nd," continued Hemmerde, "Wallace called at the CID offices in Dale Street at 10.45am and said: 'I have some important information for you.' This was the information given in a statement by Wallace, and my learned friend for the Defence suggests that none of the names in this information should be mentioned."

"Very well," replied Justice Wright, "they will not be mentioned."

Hemmerde then read what he described as a long statement by Wallace, with the following extracts:

> "Mr 'P'[279] is an old friend of my wife and myself. He was employed by the Prudential until he resigned to improve his position. I knew this man had collected premiums which he did not pay in, and the Superintendent[280] has told me that 'P"s parents paid about £30.[281] 'P' is a single man about 22 and I have known him some years. When I was ill with bronchitis in December 1928, 'P' did part of my work, and I discovered slight discrepancies and spoke to 'P' about it. 'P' has called at my house, and he was acquainted with my domestic arrangements.
>
> 'P' has been up to the middle bedroom when I was ill in bed. I do not think he called on me after I resumed duty, but if he did call, Mrs Wallace would have had no hesitation in letting him in. I have seen 'P' since then, working with his new company, and I have even spoken to him. I saw 'P' in the City Café only in December last. I was playing chess and he returned my greeting.
>
> Another man called 'M'[282] has also done part of my work while I was ill in December 1928. He had previously been in the employment of the Prudential, and was then out of work. I have heard that this man left because of financial irregularities. He visited my house and knew the internal arrangements and Mrs Wallace would have invited him in if he had called subsequently. Both these men knew my business arrangements, and that I kept Prudential money in a cash-box on the bookcase during the

279 Richard Gordon Parry.
280 Joseph Crewe.
281 'Not as much as that. £30 is a little bit exaggerated.' [Joseph Crewe Trial Transcript pp.70].
282 Joseph Caleb Marsden.

daytime and upstairs at night."

Hemmerde added that the statement also gave a list of business associates and friends who would be admitted to the house without hesitation by Mrs Wallace if they called.

> "Wallace says that he left the house about 6.45 on January 20th and that his wife came down the yard with him as far as the back door. She closed the yard door and locked it,"[283] continued Hemmerde. "That statement was made on January 22nd, but two days before Wallace told the police that he was not sure whether his wife locked the yard door or not. It is curious that in matters where you would have thought every detail would be clear in Wallace's mind, he should give two different accounts."

Hemmerde said that there they had Wallace volunteering the information about three people[284] who might have been admitted by his wife without question, and the inference they were asked to draw from that by Wallace was that they might possibly have committed this atrocious crime.

"Needless to say," continued Hemmerde, "these matters have been fully investigated."

> "About 10.20 on January 22nd, Wallace met Mr Beattie, of the Chess Club, at the corner of Lord Street and North John Street, and Wallace said to him: 'About that telephone message, can you tell me at what time you received it?' Mr Beattie said: 'About seven o'clock or shortly after.' Wallace then said: 'Can you get nearer than that to it?' and Mr Beattie replied: 'I am sorry, but I cannot.' Wallace remarked: 'It is of great importance to me, and I should like you to be more exact and more definite.'
>
> Why was it of great importance to Wallace?
>
> You may say, because he had heard rumours that he might be connected with the business, and that he wanted to know what time the call was made so that he might be able to say perfectly properly that it could not be him, because at that time he was in another place.

283 Wallace did not say that. In actual fact he said 'My wife came down the back yard with me as far as the yard door. She closed the yard door. I do not remember her bolt it.' [Witness Statement William Herbert Wallace, 22nd January 1931].

284 Wallace actually named 14, plus some of their family members.

That might be a perfectly proper and reasonable explanation, and although you may gather from the police that at that time they certainly had not given him any information that they thought he was the person who had rung up,[285] it is possible that Wallace may have thought there was a danger of the police thinking so.

Wallace may have said to himself: 'Well, if that telephone message came when I was at another place, then there is an end of the case.'

It is only when you follow out what happened afterwards that you see the full significance of this remark, because on the next day Superintendent Moore and Inspector Gold saw Wallace at Dale Street. Superintendent Moore said to Wallace: 'You saw Mr Beattie of the Chess Club last night?' and Wallace said: 'Yes.' The officer said: 'You asked him about the telephone message and the time he received it?' Wallace agreed, and the officer said: 'You told him the time was important? What did you mean that the time was important?' Wallace's reply was: 'I have an idea. We all have ideas. It was indiscreet of me.' What does he mean by saying, 'I have an idea. We all have ideas. It was indiscreet of me?'

If the facts are as the Crown suggest, it was indiscreet of Wallace, then that is an admirable description of his conversation.

There is one other curious feature about that conversation with Mr Beattie, because Wallace told Mr Beattie that he had just left the police and they had cleared him. Mr Beattie said: 'Is that so? I am pleased to hear it.'

You will hear from the police that at that time no charge whatever had been made against Wallace, and certainly nothing had been said to him to suggest that they suspected him.[286] So there was no justification for Wallace saying he was cleared.

On January 27th, Wallace went to the CID office where Superintendent Moore asked him: 'Did you speak to any person on the way home on the night of the murder, after leaving the tramcar?' and Wallace said: 'No.' The officer asked: 'Are you sure?'

285 This is ludicrous. The police themselves were not looking at anyone other than Wallace being the culprit, even as early as the evening of the murder.

286 Wallace claimed he only realised for definite that he was suspected the day after Julia's funeral. He must have had an idea that he was a suspect before this though. He was, after all, the husband of the deceased. The police have and always will look at a high percentage of murders being committed within the confines of a family. A guilty Wallace would have wanted to glean as much information from Beattie as possible with regards to the telephone call. There is no doubt he went to the tram stop at the corner of Lord Street and North John Street on the Thursday night with the intention of seeing the club captain.

> and Wallace replied: 'I am certain.'
>
> Superintendent Moore informed Wallace that a woman named Lily Hall had seen him speaking to someone quite near his house on the night of the murder, but Wallace persisted in his denial."

Hemmerde said that the jury would hear more details in full from witnesses and that he had just outlined a few points that the jury should bear in mind.

> "I tell you quite frankly the Crown can suggest no motive for this crime. It would be most unsafe for you or any jury to pay too much attention to motive. Motive may be of great importance in helping you to find out who is the likely man to have done something. Suppose, however, to take an extreme case, you saw a murder committed. You would be unimpressed if someone said afterwards, 'There is no motive,' and you would say, 'I cannot help that; I saw it done.' Therefore, although there is no motive apparent to the Crown or to you that does not mean that a man may not have done something he ought not to have done. If the facts seem to you to point irresistibly to the conclusion that Wallace committed this crime, then motive has nothing to do with the question.[287]
>
> What are the facts? Here you have a woman of 53. What enemies would she be likely to have who would come and crush her to death like that with some iron bar? Who would trick her husband out of the way, so that they could complete this work? Who has any motive in the world for committing this atrocious crime against this woman left alone that night?
>
> In all cases of criminal charges, and above all of murder, you have got to be satisfied beyond all reasonable doubt that the person charged is guilty, and you must not be led away by this coincidence or that coincidence, or by slight discrepancies, or slight inconsistencies in evidence. You have got to be satisfied, looking at the thing cautiously, carefully, and above all, fairly in the accused's interests, that you do not lay too much stress on points for which explanation cannot be given.
>
> But you start here with the case of a woman who apparently has no enemies in the world. Who would have thought there was

287 As in the cases of Nathan Leopold and Richard Loeb; Ronald Light; The Ratcliffe Highway murders of 1811, and of course the murders attributed to the Whitechapel Murderer.

much or any money in this house?[288] It is not suggested that much money was taken, and indeed, apparently, the person who did the murder must have handled the notes found in the middle bedroom upstairs,[289] because there is blood upon them, and, therefore, it is incredible that money, or anything whatever, could have been responsible for this ghastly tragedy.

When you eliminate money, what are you left with? That someone did this woman to death in that room, almost certainly wearing that raincoat, and that someone tried to destroy that raincoat. Who could have any interest in destroying it? Any casual person or any persons whose names I have not disclosed who might possibly have persuaded this woman to let them in – could they have done this crime?

If they did, why should they have wanted to tamper with or destroy the raincoat, in which they did this murder? If you think the raincoat bears signs of attempted destruction, then the person who was in the room, or has done this deed, went upstairs to remove some bloody traces of the deed. But there is not a sign of blood anywhere on the stairs, and not a sign of anything, except just where a man might be cleaning his weapon, or his hands, only one drop of this woman's blood. Why should a thief have come into that house and wanting to wash his hands not done it with the running water in the kitchen, opening just out of the sitting-room?[290] Someone who went upstairs went for a deliberate purpose, and you will hear that there is no evidence of any attempt to rifle drawers with a view to robbery, although there is some evidence that things have been huddled about just to show that someone has been pretending to look for money. Who would be likely to do this deed, and gone upstairs knowing the interior arrangements of the house? Who would have taken care that no traces should be left on the stairs, or indeed outside the sitting-room?[291]

If this case is true that the Crown seeks to lay against Wallace, then you are dealing with no ordinary criminal who, in a moment of heat or passion, strikes a foul blow. You are dealing with a man who must have cunningly planned the whole thing; a man who

288 Anyone who knew that Wallace was a Prudential agent could have surmised it. As noted earlier, the fact that burglars are opportunists as well should not rule this point out, although the crime scene does not suggest a burglary.

289 This is inconclusive – Wallace or otherwise.

290 The same could apply to Wallace.

291 It would be a natural reaction for anyone to try to avoid blood contamination.

rang up the night before, if he was the murderer, who must have planned to get Wallace away, or, if it was Wallace himself, who must have planned to create the best possible alibi for himself the next night.

Do you think someone was waiting outside to see Wallace go out? How could they know whether Wallace was going out the back or front door?[292]

Look at the probabilities. Look also, to some extent, at the demeanour of this man. Look at his careful inquiries and, if I may say so, the over-emphasised inquiries in the Menlove Gardens district.

Consider the account of his alleged difficulty in getting into the house. When you have heard the evidence of the police and a locksmith, you may form your own opinion whether Wallace really experienced any difficulty in getting in that night, especially noting what happened when Mr and Mrs Johnston came on the scene.

If the accused knew what happened in the house before he returned, it may strike you as a curious coincidence that he should go first into every other room except that in which his companion lay dead. There is no cry of horror, no calling out to Mr and Mrs Johnston to come in and look what he had found. Instead, Wallace comes to the door and says: 'She is dead. Come and see.' You will see how he behaved in the house during the time after the discovery of the body. You will hear as to whether he showed the signs of a heart-broken husband, or whether he remained apparently all through extremely cool and collected.

If you think that the evidence laid before you leads to the conclusion beyond all reasonable doubt, that Wallace, for some reason that we cannot define, killed his wife that night, you will have no hesitation in doing your duty. If, on the other hand, you think there is some reasonable doubt, you will have no hesitation in doing your duty and returning a verdict of Not Guilty.

This case is a difficult and painful one. It is not a case where you will be in any way concerned with other possible verdicts such as manslaughter. If he did what he is accused of doing, then it is murder, foul and unpardonable. Few more brutal murders can ever have been committed as this – an elderly, lonely woman

292 Not to mention the possibility that Wallace could also have gone straight to Menlove Gardens from his afternoon collecting round.

> literally hacked to death for apparently no reason at all. Without apparently an enemy in the world she goes to her account, and if you think that the case is fairly established against Wallace – that brutally and wantonly he sent this unfortunate woman to her account – it will be your duty to call him to his account."

This was the dramatic coda to Hemmerde's formidable opening speech, which had lasted almost two and a half hours.

The first witness called was Police Photographer and Fingerprint expert Harry Hewitt Cooke. He said that he had taken various photographs in and around 29 Wolverton Street, and also taken the photographs of the deceased at Princes Dock Mortuary on 21st January. In reply to Oliver, Cooke said that he had taken the two photographs of the crime scene one after the other at about 1.00am on 21st January. Oliver asked if anything had been moved – Cooke said that one of the chairs was moved, allowing him to get out of the room.[293] Cooke admitted that in the Police Courts he testified that nothing had been moved.

William Henry Harrison corroborated the evidence he gave at the Police Court with regard to the distances and measurements he made.

Telephone engineer Leslie Heaton said that the he did not know if the call-box situated on the corner of Rochester Road was lighted at night. Hemmerde said that he would have it looked into.

Louisa Alfreds, Lilian Martha Kelly, Annie Robertson and Gladys Harley all repeated the evidence they gave at the Police Court with regards to the call.

Chess Club Captain Samuel Beattie was the next witness. He said that the Chess Club met usually on Mondays and Thursdays, and that he had known Wallace for about eight years.

Oliver: "At the Police Court you said it was a confident and strong

293 It is highly unlikely Cooke took the photographs one immediately after the other. On viewing, there are extreme differences with the position of several items in the room. The chair in front of the sideboard (photograph 6) is to the side of it in photograph 7. There is no doubt that it is in its original position on photograph 6. It would have been illogical for it to be to the side of the sideboard. The door would not be able to open properly (opening inwards and to the right). Also, the position of the body is different on the two photographs, as is that of the mackintosh. On photograph 6 a stack of papers are positioned to the left of a bowl on the left-hand side on the top of the sideboard, but to the right of the bowl on photograph 7.

voice."

Beattie: "That means it was not a hesitating voice in answer to some question."

Mr Justice Wright: "You used the words 'It was a confident voice.'"

Beattie: "Yes, in answer to a question it was a confident voice, sure of himself."

Oliver: "Was it a hesitating voice that seemed to speak with difficulty?"

Beattie: "No."

Oliver: "So far as you could judge was it a natural voice?"

Beattie: "That is difficult to judge."

Oliver: "I know it is, but did it occur to you it was not a natural voice at the time?"

Beattie: "No, I had no reason for thinking that."

Oliver: "Do you know Mr Wallace's voice well?"

Beattie: "Yes."

Oliver: "Did it occur to you it was anything like his voice?"

Beattie: "Certainly not."

Oliver: "Does it occur to you now it was anything like his voice?"

Beattie: "It would be a great stretch of the imagination for me to say it was anything like that."[294]

Hemmerde interjected: "I can tell your Lordship now, there is no light fitted in that telephone box at all. The nearest light is 24 feet away."

James Caird said that he had known Wallace for about 14 or 15 years, and that Wallace was an intellectual, studious and placid man. He also said that Wallace and Julia appeared a happy couple.

PC James Edward Rothwell recounted his sighting of Wallace on Maiden Lane on the afternoon of 20th January: "His face was haggard and drawn and he was distressed – unusually distressed."

294 It has been suggested that it was a bold and courageous step by Oliver to ask such a question without knowing the exact reply Beattie was to give (and that may be true to a degree), but it can also be said that the point of whether the voice was disguised or not did arise in the Police Court. Beattie made no mention of the voice sounding disguised (or anything like that of Wallace) at the Police Court. It would also seem incredulous that Beattie would say it did indeed sound like the voice of Wallace. To Oliver the word 'gruff' must have appeared to the jury as 'disguised.'

Oliver: "I wonder if it occurred to you that your eyes could water in the cold. Has that ever happened to you?"

Rothwell: "Yes, it is quite possible."

Oliver: "If I were to call about twenty five people who saw him that afternoon about that time or round about that time and they said he was just as usual, would you say you had made a mistake?"

Rothwell: "No, I should stick to my opinion."

Oliver: "Then I shall have to call them."

Alan Croxton Close was the next witness. He told of his actions on the night of 20th January and also of the following evening. He was cross-examined by Oliver:

"You have covered a distance of 500 yards and you have been to the shop. Do you really say you did that in five minutes?"

"Yes, I have been over the ground with two detectives and it took me five minutes."

"On the evening of the 21st, did you have a conversation with the girl, Elsie Wright?"

"Yes."

"I want you to try and remember a conversation that took place then. Did the boy Metcalf when you went up to the group say: 'You ought to go and tell the Police you were at Wallace's'?"

"Yes."

"Did he ask you this: 'What time were you there'?"

"I do not remember."

"Just try and remember, will you? Perhaps this next thing will bring it back to your mind. Did you say: 'At a quarter to seven'?"

"No, sir."

Close spoke so indistinctly that Oliver and Justice Wright had difficulty in actually hearing the evidence given. On occasions Close shook his head without answering.

Oliver continued:

"Did you rather make a joke about it that evening when they wanted you to go to the Police? Do you remember you put your hands in your waistcoat like that [Oliver illustrated] and say: 'Well, I am the missing link'?"

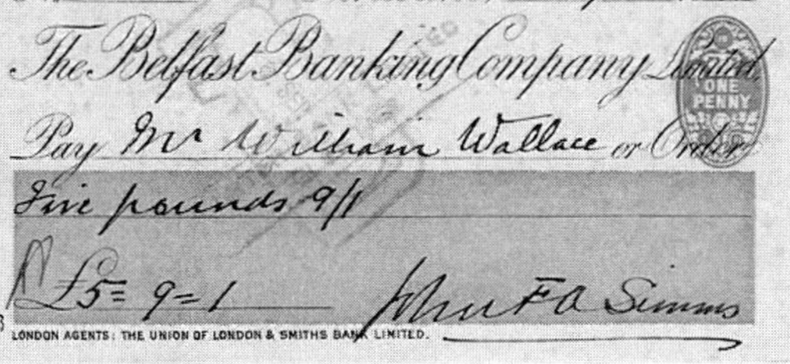
No. D2992 Strabane, 1st Sept 1911

The Belfast Banking Company Limited

ONE PENNY

Pay Mr William Wallace or Order

Five pounds 9/1

£5=9=1 F A Simms

LONDON AGENTS: THE UNION OF LONDON & SMITHS BANK LIMITED.

W. Wallace

Top: Prudential Building, Holborn (Author's Collection)
Bottom left: Hector Munro, Wallace's solicitor (Courtesy Chris Kelly)
Right: Cheque made to and signed by Wallace (Author's Collection)

St George's Hall (Author's Collection)

Above: The queue for the trial (Evening Express)

Right: Trial judge Robert Alderson Wright (National Portrait Gallery)

Left: Edward Hemmerde KC, leading counsel for the Prosecution (National Portrait Gallery)
Right: Roland Oliver KC, leading counsel for the Defence (National Portrait Gallery)

Left: Leslie Walsh, junior to Hemmerde (University of Salford Archives and Special Collections)
Right: Sydney Scholefield Allen, junior to Oliver (Liverpool Record Office)

Number 1 Court, view from the dock (Anita Smith)

Above: The holding cell at St George's Hall. A grim place that has seen suicides (Author's Collection)

Right: The steps leading up to the dock (Anita Smith)

Number 1 Court (Anita Smith)

There was a loud outburst of laughter in the courtroom and Justice Wright said that if there was any more laughter he would take steps to stop it. The police would see to it there was no unseemly merriment.[295]

"No," replied Close.

"Have you ever used such an expression?" asked Oliver.

"I do not think so."

"Nobody is saying it is very wicked if you did. I am only trying to find out what you did say."

"Well, I did not say it."

In reply to Hemmerde, Close said that he usually finished his work at about 6.30pm but was twenty to twenty-five minutes late.

John Paterson repeated the evidence he gave at the Police Court with regards to the winding and regulation of the Holy Trinity Church clock.

Examined by Hemmerde, conductor Thomas Charles Phillips said that the scheduled time the tram usually left Smithdown Lane tram stop near Lodge Lane was 7.01, and that the reason it was late was due to the subsidence in Dale Street.

Hemmerde: "Do you remember that evening having a conversation with the accused?"

Phillips: "Yes. He asked me if the car went to Menlove Gardens East and I said, 'No. You can get on No.5, 5a, 5w, or a No.7 car.'"[296]

Arthur Thompson said that he boarded the No. 5a tram at Penny Lane at 7.13pm and had a two minute wait. The accused asked him to put him off at Menlove Gardens East. When he arrived at the corner, Thompson said he beckoned the accused to the platform and told him it was the stop for Menlove Gardens.

Hemmerde: "What did he say?"

Thompson: "He said, 'Thank you, I am a complete stranger round here.'"

Katie Mather said that on the evening of 20th January she was

295 *Evening Express*, 22nd April 1931.

296 Whether it was confusion, forgetfulness or other, it seems odd that Phillips mentioned the No. 5 as that was the tram he was working [Trial Transcript pp.44].

called to the door and was asked by the caller if a man of the name of Qualtrough lived there, and if it was Menlove Gardens East. She told the caller that nobody lived there by that name and that it wasn't Menlove Gardens East.

Cross-examining, Oliver asked if it was a newly-built area. Mrs Mather concurred, saying that newly-built streets were being erected with names she did not know.

Sydney Hubert Green said that on 20th January he was approached by the accused at Menlove Gardens West at about 7.13.

Hemmerde: "He asked you where Menlove Gardens East was?"

Green: "Yes."

"What did you tell him?"

"That there was no such place."

James Edward Serjeant said that he saw the accused at the corner of Allerton Road and Green Lane at approximately 7.40.

Hemmerde: "What did he ask you?"

Serjeant: "He said: 'Do you know,' or 'Can you tell me of Menlove Gardens East?' I said: 'There is no Menlove Gardens East; only Menlove Gardens North, South and West.' He said: 'Do you know where I can see a directory?' I said: 'Yes, you can see one down Allerton Road or down at the Police Station' which I pointed out to him."

Hemmerde: "Or at the Post Office?"

Serjeant: "Or at the Post Office."

Oliver then cross-examined:

"Did you show him where the Post Office was?"

"No, I pointed down the street."

"Or the Police Station pointing back over the bridge?"

"Yes."

"Did he then say: 'It is not 8 o'clock yet'?"

"Yes."

"That would mean the Post Office would still be open, would it not?"

"I do not know what he meant by it."

"Is it the fact that the Post Office would be open till 8?"

"Not that I'm aware of."[297]

"When does it shut?"

"Seven, I believe."

"This was long after seven?"

"Yes, I know. I am not sure whether it shuts at 7 or 8 o'clock."

Justice Wright: "This was the order: 'He turned away and he then turned back again and asked where he could see a directory. I told him he could see one at the Post Office or the Police Station and he then said: 'I am an insurance agent and was looking for a Mr Qualtrough who had rung up the Club and left a message.' He then said: 'It is not 8 o'clock, just a quarter to 8' and pulled out his watch.'"

Oliver: "Is that the correct order?"

Serjeant: "Yes, that is the correct order."

Lily Pinches said that the accused entered her newsagents on 20th January sometime after 8.00pm and asked for the use of a directory.

Oliver: "How long was the prisoner in your shop, do you think?"

Pinches: "Ten minutes."

"Let us see how clear your recollection about it is. How long after 8 do you say he arrived?"

"About 10 minutes after 8."[298]

"When he arrived?"

"Yes."

"Arriving at ten minutes past 8 and stopping ten minutes he would leave at 20 past, would he not?"

"Yes."

Detective Sergeant Fothergill, Detective Constable Prendergast,

297 Which begs the question – why then did Serjeant suggest looking there if he thought it closed at 7.00pm?

298 As with most of the times involving this case, this is another unknown. If Wallace left the house at 6.49 he arrived at Menlove Gardens West at 7.20 – 31 minutes later. The Johnstons said they left the house by the back door at 8.45pm when they saw Wallace (Mrs Johnston heard him knocking at the back door minutes before). The given time for the tram test going (from Wolverton Street to Smithdown Place) was anything between 15-20 minutes. The second tram (Smithdown Lane to Penny Lane) averaged ten minutes and the five minutes from Penny Lane to Menlove Gardens West, totalling 30-35 minutes. If the Johnstons saw Wallace at 8.45, it is highly unlikely he took the No. 8 tram back much later than 8.15. Incidentally, the Police didn't conduct any tests to see what the average time returning might have been.

Detective Sergeant Hill and Detective Constables Gilroy and Oliver all gave evidence with regard to the tram tests that were conducted on the 26th and 27th January.

Joseph Crewe said that Wallace visited him on five occasions about two years previously and that the tram Wallace could take would drop him off at the corner of Green Lane and Allerton Road.

With regards to Wallace's collection, Crewe said that the weekly remittance could vary from £30 to £50; sometimes it might be even as high as £80-£100:

"On the 5th January Mr Wallace paid in £35 2s 11d. On the 12th January, that is for the Monday, he paid in £89 0s 9d."

Justice Wright: "What about the 19th January?"

Crewe: "The 19th January only £10 11s 0d was paid in, for the simple reason either the police or someone else had taken the cash and the police have a portion of that cash yet."

Hemmerde: "What makes you say that?"

Crewe: "Well, I understand the police have at least £18 cash and I have asked for it."

Hemmerde: "What makes you say that? Where did you get it from?"

Crewe: "Because they took it and I have asked for it."

Hemmerde: "Will you tell my Lord and the Jury what makes that to be different between the 5th and the 12th. I think you call that return a debit, do you not, in the Prudential?"

Crewe: "Yes, that is right."

Hemmerde: "And the return is made up from industrial subscriptions, pennies a week, and that sort of thing?"

Crewe: "Yes."

Hemmerde: "Do you find as a rule they vary as much as that?"

Crewe: "The reason they vary is this: On the 5th January he paid £35 2s 11d in. The following week, the 12th January, is what we call a monthly week. He also collects weekly premiums and monthly premiums. That accounts for £89 being paid that week."

Hemmerde: "The monthly premiums are paid in on a regular date just the same as the weekly premiums?"

Crewe: "They are paid in once a month."

Hemmerde: "And the date of the quarter's monthly premium always means a much larger sum?"

Crewe: "Yes."

Justice Wright: "All paid in the same week?"

Crewe: "The weekly and monthly are paid in at the same time."

Hemmerde: "It is always four weeks apart?"

Crewe: "Yes."

The final witness on the first day was Lily Hall. Her evidence was as ambiguous as most of the others. The following is an excerpt between Hemmerde and Hall, with a few points from Justice Wright:

Hemmerde: "When did you last see Mr Wallace before this tragedy?"

Hall: "On the 19th."

"You saw him on the 19th?"

"Yes."

"That was the Monday?"

"No, the Tuesday."

"You mean Tuesday, the 20th?"

"Yes."

"On the Tuesday, where was it you saw him?"

"The bottom of the entry to Richmond Park."[299]

"Would you look at the plan and point out where you say it is?"

Justice Wright: "Is that the passage which goes up to Wolverton Street?"

Hemmerde: "My Lord, I am told it appears better if we take the plan No, 14, where you get the entry shown there."

Hemmerde pointed out the location to Justice Wright and the witness.

Hemmerde: "There Letchworth Street comes down into Richmond Park. That is right, is it not?"

Hall: "Yes."

"Then if you turn to the left into Richmond Park is there a little

299 There are several entries in Richmond Park.

street marked or a little entry on the same side as Letchworth Street? Do you see it there?"[300]

"Yes."

"Is that the one you are alluding to?"

"Yes."

"On that day, the 20th, were you walking along Richmond Park?"

"Yes."

"In which direction?"

"Towards Letchworth Street."

"Coming towards Letchworth Street whom did you see there?"

"Mr Wallace."

"What time was that?"

"About twenty past nine."[301]

"Was Mr Wallace alone there?"

"No."

Justice Wright: "Twenty past nine at night?"

"Yes."

Hemmerde: "Who was he with?"

"Talking to a man."

"Did you pass them?"

"Yes."

"Quite close?"

"I was on the other side and I crossed over."[302]

"Could you see them quite clear?"

"Yes."

"Was it light there?"

"There was a lamp further along."

Justice Wright: "Which side was he?"

"The side of the entry."

Justice Wright: "Which side were you?"

"The passage side."

300 The one running alongside the Church Institute.

301 Another ambiguous reply. What is even stranger is that Oliver never alluded to it to discredit the witness – maybe he believed he didn't have to.

302 Lily Hall said that when the two parted one went through the passageway between numbers 79 and 81 Richmond Park, and the other towards Breck Road. She could not identify either of them at that point.

Justice Wright: "Then you had to cross over to get into Letchworth Street?"

"Yes."

Justice Wright: "Did you then cross over when you passed him?"

"Yes."

Hall was then cross-examined by Oliver:

"How long after the murder did you give your statement to the Police, about a week?"

"I think it was a week, but I am not quite sure."

"It was a long time to wait, was it not? You were living in Letchworth Street almost next to the house where the murder had been committed, were you not?"

"Yes."

"I am only suggesting you have made a mistake. What made you wait all that long time before going to the Police?"

"I was ill in bed for one thing."

"That would not prevent you from sending for them."

Hall was then re-examined by Hemmerde.

"Were you ill for two or three days?

"A week."

"Just after this?"

"I think it was on the Thursday."

"You were taken ill?"

"Yes, it was on the Thursday."

"You told your sister about this on the Tuesday morning[303] and you were taken ill on the Thursday?"[304]

"Yes."

"Was your statement actually taken by the Police when you were in bed?"

"Yes."

It was at this point that Hemmerde pointed out the next evidence was that of the Johnstons. Justice Wright said that it would be

303 Should be Wednesday morning.

304 There was nothing to stop Lily Hall informing the police on the Wednesday. She wasn't ill until the Thursday, and the police were all over the area in the days following the murder, the Wednesday in particular.

adjourned until the following morning, as that evidence would be substantial.

Wallace was taken back to Walton Gaol, but for the following nights the routine in the reception room was omitted.

Detective Superintendent Hubert Moore and Detective Inspector Herbert Gold visited 29 Wolverton Street. At about 9.30pm they made an examination of the front parlour. Using a lighted paper Moore noticed that the pictures on the walls were visible, as were the ornaments on the mantelpiece and the gas brackets. The hat stand in the hallway with a piece of glass at the centre reflected an indirect light into the room, which was minus the door.

THURSDAY 23 APRIL

It was St George's Day, and public interest was keener than that of the previous day. Many were unable to gain admission to the court, and a queue of 200-300 waited in the rain in the forlorn hope of gaining admission after lunch. Wallace looked calm and composed as he took his place in the dock. He sat between two warders with arms folded, and followed the evidence with close interest.

John Sharpe Johnston was the first witness of the day. Examined by Leslie Walsh, Johnston said at about 8.45 on the night of the murder he was going out of his house through the back door with his wife and had looked at the clock before they came out. He said that as they went through the back door he saw Mr Wallace passing.

At this juncture Justice Wright asked Johnston to repeat an answer he had not heard. "This witness box," said his Lordship, "ought to be altered and placed on a higher level. I cannot hear your voice."

Johnston said that Wallace passed his back door:

"I said: 'Good evening, Mr Wallace.' He seemed anxious. He asked: 'Have you heard anything unusual tonight?' Mrs Johnston replied: 'No. Why? What has happened?' Wallace said he had been round to the back door and also to the front but could not get in."

Justice Wright: "What were his words?"

Johnston: "As far as I can remember, he said: 'I have been to the front door and the back door and they are locked against me.'"

Johnston suggested that Wallace should try the back door again, and if he could not open it he would get his own back door key. Wallace went up to the back door of the house, leaving them standing in the entry. When he went up to the door Wallace said: 'It opens now.'

Walsh: "Were you able to hear from where you were whether he tried with his key or anything?"

Johnston: "No, he did not seem to try the key; he seemed to turn the knob in the usual way."

Walsh: "When he went in did you say anything?"

Johnston: "Yes, I said I would wait and see till he saw everything was right."

Johnston added that he noticed two lights in the windows at the back. He was still standing in the entry at that time: "After Wallace had gone into the house I heard him call out some word[305] which I could not make out. He called twice. Just after that the light in the middle bedroom was turned up and shortly afterwards a match was struck in the small room overlooking the entry."

Johnston said that that match was struck after the light had been turned up in the middle bedroom. About a minute and a half later Wallace came into the yard.

Walsh: "What did he say?"

Johnston: "He said: 'Come and see; she has been killed.'"

Johnston said that Wallace seemed a bit excited. They then all went into the house through the kitchen and into the front parlour.

"As we went in I saw the body lying diagonally across the room, the feet towards the fireplace and the head towards the door."

At this point photograph No. 7 was handed to the witness. Johnston said that the mackintosh was not in the position indicated on the photograph – the mackintosh was not visible to him. After

305 Until the evening of the murder Johnston did not know Mrs Wallace's first name.

looking at photograph No. 6 Johnston said that was the position of the body, but the right arm was not showing when he went in – he was adamant that there was no mackintosh visible.

Johnston said that in the kitchen Wallace reached up to the shelf and took the cash-box down. He asked how much was missing and Wallace replied: 'About £4', but could not say for definite until he had checked his books. Johnston then asked Wallace to have a look upstairs to see if everything was all right before he went for the police.

Cross-examined by Oliver, Johnston said that the Wallaces seemed a very happy couple, and that he had never heard any quarrelling from No. 29. When Johnston described the Wallaces as a 'very loving couple' Wallace dropped his head, swallowed hard and then regained his composure.

After being asked to look at photograph No. 6 of the room, Johnston said that he did not notice the chair in front of the sideboard.

At this point Hemmerde arrived in court. After sitting down for a few seconds he told Justice Wright that there seemed to be an unusually cold draught in the seats occupied by Counsel: "I thought it might be my imagination," said Hemmerde, "but my learned friend Mr Oliver confirms my impression."

Mr Justice Wright said that the officials would look carefully at all doors. Hemmerde, looking towards the ceiling, indicated that the draught might be coming through the open fanlights in the glass roof.

Justice Wright: "No, this place is carefully sealed up as regards the passage of air. Perhaps it is an outside door that is the cause."

Florence Sarah Johnston followed her husband into the witness box. In reply to Walsh, she confirmed her husband's account of the meeting with Wallace.

"Mr Wallace said he had been out since a quarter to seven and that on his return found both the front and back doors locked against him. My husband asked him to try again and if unsuccessful try his key. We could not see properly from where we stood, but Mr

Wallace appeared to put his hand on the knob and then called out 'It opens now.'"

Mrs Johnston said that she saw a light go up in the back bedroom, and then a match or light flickered in the room Wallace used as a laboratory. About two or three minutes later Wallace came out, distressed and agitated. Mrs Johnston then related her account on seeing the body:

"The light in the room was just a fair light, not a brilliant one. You could see everything in the room. Mr Wallace went to one side of the body and I went to the other side. I felt her left hand – I could not see her right hand."

Leslie Walsh asked a reluctant Mrs Johnston to look at the photograph.[306]

"Is it essential to look at them?"

Justice Wright: "Look at numbers 6 and 7."

Walsh: "Yes, number 7 for a moment. Is that like the room when you went in?"

Mrs Johnston: "Well the furniture is the same, but of course, as I said before in the other court, it looks like a faked room, as I call it, because it looks so very strange to me. I know it is the condition it was taken in."

Holding the photographs Mrs Johnston said that interiors always look so different on a photograph compared to the actual thing. No doubt this is what Mrs Johnston meant by being a faked room. The camera may never lie, but it can often distort the truth.

In reply to Walsh, Mrs Johnston said that the chair was in the position shown on number 6 when she entered the room and that she had to pass between that chair in front of the sideboard and the chair on the right-hand side to get to the body.[307]

Mrs Johnston then recounted going into the kitchen with Wallace and her husband, Wallace drawing their attention to the cash-box, Wallace's checking of the upstairs, and her husband's subsequent departure for the police.

306 Photograph No. 7.
307 On entering there were two chairs to the right of the doorway, one in front of the other.

Walsh: "When your husband had gone for the doctor and the police what did you and Mr Wallace do?"

Mrs Johnston: "We were in the kitchen for a few minutes then we returned to the sitting-room."

Walsh: "What did Mr Wallace do then?"

Mrs Johnston: "Mr Wallace stooped over Mrs Wallace and said, 'They have finished her. Look at the brains,' and I said, 'Whatever have they used?', glancing round the room. Mr Wallace came round the body and said 'Whatever was she doing with her mackintosh and my mackintosh?' Mr Wallace stooped and fingered the mackintosh. I asked him if it was his and he said yes."

Mrs Johnston said that they then both went into the kitchen where they made a fire. "The inaction was terrible. I felt I had to do something."[308]

In reply to Oliver, Mrs Johnston said that Wallace looked very pale and to an extent appeared to be suffering from shock, sobbing on two occasions before the arrival of the police. When they were left in the kitchen alone he appeared to break down, but seemed to pull himself together when others were present. During the time she was with Wallace, Mrs Johnston did not find anything suspicious about his manner.

The witness reiterated that the chair was in front of the sideboard as in photograph No. 6, and that there was room to get round the body. She was there twice and her husband once.

Oliver put it to Mrs Johnston that Wallace might have said, 'Whatever was she doing with a mackintosh and my mackintosh?' Mrs Johnston agreed that Wallace might have said that, but she was sure that she heard him correctly and that he said, "Whatever was she doing with her[309] mackintosh and my mackintosh."

Mrs Johnston said it appeared to her that Mrs Wallace might have thrown the mackintosh over her shoulders.[310]

308 This is somewhat contradictory to Mrs Johnston's testimony at the Committal Proceedings – there she said that both she and Wallace built the fire before they visited the parlour for the second time.

309 The question of whether or not Mrs Wallace had a mackintosh never seemed to arise – nor did the possibility of Wallace having more than one mackintosh.

310 It seems odd that Mrs Wallace would wear a mackintosh in answering the front door, yet not

Oliver: "Do you know whether or not the door was bolted?"

Mrs Johnston: "I do not."

Oliver: "If he says he undid the bolt you would not contradict him, would you?"

Mrs Johnston: "I do not know whether he did, but I cannot remember that."

Frederick Roberts Williams was the next witness. In reply to Hemmerde, Williams said that he did not hear a bolt being drawn on the front door after he had knocked. Hemmerde asked Williams to speak up, but was then informed that Williams was on sick leave. The witness declined the offer of a seat in the witness box.

The constable described his observations in the sitting-room and that the position of the body on photograph 6 was how he saw it. Williams said that when he examined the victim's right wrist for a pulse the flesh was slightly warm. Williams then recounted his discussion with Wallace on how it had happened, claiming that Wallace said he left the house at 6.45 on business to go to Menlove Gardens. When he arrived home he had found his wife in the position she was in the front parlour.

Hemmerde: "Did you make a note of that conversation at the time?"

Williams: "Not at the time. I made a rough note of the statement in the first person."

Williams then described his investigation of the house accompanied by Wallace: "In the middle bedroom the gas-jet was lit. I asked the accused if this light was burning when he entered the house. He replied, 'I changed myself in this room before leaving and probably left it on myself.' I noticed an ornament on the mantelpiece from which five or six £1 notes were protruding."

Williams identified the jar but could not identify the notes.

wear one to go down the yard with her husband on his departure to Menlove Gardens. The *Evening Express* dated 23rd April 1931 erroneously reported that Oliver asked Mrs Johnston if she had seen Julia wearing a mackintosh, to which Mrs Johnston replied 'Yes.' Oliver then stated that she had worn it the day before. But this is completely wrong – it was not regarding the mackintosh that this section of the cross-examination took place – it was with regard to Julia's health. The reporter misreported this. [*Evening Express*, 23rd April 1931, Trial Transcript pp.100].

"Accused took hold of the ornament and partly extracted the notes. I requested him to replace the notes in their original positions, which he did."

Williams said that he next went into the room which had been converted into a laboratory with Wallace. There, the accused said everything seemed all right. They next went into the bathroom where a small light was burning. Wallace informed the constable they usually kept a light burning there.

In reply to Hemmerde, Williams said they then went into the front bedroom, which was in a state of disorder. He and Wallace then went into the sitting room, where Wallace stepped round the body and lighted the other gas-jet.

Hemmerde: "Up to that time, what had been the demeanour of Wallace?"

Williams: "He was cool and calm. I think he was extraordinarily cool and calm."

Cross-examined by Oliver, Williams said that Wallace admitted ownership of the mackintosh to him and Sergeant Breslin.

Oliver went on to the one thing that he disputed:

"I am prepared to accept everything except one thing: 'My wife accompanied me to the back door' – that is not disputed – 'and walked a little way down the entry with me and she returned and bolted the backyard door.' Are you sure he said she walked down the entry with him and not down the backyard?"

Williams: "I am emphatic that he said she walked down the entry, because I thought of the probability at the time of somebody having sneaked into the house while the accused and his wife were a few yards down the entry. That is how I remember it."

Oliver: "With them in the entry?"

Williams: "It is a peculiar neighbourhood."

Oliver: "Is it a peculiar neighbourhood? What is peculiar?"

Williams: "As regards the laying out of it, the planning of it."

Oliver: "There have been troubles there occasionally, have there not?"

Williams: "I do not know."[311]

Sarah Jane Draper followed Williams into the witness box. She said she had known the Wallaces for about nine months and that she used to go cleaning there. The last time she was at 29 Wolverton Street was on 7th January. She said she accompanied Inspector Gold to the house on 21st January, when she noticed a poker was missing from the kitchen and a piece of iron from the sitting room fireplace was also missing. Mrs Draper said that the piece of iron was used for clearing cigarette stubs and spent matches from underneath the fire. It usually stood by the fire or was laid underneath the kerb. She remembered seeing it on 7th January because she used it to retrieve a screw that had fallen from the gas bracket. Hemmerde handed her several similar bars of iron, one of which she said resembled the missing one, but not as rough.

Cross-examined by Oliver Mrs Draper said she would be cleaning at the Wallace house for four hours a time, and that she always found the Wallaces on friendly terms.

Alfred William Roberts, Detective Chief Inspector in the Liverpool City Police, said that he received a lock from Inspector Gold on 26th January and handed it to locksmith James Sarginson.

Sarginson said that he was handed a lock[312] from Inspector Roberts. He examined it and found that it was dirty and rusty. The wards of the lock were stuck in a neutral position and if they were not lifted to a certain height the lock would not open. He formed the opinion from his observations that the lock had been in that condition for a considerable time.

Sarginson also said that he examined another lock,[313] and although it was rusty and stiff it appeared to be in good working order. The back kitchen door latch could be secured by the locking bolt. This necessitated the key being inserted and turned, from which the locking bolt shot out. It could then be opened inside or

311 Williams must surely have known of the exploits of the Anfield Housebreaker active at the time. The burglaries that had occurred in the area would not have escaped the notice of a policeman.

312 The lock from the front door; Exhibit 21.

313 The lock from the scullery door; Exhibit 22.

outside by the key. Sarginson said that although a portion of it was stiff, somebody accustomed to using it would find no difficulty in opening it.

Professor John Edward Whitley MacFall followed Sarginson into the witness box. He repeated the evidence he gave at the Police Court with regard to his arrival at Wolverton Street and his examination of the body, and that he formed the opinion that death had taken place four hours before ten o'clock.

Hemmerde addressed the time of death with regard to the advancement of rigor mortis: "What would you regard as the possible margin of error in that calculation?"

"It could not possibly be in this case more than an hour; it is not possible, because post-mortem rigidity is not merely beginning, it has begun and has progressed to a certain extent in the neck and in the arm."[314]

MacFall also said that it was his belief that the victim had been sitting in the chair to the left of the fireplace, with the head a little forward slightly turned to the left as if talking to somebody.[315] MacFall based this hypothesis on his examination of the blood around the chair and also the fact that there was no blood on the seat of the chair itself.[316]

MacFall said that eleven blows had been administered; the one to the front being the most severe and sufficient to cause death alone, and that all eleven could have been inflicted in half a minute.

314 This is rash in the extreme. The putting of an exact time (or even an approximate time) cannot be justified by the progression of rigor alone – there are other factors that have to be taken into consideration – body temperature, temperature of the room, the physical attributes of the victim etc. and even then it is not infallible. MacFall's insistence with regards to the actual time of death was not only irresponsible; it was also contradictory with his original report.

315 One has to ponder MacFall's remark; 'The head a little forward slightly turned to the left as if talking to somebody.' MacFall's testimony was contradictory – he said this at the trial yet said in his post-mortem report that 'it was possible for the woman to have been sitting in the chair with the head lowered and turned to the right.' MacFall meant to the victim's left (ie near the fireplace). Surely the first blow would have been almost impossible to administer from the angle perceived. It is improbable he meant towards the right from the perspective of the victim. The victim would have seen an oncoming attacker. [Trial Transcript pp.127, MacFall post-mortem report.]

316 It would appear highly unlikely that the victim was sat in the chair at the time of the assault. Surely it wouldn't have escaped the notice of the victim if they were about to be attacked, especially with regards to a naked man in a mackintosh. The burns to the lower right front of the mackintosh and three characteristic burn marks on the lower part of the skirt would also suggest that the victim had fallen onto the fire on impact.

His evidence then concerned the mackintosh and the blood splashes. He said that there appeared to be several characteristic marks, and one definite 'projection mark' on the left sleeve.[317] He thought most of the blood on the garment came from the floor, and was of the opinion that the victim had not been wearing the mackintosh as there was no suggestion of it having been on the arms. MacFall was forced to concede that the assailant would have blood on his person.[318]

In reply to Hemmerde, the Professor said that he was very much struck with Wallace's demeanour on the night of the murder. He thought it abnormal: "He was too quiet, too collected, for a person whose wife had been killed in that way that he described. He was not nearly so affected as I was myself."

Roland Oliver rose to cross-examine. He hadn't even put his first question to the witness when MacFall cut in:

> "May I put in this before that? You have not had the position of these blows put in and I have a note I made at the post-mortem showing the position. I have not given the position I found at the post-mortem examination, which is very important. This I made as I was making the post-mortem examination. It shows the position after the hair is removed and the head shaved. It shows the cuts."

"I do not want to stop anything," replied Oliver, "but how can that indicate who did it?"

"I have a great reason for this myself," countered MacFall. "I formed an idea of the mental condition of the person who committed this crime. I have seen crimes, many of them of this kind, and know what the mental condition is. I know it was not an ordinary case of assault or serious injury. It was a case of frenzy."

Justice Wright said that the Court may have already formed that opinion, but that was a matter for the jury to decide upon.

Oliver: "The fact that a man has been sane for 52 years and has been sane while in custody for the last three months would rather

317 Between the elbow and the shoulder.
318 Although MacFall was adamant that the hand that held the weapon would be free from blood.

tend to prove he has always been sane, would it not?"

MacFall: "No, not necessarily. We know very little about the private lives of people or their thoughts."

Oliver: "You have told the jury that you were very much struck with his demeanour. You noticed it at the time and were very much struck by his callous demeanour?"

MacFall: "I was."

Oliver: "Why did you not say so at the Police Court?

MacFall: "I was not asked."

Oliver: "You do not mind volunteering things. You have been volunteering things for the last five minutes."

MacFall: "There is a great deal I would like to volunteer that my Lord has pulled me up on."

The Professor was forced to agree with Oliver that there was the possibility that the mackintosh might have been thrown over the shoulders by the victim, and that the crime scene was consistent with the victim being attacked while leaning over the fire then being moved away to the position where the body was found.

Oliver then came to the subject of blood spatter: "Would you agree that it is almost certain that the assailant would have blood on his face and his clothes?"

"On his left hand, I think he would," said MacFall.

"Not on his right?"

"No. You do not find the blood so much on the hand that holds the weapon."

Oliver put the question of the 'naked man' theory to MacFall: "Was the suggestion that he was naked ever made before this Court?"

"I do not know."

MacFall said he had heard it, but not in public before.

The Professor was forced to admit that he had not made notes with regard to the rigor mortis tests during his examinations on the evening of 20th January. Oliver then put the question of rigor to MacFall: "You would agree, would you not, that the progress of rigor from the point of view of crime is important, I mean the stages that are reached during your observations are important?"

"Very."

"And not one note made?"

"No, but I know definitely."

"Let us take the question of rigor. It is a very fallible test as to the time of death?"

"Not in the present case of an ordinary person dying in health."

"It is a very fallible factor even in healthy people?"

"It is, just a little."

"Not just a little. I am putting 'very'?"

"No, not very fallible."

"Does it depend, amongst other things, upon the muscularity of the person?"

"It does."

"And the powerful and muscular body will be affected by rigor much more slowly?"

"Yes."

"Than a feeble and frail body?"

"Yes."

"Was this a feeble and frail body?"

"Yes. She was not exactly frail; she was a feeble woman."

"You have used the word 'frail'?"

"Yes, she was a weak woman."

"Frail?"

"Yes, frail."

"It is your own word?"

"Yes, my own word."

"Then we may summarise your last two answers, and it comes to this: that she was a woman who was likely to be quickly affected by rigor?"

"No, she would be rather delayed if anything."

This was another display of arrant nonsense. Even Justice Wright intervened: "I thought you said it would be quicker in a frail person and slower in a person of muscularity?"

"She would be delayed," replied MacFall.

"Do you wish to say that a feeble and frail person would have delayed rigor?" questioned Oliver.

"No." said MacFall

"Why do you say it then?" Oliver persisted.

"She was in a condition of good health, although a frail woman," answered MacFall.

"Then I will start all over again. A muscular body would take longer to be affected by rigor than a feeble and frail body?"

"Yes."

"Was this woman a feeble and frail body?"

"Yes."

"Then she would be likely, would she not, to be more quickly affected by rigor?"

"A little."

"Then why did you say rather longer just now?"

"Not rather longer than a muscular person."

"You are not arguing the case, are you?"

"No, I wish to state what I found."

"You know what is at stake here?"

"I do."

"Bearing in mind that this feeble and frail woman would be more likely to be affected by rigor, are you going to swear she was killed more than three hours before you saw her?"

"No, I am not going to swear; I am going to give an opinion and I swear that the opinion that I give shall be an honest one."

Justice Wright: "Then what is your opinion?"

"My opinion was formed at that time that the woman had been dead about four hours."

"Now that I have reminded you that she being feeble and frail rigor would come on quicker, does that move your opinion?"

"No."

"You do not think she was killed four hours before you saw her?"

"I do."

"You do?"

"Yes."

"So if she was alive at half past six your opinion is wrong, is it not?"

"Yes."

"Does that not convince you what a very fallible test rigor mortis is?"

"No, it does not. I am still of the opinion."

"Do you think the milk boy imagined seeing her alive?"

"I do not want to think about the milk boy and what he saw at all."

MacFall conceded that the spot of blood found on the lavatory rim could well have been deposited there by one of the police sometime after the murder, and although he had some blood on his hands from examining the victim it was not deposited there by him.

There is no doubt that Oliver threw considerable doubt onto MacFall's evidence, and even discredited him as a witness.

Hugh Pierce was the next witness. He said that he primarily went to Wolverton Street on the evening of the murder to test for rigor mortis and formed the opinion that death had occurred at about six o'clock, but would give two hours limit on either side.

Oliver: "You base your opinion, as to the time of death, on rigor?"

Pierce: "Yes, and the cooling of the body."

Oliver: "You know what is called the rectal temperature is considered the best test?"

Pierce: "Yes."

Oliver: "That was not done?"

Pierce: "No, it was not done. I did not do it."

Oliver: "With regard to your observations, when you got there you said that rigor was present in the neck and what else?"

Pierce: "The upper part of the left arm."

Oliver: "Do you know that is precisely the condition recorded by Professor MacFall two hours earlier?"

Pierce: "I do."

Pierce said that if a body is interfered during examination, it can affect the process of rigor.

City Analyst William Henry Roberts was the next to take the stand. He said that on 24th January he received certain articles from Inspector Gold. He said that the mackintosh was extensively and heavily bloodstained with human blood on the right side, both outside and inside, and the left side was heavily stained on the outside. In his opinion, that on the left side came from being in contact with the floor.

In reply to Hemmerde, Roberts said that the blood on the upper inner side of the right sleeve could have been caused when a person taking the coat off might touch, with the hand coming out.[319]

With regards to the hearthrug, Roberts said that there was one stain on the corner that corresponded to where the head had been, and that there were other bloodstains on the centre of it. These might have been from the killer wiping the feet clean.

Roberts came to the conclusion that the amount of blood he saw on the floor and the other things in the room and the mackintosh might have amounted from between three-quarters of a pint to a pint and a quarter, and that the smears of blood on the note were such as would be caused by drawing a slightly bloodstained thumb across it.[320]

Detective Superintendent Hubert Moore was the final witness of the day. He reiterated the evidence he gave at the Police Court; his arrival at 29 Wolverton Street on the night of the murder, his subsequent examination of the house, and Wallace's demeanour. Moore also made a point of Wallace's 'discovery' of Mrs Wallace, and that one would have to almost walk sideways to avoid the blood in the parlour.

In reply to Oliver, Moore said that Wallace had been treated as a man whose wife had been murdered up to the period of his arrest.

Oliver then went to the subject of the mackintosh:

"You now know, do you not, that before you found it the

319 This completely contradicts MacFall's opinion that the hand holding the weapon would be free from blood.

320 The question of whether it was a thumbprint is not known. Whether Harry Cooke examined it for fingerprinting is not known. If so, it amounted to nothing. At the trial, Justice Wright said the mark on the note was 'not that of a fingerprint but a mere smear.' [Trial Transcript pp. 315.]

Defendant had acknowledged it to Mrs Johnston, to Police Constable Williams and to some tall officer who had come into the kitchen. Are you surprised that he was doubtful?"

"I do not know – all the more reason why he should say at once 'It is mine.'"

"What inference do you draw from it? What do you think? That he was trying to conceal it, or what?"

"Perhaps I had better not say what I think he had in his mind," replied Moore. "What inference do you draw, was my question, from his hesitation to acknowledge that mackintosh to you when he had already acknowledged it to four different people, three of them policemen?"

"That he was beginning to think the mackintosh was dangerous and that the police had formed a certain idea."

"That would be a splendid chance for him, after he had already told four people, three of them police officers, to be suddenly doubtful about it. However, that is argument. You talked about his demeanour being quite calm, smoking cigarettes; is that true?"

"Quite."

"You have never mentioned it before today in public?"

"I was never asked it."

"It only seems to have occurred to someone quite lately to ask that question. You attach importance to it, do you not?"

"No, not that I know of."

"Have you ever heard of people smoking cigarettes to try and keep a hold on their nerves, to try and calm themselves?"

"I am not a cigarette smoker, I smoke a pipe."

Oliver then came to the cash-box on top of the cabinet.

"If someone stood on that eleven inch shelf on which stood the cash-box he could open the cash-box, could he not?"

"He would have to be a bit of an acrobat to do so," replied Moore.

"I dare say, but it is quite likely it could be done?"

"I do not think so."

Moore was forced into admitting there was the possibility that everything in the sitting-room was consistent with a knock at the front door and admission by someone being taken into the parlour.

Oliver then mentioned the striking of the match before entering the sitting-room: "You make the point that it is quite wrong to strike a match at the door to light the gas?"

"I do; there is no necessity for it. A man living sixteen years in a little room like that – it was not the natural thing."[321]

Oliver then turned to the subject of Wildman. "Do you know a boy named Wildman?"

"No, I do not."[322]

"Is he a boy of good character?"

"I do not know anything about him at all."

"I want to know, why should not that boy have been called by the Prosecution?"

Moore said that he thought the reason Wildman was not called as a witness was that his statement was taken about a fortnight or some considerable time afterwards.[323]

In reply to Hemmerde, Moore said that the weapon would go down one of the street drains easily and that the Police would have had to search all of them to find it.[324]

Moore said that the next two witnesses, Harry Bailey and Herbert Gold, would testify with regard to Wildman.

This concluded the second day of the trial.

As the jury were leaving St George's Hall after the adjournment an old beggar woman approached one of them. She was brushed aside with haste and warned by one of the court bailiffs.

FRIDAY 24 APRIL

The third day of the trial saw the same public interest. Many

321 This is double-think by Moore – in one instance we are to believe that Wallace was so familiar that he should be able to negotiate his way around a dimly-lit room, only in another instance for it to be deemed highly suspicious that he managed to evade bloodstains.

322 It seems unbelievable that Moore did not know of Wildman.

323 There can be no doubt that that was not the reason – Wildman's evidence was not favourable to the police and prosecution case. Lily Hall's statement was taken almost a week after the incident but her evidence was used.

324 The police investigations did not include the searching of the drains on the complete route from Wolverton Street to the Menlove Gardens area.

women had attended the trial, and Friday was no exception. At times chocolates and other items were passed from one to another to aid sustenance.

The first witness of the day was Detective Sergeant Harry Bailey. He said he arrived at the house at 10.25 and found no evidence of forcible entry. Near the body, in the folds of the mackintosh, he found two burnt matches.[325]

Bailey said that Wallace accompanied him and Inspector Gold to the Anfield Station, where accused made his first statement.[326]

Bailey also said that the skirt of the victim was burnt at the front but there was no sign of burning on the underskirt, and that he took possession of several items in the house, including the jar containing the £1 notes.

Walsh asked Bailey how the notes were folded. After a pause, during which barristers searched in their pockets for one pound notes, Justice Wright asked Oliver if he had four £1 notes; Oliver very much regretted that he hadn't. Bailey took four notes from his pocket and demonstrated how they were folded. Justice Wright thought that the actual notes were of no use to anybody, and Oliver agreed.

Bailey said that on 19th February he and Inspector Gold accompanied Alan Close on a reconstruction of his milk round. They began directly opposite the church clock at 7.05pm. Gold was at one side of Close, and Bailey walked behind. Close made his own pace according to his own actions, and went through his movements on the night in question when he delivered the milk. He eventually arrived at Wolverton Street at 7.10pm.

In reply to Walsh, Bailey said that the victim appeared to be poorly dressed.

Oliver cross-examined: "I am not quite sure what the point suggested is. You have been asked whether this woman was poorly dressed and you said she was, as if to give the impression of poverty."

"Not from that point of view," said Bailey, "home-made clothing."

325 Exhibit 40.
326 Exhibit 42.

"Did you by any chance know that this man had a banking account at this time?"

"Not at that time."

Oliver said that Wallace had a bank account of £152, and the Midland Bank could supply a copy of the account. Walsh agreed and said that the Prosecution did not dispute it.

In reply to Oliver, Bailey said he did not know the boy Wildman but knew of the family.

With regards to the two tram tests he conducted, Bailey again admitted that it would have been a fairer test to have got on the tram at Smithdown Lane and then taken the time.

Oliver then came to the reconstruction of the milk round and the Wallace's demeanour:

> "What the boy Close had to do was walk a distance that has been measured by the Surveyor, 500 yards, go into his shop – I mean altogether: it is not 500 yards to the shop – cover a distance of 500 yards and including in that going into his shop, putting down his empty can and picking up a fresh one, walking along the route described, calling at two houses, calling at a house and handing in his can, going on further making another delivery, coming back and taking his can to Mrs Wallace for delivery. Are you saying he did it in five minutes?"

"That is all he took."

"With regard to the Defendant's demeanour, have you ever before today in public expressed any opinion about the accused's coolness on this occasion? You never gave evidence about it before, did you?"

"I have never been asked."

"'I have never been asked', that is an answer we get from everybody."

Detective Inspector Herbert Gold followed Bailey into the witness box. He said he went to the house in Wolverton Street at 10.30 on the night of the murder. He was there when Detective Superintendent Moore tried the front door lock, and when he asked the accused if he recognised the mackintosh. He went with Wallace and Sergeant Bailey to the Anfield Station, where he took a statement from the accused. Gold asked Wallace if he had heard anybody moving about in the house on his return, and Wallace said that he thought someone was in the house when he went to the front door, due to the fact that he could not open it and could not open the back door either. Gold examined Wallace at the Anfield Station but could find no signs of blood upon him. The Detective Inspector noticed that Wallace appeared cool and calm: "He did not seem to be in the least upset. I did not see any sign of emotion in him at all at the death of his wife."

Gold said that when he first went into the house on the night of the murder Wallace was sitting in the kitchen. In fact, he had the cat on his knee and was stroking it. To him, Wallace did not look like a man who had just battered his wife to death. Cross-examined by Oliver, Gold made reference to the diaries kept by Wallace:

"I think you found an entry in January 1928,[327] that is some three years before this event, in which he recorded some kind of tiff with his wife because she had too many papers in the house. Is that right?"

"Yes, that is right."

"And does the diary say he was sorry for it and expressed his regret?"

"I have not got a note of that, but I think it does say so."

Oliver then moved to the question of the police shadowing Wallace.

"Was he followed after the 21st?"

"Not to my knowledge."

"On the 22nd?"

"Not to my knowledge."

Oliver persisted: "Mr Gold, on the 22nd was he shadowed?"

"No, not to my knowledge."

"He must have been followed when he spoke to Mr Beattie?"

"Not to my knowledge."

"Do you remember the conversation with Mr Beattie in the

327 7th January 1928.

evening?"[328]

"He was with me in the Detective Office all day on the 22nd up to twenty to ten, when I was taking a statement. Then he looked at his watch and said 'I do not want to be late to get to Ullet Road because my sister-in-law will be going to bed. I am not going to Wolverton Street', and he said 'Can I go?' and I said 'Yes', and he went and met Mr Beattie."

"Then he must have been shadowed?"

"No, I did not know it."

Re-examined by Hemmerde, Gold said that Wallace had been followed on his rounds because the police were told that people were hostile to him, and therefore a man was sent with him in case of necessity.[329]

City Analyst William Henry Roberts was recalled. He said that he made exhaustive experiments with regard to the blood on the pan on 22nd and 23rd of January.

Hemmerde: "Did you measure the height between the basin and the rim of the pan?"

Roberts: "I judged the height between the pan and the basin to be 15 inches, and it was on that I made my experiment. When the blood drops that height it forms a little clot, and when that dries it clots together and makes a little blob. It is clotted."

"This, we know, is three-eighths of an inch?"

"Yes."

Roberts was then cross-examined by Oliver.

"Have you any notes of your experiments?"

"No."

"Are you telling the Jury that within two minutes of blood being shed it would fall a height of fifteen inches on to a porcelain pan?"

"Yes."

328 In *The Killing of Julia Wallace* Jonathan Goodman claims that Gold's reply to this question was (for the fourth time) 'Not to my knowledge', but this is inaccurate [Goodman, *The Killing of Julia Wallace* pp. 214].

329 This is highly unlikely to be the reason Wallace was followed. If it *was* the reason, it seems odd that the police did not inform him of their movements. They certainly did not shadow him after his acquittal when he was subjected to hostility on his rounds.

"And remain in the position of a thing like a pea cut in half?"

"No; I said it forms a blob and afterwards it dries like that."

"I want to know what the experiment was. I have evidence about it. First of all, when it fell, what shape did it take?"

"It flattened and then formed just like a blob."

"Will you apply your mind to my question and answer it if you will. When it first fell, what shape did it assume?"

"As I say, it looked circular. From the side it was just flattened on the pan."

Justice Wright: "The drop must be more or less spherical?"

Roberts: "Yes."

Justice Wright: "And it flattened to that extent. That is your evidence?"

Roberts: "Yes."

Oliver: "I want you to understand that I am absolutely challenging it and am going to call evidence to contradict it."

Roberts: "Yes. I did a great many experiments. I did not only do one experiment."

Roberts was further re-examined by Hemmerde: "Your experiments were made on blood within two minutes of being shed?"

"Yes."

"Supposing it was a little more than two minutes, would the blood be more clotted?"

"Yes."

"And if it was a little more than two minutes would it have less tendency to splash?"

"Yes, certainly."

"Would it have more or less a tendency to flatten out?"

"It would have less tendency to flatten out. Of course I did the experiment when the blood had been drawn about fifteen minutes, and of course it clotted then to a certain extent."

Mr Justice Wright: "It did?"

"Yes, my Lord, after fifteen minutes, but the two minutes blood was quite fresh."

Hemmerde: "That, my Lord, with the accused's statement is the evidence for the Crown."

What the jury made of it all was anybody's guess.

The Clerk of Assize read out Wallace's reply to the charge that he made at the Committal Proceedings on 4th March.

Oliver rose to make his opening speech for the Defence at 11.50. Addressing the jury, he said that the terrible task had fallen upon them to try a man for his life and that they should form their own opinions on the case and not what they might have read in the newspapers:

> "It is one of the disadvantages in defending a man in a long case like this, that three days have been occupied before the Defence is allowed to be put before you in any coherent form. You have to form such impressions as you can from what the Defence is from points made in cross examination.
>
> My learned friend made a somewhat dramatic appeal, not perhaps cautioning you against forming a rash or hasty judgement, not pointing out the weight and burden of proof upon him, not pointing out to you that in our English law a man is innocent until he is proved to be guilty, but rather, at the end of his opening and impassioned speech, invoking the law against the perpetrator of this frightful deed.
>
> The frightfulness of the deed speaks for itself, but until you are satisfied that this man did it, it is rather a case of reserving your judgement. The case was rather thrown at you like this, 'If he did not do it, who did?' You should not approach it in that way. You should rather ask 'Who is this man?' "The accused is going to be put in the witness box. Who is this man who is charged with this frightful crime? You know of Wallace's history now. He is 52 years of age. There has never been a thing against him in his life. Everybody who knew him liked him. He is a man of considerable education."

At this point Wallace appeared to be moved. He leaned forward and bent his head.

> "Wallace is a refined man and, as these extracts from his diary show, he is a man with a considerable gift of expression. What were his relations with his wife? No one is in any doubt about that. You have had the evidence of people who knew them,

> you have had extracts from the diaries, and you even have the concession of my learned friend, the Recorder, who said in his opening statement that undoubtedly Mr and Mrs Wallace lived happily together. There is no sort of suggestion of ill feeling. There was some suggestion by the Crown as to money trouble, because at one time the Recorder seemed to attach importance to this statement of Wallace's insurance accounts. But we shall see there is no money trouble. Wallace has £150 in the bank. Will anyone consider that he would murder his wife for the sake of £95 in her bank?[330] There is no suggestion of any other woman. In fact, there is no other suggestion. Are you going to convict this man of murder on what I assure you is the flimsiest of circumstantial evidence?"

Oliver said that MacFall had no right to voice his opinion of frenzy, stating that the Court of Criminal Appeal laid it down in 1910 that it was not proper for the Crown to call evidence of insanity if that evidence in the possession of the Crown was not placed at the disposal of the prisoner's counsel to be used by him if he thought fit. The jury should disregard MacFall's evidence as Wallace had been under the medical supervision of doctors in the prison, and it was their duty to inquire whether people were sane or not.

Oliver was equally critical of the police:

> "Here we come to the first bit of the police evidence. This is what is called a police case. If there is one kind of crime which is the abomination of the police, it is an unsolved murder. They do everything they can to get a solution, and once they evolve a case they pursue it relentlessly. You find PC Rothwell cycling along the street and passing this man, who happens at the time to be brushing his eyes with his coat sleeve. This constable makes a report after the murder. 'I passed him when I was on my bicycle,' he said. 'I saw him distinctly, he was ghastly. He had to wipe his eyes.' The suggestion was that he was so distressed about the crime he was going to commit that evening that he had to wipe his eyes.
>
> Now, members of the Jury, I am going to ask you to say that evidence is rubbish. I can call any number of witnesses, as many

330 People have murdered for less.

> as you want, who saw him that afternoon, while making his collection. They will all say there was nothing the matter with him; that he was just as usual."

Oliver said that the Prosecution had failed to prove that Wallace sent the message himself and stressed the importance of Beattie – that the voice on the telephone was nothing remotely like that of Wallace.

> "If he did not send that message, then he is an innocent man. There are one or two things which showed that Mr Hemmerde has been curiously instructed by the police. It has been said that here is a frail, rather old-fashioned woman, who lived here alone in a street where robbers would hardly expect a rich harvest. Then Mr Hemmerde said: 'How on earth could anyone have known Wallace was going to this little chess club? I don't suppose anyone except the few members would know he was going to the chess club.'
>
> Was there no spoil to be going at 29 Wolverton Street? Wallace was a collector, and probably would have in his possession on that evening or the next anything up to £30, £50 or even £100 in cash. Have plans of that sort never been made before to rob people who have been known to have cash, especially in that convenient form, small cash?
>
> Then in the other instance what is the evidence? This appears to be one of the most populous cafés in Liverpool, and there by the door, plain for everyone to see, is the statement that probably at 7.30 on January 19th this man Wallace would be there playing a chess match.
>
> It is curious that the message happens to have been sent from a telephone box which is just under a quarter of a mile from Wallace's home and, of course, I am accepting that as the nearest telephone box that could have been used. Does it not appear to you that anyone who had plans of this coup was watching and seeing Wallace go out then go to the telephone box and ring up the Chess Club not after but before Wallace got there? He would not want to speak to Wallace himself because he might get questioned, which would show that the whole thing was a sham. He wanted to do it before.
>
> The whole of this case is argument, and there is very little proof in it. First, the robber could not be sure that Wallace had gone

to the Chess Club,[331] and the second, there was the likelihood for a better lot of money on the Tuesday evening, which was the last day of the collection, than there would be on the Monday. It has been said that this is a prepared alibi, but so far from being a prepared alibi, if the case for the Prosecution was true it is clear proof that my client was on the spot when the thing was done. What he told the police was true, you know, about the times, but so far from proving the alibi that would tend to prove he was at his house when the murder was committed.

There were two things in the evidence of Inspector Gold this morning who said that when questioned Wallace said that Mrs Wallace would admit Qualtrough coming to the house and make a note. Gold said he asked Wallace whether Mrs Wallace would admit anyone while Wallace was away and Wallace said, 'Not unless she knew them personally, and then she would let them in through the parlour.' Wallace admits, on Inspector Gold's evidence, that Mrs Wallace would have admitted Qualtrough. Wallace also said to Inspector Gold: 'I did not tell anyone I was going to the club or cannot think of anyone who knew I was going.' The man who gave the name of Qualtrough must have called and got in through the parlour, and that's how the thing happened. That speaks loudly against the theory that this was a concocted, prepared alibi, a preparation to put up a defence before the crime.[332]

At 6.45 he leaves to carry out his appointment with Qualtrough, and when I said he left at 6.45 I think it must be common ground between my learned friend and myself that it is within a minute or two of 6.45,[333] when my client got to the tram that night, whether it was at the church or the bottom of the street. Why is there no evidence of his demeanour on the tram? You hear nothing of him until he gets to Smithdown Road. It is suggested that he ran and got on to the moving tram immediately after he committed a murder, and no one noticed it?

Members of the Jury, the crucial point in this case is: When was Mrs Wallace last seen alive? That is absolutely vital. If she was last seen alive at 6.45 and he left the house a minute or so after, he is innocent. He was searched the same night by the police and there was not a trace on him or his clothes, boots, hair, hands or face of

331 But leave a message in the hope that he would attend and receive it.
332 It also speaks loudly against the theory that this was a concocted, prepared burglary.
333 Possibly even six minutes later than 6.45.

any blood. Before he gets away he had got to be absolutely clean as he was before. If he was wearing clothes they could not be washed, they would have to be got rid of. We have heard nothing before, and for the first time we have it here, a suggestion put before you that he was naked in a mackintosh. His face, hair, hands would be covered with blood and so would his legs from the knees downwards. He has got to have a bath. There is no sign of anyone having had a bath. That was given in evidence by the Prosecution. There was no towel which has been suggested to be damp."

Oliver said that Wallace could not have carried out the actions necessary post-murder in the time available, and also told the jury that the evidence of milk boy Alan Close was questionable:

"You are not bound to believe anything unless you want. Here is a boy on his round. He has got to cover the distance of 500 yards in five minutes. Just about 3½ miles an hour. Probably you will not think that that boy would go much more than 3½ miles an hour if he had nothing else to do, but he has got to go to the dairy. It so happens – another coincidence – that his cans are all ready for him. He has got to take his fresh cans, put the old ones away, and go on a round, calling at two houses, ringing or knocking at Mrs Wallace's door, waiting for her to answer, handing in the milk, delivering more milk, it may be only next-door, coming back and collecting the can. All in five minutes. Do you believe it? You are not bound to believe it.

I am going to call one boy, whose name we gave to the police, and he came forward the moment he read in the paper that Close had said it was 6.30 to say, 'Why he told us the day after it was 6.45.' You will have no doubt that they are telling you the truth when they say that the boy said it was 6.45. If it was 6.45, Wallace is innocent.

How about the other man? If there was another man who did it. No one searched him that night. All he would have to do is wash his hands and face – you cannot walk through the streets with bloody hands and face – he would of course do that before he touched anything, because you know bloody fingers have brought many a man within the reach of the law.[334]

What evidence is there on which you can safely say that Wallace

334 Bloody fingers that left no trace of blood on the cash-box (which would rule out burglary).

was the murderer? Let us take his journey to Menlove Avenue. It has been asked, 'Why did he want to go there at all on a message from someone he never knew?' That's a question for you. Here is a man who has been told of business on which you know he would draw 20% of the first premium. Anything up to a £5 note, perhaps. Do you think it unlikely that he would go? It is said 'how would the thief know that he had gone?' It is not difficult. The man who sent the message for him the night before would, of course, be watching to see if Wallace went off at the time, and could even follow him as far as the tram.[335]

I submit to you that Wallace's course that night was absolutely the course and behaviour of an innocent man. Comment is made about everything. It is funny that he told the tram driver that he was a stranger. It is almost a form of politeness, if you are bothering someone to tell you where a place is. That is said to be dreadfully suspicious. Why? He was a stranger and did not know the district at all.[336] It is said because two years ago he had five violin lessons in a street which you don't have to go to to reach Menlove Avenue that he knew the whole district. Menlove Avenue is miles long. Of course he was asking, and why should he not?

I am going to ask you to say it is a perfectly rational account, everything he did from the moment he started up dark Menlove Avenue to the moment he found himself talking to a police constable near the police station. Comment is made on the fact that he pulled out his watch. That was after he had found there was no Menlove Gardens East, but he still had this peculiar name Qualtrough to follow. He asked about a directory. The shop was open and the post office part was shut. He goes to the newsagent.

In my submission there is not a rag there except police suspicion to fasten upon him. The police have not made any experiment to show how long it takes to get from the newsagent's shop to Wolverton Street. That has been left to us.

Why have not the police called some of these people? It is not for them to pick and choose. Here is a man on trial for his life. Why would they not give us the names of people they were not calling, that we might follow things up?

What excuse is there? They are all-powerful, these police people.

335 He would have to have been in two different places at once; a physical impossibility.

336 Wallace's visits to Ullet Road would suggest he was certainly no stranger along the Smithdown Road route.

> They can comb out Liverpool. We are wretchedly hampered. Is it that the police are afraid to help the Defence, or is it that they won't? Why should they not have called these people? There is no reason why they have not called these boys except that they do not fit in with their case. I am asking you where there is conflict between my client and the police (there is not very much) to discount them and remember, so far from assisting, the police have done everything in the case they could to throw ropes in front of us and to prevent facts coming."

Oliver suggested that Lily Hall was mistaken in her alleged sighting of Wallace with another man.

> "What happens next? Wallace finds that he cannot get into his house. Please remember this, what object could he have in pretending that he could not get into his house? Wallace was heard knocking at the door by Mrs Johnston, and it was his ordinary knocking. Why should he not call the Johnston's first if he wanted someone to see him? Both the front and the back locks of Wallace's house are defective, and he will tell you that the front door was bolted and the back door locked.
>
> If Wallace could not get in, what was he to do? If he wanted witnesses it would be no use waiting until someone was coming out. He did not know the Johnston's were coming out, because they came out by accident at that moment.
>
> Mr Hemmerde said in opening, 'Why does Wallace not go to the sitting-room first instead of going upstairs?' The sitting-room is one that Wallace never used except when company was there, or when he wanted to play the violin, with his wife playing the piano. Therefore, he went straight upstairs to the bedroom after passing through the kitchen to see if Mrs Wallace had gone to bed. He went upstairs calling her name and finds she is not there. Then he goes to the last place, the sitting-room. He strikes a match and sees her body on the floor, in a fit, he thinks. He walks round the body because he would not walk over it. He lights the customary gas-jet over the fireplace.
>
> The boy Close gave evidence as to the earliest possible time that this crime could have been committed, and that is in the region of 6.30 or 6.35. It does not follow, however, that death took place at all then. You might think it extremely improbable that the woman took the milk from the boy at that time because I am going to call a boy who delivered a newspaper between 6.30

and 6.35.[337] There is evidence that tends to put the time of death as far back as possible, and that is given by Professor MacFall. He bases his estimate of the time of death upon post-mortem rigidity, coupled with the appearance of the blood. Still, so far as post-mortem rigidity is concerned, he purports to give you evidence of a course of observation lasting from 9.50pm until 1am, of varying stages of post-mortem rigidity.

Professor MacFall says he did not make a single note about that rigidity. Why was that? Quite obviously because post-mortem rigidity did not interest him particularly that evening. Their information at that time was that Mrs Wallace was last seen alive about four o'clock. They did not get the statement from the boy Close until the next night. How comes it that the Professor has not a single note about post-mortem rigidity? There is no note either about the condition of the blood. There was, he says, some small quantity of serum present. I will call a pathologist who will say that even if death had taken place anything like three or four hours before there would be an enormous quantity of serum.

So far as fixing the time by post-mortem rigidity is concerned, it is almost hopeless to get within an hour or two. Even Dr Pierce allows a margin of error of two hours in his estimate of the time of death, which he agrees might have occurred at 4pm or 8pm. You have been told by a Police Sergeant and by Professor MacFall about Wallace's unnaturally calm demeanour. Whom do you believe? Mr and Mrs Johnston say that Wallace appeared to be suffering from a shock, and that when Mrs Johnston was sitting with him in the kitchen for a quarter of an hour Wallace was then in a condition bordering upon breakdown, while he actually burst out sobbing.

When the police came, whether from an instinct of dignity at their appearance or from some other cause, Wallace, they say, becomes calm. Do you believe Mrs Johnston or the Professor, with all his force of didactic power – he is accustomed to lecturing people – or all the satellites of the police who came and went one after the other, and say that Wallace was very cool and collected?

Not one word was said at the Police Court in all this great mass of depositions about Wallace's demeanour being unnaturally calm or about him being very cool and collected. That has all been thought of since. I wonder whose brain devised it. A very subtle

337 The *Evening Express* of 24th April reported 6.20 to 6.25, but Oliver must surely have said 6.30 to 6.35.

form of attack this, all thought of since the Police Court. Do you think the police do not know the value of that sort of evidence? What is the excuse for not giving it before? Professor MacFall says: 'I was not asked.' He does not mind volunteering things. Superintendent Moore says: 'I was not asked.' That is nice stuff to bring out against a man who is on trial for his life.

Now for the mackintosh. How on earth could he at first see that it was a mackintosh that had been wrapped up under her head? The ordinary policeman out in the street, PC Williams says: 'That looks like a mackintosh.' Wallace says: 'Yes, it is mine.' Where was the mackintosh lying? According to the Crown Wallace put it on to murder his wife, and when he is finished he puts it under the body. We have a photograph produced in which the mackintosh has been specially put there for you to look at. Why was it photographed like that? The superintendent of police says: 'The photographer must have caught his foot in it as he went out of the door.' Does Mrs Johnston's suggestion not impress you when she says that the mackintosh was the sort of thing that Mrs Wallace might have put over her shoulders to go to the door?

Professor MacFall, for the first time, here says: 'I find typical blood spots marked upon it.' That suggests the mackintosh was worn by the murderer. I will call evidence[338] to show you that that blood has obviously just dripped down from the head of the woman on to the mackintosh. Yet that is put before you as evidence that the mackintosh was on the striker.

I have already pointed out the significance of the fingerprints, and I have pointed out that no professional criminal would think of leaving his identification marks on the box. The first thing he would do would be to go to the scullery and wash his hands before he touched anything.[339] The next point that was made was the blood on the notes in the jar upstairs. I wish I could understand what the theory of the Prosecution is about the blood on those notes. Were they put there after the murder as it is suggested? What on earth could the murderer's object be in putting four £1 notes into a jar on the bedroom mantelpiece? What does that prove and why did he do it? My client will tell you that that jar was a temporary savings bank. My client twice that

338 During Oliver's opening speech for the defence, a juryman sitting in the back row on the left interrupted with a hostile remark. Oliver said that three or four in the court heard the comment, although Hemmerde did not.

339 There was no evidence that the scullery sink had been used.

evening went up to that jar, once before the police arrived, when Mr Johnston asked him to go upstairs to see if they had touched anything. Honest as he is, or at least as I want you to believe that he is, he will tell you that he does not distinctly remember whether he took the notes out on that occasion or not, but he probably would. He had just come up from the body, and had been handling Mrs Wallace's hand. Do you not see the likelihood that there would be a little blood on his finger, or his thumb, and if he did take hold of those notes it would get off?[340]

If these notes were in the jar before the murder, then there was no blood on them. If they were put there after the murder, why were they taken from the cash-box? I ask you to say that there is no question whatever that that smear got on accidentally during one or other of those handlings by Wallace.[341]

Referring to the discovery of the clot of blood on the pan Professor Roberts tells you that last January, within a day or two of the murder he made an experiment which satisfies him that that blood fell on the pan within two minutes of the murder. Why have they waited until this morning to give it? Can you imagine anything more utterly vital than to be able to prove that that blood fell in that position, and in that shape, within two minutes or so of the murder.

I am going to call before you a gentleman[342] who has made countless experiments, and who will tell you that in his opinion a clot of blood of that size and shape must have been at least an hour before it could have been dropped upon that pan and retain that shape.

If this man went upstairs to wash himself after the crime the blood clot must have been dropped within a minute or two. Do you believe anyone went upstairs after that crime? Do you think it has been proved? No one has had a bath. I ask you to say you are satisfied as the jury can be that that clot on that pan was carried up by accident by someone or other of the twelve police officers or Professor MacFall or Dr Pierce.

If they leave you in this state of mind, 'Wallace might be guilty, but on the other hand, his story might be true and someone else might be guilty,' then you will acquit him. I am not bound to but

340 No blood was found on Wallace when examined by Superintendent Moore and Inspector Gold.

341 There is also the possibility that the smear was already on the note.

342 Dr Robert Coope.

> I will put before you an alternative theory for your judgement. At 6.45 Wallace had gone out. He has been watched, of course, and when he is safely on the tram, bound for Menlove Gardens, there comes a knock at the door. Mrs Wallace goes, picking up as she goes past the rack that mackintosh that hung there, and throws it over her shoulders. She opens the door:
>
> 'Good evening, Mrs Wallace. I am Mr Qualtrough. Has your husband gone?'
>
> 'Oh, he has just gone.'
>
> 'Oh, what a pity. I thought I might have been able to save him a journey; now I shall miss him. Can I come in and leave a note?'[343]
>
> 'Yes, certainly.'
>
> She knew her husband had gone, of course. They come into the parlour. That is where the visitors come, not into the kitchen. She lights the gas…Lights the fire…Just as she rises he hacks her to the ground.
>
> That is the theory which fits in with every fact in this strange case. The burned skirt, the burned mackintosh.
>
> Up to the very last moment before his arrest the police were taking statements from Wallace. I do not think there has ever been a case in which so many statements were taken from a man. If he is an innocent man, consider what his condition of mind must have been. He was quiet, stunned by shock. He sobbed, as Mrs Johnston says, when he was alone. If he has made a slip or two, remember the circumstances."

Oliver then called Wallace. The accused man rose and went into the witness box. The time was 2.20. On taking the oath Wallace spoke in such a low voice that Oliver asked him if he could speak a little louder. Wallace explained that he was a bit hoarse. After he had cleared his throat he gave his evidence in a clear tone and with a cultured voice. Justice Wright said that Wallace could sit down to give evidence but he declined, and remained standing.

Wallace said that he had lived in Wolverton Street for 16 years and that it was a rented property. He said that he had been married just over eighteen years[344] at the time of his wife's death, and that he

343 It could also be said that Qualtrough could have easily followed Wallace up to Menlove Gardens if he was that desperate to contact him.

344 In actuality almost 17 years.

had been an agent for the Prudential since 1915.

Oliver: "What were your relations with your wife?"

Wallace: "What I should describe as perfect."

Oliver: "Were you in any sort of financial difficulty?"

Wallace: "None whatever."

Oliver said that they had a note from the Bank that morning stating his account was £152.[345] Wallace accepted the figure.

Oliver: "Had you any motive whatever in the death of your wife?"

Wallace: "None whatever."

Wallace said that the area he collected in was Clubmoor and that he could make over 560 calls a week, and in reply to Oliver said three weeks out of the four that he collected the amount might be anything between £30 and £40; each fourth week it might be anything between £80 and £100, and that it could even be higher on occasions. He didn't collect on Fridays, and on Saturday 17th he was laid up in bed with influenza. He had collected on the Monday morning and the whole of Tuesday, and had collected about £14. He had paid out about £10 10s in sickness benefits, which left him with about £4 in cash.

Hemmerde said that the Prosecution did not dispute any of this, of which Oliver was obliged.

Wallace recounted his journey to the Chess Club on the Monday night and the subsequent discussion with Beattie with regard to the message.

Oliver: "It has been suggested that you used the telephone box to telephone a message to yourself. Is there a word of truth in that?"

Wallace: "Absolutely none."

Oliver: "Did you understand that there was a possibility of business from the message?"

Wallace: "Yes, I understood it so."

Oliver: "What sort of policy might you expect a father to give a son who has just come of age? What type of policy do you get for that, an endowment policy or a life policy?"

345 The Midland Bank, 152 Breck Road. £152 in 1931 amounted to approximately £6,960 in today's financial climate (National Archives).

Wallace: "Seeing the name and the daughter coming of age had been suggested I considered it might result in a policy of something like £100 endowment, or something of that nature. I did not expect it would be less than that."

Oliver: "We have been told you would get 20 per cent of the first payment. Would that be worth having on such a policy?"

Wallace: "Yes."

Oliver then came to the events of 20th January.

"Were you your usual self that afternoon?"

"Quite."

"It has been suggested by a policeman that as he bicycled past you at about half past three you had a ghastly appearance and were wiping your eyes with your sleeve."

"I heard the suggestion."

"Is that true?"

"No, it is not."

"Do your eyes ever water in January?"

"They may do, yes."

"If they did, what would you do?"

"Probably take out my handkerchief and insert it under my glasses and just wipe them."

Wallace's voice seemed to become clearer as Oliver continued to examine him. He had his hands clasped behind him and seemed calm in his demeanour.

Oliver: "When you went out was your wife alive?"

Wallace: "Certainly."

Oliver: "Did she come with you?"

Wallace: "She came down the backyard as far as the backyard door and I left her standing there with an instruction to her to bolt the door after me. That was our usual practice."

Oliver: "Did you hear her bolt it?"

Wallace: "I did not."

Oliver: "The police officer Williams says you told him she walked some of the way down the entry with you and then went back and you heard her bolt the door. Is that right?"

Wallace: "No."

Oliver: "I suppose I must put this question to you. I think it follows from what you have said. Did you lay a finger upon her; did you lay a hand upon your wife at all that night?"

Wallace: "I think in going out of the back door I did what I often enough did, I just patted her on the shoulder and said: 'I won't be longer than I can help.'"[346]

Oliver: "I did not mean that. Did you do anything to injure her?"

Wallace: "Oh no, certainly not."

In reply to Oliver, Wallace said he did not dispute the evidence of the tramcar conductors. He then gave an account of his actions in the Menlove Gardens area, the people he had conversed with, his search for a directory and his conversation with PC Serjeant.

Oliver: "Did he tell you there was no Menlove Gardens East?"

Wallace: "Yes."

Wallace said that the reason he checked the time with PC Serjeant was because he wanted to know how much time he had to spare. He thought if it was a local post office it would also be a shop and if he left it until after eight it would be closed, so he looked to see what time it was.

In reply to further questions Wallace said that he did not know Lily Hall, and that he did not speak to anyone on his return other than the tram conductors.

Oliver then questioned Wallace about his return to 29 Wolverton Street.

"When you found you could not get into your house, did you feel anxious at all?"

"Well, when I went to the front door the first time I was a little bit uneasy, but I did not attach any great importance to it. I thought she might have gone upstairs and not heard me, and I thought I would slip round to the back and try and get in there."

346 'I won't be any longer than I can help.' Surely an innocent Wallace would have immediately returned home when he was notified that Menlove Gardens East did not exist. Why then did he embroil himself in actually taking an age in Mossley Hill? He had been told on several occasions that the address did not exist – he even accepted the fact, saying to Katie Mather; 'It's funny isn't it, there is no East.' [Witness Statement Katie Mather.]

"When you knocked and got no answer did that have any effect upon you?"

"I thought at the time she might have slipped out to the post. There is a post box close at hand and she might have slipped out to post a letter. She often did that."

Wallace said that they used the middle kitchen for sitting in for meals and that the front sitting-room was used whenever they had any visitors, if anybody came on business or if they decided to play music.

He also said that he had discussed the business proposition with his wife, and that he finally decided to go after discussing it with her.

Oliver: "Going into the house you came into the kitchen?"

Wallace: "Yes, the back kitchen."

Oliver: "Was there any light there?"

Wallace: "A small light by the gas over the sink."

Wallace said that he next went upstairs, calling out his wife's name twice as he did so. He went into the middle bedroom, the light being turned down. He turned it up. He could not account for the state of the front bedroom.

Wallace then told of his discovery of his wife's body in the sitting-room. "The door was closed to and I pushed it a little open and then I struck a match in quite the ordinary way. That I probably did every night I went into the room in the dark. I held it up and as I held it up I could see my wife was lying there on the floor."

"You told the Officer you thought she was in a fit?" said Oliver.

"That was my first impression, but it only lasted possibly a fraction of a second, because I stooped down with the same match and I could see there was evidence of signs of a disturbance and blood, and I saw that she had been hit."

Wallace said that he then lit the customary right-hand gas-jet over the fireplace.

Oliver: "When you saw your wife lying there I suppose it follows you avoided treading on her as you went past?"

Wallace: "Certainly."

Wallace said that he then examined his wife and checked her pulse, and then went to notify the Johnstons.

With regard to the piece of iron that had been suggested to have been used for cleaning under the gas fire, Wallace vehemently denied any knowledge of it.

Oliver then questioned Wallace about his demeanour on the evening of the murder.

"It was said you were extremely quiet, or cool and collected. One witness said you occasionally broke down, other witnesses say you smoked cigarettes. Do you really remember what your demeanour was?"

"Well, I remember that I was extremely agitated and that I was trying to keep as calm and as cool as possible. Probably I was smoking cigarettes for something to do, I mean to say, the inaction was more than I could stand. I had to do something to avoid breaking down. I did sit down in a chair on one or two occasions, and I do remember I did break down absolutely; I could not help it or avoid it. I tried to be as calm and cool as possible."

"Is there anyone in the world who could take the place of your wife in your life?"

"No, there is not."

"Have you got anyone to live with now?"

"No."

"Or to live for?"

"No."

Oliver asked Wallace about the notes in the jar.

"Do you remember whether or not you put your hands on the notes in the jar?"

"Yes, I probably took them out and handled them; counted them."

"You say 'probably'. Do you remember doing it?"

"Yes, I think I can say that."

Oliver then came to the question of the mackintosh.

"You had already seen it and identified it to Mrs Johnston. The point is this: that it was the police constable who said to you, 'That looks like a mackintosh'?"

"Yes."

"Before that had you moved it at all?"

"No. I just fingered it."

"You have told the Jury the only point about your statement to Williams that you dispute, namely, you said that your wife had come down the entry with you?"

"That is so, I do dispute that. I think he must have misheard me."

Oliver then moved on to the question of the giving of names by Wallace of those that would be admitted into the house by Mrs Wallace.

"You mentioned the names of people who might have done this. Had you been pressed by Inspector Gold to give the names of people who could possibly have done it by the questions he asked you on the night of the 21st?"

"Yes. The questions were put to me in such a way that I felt that I had to give the names of people."

"Had you at that time considered the possibility of a man coming and giving the name Qualtrough to your wife? Looking at it now, if someone did come and give the name of Qualtrough to your wife on that night, do you think she would have let him in?"

"Seeing I had gone to meet a Mr Qualtrough I think she would, because she knew all about the business. If a visitor did call she would have shown them into the front room. There is no question about that."

Wallace said that he stayed at the Detective Office until about 10.00pm on the Wednesday night and that he practically lived at the Detective Office all that week.

Oliver then asked Wallace about suspicion and the 'indiscreet' conversation with Beattie.

"Did you realise at some time or other that there were people who suspected you of having done this?"

"I did, yes. Within three or four days I began to suspect that might be the case."

"Did the police ask you about a conversation you had with Mr Beattie on the 22nd, two days afterwards?"

"Yes."

"Had Mr Beattie said anything about the night before? I do not know whether you remember what he said?"

"I cannot give the words but he advised me to say as little about this case as possible to outsiders."

"Because I think he said what you said might be misconstrued?"

"Yes."

"Do you agree with that?"

"I agree it was misconstrued."

This concluded Oliver's questioning of Wallace. There was a stir in court when Hemmerde rose to cross-examine. The opening lines of questioning were, without doubt, set to confuse Wallace:

"I want to ask you first a few general questions. Where was your wife on Monday evening, the 19th January?"

"She was in the house."

"Quite well?"

"Yes, except for the cold that she had."

"Where was Mr Crewe on Tuesday, 20th January?"

"I understood that he had gone to the cinema."

"On that night, the 20th?"

"On the Monday night."

"I am not talking of the Monday; I am talking of the Tuesday."

"On the Tuesday I do not know where he was."

"I thought you did know. On the Monday night you say you knew he had been to the cinema?"

"No. I am wrong. On the Monday night I do not know where he was."

"You are a friend of his?"

"Yes."

"This must have been quite a slight cold of your wife's, was it not?"

"We did not regard it as a serious matter."

Hemmerde then asked Wallace about the use of the sitting-room.

"So far as the use of your parlour was concerned, did you use it much for music?"

"Yes, quite a fair amount."

"When you had an off evening I suppose, both being musical, you were inclined to spend it with music?"

"Yes."

"And I suppose being, to some extent, a musician you did not leave your piano open when you were not using it?"

"Yes, we did."

"One sees it open in the photograph taken after the murder?"

"Yes."

"And one sees music upon it?"

"Quite possible."

"Have you the book of photographs there?"

"No, that is a plan."

Wallace was then handed the photograph.[347]

Hemmerde continued: "Can your knowledge of music tell you what that was on the piano?"

Wallace studied the photograph for some moments, and then replied: "No, I cannot, except it might be two pieces of music."

"When you used the piano for music on a night in January, you would naturally have the fire lighted?"

"Yes, we did."

"And the gas?"

"Yes."

"Then if you had been going that night to stay at home it would have been quite natural that the piano should be open and the fire lit, and you would be having your ordinary musical evening, if you had not had your appointment with Mr Qualtrough?"

"No, probably we should not have had any music that evening. Her cold would have made her say: 'It will be rather cold in the front room, I do not think we will bother tonight with music.'"[348]

Hemmerde next came to the subject of the notes in the jar.

"Just one point you made about the notes upstairs. You said that you counted the notes when you went up with Police Constable

347 Photograph No.7.

348 Yet Wallace thought his wife might have gone to post a letter on his return.

Williams?"

Roland Oliver interjected: "I do not remember his saying that."

Justice Wright intervened: "If there is any question I will ask the Shorthand Writer[349] to read it. I do not quite remember that."

The shorthand writer read question 3229 down to question 3234 and gave the answer thereto, which did indeed confirm that Wallace admitted to counting the notes.

Hemmerde continued: "You see the surprise it has caused. Have you ever said such a thing before, even to your Solicitor or Counsel?"

"I do not know."

"Throughout that evening did you ever find blood on your hands?"

"I did not observe it."

"Then so far as you know, no blood from your hands could have got on those notes?"

"Yes, I think I can say that."

Hemmerde then asked Wallace about his visit to the Chess Club and the conveyance of the telephone message to him.

"No one could possibly have known that you would be at the café that night?"

"Nobody could say absolutely, certainly, that I would be there, no."

"You told no one you were going to be there?"

"That is so."

"Did you put in the 'East' in block letters after you had written 'Mossley Hill'?"

"Yes."

"Why in these block letters?"

"Because in writing it down I took the name from Mr Beattie and I repeated it afterwards: 'R.M. Qualtrough, 25 Menlove Gardens West, Mossley Hill', and he said 'Not West, East'"

"You had not begun to write West, had you?"

"I had not got to that point and he corrected me, and I wrote

349 Messrs Barnett Lenton & Co., 40 Chancery Lane, London WC2.

'East' in block letters in order that I myself would be reminded it is correct."

Hemmerde then asked Wallace if he had ever used the telephone box on Rochester Road.

"Yes."

"How many times do you think you have used it?"

"Once or perhaps twice."

Wallace said that he generally used the telephone in the library as it was more convenient.

Hemmerde then came to the subject of Menlove Gardens East.

"You could have found out at once if you had looked up in the directory where Menlove Gardens East was or was not?"

"I could have done."

"And I suppose an enquiry at the Prudential Offices would have told you whether there was such a place?"

"It was not necessary."

"Did it not occur to you to ask the policeman on point duty near Penny Lane where it was?"

"No."

"You only had to ring up Mr Crewe and find out where Menlove Gardens East was, if it was near him?"

"I could have done that but I did not think of it."

"Does not the whole thing strike you as very remarkable that a man who does not know you should ring you up for business in another district and expect you to go there, and yet without knowing whether you had gone there or not come and wait outside your house for the chance of murdering your wife?"

"Yes."

"A wrong address is essential to the creation of an alibi?"

"I do not follow you."

"If you had been told Menlove Gardens West, the first enquiry would have landed you there?"

"Yes."

"If you are told of an address that does not exist, you can ask seven or eight people, every one of whom would be witness where you were?"

"Yes."

"So to a man who was planning to do this a wrong address would be essential to his alibi?"

"Yes."

Hemmerde moved on to the subject of Wallace's conversation on the Thursday evening of 22nd January.

"Now I want to come to the case of Mr Beattie. Why should you recognise it as an indiscretion to press Mr Beattie as to the time of the call?"

"If I was a suspected person I realised that it was unwise for me to be discussing the case with a man who might possibly be called as a witness in any charge."

"Do you mean to suggest to my Lord and the Jury that you ever had the slightest fear of anything the police should find out?"

"No, I have no fear at all of what the police could find out."

"Then why should you have been in the slightest degree worried about any indiscretion?"

"Because I realised that I was being suspected, and anything I might have done or might have said might be misconstrued."

Hemmerde next asked Wallace about the telephone message.

"When you got that message originally from that telephone box, it being a totally unusual thing in your life, did it ever strike you at all to make any investigation before you went the next day?"

"Yes, it did occur to me."

"But you did not make them?"

"I did not make them."[350]

Hemmerde then asked Wallace about his attempts to gain entry into his house.

"How long were you trying altogether to get in that night?"

"Not many minutes – possibly half a minute on the first occasion, and I would go round to the back, possibly four or five minutes

350 Much has been said that Wallace should have consulted a directory prior to his visit. He had enough time earlier that day to have looked the address up. His reply to Hemmerde that he did not think of it seems contradictory to his character.

altogether, not more, till the Johnstons came out of their house."

"You could not open the front door?"

"No, I could not get it open."

"But you saw the Superintendent go out in the street and without any difficulty open it at the very first time?"

"Yes, that is true."

"Close the door and open it?"

"But I could not open it because the bolt was on it."[351]

Wallace was then re-examined by Oliver.

"When you were playing the violin with your wife, were you accustomed to do it when you were naked in a mackintosh; was that your habit?"

"What was that?"

"To play naked in a mackintosh?"

"I have never played naked in my life."

"It is suggested that you never told the police about having visited Mr Crewe's house on the evening of the 20th when you found yourself in Green Lane. It seems you never did mention it in any of your statements, but were you telling the police the names of all the people you had spoken to in order that they might trace your movements: is that what you were doing?"

"Yes."

"It has been finally suggested to you that the front is a curious place for your wife's skirt to be burned if she fell on the floor. Did Bailey give this evidence at the Police Court: 'There were three horizontal burns which could have been caused by contact with fireclay of a gas fire such as is at Wolverton Street.' Do you remember that?"

"Yes, I remember that evidence."

"That is your own Case?"

"Yes."

After three hours in the witness box Wallace's ordeal was over. He had answered more than 700 questions – over 400 of them from

351 Wallace's claims regarding the doors were extremely questionable. At no time did he tell Detective Superintendent Moore that the front door had been bolted.

the prosecution. When he left the dock he looked slightly feeble.

Professor James Henry Dible[352] was the next to take the stand. In reply to Oliver, he said that taken by itself, rigor mortis was a very unreliable and inaccurate guide to the exact time of death, and that it varied with intervals. Dible also said that a frail, ill-developed body (such as that of the victim) would also tend to accelerate rigor. The Professor also said that, putting himself in MacFall's position, he would be inclined to estimate death at something under three hours or four hours previously.[353] Dible said that he would not set out to express an opinion from rigor alone as to the time of death, but would take all other possible means into consideration and that the rectal temperature should have been taken.

Oliver then asked Dible about MacFall's reliance on serum exudation as to the time of death: "There was only a little serum exuded in the room. What do you say to the amount you would expect after giving your own time, three hours?"

"I should expect a considerable amount of exudation of serum."

Dible said that he had conducted experiments on a case during the trial with the purpose of observing the exudation of serum, and after two and a half hours there was an abundance of it around the head.

With regard to the drop of blood on the pan of the toilet, Dible said that blood shed only two minutes and dropped from a height of fifteen inches on to a hard substance would flatten – it would not form the shape described.

In reply to Hemmerde, Dible said that he conducted his experiments of dropping blood from different heights onto a dry porcelain surface and that his results completely contradicted those given by Roberts.

Justice Wright: "You say unless the blood coagulated possibly it would to some extent. What time do you think is necessary to produce that coagulation?"

352 James Henry Dible was born in Southampton on 29th October 1889. A Fellow of the Royal College of Surgeons, he was also a Professor of Pathology at London University from 1925-28 and Liverpool University from 1929-37. He died on 1st July 1971.

353 In other words, before 6.00pm or after 7.00pm.

Dible: "If you use a conical clot I think a question of hours, my Lord; at least an hour."

"That means the coagulated little bit of blood dropped from a height of a couple of feet or so would form not exactly a hemisphere, but something such as was found here?"

"Yes, my Lord."

"You say not less than an hour?"

"That is my experience, my Lord."

Dr Robert Coope[354] followed Dible onto the witness stand. He said that he had made 115 experiments in all with regard to the clotting of human blood.

Justice Wright: "Had the drop of blood which formed that little thing been coagulated, or was it fresh when it fell on that pan?"

Coope: "I should say, my Lord, it was at least an hour coagulated or I think considerably longer; and the reason I give for thinking it considerably longer is in the drying of it. Certain experiments have been made."

Oliver: "In your view, that clot must have been an hour at least away from the hand that shed it before it fell from that hand?"

Coope: "Yes, an hour."

In reply to Hemmerde, Coope said that he found Roberts' tests surprising, and that his tests yielded completely different results.

This concluded Coope's evidence.

Roland Oliver then made reference to Wallace's haggard appearance: "I have here a number of people who saw him that afternoon."

Justice Wright: "I do not suppose the Jury would want to see them."

Oliver: "If it is indicated to me that I need not trouble with that part of the case, I will not do so."

Hemmerde: "I shall make no point of the Rothwell part of the

354 Robert Coope was born in Pilsley, Derbyshire on 26th December 1892. An Honorary Assistant Physician to the Liverpool Royal Infirmary, he was also Physician to the Liverpool Hospital for Diseases of the Chest, Lecturer in Clinical Chemistry and Acting Demonstrator in Medical Pathology at the University of Liverpool. His medical practice was at 13 Rodney Street. He died on 17th February 1972.

case."

Oliver: "If that is understood, and the Prosecution will not comment on it, I will not trouble to call them."

Justice Wright: "No; the Prosecution will not say that a man looks rather haggard."

Hemmerde: "If he had not been called at the Police Court I should not have mentioned it."

Oliver: "I would like to call the last two of them in point of fact to show what his demeanour was at six o'clock."

Justice Wright: "That is not unreasonable."

James Allison Wildman said that he delivered the newspaper to 27 Wolverton Street on the evening of 20th January, and that he saw a boy wearing a Collegiate cap delivering the milk to No. 29 at about 6.37pm. Wildman said that he passed Holy Trinity Church and noticed the clock at 6.35, and that it took him two minutes to walk to Wolverton Street. Although it was several weeks later that he was interviewed by Hector Munro, he distinctly remembered the time being 6.35 by the church clock.

Elsie Wright said that on the evening of 20th January she was at the bottom of Richmond Park when the half-past six bells were ringing in the Belmont Institution. She said she then went to the Vicarage of Holy Trinity in Richmond Park to deliver milk, and was kept there for five minutes. She then walked along Richmond Park and saw Alan Close at the bottom of Letchworth Street at 6.40. She said that on the following evening, Alan Close said he had been at 29 Wolverton Street at 'about a quarter to seven.'

Douglas Metcalf said that on the evening of 20th January he had to go to the Parochial Hall to deliver a paper to Mrs Davies. There he asked one of the men what time it was. One of the men told him it was twenty to seven. Metcalf said he then went to Campbell's and stood talking to some boys outside. Whilst standing he saw Wildman going down an entry leading off Wolverton Street. Metcalf said that he was standing with the group of other children on the night after the murder, and had no doubt that Alan Close said it was 6.45 when he had seen Mrs Wallace alive.

Kenneth Caird was next sworn.

Oliver: "Did you, on the evening of the 21st January last, hear Alan Close say what time he last saw Mrs Wallace alive?"

Caird: "Yes; he said a quarter to seven."

Oliver: "Have you any doubt about that?"

Caird: "No, not the least."

David Jones said that he delivered the *Echo* through the letterbox of No. 29 on the evening of the killing at about 6.35.[355]

The final three witnesses were the women who gave evidence with regard to Wallace's demeanour on his round on the afternoon of 20th January.

Letitia Harrison said that she did not notice anything unusual in Wallace's manner, and that he was joking with her.

Amy Lawrence said that she asked Wallace in and her husband offered him a cup of tea, which Wallace accepted, and that he was 'the same as usual.'

Margaret Martin said that Wallace called at her house sometime after 5.30 and that he was just the same as he had ever been since he collected – calm, and the same in appearance.

Roland Oliver: That is the case, my Lord.

Justice Wright: I think the speeches had better be made tomorrow morning.

This concluded the penultimate day.

SATURDAY 25 APRIL

It was the day of the F.A. Cup Final – West Bromwich Albion v Birmingham City. The only result the Liverpool public was interested in though was that of the trial. The atmosphere was electric, the whole city buzzing in the build-up to the eventual verdict.

The queue outside St George's Hall began to form as early as 3.00am. The first arrivals were two Mersey Tunnel employees who

355 In his statement Jones said that he delivered the *Echo* at 6.30. [Witness Statement David Jones 22nd January 1931.]

had just left work, and they were followed by two youths and a girl, who brought with them thermos flasks and sandwiches. At 4.30am there were more than forty people lined up, and long before nine o'clock well over 200. All types of people made up the queue. There were many well-dressed women in the ranks and city business men. Three women who attended outside the court every morning at seven o'clock must have learned from experience, because they just managed to gain admission to the public gallery, having arrived at six o'clock. When the doors were closed the public gallery was filled to its limit, less than half the queue had gained entry. On a humorous note, a Lascar[356] walked leisurely up the steps past the disappointed crowd who looked on in astonishment. At the door he met a constable who had a short conversation with him. The Lascar walked back down the steps and disappeared. He was apparently looking for St Martin's Hall.

In reference to the trial, the *Liverpool Echo* reported that:

> 'It seemed like a stage play in a real-life setting, in which during this the climax that precedes the denouement the principal characters were all keyed up to the highest possible pitch of anxiety and excitement, with two exceptions: Mr Justice Wright, who, during his summing up, never once raised his voice beyond a pitch adequate for the jury's hearing, was calm with the self-possession of long experience. The only other person in court who, to all intents, seemed perfectly oblivious to what was going on, seemingly unconscious that he was the cynosure of hundreds of pairs of eyes, was the prisoner himself.'[357]

At 10.00am Roland Oliver rose to make his final speech on behalf of the defence. He said that by the rules of the procedure in the courts, as he had called witnesses in the case, he had to address the jury before his learned friend. That meant that the prosecution would have an opportunity of replying to any argument the defence used, and there would be no opportunity of answering the Recorder back.

356 A sailor or militiaman from the Indian Subcontinent.
357 *Liverpool Echo*, 25th April 1931.

Oliver began:

> "There are two points in this case which are essential in determining guilt. One is: Who sent the telephone message? The other is: At what time has the prosecution proved that Mrs Wallace was killed? In regard to who sent the telephone message, I ask you to ask yourselves whether upon the evidence you can possibly say if Wallace sent the telephone message. Regarding the second essential question, 'At what time has the Prosecution proved Mrs Wallace was killed?' There are two branches of evidence upon that; one is medical and the other is that of the boy Close.
>
> In regard to the medical evidence you have got such deductions as can be drawn from the state of rigor mortis. You have Professor MacFall saying that in his opinion death was caused four hours at least before 10.00pm. Well, that is wrong. I say it is wrong because she was seen alive long after six, and the solution of the matter is, as Professor Dible says, that rigor mortis is a hopelessly fallible test. It is not a test at all. You have got to take it with all sorts of other things including the temperature of the body, which was never taken at all, and accurate observations which were never taken at all.
>
> There are pictures of the position of the body and pictures of the direction of the blood splashes. These are the things that interested him that night, not rigor mortis. Can you conceive a man of science professing to make observations every quarter of an hour or so, and not making a single note? The question of the time of death was not seriously disturbing him at that time. Of course, it became vital when they decided to accuse Wallace.
>
> With regard to rigor mortis, there is an admission of error of at least an hour either way, and that is how I ask you to treat it. I accept, quite candidly, that upon the medical evidence death might have taken place at such a time as Wallace was there.[358] But I ask you, looking at the whole of it, to say it is not a bit more likely to have taken place then than after Wallace had gone."

Oliver then came to the evidence of Close:

> "Did they all appreciate that the whole question of when the woman was last seen alive, so far as the Prosecution case went,

358 One cannot imagine Edward Marshall Hall, Edward Clarke or Norman Birkett even contemplating making a statement of this nature in the defence of their client.

> rested on the evidence of that boy and the value of his recollection that at a particular time on that evening he looked at the clock? It was significant that within twenty-four hours of the crime, when he had no interests either way, the police elicited from him the information that he last saw her alive at a quarter to seven. He told this to other people and they were so impressed that they told him he ought to go to the police because the papers said that Mr Wallace went out at a quarter past six, and if the boy saw her alive at a quarter to seven then he could not have done it."

Oliver was then scathing of the police:

> "The fact was that when the police came to charge Wallace the quarter to seven became a hopeless time to them because Wallace established, by his evidence, that it could not be controverted that he left the house at a quarter to seven. On this boy's evidence the police elected to leave the question of the time Mrs Wallace was last seen alive. The jury knew the powers of the police. They could go to any citizen and ask him to make a statement.
>
> You saw Wildman. You had an opportunity judging his demeanour. On that boy's evidence the police elected to leave the question of the time when Mrs Wallace was last seen alive. Why? The police wield great powers and they ought to be exercised fairly. Here is a man on trial for his life. Why have not the police called all the witnesses who can assist him? There was another boy, named David Jones, who delivered an *Echo* that night at the house, not by ringing the bell but by putting it into the letterbox and leaving it. The police took a statement from him within two days, and he told them that he delivered it at 6.30. He had told the jury yesterday that it was twenty-five to seven.
>
> That paper, open and apparently read, was lying on the kitchen table. It had been taken in and for all they knew, read. Did that throw no light on the time the woman was last seen alive?"

Oliver said he did not suppose anyone would suggest that after committing the murder Wallace took the paper from the letterbox and laid it on the table.[359]

> "What was the case for the police? It varied from day-to-day. At the police court it was Wallace in a mackintosh who killed his

359 It could certainly be suggested. A guilty Wallace could have placed it there to create the illusion that Julia had been reading it before she admitted the murderer into the parlour.

> wife; no suggestion then that he was naked. Professor MacFall has sought to impress with the suggestion that there were stains of blood on the mackintosh, showing how the blood had squirted but if there was one word of truth in that why was it left until the trial? Not a word of such a suggestion was made at the police court."

Oliver asked the jury to dismiss the evidence of City Analyst William Henry Roberts with regard to his tests with blood in order to show how a clot could be formed, and said that that evidence should have been given two months before. It was perfectly obvious that the clot had been transferred to the rim of the lavatory by one of the dozen or so people in the house that night.

Referring to the blood smear on one of the notes found in the jar in the middle bedroom, Oliver said Wallace said that he probably picked them up and might have counted them.

He continued:

> "Before I called Wallace, I asked you to observe him in the witness box, and I know you did. I suppose it will be said by the Recorder, 'What a cool man.' On the other hand, if he had been agitated I suppose the Recorder would have said, 'Do you think that was the demeanour of an innocent man?' Is there no such thing as the calmness of innocence?
>
> Did you notice the way that man answered questions? Did you hear him fence once or prevaricate? Did you hear the frankness of his admissions? Absolutely frank, and apparently entirely untroubled. If my learned friend is going to argue against his demeanour in the witness box, I ask you to say it was absolutely consistent with his innocence.
>
> When he first of all said he collected on Saturday, and then corrected himself, his diary showed that this was perfectly right. Are you going to convict that man? Has the case been proved against him? How frank he was under cross-examination. It was put to him by Mr Hemmerde that when the telephoning took place on January 19th that would have been a splendid opportunity for someone to have gone in and rob the house – while Wallace was known to be at the Chess Club. Wallace frankly said it would have been. He was not arguing the case, he was answering questions, but don't forget the argument against

> that was that they could not know when they saw him go out that he was going to the Chess Club.[360]
>
> Further, Wednesday being the paying in day of the Prudential, Tuesday would be the most likely day for them to get a good haul. It was suggested to him, 'You have two doors, so there must have been two watchers?' Do you think that is unlikely? Do these sort of people never work in pairs?[361]
>
> The next thing was the evidence that Wallace had paid two visits to Calderstones and some to Woolton. Of course he had been in Menlove Avenue. But when they were going along streets did they memorise the names of side streets? The suggestion was farcical."

Oliver said that the giving of a wrong address in the telephone message was that of a person who was preparing an alibi. If that telephone message was sent by a criminal, did the jury see no value in his giving the wrong address? After all, that would keep Wallace away from the house for a longer period of time.[362]

> "There was the point of the turning out of the light, and it had been asked why should a criminal turn out the light? If that was to be said, why should Wallace turn out the light?"[363]

Referring to Wallace's search of the rooms in the house, Oliver said there was nothing extraordinary about the fact that the sitting-room was the last room he went into, because that was the last place in which he expected to find his wife.

In conclusion, Oliver said the burden of proof in the case lay on the Crown. Here they had a case of a crime without motive, a man against whose character there was no word to be said. A man

360 Yet be expected to know that when they saw him go out on the Tuesday night that he was going to Menlove Gardens.

361 One would have thought a crime devised by two people would have been more foolproof. The diversionary telephone call and fake address were extremely lax. The conveyor was relying solely on chance that Wallace would fall for it.

362 The using of a genuine address would have been adequate in keeping Wallace away for a sufficient amount of time.

363 There is the possibility that the light was on when Wallace left to go to Menlove Gardens. This would justify his ability in avoiding bloodstains. Both Alan Close and David Jones said that the front room of the house was in darkness when they called, but Julia was murdered *after* both had called, so the light could have been on then. The thickness of the curtains/blinds more than likely stopped any light from showing through.

whose affection for his wife could not be doubted, a man charged with the murder of the woman who was his only companion.

> "The Romans had a maxim which is as true today as it was then: 'No one ever suddenly became the basest of men.' How can you conceive such a man with these antecedents doing such a thing as this? Finally, if I may say so, it is not enough that you should think it possible that he did this – not merely enough, but it is not nearly enough. On looking at the two stories, you may say: 'Well, the story of the Defence does not sound very likely, but the story of the Prosecution does not sound very likely either'; and if that be the state of your minds, then he is entitled to be acquitted. I suggest that this should be the state of your minds: The story for the Defence is not very likely,[364] but at least it is consistent with all the facts; the story for the Prosecution sounds impossible."

Oliver's address had lasted an hour. He was followed immediately by Hemmerde.

> "Members of the Jury, it now becomes my duty to address you finally on behalf of the Prosecution. My learned friend need have no doubt. If you are dissatisfied with the story of the Prosecution and the story for the Defence, the Prosecution have failed to make out their case. I do not think any of you, having heard my opening speech in this case, could readily have been in doubt after you had heard it that, in accordance with what I regard as my duty, I put before you that the burden of proof was on the Prosecution, and you could not convict this man merely upon coincidences.
>
> I take my learned friend's two points – 'Who sent the telephone message?' And what time have the Prosecution established that Mrs Wallace was killed? Let us take the facts. The prisoner admits that on the Monday he left the house at about 7.15pm. Obviously that may mean two or three minutes one way or another. The telephone box is 400 yards from his house. Walking five miles an hour, one would do that in rather under three minutes; walking four miles an hour, in rather over.
>
> My learned friend said: 'How did the Recorder get the fact that nobody knew or could know he was going to be there? He must have got it from the police.' I did not; I got it from his client.

364 See note 358.

> Inspector Gold, giving evidence before the Magistrates, and again here, said he asked Wallace whether he knew of anyone who knew he was going to the club. Wallace said: 'No, I had not told anyone I was going, and I cannot think of anyone who knew I was going'; and upon that I based the statement that nobody would know that he was going or could know.
>
> You have a man ringing up at a time when, on Wallace's own time, he might perfectly well have been there, and it was a box that he has used. Whoever it was went to a box where there is no light except a reflected indirect light and where anybody could perfectly well telephone without drawing any attention.
>
> The man in the box telephoned to the City Café. Nobody but Wallace knew that Wallace was going to be at the café – no one. That is on his own story."

Hemmerde said that the voice on the telephone was confident and strong and inclined to be gruff. If a person was imitating another person's voice, one might imagine he would do so in a voice with those characteristics. That was the suggestion of the Prosecution; that the man who rang up the club was Wallace, no doubt disguising his voice.

> "What happened the next night? He says he leaves the house at 6.45, and takes two trams.[365] On one of them he actually mentions the address, Menlove Gardens East, three times to the conductor. He tells two of them that he is a stranger in the district – a man who had had music lessons a couple of hundred yards away from Menlove Avenue, a man who must have gone there going to Calderstones, as his diary points out.
>
> He proceeds to talk to Green, to the officer, and Miss Pinches, again asking for Menlove Gardens East, having been told by the officer and Green that there was no such place. We have no evidence that he goes to his superintendent except his statement at the last moment, because he says he had heard that the superintendent was not in. If he had gone and asked Mr Crewe where Menlove Gardens East was, he would have known at once.[366]
>
> But remember, according to his story, he has been induced to leave his house by a false address and false business being

365 Obviously Hemmerde meant three trams.
366 Hemmerde meant that Crewe would have looked up the address.

> suggested to him. Supposing that he had looked it up in the directory or spoken to Mr Crewe of the Prudential, and found there was no such place, he naturally would not have gone there, and yet this murderer, Qualtrough, must have assumed he would go, although the slightest thought, even if he believed his message had got home to him, would have told him he need not go at all, and, further than that, Menlove Gardens East or Menlove Gardens, let us say, is barely twenty minutes away by tram. Supposing Wallace thinks –"

Oliver interrupted: "Mr Recorder, that is quite wrong, not twenty minutes, it is more than half an hour according to your witnesses' test."

Hemmerde continued: "I am obliged to my friend. I want to get my figures exactly accurate because I want you to see what this means. A man is waiting to murder this woman, he is getting another man out of the way, he sends him off a distance, I think we had it roughly, of about three miles."

Oliver again cut in: "About four."

"About four," continued Hemmerde. "It takes just over half an hour. At any moment an enquiry might tell him that there was no such place."

Hemmerde then spoke of Wallace's return to the house:

> "When he reached the house he found, according to his own expression, that the door was locked against him. Do you believe for one moment that he could not get in through the front door or into the back door? He knew the condition of the locks, and it was significant that when Mr Johnston said he would get their key, Wallace replied: 'It opens now.'
>
> Later in the evening we find him suggesting to the police that someone must have been in the house – he does not suggest that now. If he is not really trying to get into that house, but trying to create an impression that he cannot get into the house, is not that a vital circumstance? Would he ever have said to Police Superintendent Moore when he is trying the lock: 'It was not like that this morning'? Is he not trying to suggest that the lock is in a different condition then to what the locksmith said it might have been in for quite a long time?
>
> You remember he said that there was £4 missing from the cash-

box, and taken it down – because they must actually have taken down the cash-box – and taken out the money and put it up again. As one of the police officers said, would a thief be likely to do that?

£4 is found upstairs. Why should anyone having taken money have put it back? How do you think that blood got on these notes? At no time did Wallace ever notice blood on his hands. At no time did Constable Williams see Wallace lift them out and count them.

Supposing that Wallace had never told his wife he was going out, and she had lighted the fire, prepared the room for an evening of music, and was then struck down in that room. You have got there the possibility; the burning of her dress and the burning of the raincoat, but who was wearing the raincoat?

If this murder was done by the prisoner, it is admitted by my friend it was thought out in every detail. He must have made up his mind exactly when he was going to do it, how he was going to do it, and with what weapon he was going to do it. A weapon like that would easily go into the ground or a drain.[367] But in this case you are dealing with a man – if it was the man who telephoned up the night before – who will think out everything.

For nine months, Mrs Draper had visited that house; an iron bar had been standing up by the gas stove.[368] It was there on January 7th when she was last there, because she was trying to rake underneath to find a screw that had fallen out of the gas bracket, so she remembered it. Do you think it possible that the prisoner, living in that house, has never known that that thing, which was there when Mrs Draper first came, had been there?

He does not say: 'I have seen it, but do not know where it has gone.' He says: 'I never saw it in my life.' Do you believe that?

Now, members of the Jury, the points I want to draw your attention to in conclusion are these: First of all, the overwhelming probability that the man who left this house at 7.15 on the evening of the 19th was the man who was in the telephone box at about 7.15. Only three minutes' walk from his house there is a telephone box from which this call goes through. I suggest to you

367 It would seem highly unlikely the weapon would have gone easily into the ground. It was mid-January, the ground being hard, and most of the area in and around Wolverton Street was paved. Although the drains in the Wolverton Street area were searched, the possibility that the weapon could have been deposited down one of them further outside the area cannot be dismissed.

368 Gas fire.

that on that part of the case a great deal points, if not everything, to the man there being the prisoner.

As regards the time of death, the other point that my learned friend said was so vital, I submit that that is also easily established.[369] The man who had made his plans had between 6.30 or 6.35 up to 6.49, practically twenty minutes, and there is no reason to suppose that a man who had done a thing like that would go very slowly. If he did it, he was trying to create an alibi, and he would go as fast as he could. I say there is ample time for it.

Then you come back to this, which is the vital point: Those things being possible, are you satisfied beyond all reasonable doubt from things, one of which alone might not be sufficient but from all of them put together, are you satisfied beyond all reasonable doubt that this is the man who did that murder? Never mind about the clot of blood upstairs, never mind about any fine points about the notes. Can you believe that anyone would have ever committed such a crime merely for gain – the small gains in a Prudential agent's house?

Are you satisfied from the prisoner's attitude that he was an innocent man? Firstly, were his repeated enquiries about Menlove Gardens East natural? Was it natural, or true, that he came back and could not get into the house? – Or was he pretending he could not get into the house?

Do you believe afterwards, the two days later on the 22nd, when he is speaking to Mr Beattie, and asking him if he could tell him exactly what the time was when the telephone message came, do you believe, when he subsequently said: 'Oh, that was an indiscretion', that he really meant what he said he meant here, or do you attach importance to their conversation?

You can only convict this man if you are satisfied beyond all reasonable doubt on all these facts. Of course, the last word in this case comes not from me but from my Lord. You cannot convict him unless you are perfectly clear beyond all reasonable doubt that these matters to which I have been drawing your attention point with almost irresistible emphasis to the conclusion that he is guilty. If you do not think so, of course it will be your duty to acquit him.

I am bound to suggest to you, on behalf of the Crown, that

369 Although Hemmerde advanced the theory of the possibility of the murder being committed between 6.30 and 6.49, he did not establish the time of death.

> the evidence connecting this man with that message is strong evidence; the evidence that this woman was alive round about 6.30 is strong evidence; of what that man did when he came back to the house is strong evidence that he was not acting then as an innocent man. I also ask you, having regard to what had happened, when he saw Mr Beattie on that night of the 22nd, when he said: 'They have cleared me'; and Mr Beattie replied: 'I am glad to hear it.' What did he mean by that? Is that the attitude of a man who has known he is under suspicion?
>
> I am sorry to have detained you so long, but in a case of this length I have felt it my duty to lay before you in considerable detail what I submit is the case for the Crown."

Hemmerde's speech lasted an hour. It was just after midday when Justice Wright began his summing up:

> "Members of the Jury, we have now reached the last stage but one in this somewhat long, but not too long, trial. As you all know, the crime of murder means the premeditated and deliberate and wrongful and felonious killing of another person. There can be no doubt at all here, that this poor woman was done to death, by first, a very crushing blow, and then ten other blows."

Justice Wright then told the jury that he came here as a stranger, knowing nothing about the case, and that they must approach it in the same way[370] and without any preconceived notions at all:

> "Your business here is to listen to the evidence, and to consider the evidence and nothing else. You are not even entitled to act; in fact you would not act, upon the speeches of counsel.[371] You will come with an open and unprejudiced mind to consider this evidence which has been put before you.
>
> This murder, I should imagine, must be almost unexampled in the annals of crime. Here you have a murder so devised and arranged that nothing remains which would point to anyone as the murderer; no signs of forcible entry, no fingerprints, and other than the marks to the actual commission of the crime round the woman's head, no marks of blood anywhere in the house. It is a most remarkable murder, but there it is. There is certainly

370 It would seem problematic for the jury to have approached it in the same way as his Lordship, in that the case had been well reported in the Liverpool and surrounding area newspapers.

371 Surely a jury will be influenced by what is said by counsel one way or the other?

no eyewitness, and therefore, the evidence in this case is purely circumstantial. There is some circumstantial evidence which is as good and conclusive as the evidence of actual eyewitnesses. In other cases, the only circumstantial evidence which anyone can present still leaves loopholes and doubts. The real test of the value of circumstantial evidence is: Does it exclude every reasonable possibility? I can put it even higher: Does it exclude other theories or possibilities? Is it proved to your reasonable satisfaction and beyond all reasonable doubt that the prisoner did it?

With regard to motive I do not think I can say anything at all. All the evidence is that the prisoner and his wife, to all appearances, were living together in happiness. There was no pecuniary inducement that one can see for the prisoner to desire the death of his wife. There was nothing that he could gain, so far as one can see, by her death. It can also be pointed out that there is no one else, as far as can be seen, who had anything to gain by her death if you exclude the hypothesis of the unknown robber."

Justice Wright then came to the telephone message:

"Dealing with the main lines of evidence we start with January 19th, the day before the murder. It has been said that if you are satisfied beyond all reasonable doubt that it was the accused that sent that telephone call, a bogus call, in order to establish an alibi, then you have some ground upon which to proceed. The evidence upon this, as it is throughout, is purely circumstantial. Here is a kiosk 400 yards from the accused's house. The café waitress and the telephone operator both said the voice to them sounded like an ordinary voice, while Mr Beattie, who had known the prisoner for a great many years, said it was a strong, gruff, confident voice. When asked if the voice appeared to resemble the prisoner's, Mr Beattie said it did not, and by no stretch of imagination could he associate the voice he heard with that of the prisoner.

Before I leave this aspect of the case, let me say a word about the conversation a day or two afterwards when the prisoner asked Mr Beattie to be as definite as he could about the time when the telephone message was sent. It is said that was the mark of an uneasy conscience, and that point has been somewhat stressed. Well, it may be; but, on the other hand, if the prisoner was then already feeling that he was the subject of suspicion, he might perfectly well have made these enquiries simply to impress upon

> Mr Beattie the importance of being accurate if any question should arise. It would be very dangerous to draw any inference seriously adverse to the prisoner from that conversation."

Justice Wright then spoke of the events on the night of the tragedy:

> "It is a crime which involves apparently some speculation. It must have involved this woman going into the sitting-room, turning on the light and lighting the stove. There are two theories how she was struck. One of them is that she was sitting in the armchair by the fireplace and was struck down with a blow. On that view it is difficult to think that the assailant was the husband wearing a mackintosh if he was going out there and then. It then appears that the more probable reconstruction of the tragedy is that she was struck down when stooping over the fire. You have the burning of the skirt and the burning of the mackintosh."

Mr Wright came to the question of Wallace's uncertainty in identifying the mackintosh:

> "The prisoner never disowned the mackintosh. He drew Mrs Johnston's attention to it and said it was his own. He mentioned it to Police Constable Williams and after some doubt mentioned it to Superintendent Moore. One must be careful not to pay too much attention to these things. He had been, on that night, interviewed, and when reference is made to discrepancies in his statement, I cannot help thinking it is wonderful how his statements are as lucid and consistent as they have been.
>
> With regard to the blood on the pan, I think that may be disregarded. No one knows how it got there, and it is difficult to see how it has any connection with the murder. With regard to the smear of blood on the notes in the jar, I frankly confess that I cannot understand what inference is to be drawn from that. You have heard the evidence about it, and if you can draw any inference from it you will do so."

Mr Wright then came to the various time factors, referring to the tramcar journeys to Lodge Lane, pointing out that the experiments made varied from 15 to 20 minutes. He said the case for the prosecution was based entirely on the evidence of Close. His time was a reconstructed time and the defence had called two witnesses who contradicted the evidence of Close.

Mr Wright refuted Oliver's criticism of the police:

> "I cannot say I agree with the attack on the police, because I think they have done their duty with enthusiasm and ability; however I do think they were guilty of an error of judgement in not calling the two witnesses David Jones and the boy Wildman, for the prosecution.
>
> If you think that the time was something like 6.35 when Close delivered the milk, you get a very narrow limit of time for the prisoner, if it were the prisoner who did this, to do all that he must have done. You will have to consider very carefully whether the narrow limits of time allowed, possibly of not more than ten minutes, would be sufficient for the prisoner to carry out his purpose. It is perfectly true that if he planned and executed this scheme he would have had everything ready and everything would have gone, in the way of execution, with the utmost precision and rapidity. But there was a lot to do; therefore he must have worked with lightning rapidity and effectiveness."

Mr Wright referred to the medical evidence regarding the time of death and rigor mortis. He said that with the conflicting views, the jury may not think they could derive any assistance in that area. With regard to the weapon Mr Wright said that although Mrs Draper said two things were missing from the house, the jury had to consider whether the evidence afforded them any clue from which they could infer that the prisoner used one or the other of those possible weapons. How the weapon had been disposed of was a mystery.

His Lordship then came to Wallace's journey to Menlove Gardens:

> "The learned Recorder pointed out with considerable force, that it was very foolish for Wallace to go on like that, that he might have taken steps through his friends to see whether there was a Mr Qualtrough and a 25 Menlove Gardens East. The learned Recorder pointed out that if this was an alibi two things would be natural; first, that he should speak to his friends in such a way as would impress upon them that he was there at that time; and that he should tell the police as soon as the crime was discovered what he had been doing so that they could help him to establish his alibi. Of course that is a possible view, and you

> have to consider that. But it is one aspect of the case, and there is another view. If he was going quite honestly to search for Mr Qualtrough in Menlove Gardens East in the hope of getting a useful commission, having come so far he may not have gone home but probed the matter to the bottom. It may be that he was very foolish but on the other hand it is very difficult to say that his doing so points to his guilt."

On the subject of Wallace's return and the evidence of Lily Hall, Justice Wright had this to say:

> "She says she saw the prisoner at 8.35. The prisoner says he was not there, so it is word against word. Then we come to 8.45, when he came to the house. The prosecution says it is all a preconceived scheme and he faked the discovery of the crime. As to whether the front door was locked, you will remember the evidence. He said to Police Constable Williams that the front door was bolted. Williams said he did not hear any bolt drawn.
>
> When the prisoner got in, various criticisms have been made as to what he did; he went through the kitchen and found no one there, and then he went upstairs; then he did not go to the sitting-room until after he had been upstairs. It is not very easy to see what significance can be attached to that, or indeed to the fact that he lighted the right-hand jet instead of the left-hand jet. It is difficult to see that any idea can be obtained of his guilt from the mere fact that he did not step on the body or step in the blood. I have not heard that any one of the police officers or doctors did actually step in the blood, and if they did not I do not see why he should.
>
> In conclusion, I will only remind you what the question you have to determine is. Can you have any doubt that the prisoner did do it? You may well think: 'Well, someone did it.' Human nature is very strange. You may have a man send a bogus message and having sent the message he might go to the house and be admitted by Mrs Wallace. If she had been told that the prisoner was seeking an interview with Qualtrough, and if he was admitted, he would soon find out where the prisoner was, and find out that he was not in the house. On the other hand, if he found out he was in the house he could go away. It is difficult to see how the man could have got away leaving no trace; it is equally difficult with regard to the prisoner. However you regard the matter, the whole crime was so skilfully devised and so skilfully executed, and there is

> such an absence of any trace to incriminate anybody, as to make it very difficult to say, although it is a matter entirely for you, that it can be brought home to anybody in particular.[372]
>
> If there was an unknown murderer, he has covered up his traces. Can you say it is absolutely impossible that there was no such person? But putting that aside as not being the real question, can you say, taking all this evidence as a whole, bearing in mind the strength of the case put forward by the police and the prosecution, that you are satisfied beyond reasonable doubt that it was the hand of the prisoner, and no other hand that murdered this woman? If you are not so satisfied, whatever your suspicions may be, if it is not established to your reasonable satisfaction as a matter of evidence then it is your duty to find the prisoner not guilty. Of course, if you are satisfied, equally it is your duty to find him guilty. But it is your duty to decide on the evidence which has been given before you during these three days, and, whatever your verdict is, that is the acid test which you must apply. Will you consider your verdict and say whether you find the prisoner guilty or not guilty?"

The jury[373] retired at 1.20. As they were leaving the box the two women members were in tears, one holding a handkerchief to her eyes.

With regard to Wallace's demeanour during the trial, the

372 There can be no doubt that Mr Wright's summing-up was in favour of Wallace.

373 During the trial the jury members were put up at the North Western Hotel (opposite St George's Hall) and were walked to it escorted by the bailiffs every day. Their evenings were their own, except that they were not allowed to mix with the public. They were not allowed visits from relatives or friends, but were entitled to receive and write letters. They spent the evening in playing cards (whist and bridge being popular) or reading. If they expressed a wish for fresh air a charabanc was procured and they would be taken out for an airing en masse. At the luncheon adjournment the jury was shepherded to its own room in St George's Hall, where lunch would be served under the strictest surveillance of the two court bailiffs, one of whom, a lady, was authorised to look after the needs of the two ladies serving in the case. The bailiff's job was an extremely serious one – they alone were responsible to the Sheriff and the Court for their charges; it was their duty to be continually on the watch in case any person attempted to get into conversation with the jury whilst they were leaving the court. They had to keep a strict and continuous watch in case messages of some sort were smuggled to their charges. The pains and penalties to which a member of the public would be liable should they have attempted to corrupt one of the twelve were very severe. Even to hold conversation with a member of the jury would have involved commitment for contempt of court. This was in evidence in the case of the old beggar woman on the evening of 23rd April. Even when they retired for the night the responsibility of the court bailiffs was not over. It was their duty to lock each member in his or her room for the night, and to see that no attempt was made to stir from their rooms. It wasn't only the jury that were kept under close scrutiny. When the trial date arrived all the young witnesses were taken to a large games room at the top of St George's Hall. There they were allowed to go out for lunch, but other than that, they were confined to the room.

Liverpool Echo reported:

> 'Never once during the trial did it appear to those who watched him closely and continuously that Wallace could be brought to display the slightest sign of emotion. His outward attitude was that of a man resigned to whatever fate might have in store for him. His customary attitude – his arms folded his head slightly on one side as though with weariness – remained unchanged. The many references to his dead wife left him apparently unmoved. The details of her death appeared to affect him not a whit. Only when Mr Justice Wright commenced his low voiced summing-up did Wallace betray any sign that he was more than an ordinary spectator of the drama. He leaned forward more intently, his right arm doubled up beneath him on the rail of the dock, his fist clasped beneath his chin, listening closely to all that the judge said.'[374]

As Justice Wright left the court a large body of spectators, half of whom were women, broke into a buzz of conversation. They were silenced on two occasions by court ushers, but as the fateful moments crept by people could not refrain from talking and gradually the hum broke into a crescendo in which men's and women's voices were mingled. The impression was heightened by the Judge's empty bench, the empty witness box, and the knowledge that now was the time above all others that a man's life hung in the balance. The conversation was grim. A man in the distinguished visitors' gallery remarked to a fellow spectator; "Have you ever seen the black cap donned?" "No, never," was the reply. "I have been to four trials for murder, and they have always got off."

It seemed all of Anfield was present in the public gallery, some even taking refreshment in the form of apples, oranges or a sandwich. The general consensus among the Press was the verdict would be one of acquittal.

The appearance of an usher in Court at 2.20 was the signal for a burst of renewed excitement on the part of the crowd in the court. A door clanged in the Press box. There was an audible gasp, nerves strung to fever pitch. The usher told the court officials that the jury

374 *Liverpool Echo*, 25th April 1931.

was ready to return.

The Clerk of Assize, W.J.H. Graham, then returned to his seat in the court and the jury filed slowly into their places in the box, one of them casting a furtive glance at Wallace, who had quietly re-entered the dock. Headed by the two women jurors, it appeared at once that their demeanour was most serious. After the Clerk of Assize had called the roll of jurors the court awaited the entrance of Justice Wright. He appeared almost immediately, followed by the High Sheriff, the High Sheriff's Chaplain, and the Under Sheriff.

Wallace, hands clasped behind his back, stood with a warder on each side and another warder behind him. The chief warder was also in attendance. "Optimistic, eh?" he uttered to Wallace who, carrying his hat and overcoat, gave a slight nod in reply. The Medical Officer at Walton Gaol, Dr Higson, sat in a corner of the dock. The Clerk of Assize, having ascertained who would speak as the jury's foreman was answered by one of the jurymen, who stood up in the middle of the front row:

The Clerk of Assize: "Gentlemen of the Jury, are you agreed upon your verdict?"

A rustle of papers could be heard from one of the solicitor's clerks.

The Foreman of the Jury: "We are."

The Clerk of Assize: "Do you find the prisoner Guilty, or Not Guilty of murder?"

The Foreman of the Jury: "Guilty."

Wallace swayed. There was an audible gasp around the Court. Someone at the back whistled in surprise. The noise was promptly suppressed by court officials.

The Clerk of Assize then spoke.

"Prisoner at the Bar, you have been arraigned upon a charge of murder, and have placed yourself upon your country. That country has now found you guilty. Have you anything to say why judgement of death should not be pronounced upon you, and why you should not die according to law?"

There was complete silence in the court. Everyone present was anticipating the guilty man's reply.

In a firm voice, Wallace replied: "I am not guilty. I don't want to say anything else."

The Judge's clerk placed the black cap over Mr Wright's head. Then sentence was passed:

> "William Herbert Wallace, the Jury, after a very careful hearing, have found you guilty of the murder of your wife. For the crime of murder by the law of this country there is only one sentence, and that sentence I now pass upon you. It is that you be taken from hence to a place of lawful execution, and you be there hanged by the neck until you be dead, and that your body be afterwards buried within the precincts of the prison in which you shall last have been confined. And may the Lord have mercy on your soul."

The High Sheriff's Chaplain, Canon Dwelly added: "Amen."

Wallace appeared as calm as he had throughout the trial.[375] He turned slowly and walked down the dock steps, still with his hands clasped behind his back. One warder preceded him as he walked slowly out of view. As he reached the lower steps before going to the cells, Dr Higson placed a hand on his arm, helping him gently along. There was another burst of conversation among the crowd in court, but silence was quickly restored.

Justice Wright, addressing the jury, said that they had had a very arduous sitting, and recommended that they should be exempted from further jury service for the next seven years. It was noteworthy that in passing sentence the judge did not make any comment about being in agreement with their verdict. Wallace was hustled down the steps into a cell below where dinner was brought to him, but he could eat nothing.

In the public gallery there was a rush for the exits, but the police officers had anticipated it and the passage of people onto the plateau had been controlled. The majority dispersed quietly, but others stood in groups talking excitedly. Large crowds of people who were unable to gain admission to the court when the trial

375 Wallace would later say that it was at the point when he had been sentenced and just before he was taken to prison that his stoicism could not be maintained.

resumed that morning had waited outside in the hope of gleaning some account of the progress of the proceedings. With the first rush of people through the great doors of the Hall they clamoured forward to inquire of the jury's verdict. The cries of newsboys echoed around: "Wallace Verdict...Wallace to Hang."

As Justice Wright left St George's Hall,[376] the Assize trumpeters played the National Anthem, and the large crowds who lined the streets outside bared their heads.

The prison van carrying Wallace emerged from the entrance gate almost unnoticed. He was driven back to Walton Gaol, where he was taken direct to the cell reserved for those prisoners condemned to death and dressed in the grey uniform of a prisoner awaiting execution.

Governor of Walton Gaol Major A.C.H. Benke[377] notified the Prison Commissioners, requesting a list of possible candidates for the office of executioner.[378]

376 During the trial Justice Wright stayed at the judge's residence in Newsham Park. Situated in the grounds of the sweeping arc of Judge's Drive (and a few hundred yards from the tram stop near St Margaret's Church on the corner of Belmont Road), Newsham House was built by Thomas Molyneux. In 1868 it was altered and enlarged to accommodate the judges and their staff when staying in Liverpool during the Assizes. It has 26 rooms, 17 of which are bedrooms. The Blue Room was used by Queen Victoria. Other notables who stayed there were George V and the Shah of Persia.

377 Augustus Charles Herbert Benke was born in Galway in 1889. Prior to his appointment as Governor of Walton he was Governor of Pentonville Prison 1925-30.

378 Lionel Sydney Mann was recommended for the role of Assistant Executioner.

6

THE APPEAL

Wallace spent a restless night in the condemned cell, tossing and turning but unable to sleep. There, he was watched over by the two warders who were sitting in easy chairs reading (they would work eight-hour shifts). The size of the main cell was some thirteen feet by ten or eleven. A small adjoining cell contained a bath, lavatory and wash-basin, and a gas-ring on which to boil a kettle. The main cell contained a bed, a fair-sized table and three easy armchairs. The floor of stone tiles was covered with a carpet. The walls were white distempered. From the cell a door led into another, smaller cell, where Wallace was allowed to see visitors, although no one was permitted to come within touching distance of a prisoner condemned to death, for obvious reasons. The visitor sat in another cell. A glass window surrounded by close-meshed double wire gauze through which conversation was perfectly audible was let into the wall between. The two warders always sat with the prisoner, and the visitor had one attendant officer.

There was a complete change in diet and the restrictions which Wallace had previously been used to. The medical officer now permitted him to have all he might reasonably desire in the way of varied food. Although he didn't drink to excess, avid smoker Wallace must have been relieved to learn that he was now permitted to smoke a daily allowance of ten cigarettes. Smoking was completely forbidden in every other part of the prison. He could also write as many letters as he pleased, subject of course to the usual censorship regulations, and this he did. He also spent a lot of time reading. A chessboard and pieces were brought in, and Wallace even taught one warder the basics of the game. Ring board and quoits were two games he also played with the warders in his cell (Wallace later claimed with pride that he was never beaten playing ring board in the cell).

His daily routine began with breakfast at about 7.00am. This consisted of porridge and milk, bacon and eggs, tea and bread and butter. Wallace would also make his own bed. He would then have a friendly chat with the changed guard, who had relieved the other two watchers at six thirty. About eight o'clock one of the chief officers would look in and ask if everything was all right. At nine-thirty the medical officer would come along with a similar query: "Everything all right? Anything I can do? Anything you want?" Between ten-thirty and eleven o'clock, the Governor of the jail, accompanied by one of the chief officers, would come into the cell and make a kindly inquiry: "Anything you want? Sure you're quite all right? Anything I can do for you?" Wallace was treated extremely well by the prison staff, for which he was very grateful.

Midday brought dinner, which might be boiled mutton, cabbage and potatoes. The prisoner was not allowed the use of a knife or fork, however; everything was cut up, with Wallace only being permitted the use of a spoon. A generous-sized rice pudding completed the meal. Another day it might be beef or minced meat or a stew, and the vegetables, too, would be varied. There would be another change of guard at half past two. When Wallace took a bath the warders would stand just outside the open door of the little cell, making themselves as unobtrusive as the regulations permitted. About three o'clock visitors usually arrived, and Wallace was allowed a half-hour interview each day. These visits would lift Wallace's spirits.

Four o'clock would see tea served (which was referred to as 'supper' in prison). This consisted of a plate of bread and butter, a boiled egg, a small portion of jam and a quart of tea in a large jug. The crockery necessary for all meals was kept in the main cell and Wallace himself did the washing-up. The warders, who brought their meals with them, often joined him, and very often handed him pieces of cake. As the quantity of food supplied was generally more than plenty, Wallace frequently saved some to eat at a later hour, making use of the kettle to re-heat the tea or brew some fresh from the officers' private store.

Weather permitting, another walk of an hour's duration followed this afternoon supper. During these walks Wallace would walk back and forth along a garden path alongside what was known as 'the Ropery,' looking at the hollyhocks, irises, delphiniums, and other flowers in bud, wondering if they would be in flower before he died. Before leaving his cell, every precaution was taken to see that all other prisoners were safe in their cells, and no-one with the exception of the uniformed staff ever succeeded in catching a glimpse of Wallace. A second visit from the Governor and the doctor followed. On returning to his cell at approximately six to six-thirty, Wallace would play a game of chess or ring quoits or sit quietly reading until any time after eight o'clock. At that time a cup of tea was usually served. Wallace would discuss many topics with the warders; they would recount many interesting episodes of life in the service. At half-past ten another change of guard took place, the last for the day. In the death cell a prisoner would be permitted to retire to bed when he liked, and being something of a night owl Wallace took advantage of the privilege.

On 27th April Liverpool City Police received a letter from Redcar, North Yorkshire. It was from Julia's nearest surviving relative, George Smith Dennis. He was enquiring about the belongings of his late sister and in particular the £90 in her savings account, of which he had read in the newspapers. Smith was referred to Herbert J. Davis, Berthen and Munro regarding the matter. On the same day Hector Munro informed the *Evening Express* that an appeal[379] would be made on the grounds that the verdict was against the weight of the evidence. In actual fact, the draft written out listed ten points with numerous sub-divisions, which included possible

379 A convicted person had to lodge application for appeal against conviction within ten days from the sentence.

misdirection by Justice Wright, prejudice by the Prosecution, that the Judge should have withdrawn the case from the jury, and that Professor MacFall had no right to force his opinion onto the jury regarding frenzy. The papers were subsequently signed by Wallace in Walton Gaol.

The date and time of Wallace's execution was provisionally set for 12th May at 8.00am. The discontinuance of the practice of tolling the bell was approved by the prison authorities.

On 30th April, Assistant Chief Constable Herbert Winstanley notified the Director of Public Prosecutions that Wallace had been found Guilty and sentenced to death.

On 1st May a front page appeal appeared on both the *Echo* and *Daily Post & Mercury* newspapers. A Committee[380] was formed for the purpose of raising funds in aid of Wallace. On the following day, the *Evening Express* reported that Wallace's appeal would be heard on Monday 18th May at the Court of Criminal Appeal in London.

On 2nd May Louis Curwen[381] was interviewed by Sergeant Harry Bailey. Curwen, who had been the Wallace's doctor for five years, said that he had thought the matter over since the tragedy and came to the conclusion that the Wallaces didn't appear to be the happy couple that others supposed they were.

There was an influx of letters in the press voicing the concerns of their writers and injustice at the verdict. Meanwhile a story was circulating that Wallace was on hunger strike, but these rumours were quashed by the prison authorities. Senior Medical Officer William Davies Higson said that Wallace had requested extra food to the ordinary hospital diet. Hector Munro claimed the reports were absurd.

Wallace requested a list of books,[382] but to his disappointment he could not obtain 'The Golden Book of all Books' – his copy of *Meditations* by Marcus Aurelius.

380 Apart from Wallace's brother Joseph, the Appeal Fund Committee was made of Mrs Norman Fraser, R.W. Sawney, Duncan S. Davies and E. Norman Torry.

381 Curwen had been subpoenaed by the defence and attended the trial, but did not give evidence.

382 Some of these fourteen titles covered the subjects of chess, science, physics and astronomy.

On Friday 15th May Norman Wheeler visited Wallace at Walton (and had done so on an almost daily basis). Wallace, who was cheerful, was confident that the Court of Appeal would reverse the verdict. Being the avowed agnostic, he refused to see a Parson the whole time he was in prison.

On Saturday 16th May, handcuffed and dressed in civilian clothes Wallace was driven to Lime Street Station by taxicab (Detective Superintendent Moore and other officials of the police had left for London the day before). A number of railway officials and a few members of the public were present on the platform as Wallace was taken to a reserved carriage near the front of the train. On arrival at Euston he was driven to Pentonville Prison, where he was taken to the customary reception office. On the floor was spread a large, coarse white sheet, on which stood a small chair. Wallace was ordered to strip completely. Silently, Wallace discarded his clothing. In front of him stood the official whose duty it was to search him, together with the Chief Officer and the Deputy Governor of the prison. Once stripped, a search of Wallace's person was made. His hair was combed thoroughly, hands passed over the ears, under the armpits, down the legs, under the soles of the feet, and even between the toes. Wallace was then dressed in the blue uniform of an appellant and marched off to the condemned cell.

The following day special prayers under the aegis of Canon Dwelly were given at the Anglican Cathedral in Liverpool. Described as 'intercessions extraordinary', these were offered during the morning, afternoon and evening services, and were fully endorsed by the Bishop of Liverpool Dr David. They read:

> "You shall pray for them that are set by God's mercy to secure the administration of true justice in our land. Particularly this day you shall pray for his Majesty's Judges of Appeal, that they may be guided in true judgement. And you shall pray for the learned counsels of our Sovereign Lord the King, that they may be faithful to the Christian injunction of the apostle Paul: 'Judge nothing until God brings to light hidden things of darkness and makes manifest the counsels of the heart.' And you shall pray for the people of this County Palatine that their confidence in

> the fair dealings of their fellow man may be restored – and that truth and justice, religion and piety may be established among us. Finally, you shall pray for all who await the judgement of their fellow man, and commit them to the perfect justice of Almighty God."

The prayers were not confined to the Cathedral; they were also offered up in other Nonconformist churches.

The proceedings opened on Monday 18th May 1931 at the Royal Courts of Justice, the Strand.[383]

Since its inception in 1907, the Court of Criminal Appeal had never overturned a verdict on the grounds that it could not be supported with regard to the evidence. There was also another concern for the supporters of Wallace; overseeing the proceedings would be Lord Chief Justice Hewart,[384] who happened to be one of the most vociferous proponents of the jury system. Despite these obstacles Wallace remained optimistic. Accompanying Hewart were Justices Branson[385] and Hawke.[386]

As at the trial, Roland Oliver K.C. and Sydney Scholefield Allen would be representing Wallace. Edward Hemmerde K.C. and Leslie Walsh would be appearing on behalf of the Crown.

Liverpool Chief Constable Lionel Everett was not at the Appeal, but was represented by J.R. Bishop. Also in attendance were Detective Superintendent Hubert Moore and Detective Inspector Herbert Gold.

Wallace was ushered into the court, his being the second appeal

383 Opened by Queen Victoria on 4th December 1882. At the time the buildings comprised twenty law courts, over 1,000 rooms and nine miles of corridors.

384 A native of Bury, Gordon Hewart was a journalist before he became a barrister. He practised as a Manchester local with considerable success. Called to the Bar, Inner Temple in 1902 he became Lord Chief Justice of England in 1921. A somewhat controversial character, he was famous for his feuds in the 1920s and '30s, as well as his changes in politics. It was said that he made up his mind early, could be rude to counsel and lacked many basic judicial qualities.

385 The grandfather of businessman Richard Branson, George Arthur Harwin Branson was educated at Trinity College Cambridge. He was called to the Bar, Inner Temple in 1899 and was Junior Counsel to the Treasury 1912-21. From 1921-39 he was a judge at the High Court of Justice, King's Bench Division. In 1929 Branson's cousin Olive was found shot through the head and dumped in a water tank near her home in Les Baux, just outside of Marseille. It was first thought to be suicide, but French police believed it murder. Miss Branson's lover François Pinet was arrested and stood trial but was acquitted.

386 John Anthony Hawke was called to the Bar, Middle Temple in 1892. He became a Judge of the King's Bench Division in 1928.

that morning.[387]

The lofty, dimly-lit court was crowded when Wallace, dressed in sombre garb, entered from an opening at the rear of the dock. He stood for a moment or two then was permitted to sit. He took his seat between two warders. The public gallery – the largest in the Law Courts – was thronged with spectators who followed with keen interest the drama which was being enacted, among them members of the Bar, law students, friends of Wallace and some of the general public. Interest had been stimulated further by the reports of the previous day's intercessions at Liverpool Cathedral.

Shortly after 11.00am Roland Oliver rose to give his speech. He said the notice of appeal before the court comprised many grounds, but insofar as those grounds consisted of criticisms upon the summing up, he said at once that several of them were misconceived. He wanted the court to know that when the notice of appeal was drawn up, no transcript of the shorthand note of the summing up was available and criticisms were made which he would not now seek to support.

The main ground of the appeal might be put in various ways. It might be said that the prosecution never sustained the onus of proof. It could be said that the evidence, taken as a whole, was consistent with guilt or with innocence, or it might be said that as the prosecution were relying on circumstantial evidence; that circumstantial evidence must at least be sufficient to exclude the possibility of someone other than the appellant having committed the crime.

Whatever formula was used, the real ground of the appeal was that a man who might well be innocent had been convicted of murder and sentenced to death. Referring to Justice Wright's summing up, Oliver said that if the statement of law given was correct, the case should never have gone to the jury.

There was certainly no eyewitness of the murder except the

387 The first was the appeal of 23-year-old Alexander Anastassiou, a Cypriot who had been convicted at the Central Criminal Court for the murder of waitress Evelyn Victoria Holt at Warren Street, London on 26th February 1931. His appeal was unsuccessful and he was hanged at Pentonville Prison on 3rd June 1931.

murdered and the murderer, therefore the evidence was purely circumstantial. Justice Wright had directed the jury on the value of such evidence, and Oliver said that was the direction he wished to take:

> "Mr Justice Wright had said that the real test of the value of circumstantial evidence was whether it excluded every reasonable possibility of anyone else, except the accused, having committed the murder. If the circumstances in this case, as I hope to persuade the court, were such that they did not exclude every reasonable possibility, then the jury ought not to have been allowed to find Wallace guilty."

Lord Hewart: "You say that the case ought to have been withdrawn from the jury?"

Oliver: "Yes, I am saying that."

"But no submission of the kind was made to the judge."

"No, with the jury I had before me I did not wish to make that submission, and assumed that if Justice Wright had been of the opinion he himself would have withdrawn the case."

Oliver said that no support for the case for the prosecution was obtained from Wallace. No admission of any sort, no further material to assist the prosecution was obtained from him in the witness box. No semblance of a motive existed for the murder, which had been a cold-blooded and callous one, carried out with extreme ferocity.

> "The evidence was that Wallace was a placid man with no sort of violence about him," said Oliver, "and yet it is said that he battered his wife to death as the result of a plot at least 24 hours old."

Oliver then came to the telephone message:

> "Someone rang up a chess club in a restaurant about 400 yards from Wallace's house and left a message for Wallace to call on a man at Menlove Gardens the following evening which may have resulted in business. It afterwards turned out that the address was non-existent and that the message was bogus."

Oliver said it was the case for the prosecution that Wallace sent the telephone message himself, but in actual fact there wasn't a shred of evidence to support this notion. On the contrary, Samuel Beattie had known Wallace for eight years, and said the voice he heard on the telephone was nothing like that of Wallace.

The *Daily Post and Mercury* reported that:

> "Wallace sat quietly. Occasionally he looked around the court and once for several moments ran his eyes over the bookshelves at the side of the bench. For the most part, he gave his council all his attention, his chin resting on his hand, and his hand gripping the ledge of the little gallery where the appellant sits."

In the Court of Appeal, Wallace was no longer the 'defendant' or 'prisoner'; it was the procedure to refer to him as 'the appellant.'[388]

Oliver produced the large ordnance map[389] and explained the two different routes which had been drawn on it. He said that Wallace left the house at about 6.45 and was recognised at 7.06 at the tram stop on Smithdown Lane. From there he went to Menlove Gardens, which he reached at about 7.20. He made enquiries in the area until about 8.00pm, trying to find the address of the man who had sent him the message.

At 8.45 he was seen outside the back of his house by his neighbours, the Johnstons. He was unable to gain entry. They waited whilst he succeeded in getting in, where he discovered his wife. Oliver said that it was the suggestion of the prosecution that the difficulty Wallace had in gaining admission to the house was feigned, but what the object was in pretending he could not get in was never made clear by the prosecution: "If he wanted a companion when entering the house, one would have thought he would have roused his neighbours instead of waiting outside."

After describing the position and condition in which the body was found, Oliver said the prosecution argued that, because blood marks were found on the notes upstairs, the murderer must have had knowledge of the internal ways of the house and would be careful to leave very little blood marks. That view was entirely disposed of in any fair view of the evidence.

388 *Daily Post & Mercury*, 19th May 1931.
389 Exhibit 50.

Oliver then dealt with the absence of bloodstained clothing: "It would have been impossible for any clothing to have been washed or destroyed by Wallace between 6.30 and 6.45."

At the trial, the prosecution for the first time suggested that the assailant was naked but covered with a mackintosh. That showed how the hopeless difficulty about the clothing had impressed itself on the prosecution.

> "The fact that the mackintosh was burned on the right side and that Mrs Wallace's skirt was burned also was consistent with her having put the mackintosh over her shoulders when opening the door to the man who had decoyed her husband away, and had fallen on the gas fire when she was attacked."

Oliver said that he had never known a case where so many statements were taken from an accused man as in this case, and alluded to Justice Wright's remark of how wonderfully consistent they were.

> "No jury could say that it was impossible that some criminal, knowing Mr Wallace might be expected to be in possession of between £30 and £100, had the means of knowing where the appellant would likely be on the evening of the 19th, the evening when the message was sent, having the means of watching him leave the house, and being, if he were watching him, then in the position to go and use the very telephone box that was used.
>
> If that were so, the prosecution had not satisfied the onus of proof that was upon them. It was often said that juries could be trusted not to go wrong in matters of that kind. But in that case which had been a nine days wonder in the Liverpool district, and in which reports of the police court proceedings had been circulated by and large, it was as certain as could be that if not the whole, then a majority of the jurors had read and steeped themselves in the prosecution, little dreaming that they would ever be called upon to be jurymen."

Oliver said that some of the jury members must have formed their own ideas one way or the other before they even knew they would be trying the accused, and that they must have had their minds set and not decided by evidence at the trial. Wallace and his wife lived on the best of terms, and the testimony of witnesses called at the trial showed that they were a happy couple and that they appeared to be all in all to one another.

Wallace's own diary did not suggest that their relations were otherwise than perfect. He had about £150 in the bank, and there was no suggestion at all that there was another woman in the case. No motive was found regarding any of these matters. Oliver said that there might well have been a motive for another person. The mere fact that Wallace might have been supposed to have money in the house would have furnished a motive for another person. In fact a small sum – £4 – was missing.

Oliver said that he made a serious complaint with regards the evidence of MacFall, and that the Professor went out of his way to force on the court and jury the view that the blows which killed the woman were those by a frenzied man, who was insane.

Lord Hewart: "Suppose for a moment that this witness was right in inferring from the blows that the person who had committed the crime was in a frenzy, how does that theory point to Wallace more than to somebody else?"

Oliver: "The person who did this murder had planned it, and what this witness was obviously trying to do was to let the jury know that..."

"I was not putting the point against you."

"I appreciate that, and I should suggest that the whole of this was most mischievous. The police did press this case. I suggest that this was introduced in a spirit of malevolence. No, malevolence would be wrong; I withdraw that and substitute zeal."

Wallace closely followed the proceedings, his chin resting on his right hand.

Continuing, Oliver said that much had been made at the trial about Wallace's demeanour on the night of the murder, yet there was no mention of it at the Committal Proceedings:

> "Detective Superintendent Moore, Professor MacFall and the rest of them who were called at the Police Court, had not one word to say about the Appellant's demeanour, yet at the trial, the same

> witnesses commented about his cool, calm and callous manner. It was most mischievous and most unfair."

Oliver said that there were certain facts which were absolutely crucial, the first being: 'Who sent the telephone message, or rather, did the prosecution prove that the appellant sent the telephone message?' If he did, he is guilty. If he did not, he is innocent. The second vital fact is this: 'At what time was Mrs Wallace last seen alive?' Oliver submitted that there were many reputable witnesses who could have given evidence that she was seen alive considerably later than 6.30, but the police did not call them. Instead, they elected to stand on the evidence of one little milkboy, the whole of whose evidence depended on his reliability when he said that, going round with the milk, he noticed the time by a certain clock. It was left for the defence to call the other evidence.

"The prosecution never got within arm's-length of what is called proof. At every stage of the case all the prosecution did was say; 'You might have done. It is consistent with your having done.' Surely I am entitled to insist that the prosecution prove their case," said Oliver.

Reverting to the milkboy's evidence, Oliver said that within twenty-four hours of the murder, Close told three other people that he had seen Mrs Wallace alive at about 6.45. A newspaper which was put through the letterbox at about 6.30 was later found on the table.

"Was it suggested that after committing the murder," said Oliver, "Wallace had taken the paper and laid it on the table?"

Oliver suggested that in this case, the jury were inflamed against Wallace by the way in which it was pressed. He said that it had been conducted in an oppressive manner:

"If you are in any doubt as to whether there was a miscarriage of justice or not, that is a matter to which weight must be given."

Oliver submitted that the evidence showed that the 6.30 time given by Close was questionable. At the time it was reported in the Press that Wallace left the house at about 6.15.

The Court adjourned for lunch.

Continuing his speech, Oliver examined in detail the evidence given by James Allison Wildman and Elsie Wright then came to the tram tests conducted by the police:

> "These young people covered the distance from 17 to 20 minutes, and one, by following a different route, did it in 15 minutes but I ignore these times as they do not apply.[390] Were the jury intended to understand that Wallace, an elderly man, rushed straight from the horrible murder of his wife, without waiting to cleanse himself or his clothing, and jumped straight on a tram?"[391]

The Lord Chief Justice: "You say 'elderly.' He is only 52."

Oliver: "Yes, my Lord, I said so because I am approaching that time of life myself."

Justice Branson: "It looks different when you are approaching it from what it does when you have passed it."[392]

Oliver continued: "The time at which he reached the Lodge Lane point was fixed at 7.06 as near as could be, and Wallace must have left his house at 6.45 or thereabouts."

With regards the time of Mrs Wallace's death, Oliver submitted that all the prosecution could say was that she might possibly have been alive at the time when Wallace was in the house. That, he averred, did not even begin to go in the direction of proof.

As for Wallace spending time looking for the address in Menlove Gardens, Oliver submitted that it was reasonable, as it had been suggested by the telephone call, that there was valuable business to be gained. The evidence was consistent with seeking a man who could give him such business.

Oliver said that the evidence of Lily Hall should not have been taken seriously:

> "She had every reason to exercise her imagination after this event had happened, which must have stirred the whole of this neighbourhood. There is a type of mentality which likes to be

390 They most certainly can be applied to the case.

391 Wallace, being a collection agent, was used to walking. He had spent nearly 16 years of his life walking his rounds.

392 Amid the sombre surroundings of the Law Courts and the seriousness of the occasion this was the one instance of humour over the two days.

associated with stirring events."[393]

In dealing with the suggestion that the alibi was a fictitious one, Oliver questioned why Wallace would try to establish an alibi at the end of the final tram journey and not at the start of the first one.[394]

> "In my submission what one looks for in this case and completely fails to find is any piece of evidence which is not consistent with innocence. If that be the result of the investigation of the evidence, then, in my submission, this verdict is unreasonable and cannot be supported, having regard to the evidence. There is grave danger that there may have been a miscarriage of justice.

393 Whenever a murder occurs the usual phenomenon arises – namely that of the publicity seeker, and the Wallace murder was no different. It attracted its fair share of crank attention-seekers. The evidence of Lilian Hall should have been dismissed. At the trial she not only got the time that she claimed to have seen Wallace and the stranger wrong, but also the day. The idea that Wallace would be seen talking to someone in the area and not admit it was highly unlikely. It would have been the ideal scenario for him to establish his whereabouts at the exact time, yet he did not. He would have had no reason to deny encountering an acquaintance. If, as the prosecution suggested, Wallace was going out of his way to make his return noticed, it would seem strange that he would give up such an opportunity. On 20th April 32-year-old James Gilmore walked into the Walton Bridewell and confessed to the murder of Julia Wallace. He was examined the following day. Found to be suffering from delusions, he was removed to Mill Road Hospital. On the 23rd he was sent to Rainhill Mental Hospital. On 14th May, 32-year-old Ian Forbes walked into Prescot Street Bridewell and also confessed to the murder. He was examined by the Bridewell surgeon and found to be delusional (and had been for some time, according to his family). He was sent to Mill Road Institution. Robert Carr of Moss Grove said that he encountered a man and woman in Scotland Road at about 8.10 on the night of the killing. He claimed they asked him where the landing stage was, and that both appeared peculiar in their actions. Carr later claimed that it was Wallace he had spoken to, and that the woman accompanying him was Wallace's sister-in-law Amy. Carr based this whole pretence on the second part of Wallace's John Bull articles, claiming three photos that appeared accompanying that article were those of Wallace, Julia and Amy Wallace. The three photographs weren't even photographs but merely illustrations, and certainly not those of Julia or Amy Wallace. Carr was still fantasising about his sighting nearly three years after the event. At the time of the murder 21-year-old John Parkes was a garage hand at Atkinson's Garage, Moscow Drive in the Stoneycroft area of Old Swan. Parkes lived a street away from Richard Gordon Parry. They were not friends, but well-acquainted and had attended the nearby Lister Drive School together. In 1980 Parkes claimed Parry drove a bloodstained car into the garage in the early hours of 20th/21st January 1931 and ordered him to hose down the car, during which time Parkes noticed a bloodstained glove. Parry snatched it from him, claiming that if it was found, it would hang him. There is nothing at all to substantiate this nonsense except the word of an elderly man fifty years after the event in question. I have accessed all the police files, defence records and archive files, and there is nothing amongst any of them to corroborate the so called evidence of John Parkes – no statements or police interviews whatsoever. The whole premise of Parry indulging in a midnight flit in a bloodstained car is ludicrous.

394 It could be said that Wallace knew the first leg of the journey to Smithdown Lane, therefore did not try to establish his whereabouts. There is also the possibility that he might well have tried to establish his whereabouts. It just might have been that the conductor did not remember Wallace.

> This court has on many occasions upset the verdict of juries on that very ground."

Oliver submitted that a verdict which shocked the sense of justice could not stand, and complained with regard to the naked man in the mackintosh; it was first advanced in court, and the defence, having had no notice, were unable to examine the garment properly. Oliver said that a hostile interruption by a juryman during his opening speech showed how much the production of the mackintosh had affected the jury. But what happened to the mackintosh was purely speculation. The police theory was that the murderer was naked except for the mackintosh, but the evidence he submitted was entirely in favour of it having been worn by the victim and burnt when she fell near the gas fire.

With regards the iron bar, Oliver suggested that it would be logical for an outside killer to take the weapon away with him, due to the possibility of bloodied fingerprints left upon it.

Oliver had been speaking for 3½ hours when he began to deal with the evidence given by Mrs Johnston. He said that Wallace had admitted ownership of the mackintosh to four people, three of whom were police officers. Yet the prosecution made it a strong point against him that, when three other officers subsequently demanded to know whose garment it was, he hesitated:

"Points like that, put forward by responsible counsel to a jury who, for any reason were not well disposed towards a prisoner were noticed. That sort of point was made and pressed against the appellant to the end of the case."

Oliver apologised for taking up so much time, but said he was compelled to go into every matter. "You cannot have a man convicted of murder on this sort of thing."

Oliver's speech had lasted nearly four hours.

The case was adjourned until the following day.

TUESDAY 19 MAY 1931

The second day of the appeal would see Hemmerde's reply.

Wallace again closely followed the proceedings with great interest. The court was crowded and even the gangways were packed.

Hemmerde dealt with points raised by Oliver the previous day, commenting on his claim that a member of the jury interrupted him:

> "One of the jury then said something which he heard, but neither I nor my learned junior heard. He will not mind my saying that he had made a really strong attack on the Professor, and that it was not perhaps surprising that someone may have resented it."[395]

Hemmerde said he could not understand where Oliver got his idea that the jury were not particularly friendly or prejudiced. In fact, Hemmerde made the point that the jury were chosen at the request of the defence, from the surrounding areas:

> "They came from Widnes, Southport and Warrington. There could be no question that I was talking to a jury of the city of Liverpool. It was a jury of the County of Lancaster."[396]

Hemmerde referred to the suggestion that the prosecution refused to help the defence by withholding statements made by various witnesses. He said that all the statements that were considered serious were shown to the defence:

> "In a case like this, the most extraordinary and wild statements are made by people of questionable sanity."[397]

Continuing, Hemmerde said that when the prosecution first heard of Wildman and David Jones, they knew that the defence had taken statements from both. In actual fact, the prosecution deemed the evidence of Jones worthless.

Hemmerde then came to the attacks made upon the police – attacks with which Justice Wright completely disassociated himself with in the summing up:

> "It was said that the police had coached witnesses, that the witnesses had been brought into line, and that the police had

395 Oliver's attack on MacFall was a perfectly valid one.
396 The murder and subsequent committal were widely publicised.
397 The statement of Wildman was far more credible than that of Lilian Hall.

> suppressed witnesses. I want to say here and now that as far as the police are concerned, I took charge of this case at least a week before, and if this case was pressed I pressed it. You have my opening speech, my closing speech, and my cross-examination and you have no doubt had the advantage of any communication the Judge at the trial had to make. I take full responsibility for everything that was done in this case, and the police had nothing whatever to do with the conduct of it."[398]

With regards to Wallace's demeanour, Hemmerde said that the evidence on that point might be important. In fact when the case first came to him he asked about demeanour, as he believed that was to be a vital point:

> "The Johnstons were called and asked questions without any previous interviewing to find out what they would say. There were some slight differences between what Mr Johnston said and what his wife said but on the whole there was very little in it. I thought that the evidence of all these witnesses as to his demeanour was important and I still think so."

There were one or two matters that Hemmerde said he would like to deal with. It was suggested that he said repeatedly that there was no motive, but this was incorrect:

> "I did not say that there was not much money in the house. What I said was 'Can you believe that anyone would have committed this crime for such a small gain?'"

Hemmerde said that the jury were warned of the seriousness of their responsibility not only by the Judge, but also by he himself. After four days' trial they came to a conclusion hostile to the prisoner. It was his duty now to put before the court what he thought were the determining factors that led the jury to their verdict.

The person who murdered the unfortunate woman was either the one who sent the telephone message or the person who had been convicted. The jury was asked to assume that a man unknown to

398 The zeal Oliver referred to with regards to the police investigations commenced on the very evening of the murder.

Wallace went into the City Café and read a notice about Wallace – a man he did not know and who was but one of 10,000 Prudential agents and who might be expected to have a weekly collection of about £30. Apart from that, no one could possibly know that Wallace was likely to be there that night. Wallace himself had told detectives that he had not told anyone where he was going, and that so far as he knew no one could know where he would be going. In fact, there was no guarantee that Wallace would get the message or that he would not consult a directory:

> "If he consulted a directory he would find the address non-existent, or he might have consulted some other insurance officer and not proceeded with the enquiry."

Hemmerde suggested that there was nothing to ensure that neither Wallace nor his wife had a prior engagement the following evening. He also suggested that there was no sign of a break in, and that a visitor must have gained admission peaceably on some pretence to steal money. Other considerations were ruled out. Apparently, Mrs Wallace had no enemies. There were no signs that any effort was made to find money in the house.

Dealing with the bloodstains, Hemmerde said that with the exceptions of those found in the fatal room, nothing was found elsewhere and that anyone else committing the murder would have absolutely no reason for fearing to leave blood traces in the kitchen or on the stairs:

> "Whoever it was, if he was a stranger, had nothing to fear from leaving blood about. There was no trace and yet there was undoubtedly evidence that front room had been seriously, if not dramatically disturbed.[399]

Now suppose the man had found only £4 in the cash-box, would not one have expected him to make a complete search of the house? He would have searched the whole place. Is there any evidence that he searched the place at all?"

Hemmerde next dealt with the telephone incident:

399 Obviously Hemmerde was referring to the blood.

> "The man must have rung up that night either with a bent for senseless murder or with the object of getting this man out so that he could rob. Eliminating the question of senseless murder, what conceivable reason could this man have found to behave in the way that the person did behave that got into this house? There was apparently no genuine search for money."

Hemmerde then moved onto the cash-box: "It was a very odd cash-box for a man who wants any protection. Its lid came off without it being unlocked."

At this stage the cash-box was produced, and Hemmerde demonstrated his point to the judges:

> "The cash-box was on a shelf seven feet two inches from the ground. Apparently the man took the box from the shelf, extracted some money, and then returned the box to the shelf."

Hemmerde said that it was the prosecution's suggestion that a burglar would not do this. On the question of the bloodstain on the Treasury note, Hemmerde said that if the stain was caused in daylight the man who caused it would have seen it. In all likelihood the man who had taken the notes from the cash-box would have seen that he had smeared them with blood:

> "If he saw that, what more likely than that he would put it in the first receptacle there was?[400] Anything more fatal than to have taken the bloodstained note that night can hardly be imagined."[401]

Hemmerde submitted the story for the defence was a story the jury was bound to reject, and that the case he put was a case in which the evidence was strong.

The Lord Chief Justice: "When you say the story for the defence is a story the jury is bound to reject, do you mean – Bound to reject?"

Hemmerde: "Well, bound to reject is putting it too high. No jury

400 This could apply to Wallace. It could have been part of the plan to make it look like the burglar had been disturbed by Wallace's return, panicked and put the bloodied note in the nearest receptacle.

401 Hemmerde continued in his misconception that the money taken from the cash-box was that deposited in the ornament in the middle bedroom.

is bound to reject anything. Perhaps I should say the jury would be reasonable in rejecting on the evidence. I would submit it would be right to reject."

Hemmerde said that Wallace left the house around 7.15 on the evening of 19th January, but he could have left three minutes earlier. He would reach the telephone box in three minutes. The first call was at 7.15, then the call was put through at 7.20. He also said that nothing was easier than to change one's voice on the telephone, and in fact there were occasions when it was difficult to recognise a voice. The gruff, confident voice was the easiest sort to simulate if one were bent on disguising their voice.

Hemmerde suggested that to get to the Club would take nearer twenty minutes than thirty, and that the difficulty in the case was the time between the hour at which Mrs Wallace was last seen alive and the time Wallace left the house. If Mrs Wallace was seen at the door at about 6.30, and Wallace could get out of the house by 6.45, many people might ask, 'How could he have done it in the time?'

"I submit," said Hemmerde, "ten minutes would be ample for Wallace to do everything that was to be done in the house. How could there be so little blood outside the room?"

The Lord Chief Justice: "There is the question of the time taken for dressing. Would not the appellant have to take off his clothes as well as put them on again?"

Hemmerde: "Not as he himself visualised it."

Justice Hawke: "At any rate, your theory involves that the appellant would have to put on his clothes."

Hemmerde: "I shall not shirk any issue. I pointed out at the beginning that this case was an extremely difficult one."

Justice Branson: "And then as to the telephone call, assuming that the murder had not been committed, what was there to connect it with the appellant?"

Hemmerde admitted that the evidence that the telephone call was put through by the appellant would be just the same.

Justice Branson: "And as evidence, what is it? Who could know he would be there?"

Hemmerde said that he could not take that matter further.

Justice Branson asked what evidence there was that the call had been made by Wallace. Hemmerde agreed it was a very difficult case and that the evidence was circumstantial. Essentially, there could not be direct evidence if a man chose to make a bogus call to himself.

There were two possibilities, and a mass of detail pointed to the fact that the person who was in the telephone box was Wallace. When what the man did afterwards was considered they were brought irresistibly to the conclusion that it all fitted together like a jigsaw puzzle. One could only find out who was in the telephone box by working it out to the conclusion. There were a dozen things inconsistent with innocence, and the cumulative effect of them was extremely strong.

Hemmerde went on to deal with the question of the garments worn by the murderer. During this argument, a long bar of iron similar to that with which it was suggested the crime was committed was produced. Wallace leaned forward in his seat in the dock, arm resting on the ledge, his hand cupping his chin, following with the utmost attention.

Hemmerde told the jury that they must not lose sight of the possibility that the murderer was naked, and that the room was set for a musical evening with music on the piano and the gas fire lit. After the murderer had struck Mrs Wallace down while wearing the mackintosh, he would get rid of the garment, and that was left in the room. He would then have to cleanse himself. Whoever did the deed took good care that there was no blood on his feet.

"What conceivable casual murderer would have cared what traces were left by his boots or anything of that sort?"

Hemmerde said that the man who sent the telephone message the night before would have left nothing to chance. He would have prepared for the possibility of blood being on his feet.

Oliver interjected: "It ought to be said that he was most carefully searched that night for traces of blood."

Hemmerde: "I do not think I am saying anything wrong. As a

matter of fact he was not undressed that night, was he?"

Oliver said that Wallace had been carefully searched, and a moment later read the shorthand note part of the evidence of Inspector Gold, who said he examined Wallace's clothing, hands and boots but found no sign of blood.

Hemmerde said that he did not take that to mean that Wallace was stripped.[402]

"I have never heard of a man in these circumstances being searched, for he was not even under suspicion,"[403] said Hemmerde.

As to the place where Wallace could have cleansed himself, Hemmerde suggested that he had ample time to have used the bathroom.

"One man shows emotion more than another, but only two cries[404] were heard by the Johnstons.[405] There was no cry of anguish or sorrow, audible at any rate. He may be a man of iron control."

The court adjourned for lunch.

On the resumption, Justice Branson asked Hemmerde to make clear the point he was making with regard to Wallace stepping into the room and lighting the match.

Hemmerde:

> "It is this: that the prisoner, who had every reason to believe that his wife was in the house and quite well – there was no reason to suspect foul play – coming to the door of the parlour, where the light was sufficient to show the pictures on the wall, would naturally have walked straight to the gas and lighted it. He could not have done that without stepping over the body."[406]

Justice Branson: "There was sufficient light, you say, to see the

402 Surely a guilty Wallace would not take that risk.

403 This was nonsense. All of those present gave their opinions on the demeanour of Wallace, and it can be said without fear of contradiction that Wallace was most certainly under suspicion the very evening of the murder.

404 Wallace uttering Julia's name twice.

405 At the committal proceedings and the trial Florence Johnston claimed she did not hear any noise from the house when stood in the entryway of 29 Wolverton Street. [Witness Evidence 23rd February 1931, Trial Transcript p.89.]

406 There was room between the sideboard and the blood, although it would have necessitated stepping over the chair alongside the sideboard. It could be argued though that the subsequent visitors who set foot in the front parlour and managed to avoid stepping in it knew it was there to avoid, whereas Wallace walked into a darkened room albeit with a lighted match.

groups on the pictures on the walls. Would not that give sufficient light to anybody opening the door to see the body lying on the floor?"

Hemmerde said that it might, but it was very doubtful. The point was that the striking of the match was quite unnecessary.

In reply to Justice Branson, Hemmerde was forced to admit that it might be natural for a man to light a match before stepping into the room.

With regards to the blood, Oliver made the point that it could be avoided, and in fact nobody else had stepped on it.

Hemmerde then moved on to Wallace's encounter with the Johnstons.

"Both Mr and Mrs Johnston declared that Wallace said 'The doors are fashioned against me. Have you heard anything unusual tonight?' When Mr Johnston suggested he try the door again, Wallace looked over his shoulder and said 'She will not be out – she has such a bad cold.' That hardly looked like uneasiness."

Hemmerde said it was suspicious that Wallace was reluctant to admit ownership of the mackintosh.

Justice Branson: "What inference do you draw from the hesitation in acknowledging the ownership of the mackintosh?"

Justice Hawke: "If they kept on asking you 'Is this your coat?' might you not say, 'If there is a patch it is mine'?"

The Lord Chief Justice: "Do you mean that the appellant repudiated having said that the mackintosh was his?"

Hemmerde: "That is what the inspector suggested and I am inclined to agree with him."

Justice Branson: "It appears that if he had already admitted that the mackintosh was his, he was only clinching it by saying that if it had two patches it was his."

Justice Hawke suggested that it was possible to read too much into a casual answer.

Hemmerde went on to refer to the importance of Wallace's conversation with Mrs Johnston, and his statement about the mackintosh. The garment had been roughly used, and it was not possible to say definitely what its condition was at the time of the murder. He suggested that if the man were wearing the mackintosh there would be a number of direct spurts of blood on it.

Oliver said that no medical expert had examined the mackintosh. Hemmerde said he thought that was a matter beyond controversy, but would drop it. He then moved on to the iron bar, holding up one similar: "Nothing could be much easier to get rid of than a bar of iron such as this. It could be pushed into the earth anywhere."

Hemmerde said that the remark uttered by Wallace – 'Whatever have they used?'[407] – was not a natural remark for a man with his wife in that position. It suggested that he was referring to something that had been in the room, knowing that it had gone.

With that, Hemmerde said that he came to the end of the evidence to which he felt it his duty to call the attention of the court. He submitted that upon it there was abundant evidence on which a jury could come to the conclusion to which this jury came. The jury had said the evidence satisfied them. They had heard the answers of the accused, and he submitted there was enough to justify the Guilty verdict. There were certain outstanding things which showed that something strange had happened– the business of the locks and gaining admission to the house – but when all these things were put together they made a strong case which the jury were entitled to rely on.

> "There was an extraordinary reluctance on the part of juries to convict, but with full consideration of the facts they had done so here. I have no interest in pressing the court in a matter like this. I am simply here representing the Director of Public Prosecutions but I submit that the jury have done what they conceive to be their duty upon evidence that is amply sufficient to justify them in doing so. Their verdict should not be disturbed."

Hemmerde's speech lasted four hours.

Oliver had the last word. He quoted part of Hemmerde's address to the jury. He also dealt with the statement that the police had

407 Another mystery of the case – the uttering of the phrase 'Whatever have they used?' It is generally accepted to have been uttered by Florence Johnston.

declined to help the defence and had withheld statements.

Justice Branson said he wondered whether they were really trying the case of Wallace, or trying the Liverpool police.

The Lord Chief Justice said the defence had to show that the prosecution had not sustained the onus of proof, and that there could not be excluded the reasonable possibility of some other person having committed the crime.

"Putting the case as it seems to me fairly," said Oliver, "there remain here a number of suspicious circumstances, but nothing in the nature of proof. There is no fact and no series of facts which you could say prove that this man committed this crime. Under those circumstances, in my submission, he is entitled to have this conviction quashed."

The court, quiet enough before, was now deathly silent. The three Judges of Appeal looked at each other and then followed a hurried whispering among them. Every eye was on the scarlet robed figure of the Lord Chief Justice.

Quietly he spoke: "We will adjourn for a little time."

The Judges left the court at 3.35. The *Daily Post and Mercury* reported:

> "The last hour of the Wallace case in the Court of Criminal Appeal will live in the memory of those present in court. The three judges retired shortly after 3.30 and Mr Wallace also retired from the side gallery where the appellant sits. But the court did not empty. It was crowded to suffocation, numerous barristers from other courts adding themselves to the congestion as time went on. There was a loud buzz of conversation, but the tense feeling died away, for everyone had an eye and an ear on the door through which the judges would re-appear. The judges were often thought to be coming before they came. There was many a reference now to the anxiety that the appellant must have been feeling."[408]

Wallace was taken out of the court to a corridor behind. There he paced back and forth, alternating between optimism and pessimism.

408 *Daily Post & Mercury*, 20th May 1931.

The judges returned at 4.17. There was an instant hush in the court after the cry of "Silence." The judges came in and bowed low in response as the court rose to its feet. When all were seated Wallace was ushered in. Looking tired and worn he swayed slightly, his eyes fixed upon the Lord Chief Justice. Only once did he lower his head.

The Lord Chief Justice delivered the judgement in a very quiet voice, speaking very slowly and with long pauses between sentences. Several times while he was giving judgement Wallace sniffed nervously. He stood with his hands clasped behind him, head bent on one side and slightly forward, the better to catch the quiet words of Lord Hewart. The court also strained its ears to hear the deliberation:

> "Three facts are obvious. The first is that at the conclusion of the case for the Crown no submission was made on behalf of the appellant that there was no case to go to the jury. The second fact is that the evidence was summed up by the learned Judge with complete fairness and accuracy, and it would not have been at all surprising if the result had been an acquittal of the prisoner. The third obvious fact is that the case is eminently one of difficulty and doubt. We are not concerned here with suspicion, however grave, or with theories however ingenious. Section 4 of the Criminal Appeal Act of 1907 provides that the Court of Criminal Appeal shall allow the appeal if they think that the verdict of the jury should be set aside on the ground that it cannot be supported having regard to the evidence."

There was one moment which was perhaps the most dramatic in the whole case. It looked as if Wallace was to be acquitted – then came the dramatic words:

> "There is not, so far as we can see, any ground…"

The Lord Chief Justice paused. There was an audible gasp from the court, and Wallace swayed in the dock. The warders closed in around him.

Lord Hewart continued:

> "…for any imputation upon the fairness of the police."

Wallace pulled himself together and leaned forward again. He regained his composure for the rest of the Lord Chief Justice's peroration:

> "The conclusion, to which we have arrived, is that the case against the appellant which we have carefully and anxiously considered and discussed was not proved with that certainty which is necessary in order to justify a verdict of Guilty…"

The whole court swayed a little as Lord Hewart continued:

> "…and therefore it is our duty to take the course indicated by the Section of the Statute to which I have referred. The result is that this appeal will be allowed…"

There was noise in the court – partly a breath of applause and partly the scurrying feet of the copy boys rushing out with the news. The court was silenced as the Lord Chief Justice continued:

> "…and this conviction quashed."

Wallace had looked deathly pale throughout Lord Hewart's speech, but a bright gleam was now visible in his eyes. He heaved a sigh and waved to Joseph. The police in the side gallery with him smiled and indicated that he was free to go. The judges were still on the bench as Wallace turned and left, a free man. The commotion followed him from the court as he was hurried through the little door in the crypt where prisoners arrived and departed.

At 4.40 the janitors opened a great gate of the Law Courts and Wallace exited, putting on his bowler hat. He was smoking a cigarette and carrying a bundle wrapped in newspaper as he stepped out into the bright spring sunshine on the Strand. Those first to greet him were his brother Joseph and Hector Munro, who was accompanied by his wife May. Suddenly he was surrounded by friends and members of the public, who grasped his hands and uttered congratulations. Wallace could hardly murmur his thanks, he was so overcome. There was the making of a smile on his face but he was obviously tired and emotionally drained. Being advised not to go into the Strand, a taxi was called for. He stood still, barely smiling, and seemed oblivious to all around him. People who did not even know him wished him good luck, and murmurs of "God bless you" rang out. They patted him on the back and tried to shake his hand.

"I just haven't had any feelings all day. I am beyond feeling. It is enough that I am back with my relatives and friends who know me."

"Are you going back home?" shouted one onlooker.

"I don't know where I am going," said Wallace. "I only know that I am free, free."

"We are going to take him away to a place where he is not known," said Joseph. "We want him to forget, if possible, the terrible ordeal through which he has passed during these weeks and months. We hope he will take a holiday before he returns once more to take up the threads of life where they were broken."

The taxi arrived and Wallace was rushed into it. For a moment it held up a bus, and the passengers looked out, wondering why there was a rather excited crowd surrounding a taxi in the Strand. Later, a telegram was sent to 31 Bentley Road from Wallace and Joseph, notifying Amy and Edwin that they were uncertain when they would be returning.

At 5.55 the train to Liverpool Lime Street left Euston Station. On board were Wallace's Defence team Sydney Scholefield Allen and Hector Munro, accompanied by Norman Wheeler. On board the same train were Detective Superintendent Hubert Moore, Detective Inspector Herbert Gold and Prosecuting Solicitor J.R. Bishop. When the train arrived at Lime Street at 9.35 the Wallace Defence team were greeted enthusiastically by relatives and friends, who congratulated them on the result of the appeal. Any of the onlookers hoping to catch a glimpse of Wallace would have to wait. He stayed the night in London with Joseph.

Top left: The Law Courts, London (Author's Collection)
Right, top: Lord Hewart; middle: Justice Hawke; bottom: Justice Branson (National Portrait Gallery)
Bottom left: Wallace leaves the courts after winning his appeal

Left: After his acquittal Wallace was given an office job at the Prudential (Author's Collection)

Below: Wallace with a co-worker after his acquittal (Author's Collection)

7

ENDGAME

The quashing of Wallace's conviction and death sentence was only the third instance of its kind since the Court of Criminal Appeal was founded.[409] It was the first in which an appeal had been granted on the grounds that the verdict could not be supported with regards to the evidence.

The result of Wallace's appeal had been anxiously awaited in Liverpool. In fact, it was the one topic of conversation everywhere in the city. At 31 Bentley Road, Amy and Edwin Wallace were informed by a *Daily Post* representative of the Appeal Court's decision.

"I am so glad," said Wallace's sister-in-law. "We have always believed in his innocence and now this suspense is over, it is a great relief."

Entering the room, Edwin was also thrilled with the news: "Oh, I am delighted. After so many disappointments we were almost frightened of hoping, yet we felt that his innocence would be established. It is fine to think we shall be seeing him again."

Hector Munro said that the most important point of the court's

409 On 28th September 1911 Charles Ellsome won the first appeal of this nature. He had been found guilty for the murder of 19-year-old Rose Render in Clerkenwell, London, but due to a judicial blunder by Justice Avory, who had misdirected the jury by introducing a statement which was not in the evidence at the trial, the death sentence was quashed at the Court of Appeal and Ellsome left the courts a free man. In December 1914 Adolf Ahlers, the German Consul at Sunderland, was found guilty of high treason. It was alleged Ahlers had been helping local German reservists to return home by paying for their passage so that they could serve in the German army. Although initially sentenced to death Ahlers appealed against the decision. His conviction was quashed on the grounds that a material part of the defence was not put before the jury.

decision was that it was a reversal of the verdict, not on legal grounds, but on the facts of the case:

> "The court decided that the facts were not sufficient for the jury to have returned a verdict of guilty against Wallace. I believe in his innocence, as all the people who have been in close touch with him do."

Herbert J. Davis concurred with his partner Munro. He said that if ever there was justification for the establishment of the Court of Criminal Appeal, it was in the Wallace case:

> "There is no doubt that everybody would have been extremely disturbed if this appeal had not been allowed."

The Bishop of Liverpool, Dr David, said he was very glad that the appeal had been allowed, as he had never been satisfied that the evidence justified the jury's verdict.

There were four points on which Wallace could have been legally relieved from prosecution: the Magistrate at the Police Court, the Grand Jury, the Trial Jury, and the Appeal Judges at the Court of Criminal Appeal. It was the fourth and final option that saw Wallace escape the gallows. Incidentally, Hemmerde was vehemently opposed to the Grand Jury system. It was, in his words, 'A futile system that served no purpose whatsoever.'[410] As is known, the burden of proof is on the prosecution. It is their duty to establish guilt – the defence does not have to prove innocence.

In the Wallace case the charge was not proven beyond a reasonable doubt, therefore the verdict was an unfair and completely unjustified one. There is also no doubt whatsoever that Justice Wright was directing the jury to a Not Guilty verdict.

That said, it would seem slightly unfair to lay blame solely on the Trial Jury. The ten men and two women probably believed that for the case to have reached thus far they had every right to find the accused Guilty (especially with regards to Justice Wright's claim that if there was no motive for Wallace to murder his wife, there was no motive for anyone else to do so). That, after all, was

410 *Evening Express*, 7th January 1932.

their entitlement. Even Roland Oliver did not offer that the case should be withdrawn, and neither did Justice Wright. It seemed throughout the proceedings that the buck was well and truly passed from one to the next.

The Justice of the Peace and Local Government Review from the time makes interesting reading:

> 'We have very carefully read and thought over the evidence. In our opinion there was not evidence sufficient to put the accused upon his trial or evidence to raise a strong or probable presumption of his guilt. It is of course, a very strong measure for justice to discharge a person accused of murder but the same principles apply to the capital felony as to the larceny of twopence-halfpenny. We suggest the Magistrate should have discharged Wallace due to insufficient evidence. Next, it was up to the Grand Jury to ignore the bill. The retention of the Grand Jury is always maintained to be necessary as a protection of the accused. If there ever was a case for its intervention it was the Wallace case. Next we come to the Trial Jury. Why they fail to acquit is known only to themselves. It is safe to assume that few of them came to the case with minds unaffected by local talk and newspaper reports. Two things are comfortable to contemplate: That the Court of Criminal Appeal has stood between a man convicted on insufficient evidence and the hangman; and that had Wallace had no means and no friends, he could still have reached the same high tribunal, without cost to himself.'[411]

Two letters also make interesting reading. The first, from Liverpool Chief Constable Lionel Everett[412] to Under Secretary of State at the Home Office Sir Ernley Blackwell, claims that, in Everett's opinion, the evidence was merely circumstantial and insufficient to justify a Guilty verdict. A series of suspicious circumstances were proved against Wallace, but there was no single outstanding act or incident which could put the decision beyond dispute.[413]

The second letter is from Montague Shearman of the Foreign

411 *Justice of the Peace and Local Government Review*, 13th June 1931.

412 Lionel Everett came to Liverpool in 1912 as Assistant Chief Constable. He was appointed Chief Constable in 1925, a position he held until his resignation (on medical advice) in October 1931. His residence was at the North Western Hotel on Lime Street.

413 Letter dated 12th May 1931.

Office to the Director of Public Prosecutions, Edward Hale Tindal Atkinson. Shearman states that after reading the shorthand transcript the evidence seemed clear that Wallace should never have been convicted, but at the same time was certainly Guilty.[414]

Wallace gained no favours from the press reports at the time either. The general opinion was that he was Guilty and the reporting was somewhat prejudicial.[415]

At the Prudential Offices in Dale Street there was jubilation when the news was received. A congratulatory telegram was sent immediately. Wallace stayed at a boarding house in the London suburb of Turnham Green. One of the first letters he wrote was to Roland Oliver, expressing his thanks.

Wednesday 20th May was an active day for Wallace. In the morning he was in Piccadilly. He then made a visit to the Prudential Head Offices in Holborn, where he was given a month's paid holiday. He then visited the Prudential Staff Union headquarters to express his thanks for their support, before going to Kew Gardens. In the evening he visited the Gaiety Theatre to see the first night of *The Millionaire Kid* at the invitation of comedian Laddie Cliff. "If only you knew how amazingly thrilling it is to laugh again, you would realise how every moment of tonight's entertainment has been to me a joy," Wallace remarked.

Meanwhile, Labour MPs John Smith Clarke (Maryhill), Derwent Hall Caine (Everton) and John Henry Hayes (Edgehill) raised the question of possible compensation for Wallace. Clarke said that a grant for Wallace for the suffering and material injury he had endured should be considered. Hall Caine was in complete agreement, and Hayes said that the least that could be done was to recoup every penny which Wallace had lost in his fight for life. Wirral Conservative MP John Grace said that the question of compensation had to be considered carefully in its bearing on

414 Letter dated 15th June 1931.

415 It should be noted that it was usual during committal proceedings that evidence given was only for the prosecution while the defence was reserved for the Higher Court. Inevitably, through the reporting in the newspapers the public would get one side of a case only, therefore possible prejudice would materialise long before the Assize Trial opened.

British justice as a whole. A Home Office official said that Home Secretary J. R. Clynes could not make comment until the question had been raised in the House of Commons. Those with an interest in the abolition of capital punishment also claimed the Wallace case supported their view. The Reverend James Barr, MP, who was former chairman on the Select Committee on Capital Punishment, said that "It required very little imagination to see that Mr Wallace ran a very grave risk of execution, although an innocent man."

21st May saw Wallace return by motor car to Liverpool. He immediately visited the Prudential Offices on Dale Street, where a party was given in his honour. He was however not present at the resumption of the inquest on Julia Wallace, but was represented by Hector Munro. There were fewer than a dozen people in the court when the proceedings, which lasted barely two minutes, began.

Immediately after taking his seat, Coroner Mort said:"Mr Munro, you are interested in this case?"

"Yes Sir."

"In accordance with Section 20 of the Coroner's Amendment Act, 1926, I have to say that I received yesterday a notice from the Court of Criminal Appeal, with regard to proceedings in that court. That notice intimates that a conviction had been quashed with regard to one, Julia Wallace. The notice is signed by Mr Leonard W. Kershaw, Registrar of the Court of Criminal Appeal, and therefore, I formally close this inquest, in accordance with that notification."[416]

The *Evening Express* reported that the police investigations would not be closed until a conviction had been secured, and that the case would remain on the books.[417] The police were still inundated with correspondence. One letter signed 'Wellwisher' advised detectives that the killer of Mrs Wallace could well have been a woman who lived nearby.

416 The inquest on 21st May 1931 recorded cause of death as fractured skull and that the conviction of murder against husband was quashed by the Court of Criminal Appeal. The document erroneously gives the address as 27 Wolverton Street.

417 It can be said that the police more than likely suggested this, but in actual fact were convinced they had arrested the right man.

On 22nd May Home Secretary Clynes announced that compensation awarded to Wallace would be declined. It was suggested that there was no precedent for a grant of compensation on such grounds, and that the situation did not differ principally from that of any other defendant who had been acquitted of a serious charge. John Smith Clarke, who had raised the issue, asked whether the case of Oscar Slater[418] was not a precedent. Clynes said that it wasn't, and that the question of compensation in this instance would conflict with the fundamental principles of English Law. Sir Lambert Ward asked whether it would not be an act of grace to give him a grant towards the cost of his defence, but the Home Secretary said that it was beyond his power to award compensation in a case of this kind.

Meanwhile, the press reports were that Wallace had taken a holiday in North Wales, but he had, in actual fact, travelled with Joseph to Broughton-in-Furness where they would spend a couple of weeks at a guesthouse called Latham House.

On 2nd June Wallace's solicitors Herbert J. Davis, Berthen and Munro contacted the police requesting that arrangements should be made immediately for the destruction of photographs and fingerprints of Wallace taken before and after his conviction. In reply, Harry Hewitt Cooke said that the negative of Wallace had been destroyed, and that four of his prints had been accounted for and also destroyed.[419]

On 8th June, the Labour MP for Greenwich, Edward Timothy Palmer[420] put the question of compensation to the Attorney-General, Sir William Jowitt. Jowitt said that there was no fund from which a successful appellant would be reimbursed, and that it would not be in the public interest to introduce legislation granting

418 In December 1908 83-year-old Marion Gilchrist was found murdered in her Glasgow apartment. Slater was arrested, found guilty and sentenced to death for the killing. The evidence that it was Slater was questionable to say the least. After a petition signed by over 20,000 people the sentence was commuted to life imprisonment. Slater served 19 years. His conviction was quashed in July 1928 and he received £6000.

419 Cooke claimed that Wallace had not been photographed or fingerprinted after his conviction. [Harry Hewitt Cooke, Studio, Police Headquarters Letter, 6th June 1931.]

420 Joint Secretary of the Prudential Staff Union.

the right in all cases, and it was undesirable to differentiate between cases.

On 12th June Wallace's solicitors wrote to the police asking them to replace the doors to the bathroom and the front parlour, and stated that as the gas fire in the front parlour was still dismantled it needed repairing immediately. They also said that the police were in possession of keys from the front door lock and they wanted them returning.[421]

On 16th June Wallace and Norman Wheeler called at the Dale Street Property Office to collect items that had been used as exhibits at the trial.[422] Wallace signed for and collected the desired belongings. Wheeler stated that Wallace also wanted the two additional keys belonging to the front door. Sergeant Fothergill informed Wheeler that, as far as he knew, the police did not have them.

Wallace had been advised by both his family and Hector Munro not to return to Wolverton Street[423] due to the probable hostility that he would encounter. Wallace ignored the advice. He would soon realise that the advice would have been better heeded, as public vitriol, rumour and scandal were aimed at him.

To some he was a promiscuous adulterer; to others the father of illegitimate children; a murderer who had dispatched his wife in order to pursue his illicit affairs. Ostracism and contempt greeted Wallace on his rounds. Customers who had been friendly with him now shunned him. Poison pen letters were sent to him on an almost daily basis from all parts of the country. Wallace handed

421 Herbert Gold reported that the two doors had been re-hung and the gas fire repaired. Incidentally, when the front door lock was removed a new one was put in its place. Two keys were supplied with it, and these were handed to Wallace after his committal. The old lock was replaced afterwards. [Herbert Gold Crime Report, 20th June 1931.]

422 A representative of landlord Samuel Evans also called at the property office to collect exhibits 22 (back kitchen door lock and key) and 23 (lavatory pan). For list of trial exhibits see Appendix V.

423 Before the trial had even commenced, Wallace's landlord Samuel Evans was inundated with requests from strangers anxious to rent the property. The reports claimed that the prospective house-hunters were convinced Wallace would not go back there to live. In all likelihood, those applying were probably of the opinion that Wallace would be found guilty and sentenced to death. Evans believed the enquiries were from genuine applicants due to the shortage of housing at the time and not sensation seekers.

these to Hector Munro. Eventually he was given an office job at the Prudential Building on Dale Street. Several articles and accounts libelled Wallace and he sued, usually resulting in out of court settlements. He received £300 from Allied Newspapers made out in accordance with an agreement made on 19th May 1931.[424] Another was against Wyman & Sons for an article that appeared in *True Detective Mysteries* Vol. 16 No.3, which appeared in December 1931. Another action was brought against printers and publishers Pickering & Inglis in January 1932 for an article that had appeared in an issue of *The Herald of Salvation* the previous September.

Wallace finally accepted the advice he had been given regarding moving away from Anfield, by moving across the River Mersey to a bungalow called The Summer House in Bromborough. The conveyance of the property from Raymond Rathbone Robinson[425] was made on 8th August 1931 for the price of £675. Wallace would make the forty-five minute journey to the Prudential Offices by suburban train and tram on a daily basis.

Wallace might have escaped the hostility of the residents of Anfield and Clubmoor, but he was also shunned by acquaintances and former colleagues. The once-friendly atmosphere of the City Café – where he would once sit and have lunch, drink coffee, smoke cigarettes and play chess – was another place where he was given the cold shoulder.[426]

On 16th October Messrs Herbert J. Davis, Berthen and Munro sent a letter on behalf of Wallace to the Liverpool Police, enquiring what measures they were doing with regard to their investigations. Chief Constable Herbert Winstanley said that they had not made any progress in the case. In a further letter he said he could not supply details of inquiries, as there were 'obvious objections to such a course.'

The last entry in Wallace's diary was made on 12th April 1932

424 The day the verdict was quashed by the Court of Appeal.
425 Robinson, an Analytical Chemist, had lived in Rock Ferry but had moved to Exeter at the time of the conveyance.
426 Wallace's death did not even render a mention in the annual chess club report obituary section.

and referred to his garden.[427] From April to May 1932 Wallace's life story appeared in five parts under the title 'The Man They Did Not Hang' in the publication *John Bull.* Whether these were written by Wallace or ghost-written is open to question. The typewritten manuscripts among the files held at Hill Dickinson are certainly signed by Wallace, so whether written by him or not they were certainly endorsed by him. They radiate an air of defiant stoicism, self-aggrandizement and romanticised martyrdom. They read like something from the pages of Kipling or Rider Haggard: of far-flung adventures and exotic images of natives dressed in colourful splendour from the days of the Raj and Empire; Wallace claimed he witnessed the preparations for the Delhi Durbar of 1903. He claimed to have also witnessed the leaving of Colonel Younghusband's forces on their expedition to Lhasa, Tibet and remembered the Curzon-Kitchener conflict.

When reading this biographical piece, one seriously doubts the believability of it. Many of the passages seem abundant in histrionics, and are all rather pretentious. Other passages claim that Wallace was refused entry to the army on six occasions due to his kidney complaint, and that he volunteered for the Calcutta Light Infantry, where he saw several skirmishes. Other passages speak of executions and torture in China. It also claims that Wallace could speak in Bengali and Hindustani, and that he went on shooting expeditions in India, bagging teal, duck and crocodile in the process.

Wallace author James Murphy refutes this:

> "Working in Calcutta, Wallace was in the 'bottom drawer' of trade and would certainly have kept his distance from the natives. Brits were not encouraged to mix with the locals, or to speak anything other than English. I worked in India for several years, out in the sticks, and know that people there speak their own languages and dialects, such as Sindhi, Punjabi and Tamil. For Wallace to have claimed he mastered Bengali and Hindi is exaggeration, to put it mildly. As for him travelling all the way from Calcutta to Delhi for the Durbar and also equipping himself for hunting

427 *The Trial of William Herbert Wallace*, W.F. Wyndham Brown, pp. 309.

> expeditions, well that is nonsense. It would have cost him a fortune. Also the fact that the ruling British, officer corps etc. would not have allowed an upstart such as Wallace to partake. He was 'trade' and didn't belong at that level of hierarchy."[428]

Earlier passages recount Wallace in his youth; of being struck down by typhoid (the first of his self-professed death sentences); of playing with childhood friends in the Dalton-in-Furness countryside where they would pretend to be Native Americans, and re-enact scalping invisible enemies; and also of his move to Blackpool (and being especially enthralled by the trams).

In the February of 1933 Wallace's recurring kidney complaint worsened and he was taken to Clatterbridge Hospital. It was there on February 9th that he made his will (the signing of which was witnessed by Dorothy Ellson and George Cecil Reginald Watts, both of Clatterbridge Institution). In it, Wallace appointed his brother Joseph as sole executor. He also left £100 to his housekeeper, Annie Catherine Mason, for her kindness and care during his illness.[429]

For a fortnight doctors tried to save his life. An operation was performed by Professor Charles Wells, but Wallace gradually deteriorated. On Saturday 25th he relapsed into a delirious state and passed into a coma at about midnight. Although he had been visited by his nephew Edwin from Scotland,[430] there were no relatives at his bedside when he died at 3.00am on 26th February, the causes being uraemia[431] and pyelonephritis.[432] Other patients in Clatterbridge Hospital awaited a deathbed confession, but none was forthcoming.

On 27th February Wallace's body was removed from Clatterbridge Infirmary to a private chapel at undertaker's Thomas Porter &

428 James Murphy. Letter to the author dated 29th June 2012.

429 Administration of the effects of the testator was granted on 21st July 1933 to Wallace's nephew Edwin on behalf of Joseph. The effects came to £1,614 7s 9d.

430 Edwin, a medical student, was living in Highburgh Road, Glasgow at the time. He served with the Medical Department Kuching, Sarawak 1948-60. He died at Queen Elizabeth Hospital, Jesselton, North Borneo on 27th December 1960 aged 49.

431 The condition in which the accumulation of waste products, normally excreted in the urine, are retained in the blood. Symptoms include severe headaches, vomiting, fatigue and loss of appetite.

432 Inflammation of the kidney and pelvis, caused by bacterial inflammation. Symptoms of acute pyelonephritis include fever and chills, burning or frequent urination, severe pain and fatigue.

Sons.[433] The following day Herbert J. Davis, Berthen and Munro received a cable from Joseph in the Malay States instructing them to act for him with regards to the will. The same day Edwin registered Wallace's death and obtained a burial certificate.

Special precautions were made to keep the funeral ceremony as secret as possible. No reference was made to the funeral on the sheets which were posted daily at the entrance of Anfield cemetery. Nevertheless, crowds visited the cemetery in a long trek to the grave but there was no sign that the funeral was to take place.[434] It was not until after the cemetery had closed to the public that night that the gravediggers reopened the grave of Julia Wallace. They carried on working aided by flares, but did not complete the opening so returned just after dawn. The residents near to the cemetery had no idea that the funeral was to take place, as the gravediggers had been working late and the sight of them working by flares was a regular occurrence. They finished their task shortly before 9.00am on the morning of 1st March.

A little later the motor cortege entered the cemetery from the back entrance in Cherry Lane. A special service had been held at Porter's private chapel and then, in accordance to the rites of the Church of England, a full service was conducted at the graveside[435] by Reverend C.H. Startup.[436] There were ten mourners present – all men – and they consisted of family and friends, among whom were Hector Munro and Norman Wheeler (representing Wallace's Solicitors), James Caird, F.W. Jenkinson[437] and Edwin. No members of the public were present. There were four wreathes, three of which were inscribed with the same handwriting. One read: 'With deepest sympathy – from Joe[438] and Amy.' Another

433 377 Park Road, Dingle.

434 *Liverpool Echo*, 1st March 1933.

435 Plot 4837 C/E Division. The cost was £3 1s; interment £1 10s, the removing and replacing of the headstone £1 1s and 10s ecclesiastical fee.

436 Charles Harry Startup. Curate of St Columba's, Anfield.

437 Frederick William Jenkinson. He was a schoolteacher who lived at 112 Moscow Drive and listed as one of those Wallace claimed Julia would have admitted into 29 Wolverton Street on the evening of the killing. His son Fred Wilson Jenkinson was also on the list of admitted persons.

438 Joseph died on 5th June 1950. He was living at Mylnebeck Lake House Road, Windermere at the time. Probate was made at Carlisle on 3rd October to Amy. Effects came to the sum of

bore a card reading 'With deepest sympathy from his colleagues of the Divisional Office, of the Prudential Assurance Ltd.' Another, with the simple inscription 'From Bert' and a large wreath, bore the inscription 'Peace after sorrow, from the housekeeper, with deepest sympathy.' The tombstone read 'In loving memory and affectionate remembrance of Julia, beloved wife of W.H. Wallace, who died 20th January 1931, aged 52 years.[439] To this would be added: 'Also of William Herbert Wallace, who died 26th February 1933, aged 54 years. "At rest."'

Wallace had lived barely two years after the brutal slaying of his wife. If he was guilty, he took her murder to the grave with him.

£10,134 12s.7d.

439 In actual fact Julia was almost 53 when she married Wallace in 1914. He was 35 at the time.

Wallace in the garden of his bungalow in Bromborough (National Archives)

Above: Wallace months before his death (Liverpool Daily Post and Echo)

Right: The grave of William and Julia Wallace, Anfield Cemetery (Author's Collection)

8

CONCLUSION

The time factor has always been the most baffling aspect of the Wallace murder. In fact, the sheer nature of the case has many factors regarding the time. In the present day, time is a concept that we can call upon more readily than those of 1931. Today we have the luxury of mobile phones, laptops, digital wristwatches and up-to-date media. Although people in 1931 had watches, the actual fact is they didn't have a perception of time like those of the present. Time was signalled by factory whistles and hooters. People set their watches and clocks by time signals on radio. A speaking clock service was first introduced in Britain in 1936.

The contradictions in the times regarding the case were evident (and abundant). Sydney Hubert Green said he left his house in Towers Road at 7.10pm and met Wallace near Menlove Gardens approximately three minutes later; therefore he met Wallace at 7.13pm. Wallace was at Penny Lane at about this time, boarding the No. 5a tram. In her statement, Lily Pinches said that Wallace entered the shop at about 8.30pm. At the trial Lily Hall said she saw Wallace in Richmond Park at about 9.20pm.

On the evening of 20th January Elsie Wright was delivering milk in the area. As she reached Richmond Park and Breck Road she claimed she heard the bells of the Belmont Road Institute ringing. When the peal ended she looked up at the Holy Trinity Church clock and noticed the time was 6.30pm. She then went to the vicarage and was five minutes there before making deliveries in Richmond Park and Letchworth Street.

Sometime between 6.30 and 6.45pm Alan Close called at 29 Wolverton Street. After delivering the milk there (and his meeting with Mrs Wallace) he walked along Wolverton Street and made his way along Richmond Park to Redford Street. There, he looked at his wristwatch (which was a minute or two fast) and the time said 6.45. It is highly unlikely that Close would have taken ten to twelve minutes to reach Redford Street if he had called at 29 Wolverton Street at 6.31. The distance from 29 Wolverton Street to Redford Street is approximately 320 yards at the most, which would take roughly about four minutes to walk. The paperboy Wildman claimed he saw the clock on the Holy Trinity Church at 6.35. It would then take him two or three minutes to reach Wolverton Street.

If we accept that the last time Mrs Wallace was seen alive was 6.31, Wallace would have had 20 minutes to commit the crime. If 6.40, he would have had 11 minutes; surely adequate time to carry out what he had to do.

Florence Johnston said that her milk had been delivered by Close at about 6.30. She heard him shut the front door and fetched her milk immediately. Sometime around 6.35 Walter Holme heard the front door of number 29 closing; his wife Bertha thought the sound was like someone falling. Mr Holme said that his paper was usually delivered at 6.40, and the noise had occurred about five minutes before that. Holme said that there were no noises for the rest of the evening. This is damning evidence against Wallace – any subsequent visitor knocking at the door of number 29 would almost certainly have been heard by Mr or Mrs Holme, but they did not hear anyone.

The complete scenario points to Wallace being the murderer. The collective evidence that he committed the murder is far stronger than the facts of him not having committed it. Let us look at it from the perspective of the killer: why would a killer take so many risks? All good plans are simple – the fewer the complications, the greater the chances of success. Yet the Qualtrough plan was anything but simple – it was in fact unnecessarily complex and complicated.

No intelligent criminal would have even contemplated it.[440] The intricacies of the Qualtrough plan would not have been attempted by a casual killer. A prospective burglar/murderer would not have been reliant on Wallace falling for the bogus business proposition, especially when it would involve murder. A murderer would not know if Wallace would be at the Club on the Monday evening. There was no guarantee Wallace would be there, just as there was no guarantee he would receive the message and make the journey on the Tuesday night.[441]

There is also the possibility that Julia might not have even opened the front door to admit a caller. She was regularly ill and could have been bedridden. Both Parry and Marsden would have been aware of this. Conversely, Julia may even have accompanied Wallace in his quest for Menlove Gardens. Whenever the Wallaces went out together, they would always take all the money in the house with them. This included the collection money. Parry and Marsden both knew this.

For all the caller knew, Wallace might have even had a prior engagement with Julia planned. Wallace receives a message from a person he doesn't know, with a name he has never heard of, to go to an address he does not know – and does not deem it suspicious. Why didn't he deem it suspicious? He should have. Didn't it occur to him that it could have been a masquerade by the caller to get him out of the house with the intention of burglary? The Anfield Housebreaker[442] was active in the area. For someone who did not like leaving his wife at home during the evening, one would have thought he might have been suspicious. It would make no sense whatsoever for a prospective murderer to get Wallace out of the house on the Tuesday night, when he had the whole of the Monday

440 Murphy, *The Murder of Julia Wallace* pp.122.

441 At the trial Hemmerde made the point that Qualtrough left a message with Beattie, who could not even tell him whether Wallace would be arriving. Qualtrough never enquired afterwards to see if Wallace received the message and 'left the whole thing there in the air.' [Edward Hemmerde KC, closing speech for the prosecution 25th April 1931.]

442 The Wallaces went on holiday on a fairly regular basis, visiting Rose Villa in Camaes Bay on the island of Anglesey. This would have been an opportune time for the Anfield Housebreaker to enter the Wallace house.

evening to carry it out. Those who suggest that there would have been a greater hoard on the Tuesday night are overlooking the fact that the biggest hoard would have been on 12th January.[443] Wallace collected over £89 for what was referred to a monthly week. It would have been more beneficial for a prospective thief to have committed it then.

Wallace was extremely meticulous in remembering his actions on the journey to, and around, Menlove Gardens. He could account for his whereabouts on practically every part of the route.[444] Interestingly, Sydney Hubert Green, Katie Mather and Lily Pinches were unsure of certain details and inaccurate with some of their evidence, yet this is human nature and can be looked upon as genuine mistakes. They were not expected to remember details, yet Wallace could. This would confirm that he was going out of his way to impress himself upon passers-by and account for his own whereabouts along the route. He had to ask the route to Allerton, yet needed no assistance on his return journey.

On his return he also went out of his way in drawing the attention of the Johnstons to the money taken from the cash-box. One would have thought that the death of a loved one would be of paramount importance, but first and foremost Wallace was trying to create the illusion of a burglary. On the subject of the cash-box, there were no fingerprints on it yet we are led to believe the killer replaced it high on the shelf. Surely the murderer would have had bloodstained fingers, yet there were none left on the box. Conversely, if he had worn gloves during the killing he would not have been bothered leaving bloodied marks on it. This would indicate that the contents of the cash-box had been tampered with *before* the murder was committed.

Why would anyone other than Wallace turn both the fire and gas-jet off? It is extremely unlikely that an intruder would do this. Also, the back kitchen door into the yard being shut – it is highly

443 Parry's 22nd birthday. Parry and Marsden would without doubt have known the dates of the monthly collection. The details were stated in the Prudential account books.

444 Yet could not remember if he had posted a letter on the previous evening on his way to the Central Chess Club.

unlikely a burglar would do this.

There was no element of panic escape associated with a burglary or an intruder committing the crime. The cash-box had been returned to the high shelf in an orderly fashion. There were no blood traces (apart from those in the parlour), and no furniture or items had been disturbed in an extremely cluttered parlour. The crime scene was consistent with the victim being at ease with the killer. The possibility of an intruder gaining access by using a duplicate key can be eliminated. It can also be said that the murder itself was carried out in an organised and clinical manner, without a trace of panic or clumsiness.

There can be no doubt that Wallace did consider taking the line that somebody was in the house on his return but thought better of it. Even he must have come to realise that a killer was not going to wait around a house for two hours after a murder. It is possible that Wallace wanted to create the impression that he had disturbed the killer, who then made his escape when Wallace came from the back to the front of the house the second time, but a startled killer would hardly stop to turn off the gas fire and light and also close both the back door and yard door on leaving in haste. The lack of smell of burning rubber from the mackintosh and the dying embers in the kitchen fire would also confirm that the killing had been carried out a good while before Wallace's arrival.

Wallace claiming he felt uneasy because he saw no light from the living kitchen is also one to ponder. Although he claimed he turned the light on in the living kitchen, the closed curtains would have stopped any light from escaping. Likewise, the door that connected the two rooms would surely have been closed if Julia had been in the living kitchen. Wallace had no reason to feel uneasy because no light emanated from there.

One of the biggest and misguided beliefs in the Wallace case is the perpetual claim that all of the evidence can point either way and is consistent with guilt or innocence. This is completely false – an example being that there was no justification for Wallace's actions on the tram from Smithdown Lane to Penny Lane. They could only be those of a guilty man. He had no reason whatsoever for acting the way he did. He knew the route – his frequent visits to 83 Ullet Road, as stated in his diaries,[445] illustrate this. His numerous visits to his boss Joseph Crewe in Green Lane, thereby knowing the area, are another example, as was Wallace's seemingly effortless opening of the back kitchen door in the presence of the John and Florence Johnston.

Only Wallace knew he would attend the Chess Club on the Monday evening. Only Wallace knew he would make the journey to Menlove Gardens. If we are to assume Qualtrough was well acquainted with Wallace, he would surely not have risked using a false address as there was a strong likelihood that Wallace knew the Menlove Gardens area.[446] There is also the possibility that Wallace would look up the address. If Qualtrough wanted Wallace out of the house he could have just loitered outside the Central Chess Club on the Monday evening, watched him go in, and know that in all probability Wallace would be playing a game for roughly two hours. Qualtrough could have then made his way to Wolverton Street to carry out the deed. If he did want to send Wallace on a wild goose chase, why not use a genuine address? It would have taken Wallace at least an hour's journey time there and back; sufficient time to have committed a burglary/murder.

The usual belief that the plan was set with precision timing is open to question. Wallace wasn't the greatest planner as has been led to be believed – he was a clumsy killer. What has been taken for cunning was really only inefficiency. It helped him to get away with murder.[447] The idea that the complete chronological set up was based on the delivery of the milk boy cannot be substantiated. Wallace did not plan it to that. The whole point that Close delivered the milk when he did was fortuitous. He was late on his round due

445 Wallace's diaries include entries of visits to Ullet Road on 3rd and 13th November 1929, and on three occasions in 1930; 20th April, 13th July and 16th November. Also included are references of visits to Calderstones Park and Woolton Woods.

446 Both Parry and Marsden would have been aware of Crewe living in the vicinity of Menlove Avenue and also his connection with Wallace.

447 Barrister, author, legal columnist and television presenter Fenton Bresler: *Who Killed Julia Wallace?* Trident Television Ltd, 1975.

to his bicycle being damaged.[448] Close's round was usually between 5.30-6.30pm. If he wouldn't have been half an hour late, he would have delivered the milk roughly between 6.05-6.15pm. If Wallace's plan had been based on the time Close concluded his round, he would have had to arrive home before 6.05pm (the time that he did). In all likelihood, Wallace's plan would to have been to murder his wife, carry out any tasks post-murder then head to Menlove Gardens and rely solely on the element of doubt concerning the time. That was the whole point of a false address – it gave him the opportunity to indulge in traipsing around, letting minutes pass in order to throw doubt upon the actual time of death. The longer Wallace stayed in Mossley Hill the better.

On the Monday night Wallace claimed that he wasn't even sure that he would go ahead with the journey to Menlove Gardens. In fact he claimed he was talked into it by Julia. We are asked to believe he would doggedly try to gain a commission, yet had to be talked into it.

Wallace claimed he said to Julia that he wouldn't be as long as necessary, yet on the contrary, he *was* longer than necessary. He had been told by two people that Menlove Gardens East did not exist within five minutes of arriving there. He even accepted this. He said to Mrs Mather 'It's funny there is no East.' Why then, did he continue in what even he knew was a fruitless search? It was all a subterfuge.

Another murderer would not have taken the weapon away with them – it would have made no sense for them to carry a blood-stained and incriminating weapon away. There is no doubt that they would have worn gloves, so would not have been bothered about leaving the weapon behind. Wallace's reluctance to admit knowledge of the iron bar in the front parlour is suspicious to say the least.[449] There is the possibility that he used it as the weapon and

448 Elsie Wright said that Close had delivered the milk by bicycle on the first part of his round but continued the rest on foot.

449 Jonathan Goodman claimed that during the mid-1930s workmen removed the fireplace and discovered the missing bar of iron between the hearth and the back wall, and that it was handed over to the police. There is nothing to substantiate this. The police investigation at the time of

disposed of it later. Alternatively, the weapon could have been from Wallace's converted laboratory – he had an abundance of tools there. One of these could possibly have been used and discarded afterwards.

James Murphy says that the whole question of the blood clot was one of the biggest red herrings in British legal history,[450] and it would be difficult to argue with him. The biggest red herrings in the whole of the Wallace Case, however, are surely Richard Gordon Parry and Joseph Caleb Marsden. The only thing that tied them to this case was Wallace's naming of them. Yes, both had worked for the Prudential and both knew Wallace's house, but neither man had anything to do with the murder. The suggestion that they did is pernicious nonsense. In his first statement[451] Wallace claimed he had no suspicion of anyone, yet within days was suddenly touting Parry[452] as a suspect. Wallace knew that the net was closing

the murder included the meticulous searching of the house, particularly the sitting room. [Goodman, *The Killing of Julia Wallace*. p.279.]

450 Murphy, *The Murder of Julia Wallace* pp.85, 87.

451 See Appendix I.

452 Parry did go on to have a criminal record. On 15th February 1932 he pleaded guilty at Dale Street Police Court to two offences regarding motor cars – the stealing of one in Sir Thomas Street on 13th January, and the attempt to steal another car on 30th January in North John Street. He was fined £5 and £6 costs. Incidentally, Constable 217H Jones witnessed Parry's actions on both occasions. Parry again appeared at the Police Court on 1st March 1932 where he was charged with three offences that occurred in the February; on the 18th he stole 1/6 from a telephone kiosk in the Crane Building, Hanover Street; on the 24th he stole 2/– from a telephone kiosk at Owen Owen Ltd, Clayton Square and 2/2 from another telephone kiosk in Reece's Building, also in Clayton Square. Parry pleaded Guilty (with four other offences taken into consideration), where he was fined £5 for each offence to be paid in 28 days. Parry's actions were witnessed by Detective Constable 418H John Tilley. The four other offences were the stealing of a motor car from School Lane on 25th January; the stealing of another car from North John Street on the 27th January; stealing 7/– from a telephone kiosk from S. Reece and Sons Ltd, 14 Castle Street on 10th February and stealing 1/– of the monies belonging to Moss Empires Ltd from the kiosk at the Empire Theatre, Lime Street on the 24th February. A much more serious charge was laid against him in 1936. On the evening of 22nd April twenty four-year-old Lily Fitzsimons met Parry at an herbalist shop in Prescot Road, Liverpool. There, Parry treated the girl to a glass of malted milk and a chocolate biscuit. Sometime after, they left the shop together in Parry's car with the purpose of taking Fitzsimons home. She said Parry drove her to her house in Burnthwaite Road but instead of stopping continued to Rainhill and drove on to a footpath between two houses where he parked the car. The girl alleged that Parry pulled her into the back of the car, and in spite of her resistance, committed the assault. Fitzsimons claimed that she was absolutely petrified and that Parry had committed the offence against her will and with physical violence. After the alleged incident they got out of the car. The girl claimed she got out with the idea of discovering the car number plate and found a tyre was punctured. Parry unsuccessfully tried to mend the puncture, so drove on the flat tyre to a garage at Knotty Ash. There the girl made an excuse for leaving him and went to a telephone box, from where she called the police. Two police officers arrived and, in the

in on him so needed possible suspects to deflect suspicion onto. His subsequent persistence with the belief that it was Parry was a smokescreen.[453] He continued with this fantasy in his diary entry of 14th September 1931, in which he pondered hiring a private detective. In his diary entry dated 6th October 1931, Wallace wrote of his fear of entering his home after dark, and in his *John Bull* article in May 1932 even alluded to the security light he had installed in the porch of his bungalow in case of imminent attack. These were all examples of sheer bravado on the part of Wallace. It also indicates that not only was he a cold-blooded calculated murderer, but also an individual who was quite willing to deviously cast suspicion and lay blame upon what he knew was a perfectly innocent man.

While the statement Parry made at Tuebrook Police Station on 23rd January contradicts that of Lilian Lloyd, there is no underlying or hidden secret. Josephine Lloyd said Parry called at about 7.15pm on the Monday evening. If Parry called at the time stated he could not have been in call-box 1627 when the Qualtrough call was put into action. Irrespective of that, the whole scenario of Parry being in the call-box is also open to question. Those who believe in Wallace's innocence state that Wallace would not have used a call-box so close to his home. While this is a valid point, it also applies to Parry. We are expected to believe that Parry would park his car

presence of Parry, Fitzsimons made the charge against him. Parry denied the charge, claimed he was taking her home and demanded to have her medically examined. He was arrested and appeared at the Liverpool Assizes on Monday 15th June, where he pleaded Not Guilty. The prosecution claimed that Parry had taken the girl to Rainhill and committed the offence against her will. The police officers who came to the garage saw red marks on the girl's face which might have been inflicted by a blow from a fist. Parry's defence said he could not possibly have started the car and driven it while controlling the left-hand gears entirely with his right hand with his left hand holding her coat. A witness saw the car parked on the night in question, but neither saw nor heard any signs of a struggle. Professor James Henry Dible examined the girl on 23rd April and found no evidence of injury or violence. He later examined Parry and found no evidence of violence or injury on his body either. Parry had barely entered the witness box to give evidence when the foreman of the jury asked if it was necessary to go on with the case. After the Judge's advice the jury immediately returned a verdict of Not Guilty, and Parry was discharged.

453 Annie Elizabeth Spencer, who was a client of Wallace's, said that about a week after the murder he called at her house at 235 Lisburn Lane to collect her premiums. During their conversation Wallace told her that a friend of his wife's had killed her because she never allowed strangers into the house. Mrs Spencer was of the idea that Wallace meant it was a friend of them both and asked him so. He replied, "No, a friend of my wife's."

close to the call-box in full view of everyone and anyone passing. Automobiles in 1931 were not a common sight, and one near the junction of Breck Road and Rochester Road would hardly have escaped notice. Someone making a telephone call to put into action a subsequent murder would be highly unlikely to take the chance. If Parry was going to use a telephone he could have used any of the others in the surrounding districts, whereas Wallace would not have had the time to do this. Joseph Marsden was in bed with flu on the evening of 20th January. As mentioned in Chapter One, the populace saw a widespread bout of illness – particularly influenza – in January 1931, and Marsden was another statistic on that list. On another point, the idea that Qualtrough mentioned the 21st birthday would indicate that it was Parry (who had mentioned in his police statement his discussion with Annie Williamson concerning a 21st birthday party) is nonsensical. People took out policies for birthdays; the whole idea of an endowment policy being a birthday (and a 21st one) was purely coincidental.

A point regarding Qualtrough asking for Wallace's address during the telephone conversation with Beattie; it would have been idiotic for Parry or Marsden to have asked for it. There would have been nothing to gain if Beattie would have replied in the affirmative. From a psychological perspective, the idea of asking for the address was more than likely fashioned to convince Beattie that the person calling did not know it, and that the last person he would therefore associate with the call would be Wallace. The asking for the address was probably used to reinforce the illusion that it was not Wallace making the call.

The idea of the voice not belonging to Wallace is also open to question. As Hemmerde suggested, the caller was asking for Wallace, so the last person Beattie was expecting to speak to on the phone was Wallace. Louisa Alfreds and Lilian Martha Kelly both claimed that the voice they heard on the telephone was an ordinary one. It must surely be accepted that this meant the voice spoke with a Liverpool accent. Wallace had lived in Liverpool for nearly sixteen years – we don't know whether he had the ability of disguising his voice, so the possibility of it being him making the call should not be ruled out.

Parry was known at the café. The Mersey Amateur Dramatic Society held its rehearsals there on Tuesdays and Thursdays. Those who claim Wallace's voice would have been recognised fail to acknowledge that Parry's could have as well. There is also the fact that a person's voice on a telephone can sound nothing like their voice as we hear it in person.

It is rightly acknowledged that the caller with the telephone message was the killer. Conversely, if the murderer was the caller then it could only be Wallace. The name Qualtrough was used to cover several areas; a) the name being quite unusual, therefore memorable to anyone being asked it; b) Richard James Qualtrough was insured for a time with the Prudential, during which Marsden collected from him. It is not inconceivable for Wallace to have known this, thereby planting a cryptic deceitful clue to deflect suspicion onto Marsden. Another point regarding the telephone call; not once did Wallace ask Beattie what the voice sounded like. Rather odd that he did not pursue this line of inquiry – Wallace was more interested in the time of it.

Louisa Alfreds claimed that at approximately 7.15pm she put the call through to Bank 3581, hearing a voice at the other end of the line. It was never determined whether the voice was male or female. It is difficult to comprehend what to make of this. Waitress Gladys Harley at the City Café said that the phone had not been in use for the previous half-hour before she answered the subsequent call, and it was certainly not engaged during that 30 minutes. Two minutes later the caller then notified Lilian Martha Kelly that he had pressed button A (for this to have happened Alfreds must have disconnected her connection, otherwise the call would have only appeared on her position on the lamp signal associated with the connecting cord). If he had pressed button A, pressing button B later on would not have returned his money. Kelly asked him to press button B to receive his two pennies back, which he did – the light in the exchange indicating so (pressing button B was possible with or without money being in the box so it would not be known if any money was returned, but the operator would have been given the indication that the button had been pressed). Kelly tried again to obtain the number but without success. Exchange Supervisor Annie Robertson was then informed, and she finally put the call through. At this point the call was connected and Kelly listened to ensure the call was made, before she dropped out of circuit. With the caller not having had his conversation for the first call, a record was made for his second call at the exchange. All calls would be recorded on a docket. Robertson made a note of it, writing the time (which was showing 7.20pm on the exchange clock) with the letters N.R. (no reply) in the margin. This allowed the money in the coinbox to be balanced for accounting purposes. There would be a docket at each exchange, and in all likelihood it was the docket that would have been traced. There was no physical path to trace, as both the calling line and lines and the two operators were known.

A connection could have failed for many reasons, but unlikely that a wrong number was called as each number had its own jack/socket on the switchboard. What could have happened is that the caller inserted the money, and when told to press button A pressed button B instead (or in error), thereby disconnecting the line and having to start again. Not wanting to admit his error/actions, he pressed button B again when asked. Alternatively, the caller inserted the money but a fault on the coinbox meant that the customer couldn't press button A the first time. He then put the phone down. The operator cleared the call down, the caller then picked up the handset and as the money was still in the box didn't need to insert any money and got an operator straight away. When told to press button B again he got his money back and under instruction from the operator reinserted it. After the messing about, the call got connected and this time pressing button A worked. It took a whole five minutes for the call to get connected. The mechanics of the coinbox and the general pounding they took meant that a mechanical failure could easily have happened. If the fault in the connection was due to mechanical failure this would dismiss the assumption that the call had been botched purposely with the intention of incriminating Wallace.

Another point with regards the telephone call – Wallace said he left the house at 7.15pm on the Monday evening and took the tram from the corner of Breck Road and Belmont Road. Several writers have erred in their belief that Qualtrough watched Wallace leave the house then made the call. Box 1627 was in the opposite direction to the way Wallace said he went, and if Wallace left the house at 7.15 (as he was punctual) Qualtrough would have had to have been in the box making the call. This is a highly unlikely scenario. In all probability Wallace left the house at about 7.10pm before making his way to the call-box. The nearest tram stop to Box 1627 was near the corner of Townsend Lane. The distance from there to Lord Street and North John Street junction was 2.5 miles. Inspector Gold said that the route took twenty to twenty five minutes by tram, and he was sure of this as he had made the journey on many occasions. While the exact working time of the number 14 tram making this journey to Lord Street was not tested by the police, it is difficult to say with certainty whether Wallace could or could not have made it in the time. The average speed at which a tram travelled was 6mph, and this would roughly make the journey one of twenty five minutes, which, on the face of it, would be in Wallace's favour. In 1931 motor buses were not numbered, but identified by their route. There was a bus service from Carr Lane to Victoria Street[454] which ran on weekdays from 7.00am to 9.00pm. It covered the route Wallace would take to North John Street from Breck Road.[455] On weekdays a bus was scheduled to leave Carr Lane at 7.14pm. This would take roughly twelve minutes to arrive at the stop on Breck Road. It is generally accepted that the Qualtrough telephone call ended at approximately 7.24pm. Wallace could have been fortunate to board a bus at 7.26pm. Travelling at ten mph,

454 This service began in February 1929. Another bus service from Carr Lane to the City Centre began in January 1931.

455 Via Everton Road, Low Hill, Erskine Street, Islington, William Brown Street, Dale Street and North John Street. There were also alternate buses on the route that incorporated travelling in via Whitechapel.

the bus would have reached North John Street at approximately 7.44pm.

In his statement Parry said he called at Miss Lloyd's house at 5.30pm on the evening of Monday 19th January and remained there until about 11.30pm, and this, taken with the statements of Josephine and Lilian Lloyd, is a contradiction. No doubt conspiracy theorists would rub their hands together at these three statements, but surely there is a simple explanation – namely the possibility that Parry was in the company of another woman at the time. There is also the possibility that people genuinely make mistakes regarding actual times. The statements of both Josephine and Lilian Lloyd include references to what clothes Parry was wearing the week of the murder – obviously the police were thoroughly checking up on him. Parry had alibis galore for the Tuesday night, and the whole premise that he was driving around heavily-policed areas in a possibly bloodstained car is idiotic. There were police patrols throughout the night of the murder, especially in and around the Anfield, Tuebrook and Old Swan areas. Police motorcycles and even the recent patrol car were fully utilised on the night in question. John Parkes even admitted that Police Constable Ken Wallace called at the garage on the night of the murder. We are led to believe that Parry would leave a bloodstained car outside his girlfriend's house for several hours before driving to a garage at the dead of night. It borders on the insane, as does the notion that Parry would confide and confess his part in a murder. How anyone can believe this unmitigated nonsense beggars belief. Parry was, therefore, rightly eliminated from the police investigations.

Revenge has also been touted as a possible reason for the killing, but surely this can be eliminated. Why take revenge on Mrs Wallace? If another person wanted revenge on William Wallace, why not murder him instead?

Eliminate Marsden and Parry from the equation and you are left with Wallace and Wallace alone, and that is by his own admission: "She would have only admitted someone she knew into the house." All of the people on the list Wallace gave to the CID were checked and rightly eliminated from their enquiries. In fact, at the committal proceedings both Parry and Marsden were alluded to, but it was decided not to mention their names in court (which Sydney Scholefield Allen agreed to). Roland Oliver was against Parry's name being mentioned during the trial itself, but was told by Justice Wright that names must not be withheld as he did not want any mystery surrounding the case. Inspector Herbert Gold said the names on the list had been fully investigated and that the evidence with regards to them was readily available if required. Therefore, there was no conspiracy whatsoever.

One wonders, though, how long it will be before the other names on the list are suddenly thrust into the suspect category.[456] The files have been decimated over the years and some of the papers and statements have gone missing, but this is more than likely through the passing of time and neglect and not because of any perceived underhand actions deployed by the police. Surely if statements had been destroyed purposely, the ones given by Parry, Lilian Lloyd and Josephine Lloyd would have been amongst those.

There is also a continuous and misguided belief that the Liverpool City Police at the time were utterly incompetent, and that the police strike of 1919 had a profound effect on the force of 1931. There is no actual proof to support this. In actual fact, police conditions improved greatly after the strike. It also increased awareness of their importance, and they were never again taken for granted as they had been previously.

While areas of the police investigation during the case may have been questionable (and, it has to be said, detrimental to their own cause in parts – particularly the intrusion of numerous police at the murder scene; proving the possibility that Wallace could have taken the tram or bus to the Chess Club in the time on the Monday evening; taking until Friday 23rd January to collect the suit of clothes Wallace wore, and the lack of investigating Julia's

456 Or the possibility that Joseph, bearing a remarkable similarity to his brother, was not in the Malay States but trudging around Menlove Gardens acting as Wallace, while his brother was committing the dreadful act (or vice versa).

background and actual age) – the fact was that the Liverpool Police Force was the largest and most important in the country outside that of London.[457] Up-to-date methods in the Criminal Department included an impressive system in which fingerprints could be sent via telegraph or wireless in secret code, which enabled police to identify international criminals captured by them. For the year 1931, 34 recruits were appointed from over 5,000 applicants. The Recruiting and Training Department examined 300 men for outside forces as to their physical suitability, and in addition to these 60 to educational standard. In the examination classes held for constables and sergeants seeking promotion, 8 sergeants and 66 constables reached the required standard.[458] Educationally and physically, the Liverpool City Police insisted on a very high standard indeed. Throughout the 1920s many university men patrolled Liverpool's streets, and in the ranks were public schoolboys, clerks, shop assistants, skilled engineers, trained mechanics and ships' stewards. The painting of the police in a negative light supports a charge of corruption:[459] demean the police and you have a case, so

457 The average daily strength of the force during the year of 1930 was 2,257. This amounted to 0.5 percent less than the full authorised strength. 7,100 men applied for recruitment, of which 506 were called up for educational and medical examinations. Of this number 73 were announced fit for service (the rest failing). The average length of service per man was 10.6 years. Recruits were given rigorous theoretical instructions in their training, which included knowledge of criminal habits; tools and methods used by criminals; the giving of evidence; demeanour to the public and extent of legal powers. They were also instructed in First Aid and swimming. Discipline on the force was generally good – no men were dismissed for the year 1930 and a mere two in 1931. [Watch Committee Annual Report 1930.]

458 The following figures give the relative sizes of the principal forces of the North in 1931, followed by population of each city/town from that year's census: Liverpool 2,268 (855,539); Manchester 1,442 (766,333); Sheffield 732 (511,742); Leeds 731 (482,789); Bradford 479 (298,041); Newcastle 450 (283,145); Salford 360 (223,442); Burnley 120 (98,259). Liverpool had practically as many police as Manchester, Sheffield and Burnley combined. The total strength of the Liverpool Force in December 1931 was 2,236. These figures included two Assistant Chief Constables (Herbert Winstanley and W.E. Glover), one Medical Officer (Hugh Pierce), three Chief Superintendents, ten Superintendents, nineteen Chief Inspectors, 48 Inspectors, five Sub-Inspectors, 313 Sergeants and 1,835 Constables. During the year a number of First Aid awards were earned. Nearly every man in the force held some sort of award, while 2,025 held medallions. Watch Committee Annual Report 1931.

459 There is also a continued assumption that the police coached witnesses and were selective in their choice of witnesses. If anything this criticism could be aimed at the defence; they called James Allison Wildman and David Jones (both of whose evidence varied from their original testimonies). The same applied to the evidence of John and Florence Johnston and Joseph Crewe [see note 48 chapter 2 and notes 185 and 221 chapter 4], and it was several weeks after the murder that Hector Munro interviewed Douglas Metcalf, Kenneth Caird and Elsie Wright.

to speak.[460] These allegations are completely unfounded, and merely the ploy of conspiracy theorists to justify their half-baked ideas. At the trial Justice Wright did not agree with the criticisms aimed at the police, and in fact thought they had investigated the case with enthusiasm and ability. At the appeal Justice Branson wondered whether they were trying Wallace or the Liverpool Police.

As for a contract killing (which was suggested by Richard Waterhouse in his 1994 account *The Insurance Man*[461]), this can be eliminated. Wallace would hardly hire a contract killer to dispatch his wife when he could do it himself. He would certainly not hire one and then name him. The idea is utterly preposterous and has no basis in reality. With regards to the alleged Hall sighting, it is idiotic to believe Wallace would be seen in the vicinity of the crime with an accomplice. Waterhouse was completely wrong to go down that avenue. With regards to the method of dispatch, Wallace said he had the means available to murder his wife (alluding to his scientific knowledge and therefore by chemical or poisonous means). This is highly unlikely. If Mrs Wallace had been poisoned a post mortem would have clearly identified the cause of death, and if it was by poisoning there would have only been one suspect and Wallace knew this. This was just another example of bravado by Wallace.

The mackintosh undoubtedly played the vital part in the avoidance of blood spatter. Wallace didn't take a bath – he didn't need to – he took precautions. MacFall claimed that most of the blood splashes were concentrated around the corner of the room by the sideboard and by the chair on which the violin case rested. The old maxim 'Prevention is better than cure' applies. As the prosecution stated, the room was set up for a musical evening and this is probably what happened. Wallace had told Julia he would not take the trip to Mossley Hill and that they should have a musical

460 During the police investigations over two hundred people were interviewed. Some of these were traced to public houses and cafés (which necessitated the spending of money), but no refund on behalf of the CID was asked for. Even the crank confessions were investigated diligently.

461 See Bibliography.

evening instead. The opening blow was more than likely inflicted as she bent over the gas-fire.[462] He then pulled the body away from the fire and stamped out the burning mackintosh[463] before administering the further ten blows. The wearing of gloves would have prevented the hands and fingernails being contaminated by blood. In all likelihood Wallace placed the mackintosh between himself and his victim while he bludgeoned her. This would have shielded him from any direct blood spatter. There were two marks on the mackintosh that could be interpreted as squirts, and during the investigation, committal and trial the mackintosh had been handled extensively, from which blood could have been rubbed from it. Wallace was forensically enough aware, and must have taken extreme precautions. Whoever murdered Julia Wallace managed to avoid blood spatter – the crime scene suggests this. There were no traces of blood anywhere in the hallway, back kitchen area, scullery and back yard. The underlying factor of the innocence of Wallace for many was always the lack of blood on his clothing/person, but murderers have managed to avoid blood spatter. Those who believe Wallace guilty could point to the Fall River Murderer's ability in avoiding heavy blood-spatter in the administering of a combined thirty strikes to the head area of the two Borden victims with an axe.

It is generally regarded that the attack was committed in a frenzy, yet with the exception of the two thumps heard by Florence Johnston sometime around 8.25-8.30pm there were no suspicious

462 When lit, naked flames burned high and often jumped forward out of the fire. There were no safety features incorporated into the design. The gas standpipe came out from under the floorboards; a 90-degree elbow turned it towards the fire, and there was a stopcock and the burner was simply a perforated pipe beneath the clay tiles. To light it one would have to switch on the gas from the cock and light the burner with a match to heat the clay tiles, and reduce the gas supply with the cock once they were glowing. When the gas was full on, the flames could easily ignite paper or cloth (clothing wasn't fireproofed at the time) and even the glowing clay tiles could burn material. The tiles, over long periods of use, often cracked and separated and in the separation naked flames would appear. It would take two or three minutes with the gas flame on full before the clay tiles started to glow. [James Murphy, Letter to the author 21st December 2011.]

463 The mackintosh material was more than likely gabardine. The best quality was usually worsted wool, and there was also an inferior type being a mix of wool and cotton. They were waterproofed but not fireproofed (which was the standard, popular material for such overcoats in those days). They scorched and burned very quickly against a naked flame or hot surface. [James Murphy, Letter to the author 21st December 2011.]

noises. This was corroborated by Walter and Bertha Holme in number 27, who also claimed they heard no suspicious sounds emanating from number 29. Although John Sharpe Johnston was slightly deaf in the left ear, he heard Wallace call out twice whilst waiting in the entry. The floors in the living kitchen, front parlour and hallway were wooden floorboards until you reached the kitchen, which was stone. Under the wooden floors there was ample space to kneel, enabling access right under the hallway and living rooms. Ten of the eleven blows were administered while the victim was on the floor. It is difficult to comprehend how a frenzied attack would not have been heard by the immediate neighbours. The dividing walls of the houses in Wolverton Street are about a foot thick – however noise could be heard from next door, be it music, singing, raised voices, doors slamming or running up and down the stairs. The cushion that was taken from the crime scene and analysed by Professor Roberts had numerous small human blood stains on one side (and also particles of burnt mackintosh). Perhaps the killer placed it under the head of the victim to muffle the sounds?

The weapon and gloves could have been discarded, possibly, as James Murphy suggests, in the grounds of the Dudlow Lane Pumping Station,[464] or even on the route somewhere, possibly to Menlove Gardens or Allerton. Just because nothing was found does not mean it was not there.

Some also make the chronic mistake that Wallace was an unfit and elderly man. Yes, he did have health problems[465] but his job

464 Murphy, *The Murder of Julia Wallace* pp.177.

465 Since the time Wallace's left kidney was removed in 1907 he would be subjected to acute pain on his right side every two or three years. These attacks would be relieved by lying down. When he was admitted to the Royal Southern Hospital on 9th June 1930 he complained of pain in the right loin brought about by walking. He also complained of frequency of urination, occasional nausea and headaches and an abnormal thirst. Examined by Surgeon Herbert Williams, there was evidence of commencing renal failure. The bladder was examined under anaesthetic. There was tenderness on palpation in the right loin, and the right kidney appeared enlarged. Dr Stanley V. Unsworth stated confidentially that the condition was frequently associated with mental changes – delusions, mania and temporary fits of insanity. Wallace was discharged the following month on 10th July. In his medical report dated 3rd February 1931, Physician and Neurologist William Johnson stated that it was possible that some seven months after admission to Hospital Wallace may have been in a 'physically debilitating state that could be contributory to the development of mental disturbance.'

involved plenty of walking. He was also fit enough to traipse around the Allerton area on a cold winter's night. By his own admission he preferred to walk the 605 yards to the tram stop at the corner of Belmont Road (near St Margaret's Church) than the much shorter distance (375 yards) at the stop 50 yards to the right of Castlewood Road.[466]

Where clear proof of murder exists, the prosecution does not have to provide a motive. But with regards to possible motive, although it is generally accepted that money was not an issue in the murder, there is a point that seems widely overlooked; the argument that Wallace would not have killed for the £20 his wife was insured for (and the £90 in her account). If we look at the other side of it, we see a different picture – he seemed to go to extreme measures to gain a commission in his quest for Menlove Gardens East. He also made the comment in his diary that their main problem in life was that of thousands of others: pounds, shillings and pence. Those who believe Wallace would not have murdered for money display chronic amnesia when they suggest he would try doggedly to gain a commission.

It could be difficult to comprehend how someone could be forensically aware and make basic errors, yet the act of murder can affect the murderer and his or her actions. An adrenalin rush will kick in – the mind will not think straight – panic ensues. Plans meticulously thought out before[467] the killing will inadvertently go wrong.

There is also the fact that murderers do actually commit idiotic actions. Why did Frederick Bywaters keep the letters he received from Edith Thompson, knowing he was going to kill Percy Thompson, thereby giving the prosecution ideal proof of her

466 Surely Wallace did use the shorter stop, as it would have been more beneficial to him whether guilty or innocent. An innocent Wallace would surely have saved himself the longer walk, and a guilty Wallace would not have missed the opportunity to board a tram, saving him precious minutes. Only a guilty Wallace would claim to have taken the tram from the further stop.

467 Hemmerde made the statement that 'The murderer must have made up his mind exactly when he was going to do it, how he was going to do it and with what weapon he was going to do it with.' This statement epitomises the case. It is consistent with a planned murder rather than a planned robbery, which would rule out anyone other than Wallace. The planning of the murder was more than likely done far in advance – possibly years.

infidelity and questionable character? Why did Crippen bury what police claimed were fragments of his wife Belle's remains in his cellar only to dispose of the majority elsewhere? Why did Henri Désiré Landru not destroy the meticulous notebooks he kept that gave the police incriminating evidence against him?

The only person that can be placed inside the telephone kiosk on the Monday evening and inside 29 Wolverton Street at the time of the killing on the following night is Wallace. Parry or Marsden cannot – ergo, Wallace was the killer.

The simplest explanation is the most plausible one.[468] Many accept that the Wallaces lived in the happiest of circumstances,[469] yet on that we only have the word of Wallace.[470] In correspondence held by the present-day incarnation of solicitors Davis, Berthen and Munro, Wallace mistakenly says he married in 1913, saying that he could not remember the exact date. Another example was his diary entry of 25th March 1929, stating that Julia had had to remind him that it was the 15th anniversary of their marriage the previous day.[471] It is also interesting to note that he forgot the house

468 You have to apply the theory of Occam's Razor; the theory that if you have a conundrum with several possible explanations the simplest one is usually the right one. [Alan Hayhurst, email to the author 21st February 2011.]

469 An entry in Wallace's diary dated Saturday 7th January 1928 includes an argument Wallace had with Julia over the buying of too many newspapers.

470 Florence Mary Wilson, matron of the Remand Police Home, 31 Derwent Road, nursed Wallace through an attack of pneumonia about eight years prior to the murder. She described the Wallaces as a very peculiar couple, and that their attitude toward each other seemed strained. She said Wallace appeared to be a man who had suffered a keen disappointment in life and that Mrs Wallace was peculiar in manner and dirty (this would completely contradict Sarah Jane Draper's evidence, who claimed Julia helped her to clean the house whenever she visited on a Wednesday). Alfred Mather, a former Prudential agent, informed Inspector Herbert Gold that he had known Wallace for about twelve years and described him as the most cool, calculating, despondent and soured man he had ever met. Mather said that Wallace was not liked by his clients, some even referring to him as a bad-tempered devil. The Wallace family physician Louis Curwen told Sergeant Harry Bailey that since Mrs Wallace's death, he had thought the situation over and came to the conclusion that they did not lead the happy and harmonious life that others supposed they did. Curwen claimed that from a number of visits he made to Wolverton Street, both Wallace and Julia appeared indifferent to each other's health. [Comments made by Florence Mary Wilson, Alfred Mather and Louis Curwen appear in Detective Inspector Gold Report Monday, 11th May 1931]. The general feeling amongst his clients towards Wallace was that he was a morose type of man, who would hardly return a greeting, but simply collect his premiums and leave immediately. I can certainly vouch for this – my great aunt always claimed he was a strange, taciturn character and rather abrupt. My grandfather said that Wallace was rather an aloof man and appeared rather conceited.

471 In *The Trial of William Herbert Wallace*, W.F. Wyndham Brown states the year of the diary as 1929 (pp.18). In the police records it is listed as 1930.

number that he lived at with Julia in St Mary's Avenue, Harrogate. There is even the possibility that the Wallaces slept in different rooms in Wolverton Street. The front bedroom was noticeably larger than the middle bedroom. It contained a bed, a mirror, a wardrobe and a dressing table containing drawers. In his statement dated 22nd January 1931, Wallace claimed that at night he always took the company's money upstairs to *his* bedroom.

At the same time others who knew him say that he was a gentle man, devoid of any feelings of antagonism or aggression, but history tells us otherwise. Nice men and women do kill, and when they do, more often than not, it is their spouses they kill. While it is said that you don't need a motive for murder, surely all murders have some sort of motive. Wallace was living a humdrum life and possibly wanted some sort of challenge or something to be remembered for. In a diary entry dated 10th April 1928 Wallace writes of the dislike of his job. In another extract dated 17th August 1928 he refers to his 51st (sic) birthday and having 'little to show for fifty-odd years.' There is also the fact that Julia was not the most honest of people, as is evidenced by the three falsehoods in her census record of 1911. Whether Wallace was aware of her actual age is something we will never know, although one would expect a person to know their partner was seventeen years older than them, particularly as they age. By 1931 Julia Wallace was incontinent; when her body was examined she was wearing a diaper-type item of cloth. Was her increasingly frail health a frustration and embarrassment to Wallace?

In the *John Bull* issue of 21st May 1932 Wallace wrote about the killing of his wife as he saw it. This has a chilling confessional aspect to it and fits in with the character of an egotistical killer having to divulge how they managed to commit the crime without actually admitting to it:

> "The crime was this – when I left the house, he would have been watching to see me depart.
>
> It was my wife's rigid rule not to admit strangers into the house when she was alone, and to this day it has been a cause

> for speculation how the man actually made his way inside. He must have been ready with a pretext to be allowed to wait until I returned.
>
> He followed my wife into the sitting-room, and as she bent down and lit the gas fire he struck her, possibly with a spanner. The implement of murder was never discovered.
>
> He had now to kill her. To strike her again while she lay on the floor and him standing over her would mean the upward spurting of blood.
>
> Two strides took him into the lobby, where he had observed my mackintosh hanging, and he held it as a shield between him and her body while he belaboured her to death.
>
> She must have been felled as soon as she lit the fire and before she could regulate the flow of gas. It would have been at full blaze, and as he bent at the fireplace the flame set light to the mackintosh.
>
> Then he would see that the bottom edge of her skirt was burning, and, throwing the mackintosh down, he must have dragged her away from the fire and on to part of the coat, leaving her in the position I found her.
>
> I have written the last word – only one name have I kept locked in my mind, the name of the man who killed my wife…"

The murder of Julia Wallace is what should be called an intellectual killing. It has all the hallmarks of that: the telephone call, the chess connection, the mysterious caller, the non-existent address, the contrived alibi. The whole plan was fraught with danger and possible disaster – another person would not have carried it out. The murder of Julia Wallace was not a robbery gone wrong, a contract killing or a pre-planned assassination by another unbeknownst to Wallace – it was a pre-planned assassination[472] by one man and one man alone: William Herbert Wallace.

472 Dr Michael Stone, Forensic Psychologist Columbia University classifies murderers belonging to different groups in his Scale of Evil. At 10 he places classic assassins – egocentric killers who dispose of a victim because they are in the way.

APPENDIX I
WALLACE STATEMENT (I)

Anfield Detective Office
Tuesday 20th January 1931

William Herbert Wallace says:

I am 52 years and by occupation an insurance agent for the Prudential Insurance Company, Dale Street. I have resided at 29 Wolverton Street with my wife Julia (deceased) age, believed 52 years, for the past sixteen years. There is no children of the marriage. My wife and I have been on the best of terms all our married life. At 10.30am today I left the house, leaving my wife indoors, doing her household duties. I went on my insurance round in Clubmoor district, my last call being 177 Lisburn Lane shortly before 2.0pm. I then took a tramcar to Trinity Church, Breck Road arriving at my house at 2.10pm. My wife was then well and I had dinner and left the house at about 3.15pm. I then returned to Clubmoor and continued my collections and finished about 5.55pm. My last call being either 19 or 21 Eastman Road. I boarded a bus at Queens Drive and Townsend Avenue, alighted at Cabbage Hall and walked up to my house at about 6.05pm. I entered my house by back door, which is my usual practice, and then had tea with my wife, who was quite well and then I left the house at 6.45pm leaving by the back door. I caught a car from Belmont Road and West Derby Road and got off at Lodge Lane and Smithdown Road and boarded a Smithdown Road car to Penny Lane. I then boarded another car up Menlove Avenue West, looking for 25 Menlove Avenue East where I had an appointment with Mr R.M. Qualtrough for 7.30pm in connection with my insurance business. I was unable to find the address and I enquired at 25 Menlove Avenue West and I also asked at the bottom of Green Lane, Allerton, a constable about the address. He told me there was no such address. I then called at a Post Office near the Plaza Cinema to look at the directory, but there was none there, and I was unable to find the address. I also visited a newsagent where there was a directory but I was unable to find the address. It was then 8pm and I caught a tramcar to Lodge Lane, and then a car to West Derby Road and Belmont Road and walked home from there.

I arrived at Wolverton Street about 8.45pm and I pulled out my key and went to open the front door and found it secure and could not open it with my key. I knocked gentle but got no answer. I could not see any light in the house. I then went around to the back, the door leading from the entry to the backyard was closed, but not bolted. I went into the back door of the house, and I was unable to get in, I do not know if the door was bolted or not, it sticks sometimes, but I think the door was bolted but I am not sure. There was a small light in the back kitchen, but no light in the kitchen. I then went back to the front, I was suspicious because I expected my wife to be in, and the light in the kitchen. I tried my key in the front door again, and found the lock did not work properly. The key would turn in it, but seemed to unturn without unlocking the door. I rushed around to the back, and saw my neighbours Mr and Mrs Johnston, coming out of 31 Wolverton Street. I said to them, "Have you heard any suspicious noises in my house during the past hours or so?" Mrs Johnston said they hadn't. I said then I couldn't get in and asked them if they would wait awhile, while I tried again. I then found the back kitchen door opened quite easily. I walked in by the back kitchen door. I found kitchen light out, I lit it and found signs of disturbance in the kitchen. A wooden case in which I keep photographic stuff in had been broken open and the lid was on the floor. I then went upstairs and entered the middle bedroom, but saw nothing unusual. I then entered the bathroom, but it was correct. I then entered the back room and found no disturbance there. I then entered the front room, struck a match, and found the bed upset, the clothes being off. I don't think my wife left it like that, I then came down and looked into the front room, after striking a match and saw my wife lying on the floor I felt her hand and concluded she was dead. I then rushed out and told Mr and Mrs Johnston what had happened, saying something but I cannot remember what I did say. After my neighbours had been in, Mr Johnston went for the police and a doctor, I asked him to go. I afterwards found that about £4 had been taken from a cash box in the kitchen but I am not sure of the amount. When I discovered my wife lying on the floor I noticed my mackintosh lying on the floor at the back of her. I wore the mackintosh up to noon today but left it off owing to the fine weather. My wife has never worn the mackintosh to my knowledge. You drew my attention to it being burnt, but it was not like that when I last saw it and I [cannot] explain it. I have no suspicion of anyone.

(Signed) William Herbert Wallace.

There was a dog whip with a lash in the house which I have not seen for 12 months but I have not found it up to now. It usually hung in the hallstand. The handle was of wood 12" long and 1" thick, I don't think there was any metal about it.

APPENDIX II: WALLACE STATEMENT (II)

Dale Street Detective Office
22.1.31

William Herbert Wallace further states: –

Mr Gordon R. Parry, of Derwent Road Stoneycroft, is a friend of my late wife and myself. He is now an agent for the Gresham Insurance Company but I'm not quite sure of the company.

He was employed by the Prudential up to about 12 or 15 months ago, and he then resigned to improve his position. Although nothing was known officially to the company detrimental to his financial affairs, it was known that he had collected premiums which he did not pay in and his Superintendent, Mr Crewe, of Green Lane, Allerton, told me that he went to Parry's parents who paid about £30 to cover the deficiency. Mr Crewe's office is at 2 Gt Nelson Street. Parry is a single man about 22 years of age. I have known him about three years and he was with my company about two years. I was ill with bronchitis in December in 1928 and Parry did part of [my] collecting for about two or three days a week for about three weeks. I discovered slight discrepancies and I spoke to him about it. He was short of small amounts when paying in and he had not entered all the amounts collected in the book. When I spoke to him he said it was an oversight and that he was sorry and he [would] put the matter right. Previous to Parry doing my work he had called at my house once on business and left a letter for me which he wrote in my front room. I was not in at the time but my wife let him in. While he was doing my work in December 1928 he called very frequently to see me about business, and he was well acquainted with our domestic arrangements. He had been in the parlour and kitchen frequently and had been upstairs in the middle bedroom a number of times to see me while I was in bed. I do not think he called to see me after I resumed duty in January 1929, but if he had have called my wife would have had no hesitation in admitting him. I have often seen him since he has been working for his new company and have spoken to him. About last November I was in the City Café one evening, I think it was on a Thursday, playing chess, and I saw Parry there. He was not playing chess. He was by himself walking across the room. I said, "Good evening" and he returned my greeting. I think that was the last time I saw him. He is a member of an amateur dramatic society which holds its meetings at the City Café on Thursday evenings. I do not think he drinks. He is engaged to a Miss Lloyd, 7 Missouri Road Clubmoor. He would be on a weekly salary from his company plus a commission on business and his earnings would be about £4 per week.

There was another man named Marsden who also did part of the work for me while I was ill in December 1928. I do not know his address. He was an agent for the Prudential Company for two or three years and had left before he did my work. I gave him the job because he was out of work. Parry recommended him. I have heard that Marsden left the Prudential on account of financial irregularities. While he was working for me he often came to my house to see me on business. He also knew the interior arrangements of my house. I have seen Marsden several times since he worked for me. I do not know if he is working now and I do not know anything about his private affairs. If he had called at my house my wife would have asked him in. Both Parry and Marsden knew the arrangements of my business with regard to the system of paying in money collected to the Head Office, Dale Street. There is a definite order of the company's that money must be paid in on Wednesday's but this is not strictly enforced and I paid in on Thursday's usually. I have had the cash-box from which the money was stolen for about 16 years. I always put the company's money in that box and it was always kept on the top of the book-case in the kitchen during the daytime. At night I always took it upstairs to my bedroom. Parry and Marsden knew I kept the money in the box because while they worked for me I always put the money into it when they called to pay over to me their collections. They had both seen me take it down and put it back to the top of the book-case in the kitchen often. Marsden is about 28 years of age, about 5 foot 6/7 inches, brown hair, and fairly well dressed. Parry is about 5 foot 10 inches, slimmish build, dark hair, rather foppish appearance, well dressed and wears spats, very plausible.

Superintendent Crewe, his assistant, Mr Wood, 26 Ellersley (sic) Road, Mr J Bamber, Assistant Superintendent, 43 Kingfield Road, Orrel Park, employees of the company, would be admitted by my wife without hesitation if they called. There are personal friends of ours who would also be admitted if they called. They are Mr F.W. Jenkinson, his son Frederick, 20 yrs? his daughter 16 and his wife. They live at 112 Moscow Drive. Mr James Caird, 3 Letchworth Street Anfield, his wife and family. He has two grown up sons. Mr Davis, music teacher of Queens Drive, Walton, who is teaching me the violin. Mr Hayes (sic) my tailor of Breck Road.

I forgot to mention that I believe Mr Parry owns a motorcar or has the use of one, because I was talking to him about Xmas time in Missouri Road and he had a car then which he was driving. He gave me one of his Company's calendars.

When I left the house at 6.45pm on Tuesday night last my wife came down the back yard with me as far as the yard door, she closed the yard door. I do not remember hearing her bolt it. On Monday night, the 19th inst. I left home about 7.15pm to go to the chess club. I got there about 7.45pm and started to play a game of chess with a man whose name I think is McCarthy, but I am not sure of him and I do not know his business. He is a member of the club. We had been playing for about 10 minutes when Captain Beattie came to me and told me there had been a telephone message for me from a Mr Qualtrough asking me to go and see him at 25, Menlove Gardens East at 7.30pm on Tuesday, the 21st inst. on a matter of business. Captain Beattie had the name Qualtrough and the address 25 Menlove Gardens East, and the time and date of the appointment written on an envelope and I copied it into my diary. Mr Caird was present and we all discussed the best way to get to Menlove Gardens. When I left home on Monday night to go to the chess club I think I walked along Richmond Park to Breck Road and then up to Belmont Road, where I boarded a tramcar and got off at the corner of Lord Street and North John Street.

When I was at Allerton looking for the address 25 Menlove Gardens East, in addition to the people I have already mentioned, I enquired from a woman in Menlove Gardens North. She came out of a house near the end by Menlove Gardens West. She told me it might be further up in continuation of Menlove Gardens West. I went along as suggested by her and came to a crossroad, I think it was Dudley Road, and I met a young man about 25 years, tall and fair, and I enquired from him but he could not inform me. I walked back down the West Gardens to the South Gardens and found all even numbers. I did not knock and came out on to Menlove Avenue itself, when I saw a man waiting for a tram by a stop where there was a shelter. I went up to him and asked him if he could tell me where Menlove Gardens East was, he said he was a stranger and did not know. I think these are all the people I spoke to that night at Allerton.

When I got back home and after getting into the house and making the discovery of my wife's death, Mr Johnston went for the doctor and police. Mrs Johnston and I stayed in, and some time after a knock came to the front door. I answered it and it was thus I found that the front door was bolted. The safety catch was not on the latch lock. I opened the door and admitted the constable. That was the first time I went to the front door after getting into the house.

When I left my house at 6.45pm, my wife was sitting in the

kitchen, that is, when I had got my hat and coat on ready to go, and as I have already said, she came down the yard with me. The tea things were still on the table. When I got back the table had been cleared of the tea things.

There is a Mr Thomas, a member of the chess club, and a Mr Stan Young who used to be an employee of our Company who would be admitted by my wife if they called. I do not know their addresses. My wife had no friends unknown to me as far as I know. I have now found by the calendar that Mr Parry's employers are the Standard Life Assurance Company, whose head office is at 3, George Street, Edinburgh.

(Signed) W.H. Wallace.

APPENDIX III
WALLACE STATEMENT (III)

Dale Street
23/1/31

William Herbert Wallace further states: –

Before I got on the tram at Smithdown Road on Tuesday night, I asked the conductor whether it went anywhere near Menlove Gardens. The conductor said I had better go to Penny Lane and have a transfer. I then boarded the car and sat inside on the first seat on the right. A few seconds later a ticket inspector entered the car and he told me to get off at Penny Lane and then take a 5a and he told me the numbers of other cars which I cannot remember and that either of those cars would get me to Menlove Gardens. I took a penny ticket and got off at Penny Lane. The conductor pointed to a tram, a 5a, which was standing there and told me that would take me to Menlove Gardens. I boarded it and took a penny ticket and asked the conductor to put me off at Menlove Gardens and he did so. I remember looking at my watch and noticing that I had about 10 minutes to spare before the appointment was due at 7.30pm, so it must have been about 7.20pm when I got off the tram.

(Signed) W.H. Wallace.

APPENDIX IV: WALLACE STATEMENT (IV)

83, Ullet Road
29.1.31

William Herbert Wallace further states: –

On Monday night the 19th inst. When I left home to go to the chess club I think I went out by the back door and up the passage to Richmond Park and then up Breck Road and got the tram at Belmont Road. I do not remember seeing anyone I know. I am not sure but I have an idea that I posted a letter in the pillar box opposite the library in Breck Road. I have a lot of correspondence and I have no special reason for remembering about whether or not I did post a letter that night because I post so many.

When I returned home at 8.40pm on Tuesday the 20th inst. I went to the front door because it was my usual practice if I was out late at night. It was my usual practice to use the back door in daylight and if I went out by the back way after dark my wife usually came down the yard and bolted the yard door after me when I went out.

As far as I can recollect I do not know anyone named Hall living in the neighbourhood of Wolverton Street or Richmond Park or any of the streets adjacent, but I have an idea that I have heard my late wife mention someone of that name in connection with Holy Trinity Church, but my recollection of that is very hazy. In the summer of 1929 I remember my wife and I had been out for a walk. I had forgotten to take my key and we had to borrow a key from Mr Gosling who lives on the opposite side of Wolverton Street and his key opened our front door. Some years ago a man named Cadwallader, who lives at 33 Wolverton Street, had a key that opened our door, because he used to drink and on several occasions he made a mistake and came into our house instead of his own. He has been dead several years and his widow and son still live at 33 Wolverton Street.

(Signed) W.H. Wallace.

APPENDIX V
TRIAL EXHIBITS

Photograph 1. This and the following four photographs were taken by Harry Hewitt Cooke on 24th January. Number 1 shows two CID officers – one on the step of 29 Wolverton Street and the other at the entry near Campbell's Dance Hall.

Photograph 2. This shows the front of 29 Wolverton Street with the front door open.

Photograph 3. An exterior shot showing the back yard door from the perspective of the back window.

Photograph 4. A reverse shot of photograph 3.

Photograph 5. Detective Sergeant Harry Bailey in the entryway outside the back door of Number 29 Wolverton Street.

Photograph 6. Crime scene photograph taken from the doorway towards the fireplace by Harry Hewitt Cooke on 21st January.

Photograph 7. The second crime scene photograph taken from the bay window moments after photograph number 6.

Photograph 8. This was taken on 23rd January in the living kitchen. Visible is the homemade cabinet belonging to Wallace and the cash-box on top of the shelf.

Photograph 9. Taken on 21st January. This is of the toilet pan with the visible blood clot on the rim.

Photograph 10. Photograph of victim taken at Princes Dock Mortuary (as were the following two photographs) on 21st January.

Photograph 11. Photograph of victim.

Photograph 12. Photograph of victim.

Photograph 13. Shot of bathroom in 29 Wolverton Street taken on 18th February.

Plans of ground and first floors of 29 Wolverton Street and also the Richmond Park/Wolverton Street area.

Diagram of Wallace's journey from the back of 29 Wolverton Street to the tram stop by St Margaret's Church at the corner of Belmont Road.

Diagram of Menlove Gardens and Allerton Road area.

Ornament. This was referred to as a jam jar/pot. It contained the four £1 notes on the mantelpiece in the middle bedroom.†

Mackintosh.† Extensively and heavily bloodstained on the right side, both inside and outside, and on the upper inner side of the right sleeve. The outside of the left cuff and a large area near the left pocket were similarly stained. A considerable portion of the bottom right side had been burnt away.

Cabinet.* The homemade box belonging to Wallace.

Cash-box.* This had three compartments and had a broken hinge on the lid.

Front door lock.* Locksmith James Sarginson said that it could be opened if half turned but if opened fully, it slipped back. The lock was opened by pressing the 'snips' together.

Back kitchen door lock and key. This was rusty but in good working order. The crank which accentuated the spring lock grinded against the base of the lock, so when turned it remained in and required pressure to open. A spring had been inserted to assist the original spring.

Lavatory pan.

Nail brush.* Removed from the scene by MacFall, the bristles slightly damp.

Piece of hair. The chignon Julia wore which had become detached and was found beside her head. It was matted together with blood.†

Two pictures.* Both were spattered from all angles with human blood.

Two photographs.* One photograph had four human blood

splashes on it and the other a smear of human blood on the bottom right hand side of the glass.

Violin in case.* Extensively spattered with human blood on the upper wide end of the outside of the case.

Piece of sheet music.* The front of the outside brown paper cover was spotted with human blood.

Cushion.† There were numerous small human blood stains on one side; also particles of burnt mackintosh.

Hearthrug.* One corner was soaked in human blood, there were also numerous blood stains on other parts. The blood had not soaked right through.

Dollar bill.*

Suit of clothes.*

Piece of carpet.*

Towel.*

Skirt. Julia's dress which bore the scorch marks identical to the clays of the gas fire. The front was heavily stained with blood.†

Four £1 notes, postal order for 2/4d, half-crown.*

Copy of William Henry Roberts' blood test. Roberts conducted five tests with regard to the blood. These included the microscopic test; treatment with glacial acetic acid and a trace of salt to form haemin crystals; the spectroscopic test, the precipitin test and the guaiacum test.

Half-crown and two separate shillings.*

Two matches. These were retrieved by Detective Sergeant Bailey from the folds of the mackintosh.†

Lady's handbag. Found on one of the chairs partially under the table in the kitchen.*

Wallace's statement dated 20th January 1931. This was the statement taken at Anfield Police Station.

Underskirt worn by Mrs Wallace.†

Wallace's statement dated 22nd January 1931. Taken at Dale Street Detective Office.

Wallace's statement dated 23rd January 1931. Taken at Dale Street Detective Office.

Wallace's statement dated 29th January 1931. Taken at 83 Ullet Road.

Diary. The diary Wallace used which contained the entry for his venture to Menlove Gardens.*

Four diaries. These were dated 1928, 1929, 1930 and 1931.*

Two business diaries.*

Plan of Greater Liverpool. This showed Wallace's alleged route to the chess club on the Monday evening (coloured green) and his journey to Menlove Gardens on the Tuesday evening (coloured red).

Annie Robertson's Telephone Exchange note indicating 'No Reply.'

Photograph of chess club noticeboard.

Envelope with details of telephone message (taken by Beattie).

Photograph of notice listing the chess club fixtures/schedule.

Replica iron bar.

MacFall's sketch of room.

Same as above with notes.

Same as above with notes.

* *Collected by Wallace on 16th June 1931*

† *Wallace also signed for but did not collect*

The property office would auction those items not collected. As Wallace didn't collect the mackintosh it is highly unlikely it would have been auctioned due to its condition. Other than one of the police taking it as a memento of the crime it would more than likely have been binned.

BIBLIOGRAPHY

Abbot, Anthony: "William H. Wallace – Britain's Most Baffling Crime" *The Giant Book of True Crime* [Edited by Richard Glyn Jones] (Magpie 1992)

Abrahams, Gerald: *According to the Evidence* (Cassell 1958)

Adam, Hargrave Lee: "The Clue of the Telephone Message" *Murder Most Mysterious* (Sampson Low, Marston & Co. 1932)

Agate, James: *Ego 6* (Harrap 1944)

Allingham, Margery: "The Compassionate Machine" *Truly Criminal* [Edited by Martin Edwards] (The History Press 2015)

Bennett, Benjamin: "The Bogus 'Phone Call" *Why Did They Do It?* (Howard & Timmins 1953)

Bridges, Yseult: *Two Studies in Crime* (Hutchinson 1959)

Brophy, John: "The Liverpool Classic" *The Meaning of Murder* (Whiting-Wheaton 1966)

Burke, Vincent: "A Call to Murder" *Merseyside Murders & Trials* (The History Press 2008)

Castleden, Rodney: "The Man from the Pru" *Great Unsolved Crimes* (Futura Books 2007)

Chandler, Raymond: *Raymond Chandler Speaking* (Hamish Hamilton 1962)

Cobb, Belton: "Scapegoat" *Trials and Errors* (WH Allen 1962)

Dilnot, George: "The Perfect Murder" *Rogues March* (Bles 1934)

Duke, Winifred: "The Perfect Murder" *Six Trials* (Gollancz 1934)

Fido, Martin: "The Wallace Case" *Murders After Midnight* (Weidenfeld & Nicolson 1990)

Firman, Stanley: "Through a Little Oak Door to Freedom" *Crime Man* (Hutchinson & Co. 1950)

Gaute, J.H.H and Robin Odell: *Murder 'Whatdunit'* (Harrap 1982)

Geary, Rick: *The Wallace Mystery* (Home Town Press 2019)

Goodman, Jonathan: *The Killing of Julia Wallace* (Harrap 1969)

Goodman, Jonathan: "The Wallace Case" *Masterpieces of Murder* (Robinson 1992)

Granger, Ray, Brian Innes and Mary Meenan: *Time Enough To Kill?* (Midsummer Books Ltd 1994)

Grex, Leo: "The Address That Never Was" *Mystery Stranger Than Fiction* (Robert Hale Ltd 1979)

Gustafson, Anita: "The Body in the Parlor" *Guilty or Innocent?* (Holt, Rinehart & Winston 1985)

Hall, Angus (editor): "Dial M for Murder" *Crimes and Punishment Magazine* No. 9 (BPC Publishing 1973-75). Also appeared in *Infamous Crimes That Shocked the World* (Macdonald and Co. Publishers 1989) and *Infamous Crimes* under the title "A Mysterious Telephone Call" (Black Cat 1992)

Hayhurst, Alan: "The Man from the Pru" *Lancashire Murders* (Sutton Publishing 2004)

Hussey, Robert F.: *Murderer Scot-Free* (David & Charles 1972)

James, P.D.: "Murder, She Wrote" *Sunday Times Magazine* (27th October 2013)

Jessel, David: "The Perfect Murder" *Murder Casebook* No. 25 (Marshall Cavendish 1990)

Logan, Guy B. H.: "The Murder of Mrs Wallace" *Great Murder Mysteries* (Stanley Paul & Co 1931)

Lustgarten, Edgar: "William Herbert Wallace" *Verdict in Dispute* (Wingate 1949) (also in *Best Murder Cases* edited by Donn Russell Faber & Faber 1958)

Lustgarten, Edgar: "William Herbert Wallace" *The Murder and the Trial* (Odhams 1960)

Masters, Brian and Joanna Kennedy: "Time Enough To Kill" (Eaglemoss Publications 2004)

Midwinter, E.C.: "Murderous Echoes" *Building the Union* [Edited by Harold R. Hikins] (Toulouse Press 1973)

Moiseiwitsch, Maurice: "William Herbert Wallace" *Five Famous Trials* (Heinemann 1962)

Morland, Nigel: "The Man Behind the Mackintosh" *Background To Murder* (Werner Laurie 1955)

Moss, Andrew: "Not Quite Checkmate" *Murder, Myth and Make-Believe* (True Crime Library 2001)

Murphy, James: *The Murder of Julia Wallace* (The Bluecoat Press 2001)

O'Connell, Bernard: "A Call-Box Alibi" *The World's Strangest Murders* (Frederick Muller Ltd 1957)

Odell, Robin: *Landmarks in 20th Century Murder* (Headline 1995)

Rice, Craig: "Murder Without Motive" *45 Murderers* (Simon and Schuster 1952)

Rowland, John: *The Wallace Case* (Carroll & Nicholson 1949)

Rowland, John: "William Herbert Wallace" *More Criminal Files* (Arco Publications 1958)

Rowland, John: *Murder by Persons Unknown* (Mellifont Press 1941)

Royden, Mike: "The Murder of Julia Wallace 1931" *Tales from the 'Pool* (Creative Dreams Publishing 2017)

St Hill, Charles Arthur: "Arsenic and Old Lace" (1971) [Edited by John A. Ross] (Liverpool Medical History Papers 1976)

Sayers, Dorothy L.: "The Murder of Julia Wallace" *Great Unsolved Crimes* (Hutchinson & Co London 1935) (also in *Murder in the 1930s* edited by Colin Wilson Carroll & Graf 1992)

Sayers, Dorothy L.: "The Murder of Julia Wallace" *The Anatomy of Murder* (John Lane, 1936)

Shew, E. Spencer: "William Herbert Wallace" *A Second Companion To Murder* (Cassell 1961)

Sparrow, Gerald: "Checkmate" *Murder Parad*e (Robert Hale 1957)

Sterling, Jane: "The Murder of Julia Wallace" *Famous Northern Crimes, Trials and Criminals* (G.W. & A. Hesketh 1983)

Tennyson Jesse, F.: "Checkmate" T*he Mammoth Book of Unsolved Crimes* [Edited by Roger Wilkes] (Carroll & Graf 1999)

Veale, F.J.P.: *The Wallace Case* (Verdict in Doubt No.1) (Merrymeade Publishing) 1950 (Limited edition reprint of 25 copies) (Clifford Elmer Books April 2005)

Wade, Stephen: "The Wallace Mystery, 1931" *Foul Deeds and Suspicious Deaths in Liverpool* (Wharncliffe Books 2006)

Wade, Stephen: "The Wallace Enigma" *Notorious Murders of the Twentieth Century* (Wharncliffe Books 2011)

Waterhouse, Richard: *The Insurance Man* (Leyburn Designs 1994)

Whittington-Egan, Richard: "Death in the Parlour" *Liverpolitan* vol.16 no.8 (August 1951) (also appeared as "Corpse in the Parlour" *Liverpool Colonnade* Philip, Son & Nephew 1955)

Wilkes, Roger: *Wallace – The Final Verdict* (The Bodley Head 1984)

Wilkes, Roger: "William Herbert Wallace" *The Mammoth Book of Famous Trials* (Carroll & Graf Publishers 2006)

Wilson, Colin and Patricia Pitman: *Encyclopaedia of Murder* (Barker 1961)

Wilson, Colin: "William Herbert Wallace" *Unsolved Murders & Mysteries*

[Edited by John Canning] (Michael O'Mara Books 1987)
Wilson, Colin: *Murder in Mind* (Marshall Cavendish 1999)
Wyndham-Brown, W.F.: *The Trial of William Herbert Wallace* (Victor Gollancz 1933)

OTHER SOURCES

DPP 2/2
HO 144/17938
HO 144/17939
PCOM 9/293

Birkenhead News
Daily Mirror
Evening Express
John Bull (all 1932): 16th April; 23rd April; 30th April; 7th May; 14th May; 21st May
Liverpolitan
Liverpool Daily Courier
Liverpool Daily Post & Mercury
Liverpool Echo
Liverpool Weekly Courier
Manchester Courier
Manchester Evening News

Alan Godfrey Maps
The History of the Liverpool City Magistrates' Court, Philip Bowes (1993)
Liverpool Corporation Tramways and Motor Bus Guide
Liverpool Corporation Tramways and Motor Buses Time Tables
Liverpool Labour, Sam Davies, Keele University Press (1996)
The Liverpool Red Book
Liverpool Transport Volume 2 1900-1930, J.B. Horne & T.B. Maund Transport Publishing Company (1982)
Motor Museum Guide, Beaulieu Enterprises Limited
Watch Committee Annual Police Report 1931
Who Killed Julia Wallace? Yorkshire Television 1975
www.liverpoolcitypolice.co.uk

INDEX